HISTORY OF WOMEN IN THE UNITED STATES

HISTORY OF WOMEN IN THE UNITED STATES
Historical Articles on Women's Lives and Activities

Edited by Nancy F. Cott

Series ISBN 3-598-41454-4

1. Theory and Method in Women's History
   ISBN 3-598-41455-2 Part 1
   ISBN 3-598-41477-3 Part 2

2. Household Constitution and Family Relationships
   ISBN 3-598-41456-0

3. Domestic Relations and Law
   ISBN 3-598-41457-9

4. Domestic Ideology and Domestic Work
   ISBN 3-598-41458-7 Part 1
   ISBN 3-598-41475-7 Part 2

5. The Intersection of Work and Family Life
   ISBN 3-598-41459-5 Part 1
   ISBN 3-598-41476-5 Part 2

6. Working on the Land
   ISBN 3-598-41460-9

7. Industrial Wage Work
   ISBN 3-598-41461-7 Part 1
   ISBN 3-598-41693-8 Part 2

8. Professional and White-Collar Employments
   ISBN 3-598-41462-5 Part 1
   ISBN 3-598-41694-6 Part 2

9. Prostitution
   ISBN 3-598-41463-3

10. Sexuality and Sexual Behavior
    ISBN 3-598-41464-1

11. Women's Bodies: Health and Childbirth
    ISBN 3-598-41465-X

12. Education
    ISBN 3-598-41466-8

13. Religion
    ISBN 3-598-41467-6

14. Intercultural and Interracial Relations
    ISBN 3-598-41468-4

15. Women and War
    ISBN 3-598-41469-2

16. Women Together: Organizational Life
    ISBN 3-598-41470-6

17. Social and Moral Reform
    ISBN 3-598-41471-4 Part 1
    ISBN 3-598-41695-4 Part 2

18. Women and Politics
    ISBN 3-598-41472-2 Part 1
    ISBN 3-598-41697-0 Part 2

19. Woman Suffrage
    ISBN 3-598-41473-0 Part 1
    ISBN 3-598-41696-2 Part 2

20. Feminist Struggles for Sex Equality
    ISBN 3-598-41474-9

HISTORY OF WOMEN IN THE UNITED STATES

Historical Articles on Women's Lives and Activities

---

7. Industrial Wage Work

PART 1

Edited with an Introduction by

Nancy F. Cott

Yale University

K · G · Saur

Munich · New Providence · London · Paris · 1993

Publisher's Note

The articles and chapters which comprise this collection originally appeared in a wide variety of publications and are reproduced here in facsimile from the highest quality offprints and photocopies available. The reader will notice some occasional marginal shading and text-curl common to photocopying from tightly bound volumes. Every attempt has been made to either correct or minimize this effect.

Copyright information for articles reproduced in this collection appears at the end of this volume.

Library of Congress Cataloging-in-Publication Data

History of women in the United States : historical articles on women's lives and activities / edited with an introduction by Nancy F. Cott.

p. cm.

Includes bibliographical references and indexes.

Contents: 1. Theory and method in women's history -- 2. Household constitution and family relationships -- 3. Domestic relations and law -- 4. Domestic ideology and domestic work -- 5. The intersection of work and family life -- 6. Working on the land -- 7. Industrial wage work -- 8. Professional and white-collar employments -- 9. Prostitution -- 10. Sexuality and sexual behavior -- 11. Women's bodies -- 12. Education -- 13. Religion -- 14. Intercultural and interracial relations -- 15. Women and war -- 16. Women together -- 17. Social and moral reform -- 18. Women and politics -- 19. Woman suffrage -- 20. Feminist struggles for sex equality.

ISBN 3-598-41454-4 (set)

1. Women--United States--History. 2. Women--United States--Social conditions. I. Cott, Nancy F.

HQ1410.H57 1992

305.4'0973--dc20 92-16765

CIP

Die Deutsche Bibliothek - CIP - Einheitsaufnahme

History of Women in the United States: historical articles on women's lives and activities / ed. with an introd. by Nancy F. Cott.
- Munich ; London ; New York ; Paris : Saur.

ISBN 3-598-41454-4

NE: Cott, Nancy F. (Hrsg.)

Vol. 7. industrial wage work

Pt. 1. - (1993)

ISBN 3-598-41461-7

Printed on acid-free paper/Gedruckt auf säurefreiem Papier

Printed in the United States of America
Printed/Bound by Edwards Brothers Incorporated, Ann Arbor

ISBN 3-598-41461-7 (vol. 7/part 1)
ISBN 3-598-41454-4 (series)

Contents

CONTENTS

CONTENTS

Series Preface

In the space of one generation, women's history has become the fastest-growing area of scholarship in U.S. history. Since the resurgence of feminism in the late 1960s and 1970s, insistent questions about the historical meanings of "woman's place" have sowed and reaped a garden of scholarship. Where scholarly works used to be bare of mention of women, academic enterprise has now produced a vigorous growth of books and articles, bringing to light diverse women of every region, race, class and age. This research is marked by a renovating intent that refuses to accept as "human" history a history of men. Interest is lively and debate is stimulating and sought after: attendance at the Berkshire Conference on the History of Women rivals the size of the annual convention of the American Historical Association.

While books in women's history are daily increasing in numbers and strength, as in any fast-developing field the scholarly literature in the form of articles is most expansive and up-to-the-minute. All the history journals now publish articles on women's work, domestic settings, family relations, household matters, female politics and organizations and so forth, and new journals have sprung into being to concentrate on such topics. Women's historians publish in numerous regional and thematic history journals as well as in feminist outlets and in journals of other social science disciplines. This series brings together a collection of outstanding articles from the field, almost all written in the past twenty years and more than half published during the 1980s. It brings together, in volumes organized by topic, essays otherwise widely dispersed. These volumes reprint only articles that originally appeared in journals, not chapters of books; review articles are not included. Articles have been chosen for overall quality and for range. Each one was chosen for one or more of the following reasons: because it is the standard authority on its subject matter; represents an important statement on a topic by a recognized scholar; presages an important book to come; provides a first look at new evidence or new methods; or opens an untapped area or new controversy. Older articles have been reprinted if their data or interpretation have not been surpassed or if they marked an important stage in the historiography, even if since superseded.

The historical coverage of the series extends from the Revolutionary era to the 1960s. The articles themselves are dated from the 1940s through 1988. Volumes are organized by topic rather than time period. Within each volume, the articles are ordered chronologically (with respect to substance), so that the whole can be read as an historical overview. The only exception to this ordering principle is Volume One, on Theory and Method, in which the contents are arranged in order of publication. Within each volume there is an attempt to include articles on as diverse kinds of women as possible. None of the volume topics is regionally or racially defined; rather, all volumes are topically designed so as to afford views of women's work, family lives, and public activities which cut across races and regions. Any volume in the series stands on its own, supplying as full a treatment of a designated subject matter as the scholarly literature will provide. Several groupings of volumes also make sense; that is, volumes two through five all center around domestic and family matters; volumes five through nine consider other varieties of women's work; volumes nine through eleven concern uses and abuses of women's bodies; volumes twelve through fourteen look at major aspects of socialization; and volumes fifteen through twenty include organizational and political efforts of many sorts.

As a whole, the series displays in all its range the vitality of the field of women's history. Aside from imbuing U.S. history with new vision, scholarship in this area has informed, and should continue to inform, current public debate on issues from parental leave to the nuclear freeze. By bringing historical articles together under topical headings, these volumes both represent accurately the shape of historical controversy (or consensus) on given issues and make historians' findings most conveniently available for current reference.

Introduction

In much of conventional labor history the presence of women as industrial wage-earners has been ignored or lightly passed over as a diversion or exception. Yet women composed most of the industrial labor force first assembled in the U.S., in the cotton mills of Rhode Island and Massachusetts, beginning in the early nineteenth century. At that time agricultural production dominated the American economy and most American leaders and inhabitants wanted to keep it so. Some American manufacturers, however, saw the potential for the U.S. to rival England in industrial production; they built, on sites where river falls provided water power, factories which housed the newly-perfected machine processes of spinning and weaving under one roof and made it possible to mass-produce cloth. These manufacturers saw the girls and young women of the countryside as their likeliest labor pool. Of course spinning and weaving cloth at home was a traditional occupation of girls and women. Publicists of industry could (and did) fend off concern lest the healthy and vaunted yeoman-farmer base of the American republic be subverted by industrial development, for, they argued, textile factories would only draw off the land and provide useful work for not-yet-married young women who were "idle"— that is, working at home unpaid.

Employment of female operatives meant that for the first time on a large scale women's labor outside the homestead or farmstead had cash value. In some women's minds, this aroused the possibility of independence. An anonymous mill worker in Lowell, Massachusetts defended "the dignity of labor": "From whence originated the idea, that it was derogatory to a lady's dignity, or a blot upon the female character, to labor? and who was the first to say sneeringly, 'Oh, she *works* for a living?' Surely, such ideas and expressions ought not to grow on republican soil. . . . To be able to earn one's own living by laboring with the hands should be reckoned among female accomplishments . . . ."[1]

Manufacturers' demand for female labor offered women a new form of livelihood, and the realm of waged labor pointed a way out of women's economic dependence on kin or marriage. Yet sex-role prescriptions and gender divisions have informed the shape of the industrial work force from its inception to the present day. The extent of sex-segregation in the labor force—that is, women and men occupying different kinds of jobs—is a most striking continuity in the history of occupations. Just as in the initial textile mills, where female operatives were specifically called for, in almost all industries and trades women were not hired to do the same jobs as men had. Men trained for, and were hired into, jobs in which advancement and promotion were possible. Women, cut out of apprenticeship training by male craft tradition and neglected or resisted by male craft unions, got the lowest-paying, least skilled, routine jobs. Even when women and men did roughly the same tasks, what the women did, by virtue of being "women's" work, received less pay. The average female industrial worker received from a third to a half of the average man's industrial earnings for a century after the Lowell mills' opening.

While the number of female operatives constantly increased, the relative proportion of women in the industrial labor force declined as more numerous kinds of production, besides textiles, became industrialized, and heavy industry in iron and steel (supporting the building of railroads and urban construction), especially employed more and more men. Still, the industrial occupations of women greatly diversified. By 1882, when the fairly new Bureau of Statistics of Labor in Massachusetts issued a report on "The Working Girls of Boston," females were found in more than twenty-five different manufactures, from bookbinding, boots and shoes, brooms and bushes, to paper boxes, polishes and dressings, straw goods, and tobacco.[2] Both World War I and World War II gave great, though temporary, boosts to the employment and the pay of women in industry. The era of World War I was the first time that black women were employed in factories, from which prejudice of white employers and employees had previously excluded them; even then, however, they were compelled to work in race-segregated areas, in the jobs white women least wanted.

Like the very first mill operatives, women wage-earners in industry right through the 1920s continued to be principally young and unmarried, between the ages of fifteen and twenty-five. Though often casually assumed by middle-class observers—and employers—to be working for frivolous "pin money" or in order to buy clothes, these young women were providing as much of their own living as possible and vital support to their families or dependent relatives. Their wages, by and large, were not sufficient to support a person living alone. Employers paid women workers as though they were secondary earners with other sources of support—fathers, husbands—to rely on. Women took jobs at such pay because there were none better for women, but the consequent deprivations of those who were not members of families with other wage-earners, such as widows and single mothers, were extremely harsh.

Because most women industrial workers in the nineteenth century were in the labor force for only a phase of their lives, before marriage and childbearing, union organization among them tended to be difficult and fleeting. Male craft union leaders, by and large, saw women—even those in the industrial labor force—as actual or potential daughters, wives and mothers, rather than fellow laborers, and wished less to organize them than to see them safely out of the labor market. After the turn of the twentieth century, however, union organizing among industrial women gained new life and possibility. Reform associations such as the Women's Trade Union League invented special efforts to organize women workers; more women realized that their wage work was a recurrent necessity and not a transient phase in their lives; and the assertion of industrial rather than craft organization of unions in the 1930s, under the Congress of Industrial Organizations (C.I.O.), brought male leadership to make greater efforts among women workers. The shape of the female industrial labor force changed over the twentieth century, as mothers as well as daughters sought wage-earning outside the home. Articles in this volume investigate many of these changes over time in women workers and their work, particularly illuminating sexual segregation and pay differentials in the labor force, women's work culture on the job, and union organizing.

Notes

[1] C.B., in *Mind among the Spindles: A Miscellany wholly composed by the factory girls* (Boston, 1845), 187.

[2] "The Working Girls of Boston," from the 15th Annual Report of the Massachusetts Bureau of Statistics of Labor, for 1884, by Carroll Wright, excerpted in *Root of Bitterness: Documents of the Social History of American Women*, Nancy F. Cott, ed. (N.Y., E.P. Dutton, 1972), 311-313.

Industrial Wage Work

Claudia Goldin

The Economic Status of Women in the Early Republic: Quantitative Evidence

> That woman was the slave of man at the commencement of society is one of the most absurd notions that have come down to us from the period of the Enlightenment. . . . Woman occupied not only a free but also a highly respected position. . . . As wealth increased, it . . . gave the man a more important status in the family than the woman.[1]

> The period 1800–1840 is one in which decisive changes occurred in the status of American women . . . women were by tacit consensus, excluded from the new democracy. Indeed their actual situation had in many respects deteriorated. . . . Women's work outside the home no longer met with social approval. . . . Many business and professional occupations formerly open to women were now closed. . . . The entry of large numbers of women into low status . . . industrial work had fixed such work by definition as "woman's work."[2]

The thesis that women's status deteriorated from a "golden age" has been a compelling one, and numerous variants of it exist for the American and European cases. The most frequently cited

Claudia Goldin is Professor of Economics at the University of Pennsylvania and Research Associate of the National Bureau of Economic Research. She is the editor of the *Journal of Economic History*.

The research for this article was supported by the National Science Foundation and was carried out while the author was a member of the Institute for Advanced Study, Princeton. She would like to thank Eileen Crimmins, Stanley Engerman, Elizabeth Fox-Genovese, Morgan Kousser, and Kenneth Sokoloff for their comments and suggestions and the Philadelphia Social History Project for their household file of the 1860 Federal Population Census manuscripts.

1 Friedrich Engels, *The Origin of The Family, Private Property, and the State*, in Robert C. Tucker (ed.), *The Marx-Engels Reader* (New York, 1978; orig pub. 1884), 735.

2 Gerda Lerner, "The Lady and the Mill Girl: Changes in the Status of Women in the Age of Jackson," *Midcontinent American Studies Journal*, X (1969), 5, 7.

for the American case is that formulated by Lerner concerning change on two fronts. Barriers were erected limiting the employment of women in the marketplace; instead women were relegated to work in the home, as dictated by an oppressive ideology of domesticity. The causal mechanism is a complex one and emerges from a vaguely defined set of market and political forces.[3]

Another version of the golden age thesis links the decline of the status of women to the expansion of the economic marketplace in the mid-nineteenth century. Purchased goods were substituted for those produced in the home, reducing the sphere of female responsibility and degrading women's work. Others have pushed this transition back to the mid-eighteenth century. Both the original version and this variant have interpreted the doctrine of separate spheres and the ideology of domesticity as reflecting and enforcing the degraded status of women.[4]

The original version of the golden age thesis, which I identify with Lerner's article, continues to be widely cited, reprinted, and generally influential, despite attacks on several fronts. Many critics have termed the thesis a romantic view of the past and a naive belief that sex roles were blurred in precapitalist societies. Cross-cultural studies have raised doubts that preindustrial societies could have had less differentiated sex roles and could have ac-

3 For the American case see also Barbara J. Harris, *Beyond Her Sphere: Women and the Professions in American History* (Westport, Conn., 1978). The literature for the European case is extensive, particularly with regard to the decline in high status roles for women with the expansion of capitalist development. See, for example, the citations in Joan Hoff-Wilson, "The Illusion of Change: Women and the American Revolution," in Alfred F. Young (ed.), *The American Revolution: Explorations in the History of American Radicalism* (De Kalb, Ill., 1976); Martha Howell, "Women, the Family Economy, and the Structure of Market Production in Cities of Northern Europe during the Late Middle Ages," unpub. ms. (1983).

The word "status" has several meanings in this literature. Most generally it means the esteem with which women and their work, both in and out of the home, were held. The "decline in status" has referred to several changes: work in factories has been interpreted as degraded after the 1830s; work in the home was reduced in scope and denigrated; work in professions was severely curtailed; work elsewhere for women was supposedly scorned and ridiculed; and women were denied other political, legal, and economic rights.

4 On the expansion of the marketplace in the nineteenth century see Ann Douglas, *The Feminization of American Culture* (New York, 1977). On the eighteenth century see Hoff-Wilson, "The Illusion of Change," 402, who remarks that "except for the actual years in which the war was fought, colonial women found more and more of their traditional familial duties and responsibilities siphoned off as the economy became more commercially specialized. . . . Only women living in the most isolated frontier areas escaped their experience of declining importance and function within the family unit."

corded women higher status. Others have seized the revolutionary experience in America and its ideological aftermath to provide contradictory evidence. To Norton and Kerber, the immediate and long-run impacts of the war uplifted women's status and position; yet to others, such as Hoff-Wilson, the Revolution itself was a setback.[5]

A rather different interpretation of the doctrine of separate spheres has been used to alter, and even invert, the meaning of the golden age thesis. The expansion of the marketplace is again accorded a central role, but the critical change was outside, not within, the home. As work for men became more routinized and rationalized, the home emerged as an oasis, as a sanctuary, and as the women's sphere. "The ideology of women's sphere formed a necessary stage in the process of shattering the hierarchy of sex and, more directly, in softening the hierarchical relationship of marriage." Had these spheres not been separate, work for men outside the home might have been deemed superior, but the issue of inferiority, and thus the decline of status, was avoided by an ideology of "separate," and thus equal, spheres.[6]

None of these critics, however, has marshalled evidence of the sort demanded by Lerner's original article; nor have they scrutinized Lerner's sources. They have, instead, attacked Lerner either on broad issues of theory and interpretation or on readings of primary source material from the colonial period.

This article reviews the evidence used by Lerner and analyzes relevant quantitative sources that bear on aspects of women's economic role during the early republic. Measures of labor force

5 Elizabeth Fox-Genovese, "Placing Women's History in History," *Argument*, XXV (1983), 685–696, claims that "many historians of women . . . have been led, by their opposition to the inequities of capitalism in practice, to romanticize life in precapitalist—and especially preindustrial—societies." To Hoff-Wilson, "The Illusion of Change," 393, the argument "that during the colonial period women enjoyed a less sex-stereotyped existence than at any time until recently . . . is largely an exaggeration." Mary Beth Norton, *Liberty's Daughters: The Revolutionary Experience of American Women, 1750–1800* (Boston, 1980), xiv, concludes that "the older theory should now be abandoned. . . . Far from having a high status and an excellent opinion of themselves and their abilities, most of the white women who lived in prerevolutionary America turned out to display low self-esteem, to have very limited conceptions of themselves and their roles, and to habitually denigrate their sex in general." Linda Kerber, *Women of the Republic: Intellect and Ideology in Revolutionary America* (Chapel Hill, 1980).

6 Nancy F. Cott, *The Bonds of Womanhood: "Woman's Sphere" in New England, 1780–1835* (New Haven, 1977), 200.

participation and occupational structure are used to confront some of the issues raised by Lerner. In doing so the scope of the inquiry on the golden age for women is narrowed. But, at the same time, our understanding of the evolution of women's economic rôle is extended through a systematic study of representative individuals over time. Business and city directories and population census manuscripts are used in tandem to explore changes from 1790 to 1860 in the economic characteristics of female heads of households in Philadelphia. This evidence constitutes the only systematic data on female occupations and labor force participation that exist for the late eighteenth- and early nineteenth-century United States.

Not until 1860 did marshals of the United States Census Office ask females their occupations, and it took thirty additional years for data on women to be published with details on age, marital status, nativity, and race. The role of women in the economic marketplace remains a mystery for much of American history.

The labor market role of young, single women of the early republic has been recently explored with the records of the censuses of manufacturing from 1820 to 1850. Because population census data from 1860 indicate that married women were not in the paid labor market to any great extent, they are difficult to trace with quantitative sources, and only adult widowed and spinster women remain to be studied. Such women were probably as important numerically in the urban labor force of the early republic as were young women (fifteen to twenty-four years old); city and business directories of the period enable a systematic study of those who were heads of households. These records also yield information on the "hidden market work" of married women by linking the occupations of widows to those of their deceased husbands. In doing so, the data can be used to assess whether or not married women's labor force participation first declined with economic development, rising only later in the development process, as suggested in the work of Durand.[7]

7 Goldin and Kenneth Sokoloff, "Women, Children, and Industrialization in the Early Republic: Evidence from the Manufacturing Censuses," *Journal of Economic History*, XLII (1982), 741–774. The ratio of employed widows and single women over 24 years old to employed single women 15 to 24 years old was 0.85 across the United States. John Durand, *The Labor Force in Economic Development: A Comparison of International Census Data, 1946–66* (Princeton, 1975).

LERNER'S EVIDENCE Lerner's thesis is that between the colonial and Jacksonian periods, probably from 1800 to 1840, the status of women declined markedly. Professions, particularly those in medicine, became closed to women, and proprietorships were less available and more often confined to goods that women themselves purchased. As the spheres of home and work separated, women could not as easily participate in the business affairs of their husbands.

The first four decades of the nineteenth century had witnessed a dramatic change in the economic value of young, working-class women and the emergence of a doctrine of domesticity, affecting primarily middle-class females. Women were embraced by industry but not by the professions, according to Lerner, and the emerging ideology now known as the "cult of domesticity," the "cult of the lady," and the "cult of true womanhood" reinforced class distinctions that had arisen in the work force. Young, unmarried, working-class women were encouraged to labor for pay in the factories, but their middle-class or married counterparts were expected to be industrious only in their own homes. As the title of her article suggests, Lerner pointed to changes in the status of women that varied by age and class. Women's work, once highly esteemed in family businesses and professions, became severely limited and, with increased immigration, work in the factories became degraded.

Lerner did not analyze new sources; instead she generalized from her previous work on exceptional women and synthesized the literature on women and the family. She used information on particular professions and vague but convincing notions that change must have occurred some time after the early settlements in colonial America.[8]

This romantic interpretation of the past has been put forward so often that it need not be attributed directly to Lerner and can be summarized as follows. Equally arduous work for women and men in the early colonial period, reinforced by Puritan distaste for idleness, was sexually egalitarian. After the Revolution more formal laws, codes, and doctrines were established, for example

8 Arthur Calhoun, *A Social History of the American Family* (Cleveland, 1918), 3v.; Elisabeth A. Dexter, *Colonial Women of Affairs: Women in Business and Professions in America Before 1776* (Boston, 1924); Julia Spruill, *Women's Life and Work in the Southern Colonies* (Chapel Hill, 1938).

in the medical profession, mirroring those restrictions regulating property and eliminating suffrage for women. Also affecting the status of women, on a more or less continual basis over this period, were longer-run changes including the separation of home and work, the increase in per capita income and wealth, and the transition to more formal, less family-oriented transmission of skills. The removal of paid labor from the home redefined and polarized work roles by sex. Higher incomes enabled families to purchase both the leisure time of their members and more household production of services, thus furthering the sexual division of labor. Changes in the transmission of skills transferred decisions from families, who may have wanted to apprentice and train their daughters, to employers, who may not have.

Dexter, frequently cited as an early proponent of the notion that women's status declined around 1800, provided Lerner with general information on the economic activities pursued by urban women. Although Dexter claimed that her "evidence is too fragmentary and uneven to warrant many conclusions," she later asserted that, prior to 1800, women worked in their own taverns, shops, and hotels, and as seamstresses, nurses, and midwives attracting little attention, but that "after 1800 or thereabouts [a working woman] was self-conscious, and her neighbors critical."[9]

Evidence in Dexter led Lerner to conclude that "there were fewer female storekeepers and business women in the 1830s than there had been in colonial days" and that "after 1830 they were found mostly in businesses which served women only."[10]

Dexter's evidence on both points is quite limited, however. Buttressing the first of Lerner's points is Dexter's assertion that "anyone who has read over a file of early newspapers will be convinced that the proportion of [shopkeepers who were] women was larger in colonial days." She cites a figure of 9.5 percent for Boston in 1773, gleaned from a handful of newspaper advertisements, and compares it to one of only 4.3 percent from the 1900 Population Census. There is even less substantiating evidence in Dexter on the second point, that "a greatly increased number [of shopkeepers] specialized in dry goods and in clothing for their own sex."[11]

9 Dexter, *Career Women of America: 1776–1840* (Francestown, N.H., 1950), 219.

10 Lerner, "Lady and Mill Girl," 9.

11 Dexter, *Colonial Women of Affairs*, 37; *idem*, *Career Women of America*, 139. The

Lerner drew her impressions of women's status in the colonial period and on frontier settlements largely from the first two of Calhoun's three-volume history of the American family. But Lerner's interpretation of Calhoun seems to have reversed his intent. Their higher status, to Calhoun, implied an elevation to "lady," not to equality; neither the conditions of "old world ideals" nor the influence of "pioneer life," were interpreted by Calhoun to have favored "the inclusion of women in the circle of privilege."[12]

The term status has been used liberally in the literature just summarized. Status has frequently meant the esteem with which women's work outside the home was held, but at other times it has referred to work within the home. The term has also been used in connection with general notions of equality, whether constrained by social, legal, or ideological factors.

Among the many interpretations of the term "status" are several clearly delineated ones central to Lerner's thesis: (1) that women were excluded from certain professions, in particular that they were denied training as doctors and crowded out as midwives by male doctors; (2) that as proprietors they were reduced in number and increasingly sold goods that only women purchased; and (3) that in general they were less able and less frequently encouraged to work for pay.

The data that I use extend this inquiry into related territory. Such extensions focus on a representative cross-section of adult female heads of households in cities and address the following questions: What were the occupations available to mature women in late eighteenth- and early nineteenth-century urban America, and how did they change over time? Did the proportion of women working for pay rise or fall as the nature of work moved out of the home and as training became more structured? What impact did industrialization and the factory system have on this process?

THE DATA SOURCES City and business directories have been largely neglected as historical sources because of ambiguities and

---

comparison between the 4.3% figure and that of 9.5% is not entirely meaningful. The former, the 1900 census figure, refers to "merchants and nonwholesale dealers," whereas the later consists of store- and shopkeepers.

12 Calhoun, *History of the American Family*, II, 80.

biases in their coverage. Those for some cities appear considerably more complete than do those for others, and many directories do not include the full range of occupations known to have existed in nineteenth-century cities.[13]

The directories for Philadelphia are among the most comprehensive, extending from 1785 to the late nineteenth century. These directories were mainly alphabetical lists of "all business persons and heads of households" in Philadelphia and its environs, but they took other forms as well. On occasion they included separate listings of occupations, particularly for doctors, nurses, and midwives, and later for proprietors of all types. Several early directories, beginning with 1795, listed individuals by city block, forming a virtual walking tour of the city's residences and shops. Distinctions between dwelling houses and places of work can be readily made in the early directories and, with a bit more effort, in the later ones as well. Because the directories were compiled virtually every year, individuals can be traced through time, yielding information on the occupation of a widow and that of her deceased husband, and on occupational change and geographic mobility for an individual. In most of the directories until 1837, and then again beginning in 1858, race was noted; one directory for 1811 even compiled a separate "census of blacks" and was exceptional, as well, because its editor, Jane Aitken, had recently assumed the management of her late father's printing business.

The Philadelphia directories are particularly useful due to a peculiarity of the 1790 Federal Population Census which appears to have gone unnoticed, or at least unmentioned. The census marshals for the central portion of the capital of the United States recorded not only the names of the household heads, together with the number of occupants in each household, but also the addresses and occupations of each. Marshals took great care to distinguish between place of business and that of residence, making note of the proprietor of a shop, for example, but recording the person only at the residence. Thus Thomas Jefferson was

13 Many historical studies have used city and business directories for occupational data. Jacob M. Price, "Economic Function and the Growth of American Port Towns in the Eighteenth Century," *Perspectives in American History*, VIII (1974), 123–188, for example, used the records of New York City for the 1790s, and Sam Bass Warner, Jr., *The Private City: Philadelphia in Three Periods of Its Growth* (Philadelphia, 1968), used them for the nineteenth century. I am unaware of a study that has used them to form a time series of participation rates and occupations of women.

listed at his High Street address as Secretary of State of the United States, but was not counted as a citizen of Philadelphia, since his official home was in Virginia.

The information in the 1790 Federal Population Census allows an unambiguous linkage of names from the 1791 city directory to the 1790 census, and therefore allows an assessment of the directory's coverage. The directories generally claimed to have included all heads of households, but such claims were patently false for many cities. The 1791 Philadelphia directory, however, does appear to have been a complete listing. Of the females in the census, 99 percent appeared in the directory, and the directory included 97 percent of those in the census. Thus the data for 1791 can be treated as a very accurate base for the other directories; they demonstrate that the directory included all female heads of households and few additional women.[14]

Another linkage was performed using the 1820 Population Census manuscripts with somewhat less success, in part due to ambiguities in spelling and the absence of addresses and occupations in the census. The linkage rate was slightly over 70 percent for white females traced to directories spanning 1821 to 1823. The 1820 census was originally selected for this linkage because it was the first to ask households for summary information concerning foreign birth and employment. But 1820 was an atypical year for American cities in general, and for Philadelphia in particular. The severe depression in 1819 generated a temporary influx of women to the city, an additional factor lowering the rate of linkage. Although the linkage was not as complete as was that for 1790, it reaffirmed the general sense that there were no severe biases in the directories caused by the exclusion of particular individuals on the basis of occupation or other distinguishable indicators of status.[15]

14 The small slippage is easily explained: a few husbands died, some residents left the city, and a few entered in the period between the compilation of the two lists.

15 An appendix describing the city and business directories, the sampling procedures, and the linkage of the 1820 Population Census to the directories can be obtained from the author. On the economic crisis of 1818 to 1820 and its effect on Philadelphia, see Stanley Lebergott, *Manpower in Economic Growth: The American Record since 1800* (New York, 1964). The evidence that there was a temporary influx of female heads of households comes from the figures for the percentage of all household heads who were female, which rises from about 14 to 18% both during the trade reduction in 1813 and the commercial crisis of 1818 to 1820.

Even if the directories for Philadelphia were complete or, at least, unbiased samples of female heads of households, why should such data bear on the issues raised by Lerner and others? The occupations discussed in the literature on the changing status of women were primarily those held by mature women: proprietors, midwives, doctors, nurses, and some teachers, among others. These women need not have been heads of households, but most were. Because the directories also claimed to have included "all persons in business" as well as "all heads of households," they should have included other adult women workers. The 1820 link to the census indicates that certain occupations were included regardless of the woman's household status. The directory reported a somewhat higher proportion of women who were nurses and teachers than did the census; presumably the excess were unmarried women, living with siblings or parents.

Finally, who precisely were these female heads of households? Most were probably widows, although widows need not have used that appellation in the directory. Others were unmarried adult women, some of whom listed themselves as "the sisters . . ." Various aspects of their social and economic position can be gleaned from the structure of their households at two dates, 1820 and 1860. The linkage with the 1820 Population Census manuscripts provides data on the numbers of males and females in various age, sex, and racial categories.

Table 1 summarizes information on household and family structure in 1820, with roughly comparable statistics, where available, for 1860. The name of the household head was listed in the 1820 census together with summary information on the entire household, giving the number of individuals in various age groups. Only the sex of the household head, and not the precise individual, is known. I have assumed that the oldest female in each household was the head, thereby biasing the actual age of the household head upward. The age distribution of female heads in 1860 is almost identical to that inferred by this method for 1820 (see Part A), indicating that actual female heads in 1820 must have been somewhat younger than in 1860.

Related to this finding, and of more significance, is that the number of young children per female household head was substantially greater in 1820 than it was in 1860. Just how much greater is difficult to judge. The data in Table 1 indicate that there were, on average, 1.696 children below the age of sixteen in female-headed households in 1820. In 1860 there were 0.522 "own" children below the age of fifteen in female-headed native white households and somewhat more in those headed by a German (0.887) or Irish woman (0.992). The problem is that the 1820 data may include children belonging to other family members or boarders. But the difference in the number of young children between the two years is so great that far too many of these other family members or boarders would have needed to have been young children to equalize the figures between the two years. The child deficit would require 67 percent of other family members in the native-white case to have been children, 75 percent in the Irish case, and 55 percent for the German households. The differences in the numbers of children are reflected in household and family structure differences beween the two years, given in Table 1, Part B. Although similar proportions of female heads lived alone between the two years, only 29 percent lived with their own young children in 1860, but 69 percent lived with young children in 1820 (some of whom may not have been their own).

Despite the problems with comparability between the two years, households headed by women had far higher dependency ratios in 1820 than in 1860. Some of the difference in household composition across the two years is a function of the rapid increase, noted above, in female heads of households around 1820. The city may also have contained wider family networks in 1860, enabling younger widows with dependent children to live in households headed by an adult male.[16]

FEMALE LABOR FORCE PARTICIPATION RATES, 1790 TO 1860 The labor force participation rate is generally considered to be a primary indicator of the economic position of women in the economy. Table 2 gives female labor force participation rates derived from the directories and the censuses, 1790 to 1860, for female heads of households in Philadelphia. These data are based on over

16 Primary families are defined as the household head (in this case a female), her children, and any "other family members" living with her. Excluded are servants and boarders, even though some boarders may have been relatives. The percentage of female heads in the youngest age category (16 to 24 years) is 4.9% for all women but 9.1% for those who were not linked to the directories from the 1820 census. These young women, it is safe to assume, recently arrived in the city and were in the census but not in the directory.

Table 1 Aspects of Household and Family Structure for Female-Headed Households: Philadelphia, 1820 and 1860

A. *Age Distribution of Female Heads*

	1820 OLDEST FEMALE IN HOUSEHOLD[a]	1860 NATIVE-BORN WHITE
16–25 years	4.9%	4.7%
26–44	38.3	38.4
45+	56.8	56.9

B. *Household and Family Structure*[b]

	1820 HOUSEHOLDS		1860 HOUSEHOLDS
(1) Living alone	6.4%	(1) Living alone	7.9%
(2) "Adult" women[c]	11.8	(2) No "young own children"[d]	63.1
(3) "Adult" women and men[c]	12.8		
(4) Woman and "children"[d]	12.9	(3) With "young own children"	29.0
(5) "Adult" women and "children"	24.3		
(6) "Adult" women, men, and "children"	31.8		

C. *Household and Family Composition*

	1820 HOUSEHOLDS	1860 PRIMARY FAMILIES AND HOUSEHOLDS		
		NATIVE WHITE	IRISH	GERMAN
Mean Number of:		Primary Families[g]		
(1) "Adults"[c]	3.345	2.337	2.321	1.984
(2) "Children" (own in 1860)[d]	1.696	0.522	0.887	0.992
(3) "Adult children"[e] (own in 1860)	n.a.	(0.905)	(1.068)	(0.800)
		Households		
(4) Persons in household[f]	5.041	4.622	4.291	4.248
Number of observations	674	341	265	125

a See text. Includes only white women.
b Data for 1820 include only whites; a small number of black servants may be included in the 1860 household figures, which apply to households headed by a native-born white woman.
c "Adult" is defined as 16 years old and over due to the limitations in the 1820 census data. "Adult" women and men, therefore, could include older children. Changing the definition to 19 years old and over for males in 1820 alters the distribution only slightly.
d "Children" is defined as boys and girls under 16 years old for 1820 and under 15 years old for 1860. Note that "children" need not be the offspring of the female head in 1820, but are, in general, the offspring of the female head in 1860 (thus the term "young own children").
e "Adult children" are children over the age of 15 years. They are included in "adults" for both years because of the limitations of the 1820 census data. A figure is also given for the "adult children" in 1860 but cannot be computed for 1820.
f Equals the sum of the first two lines for 1820 and excludes blacks living in white households, for both years.
g Primary families are groups of individuals having the same last name. The 1860 Population Census manuscripts do not list the relationships to the head of the household and these have been inferred.

SOURCES: Philadelphia Social History Project, 1860 Household File; 1820 Population Census manuscripts.

Table 2 Female Labor Force Participation Rates for White Female Heads of Households and the Percentage of All Households Headed by a Female: Philadelphia 1790 to 1860

	(1) LABOR FORCE PARTICIPATION RATE			(2) # OF OBS. FOR (1)	(3) % FEMALE OF HOUSEHOLD HEADS	(4) # OF OBS. FOR (3)	(5) DIRECTORY OR CENSUS USED
YEAR	MAX.	MEAN	MIN.				
1790		(0.501)		531			1790 Census
1791		0.457		863	15.0		Biddle
1796		0.644		1019	14.9	1790	Stephens *
1800		0.640		204	13.2	1775	Staffords *
1804		0.533		197	14.3	1576	Robinson *
1808	0.529		0.484	223			Robinson
1811		0.574		589	13.0	1180	Census Directory
1813	0.399		0.333	303	17.9	792	Paxton
1814	0.467		0.444	306			Kite
1816	0.498		0.459	305			Robinson
1817	0.490		0.431	153			Robinson
1818	0.347		0.332	265	18.1	689	Paxton
1819	0.420		0.384	245			Paxton
1820		(0.393)		674	19.3	3493	1820 Census
1821		0.293		1429	20.2	1800	Whitely
1822	0.289		0.262	149	18.0	826	M'Carty and Davis

YEAR	(1) LABOR FORCE PARTICIPATION RATE MAX.	MEAN	MIN.	(2) # OF OBS. FOR (1)	(3) % FEMALE OF HOUSEHOLD HEADS	(4) # OF OBS. FOR (3)	(5) DIRECTORY OR CENSUS USED
1823	0.453		0.449	247			Desilver
1824	0.456		0.429	226			Desilver
1830		0.513		199	15.1	1316	Desilver
1833	0.493		0.478	136	15.4	881	Desilver
1837		0.414		651	12.2	5320	Desilver
1840		0.351		205	16.8	1217	McElroy *
1845		0.355		152	13.3	1140	McElroy *
1852		0.355		121	9.7	1127	McElroy *
1856		0.327		147	9.0	1480	McElroy *
1858		0.424		205	12.8	1603	McElroy
1860		0.437		1130	10.4	2484	McElroy
1860		0.435		795	9.0	1563	Cohen
1860		0.395		731	14.2	6000	Census
1860	Native white	(0.370)		341	(17.1)	2000	Census
1860	Irish	(0.470)		265	(13.3)	2000	Census
1860	German	(0.290)		125	(6.3)	2000	Census

Col. (1): Number of females with occupations divided by total number of females listed. See text for discussion of maximum and minimum figures.
Col. (2): Number of observations on which col. (1) estimate is based. The sample of pages varied over time, with about a one in two or three for the early period, increasing to one in twenty-four.
Col. (3): Number of females divided by total number of persons listed.
Col. (4): Number of observations on which col. (3) estimate is based.
Col. (5): An asterisk (*) indicates that blacks and whites were not distinguished in the directory, although blacks may have been undercounted in such directories.

Line 1790: The figure of 0.501 is only for the central section of the city, since this was the only portion which listed occupations. The occupations given, and thus the labor force participation rate, for this area are in almost perfect agreement with those in the 1791 directory. The aggregate figure is somewhat higher in the census because female labor force participation dropped as the distance from the center increased.

1820: The figure 0.393 is in parentheses because female heads of households in the 1820 census were matched to directories from 1821 to 1823 and thus reflect changes in labor force participation over that period.

1860: The figure of 0.395 in col. (1) is a weighted average for the three groups where the weights are 0.070 German, 0.299 Irish, and 0.631 native white. The figure in col. (3) of 14.2 uses the following weights: 0.159 German, 0.318 Irish, and 0.523 native white. Both sets of weights are derived from underlying sampling properties of the Philadelphia Social History Project data.

12,000 individuals across the twenty-seven individual years sampled. Because the data for 1791 have been linked to the 1790 census, they can be used to obtain an unbiased estimate of the market labor force participation rate of female heads of households. The percentage of all directory listings that were female, given in column (3), should be related to, if not identical with, the percentage of all households headed by a female.[17]

The data on labor force participation rates for the years 1791, 1811, 1821, 1830, 1836, and 1840 through 1860 are given as point estimates, whereas those for the other years are given as ranges. In the pre-1840 directories a widow was occasionally listed with the name of her deceased husband and an occupation or trade, which the widow may or may not have assumed. Such a listing might read "Sarah, widow of John, tavernkeeper" and seemed to be most frequent among recently widowed women. For various years these listings were scrutinized by searching forward in time for directories listing these women without their husbands' names. Where a point estimate is given, considerable care was taken to assess whether the occupation was the widow's or whether it had been solely that of her deceased husband. Where a range is given, the minimum value assigns all women to widow (out of the labor force) status, and the maximum value assigns them the listed occupation only if it was a conceivable female designation. The ranges are not very great, the largest being 6.6 percentage points.

The proportion of female household heads which indicated that they had an occupation varied over the period, from a low of just under .3 to a high of just over .6. There was a slight downward trend across the entire seventy-year period (see the regression in Figure 1), exaggerated somewhat by certain years in the late 1790s which contain the highest figures.

What accounts for the movement in this economic and social indicator? The strength and buoyancy of the economy was a major factor in the labor force employment of this group. The surge of demand in the period of American neutrality during the Napoleonic Wars generated the high figures from 1796 to about 1804, and the commercial crisis of 1818 to 1820 had the opposite

17 The discrepancy between the 1860 census figure of 14.2 and the directory's of about 10 suggests that the directories, in the period after the 1850s, were either listing fewer females or relatively more males.

Fig. 1 Labor Force Participation Rates for Female Heads of Households Philadelphia 1791 to 1860

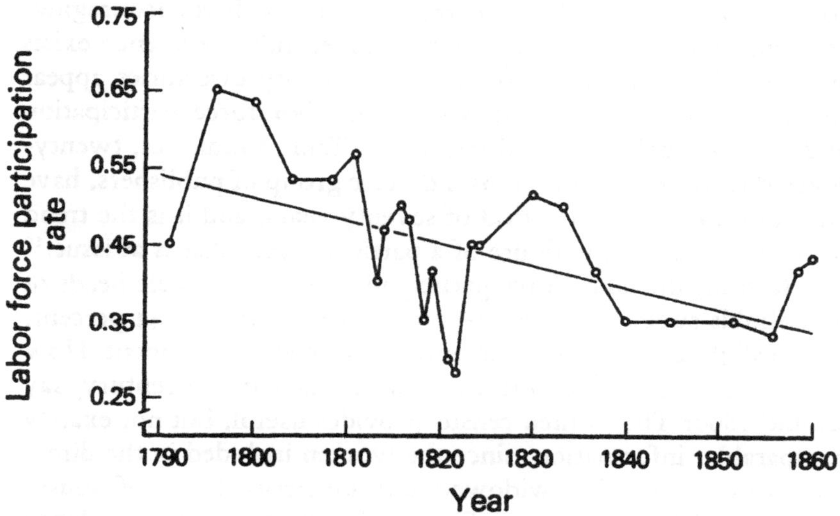

SOURCE: Table 1, col. (1), means or average of maximum and minimum figures.

NOTE: Straight line is the following ordinary least squares regression of the labor force participation rate on time:

$$\text{Labor Force Participation Rate} = \underset{(16.26)}{0.539} - \underset{(3.20)}{0.0028}\ \text{Time}$$

$R^2 = 0.31$; 't' statistics are in parentheses.

effect, one of lowering employment figures to their nadir in 1822. Indeed, the evidence suggests that labor force participation for this group of women was procyclical and that the percentage of all households headed by a female was countercyclical. If one eliminates the apparent aberrations caused by extremes in economic activity, the labor force rates, with few exceptions, range from .35 to .50, as can be seen in Figure 1.[18]

Other, complementary explanations exist for the relative volatility in the labor force participation data. The directory data were compiled by several different publishers (see col. 5, Table 2), perhaps with dissimilar survey methods and views concerning

18 Hoff-Wilson, "Illusion of Change," 397, notes that "the economic occupations of city women were negatively affected by periodic fluctuations in the commercial economy between 1763 and 1812."

the coverage of female heads and households. Such a possibility cannot entirely be rejected, as demonstrated by the two entries for 1811 which differ by 13 percentage points. It is encouraging, though, that for the years in which independent evidence exists from the Federal Population Census, the city directories appear to be accurate representations of both labor force participation and occupational data. Furthermore, as Table 2 indicates, twenty-seven directories, produced by a diverse group of publishers, have been examined over a period of seventy years, and it is the trend over time and not the figure of a particular year that is at issue.[19]

In sum, the labor force participation data for female heads of households suggest a seventy-year average of around 44 percent, with a slight downward trend and a procyclical component. How do these data compare with those much later in the century, say around 1890? The printed census provides useful, but not exactly comparable, information, since the women included in the directory were presumably widowed and unmarried heads of households. Available data give a figure of 41.8 percent for the labor force participation rate of widowed, urban women of twenty-five to thirty-four years old in 1890. Because these women, being young, were likely to have been heads of households, this figure is probably comparable to those for 1790 to 1860. Data in a special 1900 census volume on working women yield a labor force participation rate of 39 percent for female heads of households. The 1890 and 1900 figures are comparable to the long-run average for the period 1800 to 1860, but are considerably lower than the peak of labor force participation in the late eighteenth century. Furthermore, because labor force participation rates declined with age (the 1890 figure for thirty-five to forty-four year olds is only 33.1 percent), it is likely that there was a secular decline in the labor force participation of older female heads of households in cities.[20]

19 It appears that Robinson's directory was more complete than was Aitken's, which omitted many widows who did not have occupations. The occupations in the central portion of Philadelphia in 1790 are in almost perfect agreement with those in the directory.

20 U.S. Bureau of the Census, *Statistics of Women at Work: Based on Unpublished Information Derived From the Schedules of the Twelfth Census, 1900* (Washington, D.C., 1907). Figures for 1890 are derived from U.S. Census Office, *Population of the United States at the Eleventh Census: 1890* (Washington, D.C., 1895), Pt. I, for native-born women of native parents. The figure for the native born with one or more foreign-born parents is 43.4% for 25 to 34 year olds and 35.4% for 35- to 44-year-old widows. The 1900 figure is derived by

What accounted for this apparent decline in the labor force participation rate, and what might it signify with respect to the changing status of women? Several factors were acting to decrease the involvement of females in the market economy. Those operating in the opposite direction, to increase participation despite decreases on net, must also be addressed.

Two aspects of economic development and industrialization decreased the market involvement of older women. The movement of work from the household to the marketplace must surely have reduced the transmission of business and craft knowledge within the family and the ability of widows to assume the responsibilities of their husbands' shops or craft positions. In a related manner, the separation of place of work from place of residence removed the convenience, and thus increased the costs, of participating in the market economy, particularly for women with pre-adolescent children.

Of more importance to the long-run decline in the market participation of this group was the more rapid growth of industry in America's urban centers relative to that in its hinterland. This shift in industrial location, barely evident in early nineteenth-century Philadelphia, was obvious by 1860. Particular industries markedly raised the relative wages of the young compared with the old and thus altered the labor market parameters facing households. Data from the 1860 Federal Population Census suggest that families may have substituted the labor time of their younger members for that of their older ones.

The probability that a female head of household participated in the labor force is analyzed in Table 3. The included variables are age, wealth, the number and ages of the children living at home, ethnicity, and literacy. The probability that a female head of household participated in the labor force decreased with age and with wealth, over about $1,300 (1860 dollars). Female heads of household with no wealth, however, had lower reported participation rates than those in the middle range. Because many of the occupations that women held at this time were performed in the home—for example, boarding and innkeeping—those with no wealth had less opportunity to earn income. It is also possible

assuming that 15% of all households (the figure given in the 1900 census) were headed by women.

Table 3 The Determinants of Labor Force Participation of White Female Heads of Households, 1860 Philadelphia

DEPENDENT VARIABLE: LABOR FORCE PARTICIPATION (0,1)[a]
MEAN OF DEPENDENT VARIABLE: 0.390

	COEFFICIENT		MEANS[e]
Constant	0.911	(11.70)[d]*	
Age × 10^{-2}	−0.777	(5.62)*	47.3
Wealth			
No wealth	−0.107	(2.85)*	0.521
× 10^{-4}	−9.512	(3.61)*	3150[f]
Squared × 10^{-9}	3.654	(2.84)*	
Number of Children[b]			
< 15 years	−0.041	(2.53)*	0.735
Males 15–19 years	−0.062	(1.79)**	0.207
Females 15–19 years	0.031	(0.86)	0.197
Males > 19 years	−0.101	(3.54)*	0.279
Females > 19 years	−0.085	(2.97)*	0.285
Ethnicity Dummies			
Irish	0.064	(1.54)**	0.363
German	−0.109	(2.11)*	0.171
Literacy (1=illit.)[c]	0.071	(0.99)	0.063
R^2	0.149		
Number of Observations	731		

a Ordinary least squares results are given and do not differ from those produced by a logit estimating procedure.

b Interacting the children variables with the ethnic dummies does not meaningfully alter the regression.

c Illiterate is defined as not being able to write.

d Absolute values of 't' statistics are in parentheses. An asterisk (*) indicates significant at least at the 95% level; a double asterisk (**) indicates significant at least at the 90% level.

e Means are given across the three ethnic groups as compiled in the source, and the sample is not population weighted.

f Wealth includes both personal and real estate. The means by ethnicity are: Irish $441; German $695; Native-white $6,157. Average wealth per family, independent of the gender of the household head, was $3,887 in Philadelphia in 1860.

SOURCE: Philadelphia Social History Project, 1860 Household File.

that very poor women earned money in menial occupations that were underreported in the census.

The impact of industrialization on adult female labor force participation rates can be inferred from the substantial decrease in the probability of employment of women with adult children living in their households. A female head of household having a daughter over nineteen years old living at home had a decreased participation rate of 8.5 percentage points; one with a son over nineteen years old had a decreased participation rate of 10.1 percentage points and one with a son between fifteen and nineteen years of age had a decreased rate of 6.2 percentage points. Thus the presence and number of older children living in the household were important factors in the decision to participate in the market economy, even though age and wealth, both of which had reinforcing effects, are included in the equation.[21]

Industrialization within cities seems to have decreased the market participation of female heads of households but increased that of their adult children. Finally, increases in income per capita have, in the twentieth century, decreased the market involvement of females, particularly older women, and a similar factor may have operated in the early nineteenth century, as the coefficients on the wealth variables in Table 3 suggest.

Other factors operated in the opposite direction and served to increase the labor market role of female heads of households in Philadelphia. These factors render the decrease in the average labor force participation over time even more striking. The composition of the population changed with the arrival of the Irish, beginning in the late 1830s and continuing into the 1850s. The difference in participation rates between Irish and native-born white American female heads of household was about 10 percentage points in 1860 (37 percent for native born and 47 percent for the Irish). Thus the influx of the Irish served to increase female labor force participation rates. It should be noted that the difference between the Irish participation rate and that for the native born was primarily a function of relative wealth and age. Differences in the means between the Irish and the native born are virtually eliminated by standardizing for age and wealth, as can be seen in Table 3, in which the dummy variable for the Irish is small and barely significant statistically.

21 Susan Grigg, "Towards a Theory of Remarriage: Early Newburyport," *Journal of Interdisciplinary History*, VIII (1977), 183–220, analyzes the determinants of remarriage among widows. She finds a reduced probability of remarriage for widows with children of any age; however, those with children 16 to 20 years old had the lowest remarriage rates, holding the age of the widow constant. Furthermore, the coefficient on the number of children in the various age brackets is significant only for the older age group. Grigg's findings on remarriage, although they pertain to the period around 1810, reflect similar underlying causes as do those in Table 3 on labor force participation. Widows with older children could survive better than those with no children or with young children.

OCCUPATIONAL DATA, 1790 TO 1860 Several of the issues relating to the original golden age hypothesis concern the occupations that females held. Four years of occupational data (1791, 1811, 1821, and 1860) are given in Table 4 and were chosen to coincide with available census information, in particular for 1791 and 1860, and to utilize directories which indicated race. The occupational distributions indicate that a preponderance of these women worked in their own homes, as hand sewers (line 1), spinsters (3), retail dealers (4), innkeepers (5), boardinghouse keepers (6), and washerwomen (8). Fully one third were retail dealers across all four years, although the percentages in the other categories were less stable across the years.

The trend from 1791 to 1860 in occupational structure for female household heads was, in general, toward the sewing trades

Table 4 Occupational Distribution for White Female Heads of Households: Philadelphia 1791 to 1860

	(1)	(2)	(3)	(4) LINKED[b]	(5)
OCCUPATIONAL GROUP[a]:	1791	1811	1821	1821	1860
(1) Hand sewers and milliners	10.3%	19.0%	18.4%	20.3%	31.8%
(2) Craft, semiskilled, and factory jobs	1.6	2.1	3.1	4.3	6.7
(3) Spinster	15.6	2.1			
(4) Retail dealers and hucksters	32.5	31.2	28.5	29.9	32.8
(5) Innkeepers	7.2	4.5	4.8	7.5	2.2
(6) Boardinghouse keepers	18.4	16.4	16.0	17.6	6.9
(7) Teachers and nurses	14.1	20.8	23.9	14.4	11.9
(8) Domestic and personal service	0.2	3.8	5.3	5.9	7.7
Number of observations	418	605	418	187	494

a The major occupations in each group are:
(1) dressmaker, seamstress, tailoress, milliner, mantuamaker, hat and cap maker
(2) includes factory workers and craftspersons, such as upholsterer, perfumer, vest maker
(3) spinsters were home spinners
(4) shopkeeper, grocer, butcher, chinashop keeper, huckster, peddler
(5) innkeeper, tavernkeeper, restaurant keeper
(6) boardinghouse keeper
(7) teacher, nurse, midwife, librarian, governess, and semi- and quasi-professionals, such as layers out, bleeders, and herbwomen.
(8) washer, laundress, ironer, cleaner, domestic laborer.

b These data were linked from the census to the directory, and therefore include only female heads of households. They indicate that the directory listed female heads of households plus some nurses and teachers who did not head households.

and away from certain proprietorships. This movement is more easily seen when the data in columns (1), (4), and (5) are compared. As was noted above, the 1811 and 1821 directory data counted teachers and nurses even if they were not heads of households, making the data from the 1821 link to the census a more accurate source. The trend away from proprietorships was heavily influenced by decreases in the percentage that were boardinghouse keepers, a change that could have been more apparent than real. The percentage of all households with boarders was probably around 15 percent in 1860, including both female- and male-headed households, and it is likely that the figure for female-headed households was about 25 percent in 1860. Women who had several boarders, but not a substantial boardinghouse, do not appear to have stated that they ran one in the later period.[22]

This detailing of occupational change for women raises the issue of whether the entire occupational distribution for men and women was altered over time. Occupational distributions for male heads of households in 1791 and 1860 do indicate that the percentage of proprietors declined and that the percentage in manufacturing or craft positions increased. But the changes for men, although in the same direction as those for women, were not as large.[23]

22 The 1860 Federal Population Census does not give the relationship of individuals to the head of the household. This article's analysis employs a computer algorithm constructed by the Philadelphia Social History Project to infer relationships. See Theodore Hershberg et al., "Record Linkage," *Historical Methods Newsletter*, IX (1976), 137–163. The algorithm overstates "boarders" by including other family members who do not share the same last name with that of the household head. In 1860 the percentage of female-headed (native-born, primary) households with "boarders" was 36.7%, and of male-headed households (native-born, primary) households it was 27.1%. The percentage of all households with boarders was about 15% in 1880, when relationship to the head of household was given. Thus, if the bias in 1860 from including too many other family members in the boarder category were independent of the sex of the head of household, about 25% of female-headed households would have included boarders in 1860.

23 The distribution of occupations for adult males is:

	1791 Directory	1860 Census, Native White
Craft and factory	39%	44%
Laborer and unskilled	12	12
Sea related and transportation	8	5
Proprietor	28	23
Professional and commercial	7	11
No occupation given	6	6

The wide groupings utilized in Table 4 mask some of the more subtle changes over the period. Within the group of craft and semi-skilled positions found in the 1790s, several atypical positions for women existed, among them ironmonger, turner, tallow chandler, shoemaker, pewterer, cooper, tinplate worker, glass engraver, and sieve maker. By 1860 typically male occupations, such as many of these, were no longer performed by women. Although the numbers involved here are small, the implications transcend quantitative magnitudes and bear on the trends in proprietorships as well. These trades had once been transferred within the home-work environment among family members. Innkeepers and shopkeepers, as well, must have utilized family workers and thus transmitted business acumen and professional goodwill associated with a family, enhancing the probability that a widow (or an offspring) could maintain the business.

These notions are explored in Table 5 in which female heads of households in 1796 are located in the directories from 1791, 1793, 1794, and 1795, and are also linked to their husbands, if possible. The year 1796 was one in which the labor force participation rate for female heads of households was substantial (see Table 2) and the directory remarkably detailed. In addition, 1793 witnessed one of the most virulent yellow-fever epidemics in United States history, and the high mortality rate in the central portion of Philadelphia produced an abundance of recently widowed women.

Of the 1,019 female household heads who lived in Philadelphia in 1796, 83.3 percent could be traced back in time to a previous directory. Of those females who could be located at all during these years, 25.3 percent of their husbands were found over the span of four years, 1791 to 1794. Some of the 1,019 women never had husbands; a great many others had entered the city already widowed; and still others may have split off from larger households in the city too recently to be traced to earlier directories. None of these considerations affects the main finding of this exercise: widows in 1796 had a high probability of assuming their deceased husbands' businesses and craft positions.

Of the 217 husbands who could be located in the directories from 1791 to 1794, eleven had been innkeepers and six of their wives were innkeepers in 1796. (Part B of Table 5 includes the

Table 5 The Occupations of Widows and Their Husbands, 1791 to 1796

A. Sample Information

SAMPLE SIZE IN 1796	% TRACED TO 1791–1795	DISTRIBUTION OF FEMALES TRACED[a]				HUSBAND LOCATED 1791–1794[b]
		1791	1793	1794	1795	
1019	83% (849)[c]	22%	14%	14%	25%	26% (217)

B. Occupations (and Appellations) of Widows and the Husbands

WIDOW'S OCCUPATION \ HUSBAND'S OCCUPATION		Grocer & Shopkeeper	Boarding-house Keeper	Innkeeper	Baker	Tailor	Artisan	Gentleman & High Status Occupation[d]	Low Status Occupation	Other
WIDOW'S OCCUPATION		29	8	11	9	6	71	33	33	17
Grocer & Shopkeeper	33	23 (79%)[f] (70%)[g]								
Boardinghouse Keeper	32		8 (100%) (25%)							
Innkeeper	7			6 (55%) (86%)						
Baker	5				4 (44%) (80%)					
Seamstress	15					3 (50%) (20%)				
Artisan	15						14 (20%) (93%)			
Gentlewoman	40							21 (64%) (53%)		
Washer & Huckster	30								14 (42%) (47%)	
Other	40									
Total	217									

a The first year the woman is encountered in a directory from 1791. The percentages sum to 100% including the last column, "husband located."
b Regardless of which year.
c Number of observations.
d Includes attorney, esquire, clerk, physician, merchant, accountant, and gentleman.
e Includes porter, stevedore, sailor, pilot, laborer, skindresser, mariner, carter, huckster, gravedigger, sexton, and warfinger.
f Number of husbands and wives with the same occupation/Number of husbands with that occupation.
g Number of husbands and wives with the same occupation/Number of wives with that occupation.

diagonal and marginals of a matrix of the occupations of widows and their husbands.) Virtually all widowed boardinghouse keepers had husbands who had been boardinghouse keepers. There were twenty-nine husbands who were shopkeepers or grocers from 1791 to 1794, and twenty-three of their widows were similarly employed in 1796. Of the thirty-three husbands on the lower end of the income distribution who had been laborers, mariners, carters, or skindressers, about half of their wives became hucksters or washers when widowed. There were twelve cases of anomalous or atypical trades taken over by a wife: a tallow chandler, bottler, shoemaker, turner, cooper, stationer, ironmonger, tea merchant, sieve maker, tinplate worker, brewer, and a pewterer who was enumerated separately even when her husband was alive and was one of the very few cases of a married woman who was listed as employed. An upholsterer, two butchers, and four bakers, uncommon but not rare positions for women, also passed their trades on to their wives or commonly shared them when alive. Almost all fifteen widows occupying craft positions in 1796 had husbands who had been artisans.[24]

The conclusion that trades and businesses were overwhelmingly carried on by widows should not be surprising, but it does raise the issue of the amount of practical knowledge that these women had of their husbands' occupations. A study of Loyalist women has concluded that they had little knowledge of family businesses, trades, and general economic management. Loyalist women, however, were wealthier than those in this sample, many being the wives of merchants who were not involved in daily operations, and the wives of farmers who may not have been in close contact with business practices.[25]

24 Note that blacksmiths, carpenters, and scriveners—among others—did not have wives who carried on their trades after their death. The labor force participation rate of newly widowed women was higher than that for all women, suggesting that some of the inherited trades and businesses were short lived. It is possible that these women took over their deceased husbands' trades for only a brief period, perhaps until their sons' became of age to do so. But there is corroborating evidence from wills that widows actually conducted these enterprises. Lisa Waciega, "A 'Man of Business': The Widow of Means in Philadelphia and Chester County, 1750–1850," unpub. paper (1985), has uncovered substantial testimony that wives carried on businesses and trades as silent partners while their husbands were alive and were bequeathed these businesses upon their deaths.

25 Norton, "Eighteenth-Century American Women in Peace and War: The Case of the Loyalists," *William and Mary Quarterly*, XXXIII (1976), 386–409.

Although it is possible that women with little prior business knowledge were hastily put in command, it is more likely that many of the women in the 1796 directory were actively engaged in "hidden market work" when they were married, and that the decrease over time in proprietorships and occupations of a craft nature is linked to the progressive separation of home and work. Benjamin Franklin wrote of the hidden market work of his own wife. "She assisted me cheerfully in my business, folding and stitching pamphlets, tending shop, purchasing old linen rags for the papermakers, etc." Franklin's wife was able to do all of this despite her duties as a mother because the printing shop was a part of their house. Deborah relieved Benjamin from the everyday chores of printing and enabled him to become the editor and statesman for which he is remembered.[26]

Within the group of occupations that women have held, those stressed by Lerner and Dexter as having been eliminated from their domain include, most prominently, midwifery and proprietorships. Conditions relating to the latter set of occupations have already been addressed. The former, midwifery, has been discussed at length elsewhere, and the Philadelphia directories reflect the more universal decline of this profession and the rise of male midwives, accoucheurs, and doctors of obstetrics. This transition, at least in urban areas and among middle- to upper-class women, occurred at different times in both Europe and America. It is evident that by 1820 the obstetrics profession in Philadelphia had undergone vast changes. The directory of 1803 listed twenty-two midwives, practically all of whom were female. But by 1820, forty-five physicians, almost one third of the total number of doctors, were listed as practicing midwifery.[27]

What of the percentage of women within various classes of occupations? Not only were many women supposedly forced out of the paid labor force by social and political means, but those

26 Benjamin Franklin, *The Autobiography and Other Writings* (New York, 1961), 92.

27 Catherine Scholten, " 'On the Importance of the Obstetrick Art': Changing Customs of Childbirth in America, 1760–1825," *William and Mary Quarterly*, XXXIV (1977), 426–445, has also used city directories to show the declining female share of the midwife profession. Later in the century, when standards in the medical profession were being criticized, a movement began to reinstate women obstetricians to protect female virtue. Thus there is a certain ambiguity to the notion of "status" in this context, referring at times to the patient and at times to the midwife. Charles Rosenberg and Carol Smith-Rosenberg, *The Male Mid-Wife and the Female Doctor* (New York, 1974).

who remained were also claimed to have been confined to areas that then became their domain. Such changes would have greatly altered the social environment of women's work. Were proprietorships "feminized," with women selling women's goods?

The evidence on this issue runs counter to Dexter's assertion, despite the fact that stores in general became more specialized over time. Data from the two end years of the period analyzed, 1791 and 1860, indicate that the female share of many types of proprietorships was surprisingly stable and that women had a relatively large share of several businesses dealing solely with men's goods.

On the first point, 28 percent of all shop or storekeepers in 1791 were female; in 1860, 43 percent of all dry goods, trimmings, and fancy goods storekeepers were. In 1791 2.5 percent of all grocers were female, increasing to 9.1 percent by 1860. For butchers the respective figures are 4 percent and 3.3 percent, and for hucksters they are 63 percent and 67 percent. Fully 10 percent of all cigar dealers in 1860 were female, but we have no comparable figures for the early periods. For innkeepers the relevant percentages are 15 percent for both years, although the 1791 figure is inflated by counting all widows listed as innkeepers despite the listing of their deceased husbands' names as well.[28]

The findings of the quantitative aspects of this research are fivefold:

(1) Females headed about 15 percent of Philadelphia's households over the period 1791 to 1860, and, on average, 44 percent of these women listed an occupation in the city directories. Their labor force participation rate varied procyclically with economic fluctuations during the early period; the percentage of all households headed by a female varied countercyclically over the same period.

(2) The occupations held by these women were generally linked to the home, particularly for the early period, with the exceptions of street vendors and market women. By 1860 a greater percentage of employed women worked outside the home.

28 The 1860 data are from Boyd's Directories 1859/60 and 1860/61. The rest are from the directories listed in Table 2. The 1860 population census data for tavern and innkeepers are computed from the 1860 population census data for native-born whites.

(3) There is little evidence to substantiate many of the assertions made about changes in the structure of female occupations over this period. An important exception is that women did occupy many more atypical positions in the 1790s than they did afterwards. These atypical positions were inherited from their husbands, as can be seen by tracing widows back to their deceased husbands through the city directories of 1791 to 1796. It is reasonable to assume that many of these women were engaged in hidden market work even when their husbands were alive. This finding lends credence to the hypothesis that the labor force participation rate of married women first falls with economic development and only later rises.

(4) Female heads of household were somewhat younger in 1820 than in 1860. More striking is the difference between the two years in the number of young children per female household head, suggesting that young widows in 1860 lived with relatives far more frequently than they did in 1820.

(5) The presence of older children (over nineteen years old) in female-headed households in 1860 greatly reduced the probability that the female head had an occupation. Industrialization affected the market participation of women directly by separating home and work place, and indirectly by increasing the relative wages of young adult children.

The thesis that women suffered a decline in status sometime in the past is an important one. Rather than viewing the history of women's participation in the economy and in political life as continuous, proponents of this theory claim there was a major discontinuity, and, therefore, that a set of discriminatory forces altered the course of history.

Such a thesis, however, is not an entirely accurate description of the past, although much evidence has the appearance of being consistent with it. I have provided the first systematic data with which to understand the changes that did take place and that led some to embrace this doctrine of declining status. The data are from twenty-seven city directories and three federal population censuses, and they span the period 1790 to 1860 in what was, for a time, the largest city in and the capital of the United States.

Several elements of the original thesis are accurate and important depictions of past change. In the medical profession, for example, the professionalization of obstetrics succeeded in eliminating female midwives in cities, although only three decades later the use of female midwives was encouraged to guard the virtue of the patient. There was also a decline in certain trades and lines of business that women assumed when widowed. But these changes were far less the result of a change in ideology than a by-product of economic development. Trades moved from a home-work environment into artisanal shops and larger manufactories. Shops were more often partnerships or joint ventures and were physically removed from the home. Thus, skills may not have been passed on, and distances to work may have reduced a woman's ability to carry on a business after her husband's death.

The trends in female labor force participation and occupations over this period were brought about by industrialization, which altered the wage structure between young and old, and by economic development in general, which, together with the factory system, removed certain types of paid work from the home context. A different mechanism may have produced the results commented on by Lerner and others, and a decline in status or esteem for women may still have resulted. The occupational and labor force data, however, do not indicate a large enough shift to justify terming the early period a golden age for women.

WOMEN, WORK, AND THE FAMILY: FEMALE OPERATIVES IN THE LOWELL MILLS, 1830-1860

Thomas Dublin

In the United States between 1830 and 1860 increasing numbers of women found employment outside the home. In New England, the rise of textile manufacturing along the major rivers of Massachusetts, New Hampshire, and Maine created work for a predominantly female labor force. By taking these new jobs women chose not only to work outside their homes, but also to leave their families and to live in a radically different environment. While in the mill towns they became part of an urban working-class community.

I shall examine the nature and the transformation of the mill operative community in Lowell, Massachusetts, the leading textile center in the nation during this period. In the 1830s, the mill workforce consisted almost exclusively of young, single, native-born women. These female operatives came to form a close-knit community and the growth of community contributed, in turn, to the rise of collective labor protest. After 1845 the growth of an immigrant family workforce undermined the Yankee community and the labor movement it had nurtured. The transformation of the operative community in Lowell and the simultaneous decline in labor unrest offer important evidence of the impact of women's changing family roles on labor organization and protest under early industrial capitalism.

The female operatives in Lowell in the mid-1830s formed a community based on bonds of mutual dependence. Their experiences in Lowell were not simply similar or parallel to one another; they were inextricably intertwined. Women worked together in the mills with experienced operatives teaching newcomers work skills; in addition they lived together in company-owned boarding houses adjacent to the mills. Furthermore, the women were conscious of the existence of community and articulated this consciousness in their writings.[1] Community was both an objective and a subjective reality in the lives of female operatives.

Young women recruited from northern New England predominated in the work force of the early Lowell mills. In July 1836, for example, 74 percent of the work force of the Hamilton Manufacturing Company in Lowell was female and 96 percent native-born.[2] More than four-fifths of these women were between the ages of fifteen and thirty.[3] Almost three-fourths of female operatives at Hamilton resided in company boarding houses while in the mills.[4]

Although a quarter of the female operatives resided in private housing, the proportion living with their families was considerably smaller. Only one-ninth of female employed at Hamilton in July 1836 lived at home with their families.[5] The absence of significant numbers of workers living in families contributed to the importance of the operative peer group. Sharing work in the mills 72 hours a week and living in close quarters in company boarding houses, female operatives came to form a close-knit community.

Women were not only separated from their families while working in the mills, but were relatively isolated from men as well. The female-male division of labor insured that women and men had little contact within the mills. Men held all supervisory positions and worked in a number of skilled departments; women were confined principally to machine-tending jobs.[6] A typical workroom had two male supervisors, eighty female operatives, and a couple of children assisting the others. Women and men had little contact outside the formal overseer-operative relation. Patterns of residence further reinforced this separation. Married men lived in company tenements; single men, in all-male boarding houses; and single women, in all-female boarding houses. Even in institutions and activities open to both sexes—for instance, churches and lyceum lectures—women comprised the vast majority. In 1830, women comprised 63 percent of the population in Lowell. They made up more than 70 percent of those in the primary working population between 15 and 29 years of age.[7] Segregation at work and in housing, coupled with the predominance of women in early Lowell, contributed to the growth of a distinct female operative community.

The central institution in the female community was the corporation boarding house. There operatives escaped from the noise, cotton dust, and relentless pace of work in the mills. Relationships among women which arose within the mills were reinforced in a more relaxed setting. The boarding house, with an average of twenty-five female boarders sleeping four to six in a bedroom, was above all a collective living situation.[8]

The boarding house was also the center for the social life of operatives. After more than twelve hours a day in the mills, women spent most of their remaining hours in their boarding houses. In this setting they ate meals, rested, talked, sewed, wrote letters, and read books and magazines. From within this circle, they found friends who accompanied them to shops, to evening lectures, or to church events. On Sundays or holidays they often went out together for walks along the canals or into the nearby countryside. The community of operatives, in sum, developed in a setting in which women worked and lived together twenty-four hours a day.[9]

The boarding house provided the social context in which newcomers to Lowell made their first adjustment to urban, industrial life. Women generally did not come to Lowell entirely on their own. Usually they came because they knew someone—an older sister, cousin, or friend—who worked in Lowell. A newcomer was usually directed to a specific address, and her first contact with fellow operatives generally came in the boarding house, not in the mill.

From her arrival at the company boarding house, a newcomer felt the influence of the community of operatives. Harriet Robinson, an operative and the daughter of a boarding house keeper, described the socialization process in her autobiography, *Loom and Spindle*:

> Their [newcomers'] dialect was also very peculiar. On the broken English and Scotch of their ancestors was ingrafted the nasal Yankee twang; so that many of them when they had just come *daown*, spoke a language almost unintelligible. But the severe discipline and ridicule which met them was as good as a school education, and they were soon taught the "city way of speaking."
>
> Their dress was also peculiar, and was of the plainest homespun, cut in such an old-fashioned style that each young girl looked as if she had borrowed her grandmother's gown. Their only head-covering was a shawl, which was pinned under the chin; but after the first pay-day a 'shaker' (or 'scooter') sunbonnet usually replaced the primitive head-gear of their rural life.[10]

It was an unusual and strong-willed individual who could work and live among her fellow operatives and not conform, at least outwardly, to the customs and values of this larger community.

In addition to the pressure to conform to group patterns of speech and dress, the women enforced an unwritten code of moral conduct. Henry Miles, a minister in Lowell, described the way in which the community pressured those who deviated from accepted moral conduct:

> A girl, suspected of immoralities, or serious improprieties, at once loses caste. Her fellow boarders will at once leave the house, if the keeper does not dismiss the offender. In self-protection, therefore, the patron is obliged to put the offender away. Nor will her former companions walk with her, or work with her; till at length, finding herself everywhere talked about, and pointed at, and shunned, she is obliged to relieve her fellow-operatives of a presence which they feel brings disgrace.[11]

One should not conclude, however, that women always enforced a moral code agreeable to Lowell's clergy, or to mill agents and overseers, for that matter. The kind of peer pressure imposed on moral transgressors may also have been applied during labor struggles to women who did not participate in strikes. It would have been hard to go to work when one's roommates were marching about town and attending strike rallies. The ten-hour petition campaigns of the 1840s were similarly aided by the existence of a tightly knit community of operatives living in dense neighborhoods of boarding houses. To the extent that women could not have entirely private lives within the boarding house, they probably had to conform to group norms, whether these involved speech, clothing, relations with men, or attitudes toward the ten-hour day.

The strength of this female community was revealed in the rise of labor protest in early Lowell. In 1834 and 1836 large numbers of women operatives struck to protest wage cuts. Between 1843 and 1848 women operatives were among the most vocal advocates of a reduction in work hours. The early strikes—or "turn-outs" as they were called at the time—were above all strikes by women. Newspaper accounts specifically identified the strikers and their leaders as women.[12] Company correspondence made the point vividly when one mill agent wrote that 386 women and 3 men—out of a work force of 1300—were absent from the mills under his charge.[13] Women also dominated the Ten-Hour Movement, comprising three-fourths of petition signers in 1845.[14] They organized as well the Lowell Female Labor Reform Association, which spearheaded the Ten-Hour Movement in Lowell and worked actively to organize similar operatives' associations in other mill towns.[15]

The company boarding houses were the focal points of female labor protest in this period. Boarding house residents predominated among strikers in the mid-1830s. Of women who participated in the turnout at the Hamilton Company in October 1836, more than 95 percent lived in boarding houses. Among female boarding house residents, 28 percent went on strike; among those living at home, only 12 percent did so.[16] In other words, women living in boarding houses were more than twice as likely as those living at home to take part in the strike. Similarly, the ten-hour petition campaigns of the 1840s were promoted by numerous meetings held in company boarding houses. In these meetings, organizers from the Female Labor Reform Association recruited new members and secured additional signatures for their petitions to the state legislature.[17] The boarding houses thus provided both the participants in and the organizational structure of the labor movement in Lowell in these years.

Although these protests did not culminate in union organization the strikes were nevertheless collective actions. The mass departure of operatives to their rural homes was not simply the sum of hundreds of individual decisions of operatives who preferred to leave Lowell rather than submit to wage cuts. The words and actions of operatives make this point clear. In February 1834, eight hundred striking women paraded about Lowell and endorsed the following demands at a mass outdoor rally:

> Resolved, That we will not go back into the mills to work unless our wages are continued . . . as they have been.
>
> Resolved, That none of us will go back, unless they receive us all as one.
>
> Resolved, That if any have not money enough to carry them home, they shall be supplied.[18]

In October 1836, women formed committees within each of the mills to provide strike assistance for those in need.[19] Employers acknowledged the organization and tactical skill of the operatives. One mill agent wrote that although some operatives were willing to work, "it has been impossible to give employment to many who remained." He at attributed the difficulty to the women's tactics: "This was in many instances no doubt the result of calculation and contrivance. After the original turn-out, they [the operatives] would assail a particular room—as for instance, all the warpers, or all the warp spinners, or all the speeder and stretcher girls, and this would close the mill as effectually as if all the girls in the mills had left."[20] The demand for amnesty, the concern for the welfare of fellow operatives, and the effort to bring out workers in key departments are all indications of the organized, collective nature of these strikes.

In their protests female operatives gave expression to new values and attitudes which were clearly the product of their industrial experience. In 1834, for example, one strike leader gave a "flaming Mary Woolstonecroft [*sic*] speech on the rights of women and the the iniquities of the 'monied aristocracy.' "[21] Some operatives came to see a relation between their treatment as workers and the dominant bourgeois paternalism that affected all women. This understanding was expressed in an open letter to a state legislator who had opposed the enactment of a ten-hour law:

> Bad as is the condition of so many women, it would be much worse if they had nothing but your boasted protection to rely upon; but they have at last learnt the lesson which a bitter experience teaches, that not to those who style themselves their "natural protectors" are they to look for the needful help, but to the strong and resolute of their own sex.[22]

Women had learned to rely on one another in their daily lives and so came to depend on each other in their labor struggles as well.

The conditions that gave rise to the close-knit community among female operatives, however, did not persist unchanged in these years. The three decades before the Civil War was a period of rapid growth and change in Lowell. Between 1836 and 1850, for instance, the assets of the textile corporations almost doubled, while the number of employees increased from 6,100 to 11,400.[23] With the expansion of the mills, the population of the city grew from 17,000 in 1836 to 33,000 in 1850. After 1845 the mills attracted increasing numbers of immigrants, particularly the Irish. The 1850s saw the transformation of the labor system which had persisted in Lowell since the 1820s and the undermining of the close-knit female community which had developed during these years.

The earlier operative community was undermined by two interrelated factors: the changing make-up of the mill work force and the growing dispersal of operatives' housing. The proportion of foreign-born employed at the Hamilton Company in Lowell rose sharply, starting at only 4 percent in 1836 and reaching 62 percent in 1860. Three-fourths of all immigrants working at Hamilton were Irish; by 1860 the Irish formed the largest single ethnic group in the company's mills, comprising 47 percent of the work force.[24]

The declining importance of company boarding houses also undermined the female operative community. In 1836 almost three-fourths of operatives at Hamilton had resided in company housing. By 1860, this proportion had declined to one-third.[25] Increasing numbers of workers lived in private boarding houses or at home with their families. The new residence pattern resulted primarily from the actions of the textile corporations. In the 1840s they did not construct additional housing to keep pace with the expansion of the mill labor force. In addition, they sold off undeveloped lands to private developers. Finally, they ceased enforcing the company regulation that required operatives to reside in company housing. Without an adequate stock of company housing, newcomers came to rely on the growing supply of private tenement housing. The dispersal of housing led to a disjunction of work and living settings for operatives. The new residence pattern removed an important element in the shared experiences of female operatives.

What occurred in Lowell in the 1850s, however, was not so much the decline of community, but rather its reconstitution along new lines. As the composition and residence patterns of the mill work force changed, the locus of the operative community shifted. There remained a dwindling group of Yankee women living in company boarding houses, and by 1860 the predominant operative community was found among Irish immigrant families.

The Irish operative community differed from its Yankee predecessor in several important respects. The Irish were not exclusively a female community. As they entered the mill work force between 1836 and 1860, the proportion of males employed at the Hamilton Company increased from 15 to 30 percent.[26] Immigrant males were concentrated primarily in the mulespinning and weaving departments. The influx of immigrant families into Lowell brought large numbers of men and boys willing to work at wages comparable to those of females. The textile mills took advantage of this new supply of labor and hired increasing numbers of males to perform work formerly done by women.

Unlike the earlier Yankee operatives, large numbers of Irish came to Lowell with their families. In 1836 only 11 percent of females employed at Hamilton had resided at home. For a comparable sample of Irish female millhands in 1860, almost one-half lived with their families. After 1850 a family-labor system supplanted the earlier one based on the labor of single women. The transformation was by no means complete in 1860, and large numbers of single women—both native-born and immigrant—continued to come to Lowell on their own to work in the mills. But the decisive trend between 1836 and 1860 was the increase in the proportion of female operatives living at home with their families at the expense of the women residing in company boarding houses.[27]

In order to examine the family relationships of female millhands and the structure of their families I drew a one-in-ten systematic sample from the 1860 federal manuscript census of Lowell. Selecting every tenth millhand enumerated in the census I generated a sample of 761 female and 329 male operatives. I recorded for each of these sample members personal data—age, nativity, sex, occupation being the most important—and for females only I recorded additional information on the composition of their households and, where present, families.[28] Of the 761 females in the sample, 266—thirty-five percent—were living with their families. The remainder of this analysis will focus on these families of female millhands.

Immigrant women were much more likely to be living at home than were Yankees. More than 48 percent of the foreign-born in the 1860 Female Millhand Sample lived at home. For native-born the comparable proportion was only 23 percent. In other words, relatively twice as many immigrants as Yankees resided with their families while working in the mills.

The most striking fact about the families of female millhands is that more than half—138 of 266—were headed by females. The proportion of female-headed households was the same among native-born and immigrants, suggesting that class rather than ethnicity was primarily responsible for the observed pattern of family composition. Two interpretations may account for the high proportion of female-headed households among these families. First, it is possible that widows may have moved to Lowell to take advantage of a labor system that offered employment primarily to women and children.[29] On the other hand, a labor system offering steadier employment to women and children than to men may have undermined the economic position and authority of adult males in working-class families, thus leading to high rates of desertion. Only by tracing the histories of families over time—by linking successive manuscript censuses—will it be possible to determine the bases of the high proportion of female-headed households among operatives in Lowell.

Whether female- or male-headed, the families of millhands were dependent on the employment of several family members. In the 266 families of the 1860 Female Millhand Sample more than 70 percent of all family members were recorded by census enumerators as employed. There were few elderly and few young children in these families—the children were generally in their 'teens and twenties and parents in their their thirties and forties. The proportion in the family working varied with the earning capacity of the household head. In female-headed households 85 percent of family members were listed as employed; for male-headed, the corresponding proportion was 63 percent. These were clearly the families of workers—families forced by the low wages of parents to rely on the earnings of children to provide a subsistence.

Three-fourths—or 205 of 266—of all female millhands in the sample living at home were children. I describe them as children not so much because of their age—they were twenty years old on the average—but because they resided in the households of their parents.[30] In these 205 families there were on the average four children, making a total of somewhat more than 800 children. This population consisted of the female millhands drawn from the sample and their siblings. These children were well integrated into the Lowell labor system: three-fourths of them were employed, and 93 percent of those so recorded were millhands. Judging from the ages of children in school and of those working in the mills, it is apparent that most began working at thirteen or fourteen years of age. Of 40 fifteen-year-olds enumerated in these families 39 were listed as employed; only one attended school. On the average, the oldest children in these families were twenty-two years old, suggesting that these children worked a minimum of eight years while residing at home. Given an average spacing of nine years between youngest and eldest, one may conclude that for at least seventeen years these families could draw on the income of children to supplement adult earnings.[31]

The dependence of mill families on the earnings of their children is further underscored by two factors: the ages of working children and the occupations of parents. Although the census does not differentiate between different types of millhands—that is, between weavers, spinners, bobbin girls, and so on—one can infer from census data that most of the children held regular positions in the mills. As noted above, the oldest child in these families averaged twenty-two years of age; the youngest employed in the mills, seventeen. These ages are well above those of bobbin girls, lap boys, or back and front boys, who were low-paid and tended to be between ten and fifteen years of age. The employed children in these families probably earned regular adult wages which in 1860 averaged $0.57 per day.[32]

The parents of the female millhands were concentrated in two particularly low-paid occupations. The majority of male heads of these families were day laborers; 80 percent of female heads were listed as housekeepers. Given the seasonality of outdoor construction work, a forty-year-old Irish day laborer could expect to earn little more than his seventeen-year-old daughter. His daily wage was higher, but given the irregularity of work, his yearly earnings were likely to be only about the same as those of millhands.[33] Housekeepers earned still less, and it is even questionable whether women so designated actually worked for wages, as census enumerators also recorded some women separately as "domestic servants." Assuming, however, that housekeepers did work for wages outside their homes, it is unlikely that they earned as much as adult millhands. In these families there were, on the average, three children and one parent listed as employed in June 1860. Given the comparative wage levels described here, it is likely that children earned about three-fourths of the income of these families.

It is important to bear in mind that the conclusion regarding the dependence of mill families on the earnings of their children is based on the 1860 Female Millhand Sample described above. Obviously there were families in Lowell without any female members in the mills who would not be included in the sample considered here. This sample is by no means a random sample of Lowell families. Still it offers a view of working-class immigrant families attracted to Lowell and to the mills.

The picture of the family labor system that emerges from these data is one of family members functioning as a unit to provide for family needs. In young families with no or few children, often both husband and wife worked, and as children grew up they soon became important contributors to the family income. The earnings of children were particularly important because half of the families had no male parent living in the household. Even in two-parent families, however, it is likely that at one stage of the family cycle children earned almost 75 percent of the family income. The low wages and irregularity of day laboring jobs for Irish adult males made the earnings of children crucial to the family living standard.

The dependent position of female millhands living at home with their parents and the importance of their earnings to the subsistence of their families must have had a dampening effect on labor protest in the 1850s. Two decades earlier Yankee women lived on their own in Lowell in a community consisting of female operatives. If they contributed to the support of distant families they clearly chose to do so. When a Yankee operative "turned out" in 1834 or 1836 she had a rural home and family to which she could return. When an Irish operative living at home decided to strike or to to sign a ten-hour petition, she had to consider her parents' reaction and the loss of family income which her action might entail.

Although I do not have comparable data on the family relationships of male millhands in 1860, I would suggest that men were affected quite differently by the changes in the Lowell labor force. First, the pool of male operatives increased during this period, while the number of females declined slightly. Second, it is likely that a significantly higher proportion of single males than females lived away from their families in company or private boarding houses. Furthermore, more males than females headed their own households. In other words, fewer males than females lived with their families as dependent children.

With increasing numbers of male operatives in the mill work force and with changing housing patterns and family relations undermining the close-knit community among women operatives, it is not altogether surprising that men increasingly came to dominate the labor movement in Lowell in the 1850s. The Ten Hour Movement of the 1840s was transformed from a female-dominated educational and agitational campaign into a male-dominated political movement closely tied to electoral politics. As ward committees in the Democratic and Free Soil parties took an increasing part in the ten-hour struggle, the role of female operatives declined accordingly. After 1850 women in Lowell never again played such a dominant role in the labor movement.

Whether this pattern prevailed in later years and in other industrial communities remains unknown. The relationship between family membership and protest should be examined in more varied ethnic and industrial settings before any firm conclusions are reached. Further research into the history of working women in other mill towns and industrial centers should offer evidence bearing on the conclusions reached here.

NOTES

I would like to thank Lynn Lees and Nancy Schwartz for critical comments on earlier drafts of this article.

[1]Harriet Robinson, *Loom and Spindle, or Life Among Early Mill Girls* (New York: Thomas Y. Crowell, 1898), p. 89.

[2]The data throughout this article are taken from my dissertation, "Women at Work: The Transformation of Work and Community in Lowell, Massachusetts, 1826-1860," (Ph.D. dissertation, Columbia University, 1975). For data on the makeup of the Hamilton Company work force in 1836 see chapter 3 and appendix 2.

[3]Dublin, "Women at Work," Table 3, p. 42.

[4]Ibid., Table 2, p. 39.

[5]Ibid., p. 39.

[6]Ibid., Table 4, p. 63.

[7]Data on Lowell's population is taken from the analysis of the 1830 federal manuscript census of Lowell. The census enumerator recorded the number of males and females in specific age groups which has made possible the calculation of the proportion of females in specific age categories.

[8]Based on the analysis of the listings of residents of Hamilton boarding houses in the 1830 and 1840 manuscript censuses and the examination of photographs of the boarding houses taken in the late nineteenth century. *Locks and Canals Collection*, Lowell Technological Institute.

[9]*The Lowell Offering*, 2: 65-79; 5: 218.

[10]Robinson, *Loom and Spindle*, pp. 65-66.

[11]Henry Miles, *Lowell As It Was and As It Is* (Lowell: Powers and Bagley, 1845), pp. 144-45.

[12]Boston Evening *Transcript*, February 17 and 18, 1834; *Zion's Herald*, October 5, 1836; Boston *Daily Times*, October 6, 1836.

[13]*Lawrence Manufacturing Company Records*, vol. MAB-1, correspondence of John Aiken to Henry Hall, October 3, 1836, at Baker Library, Harvard Business School; *Lowell Directory*, 1836, p. 9.

[14]Ten Hour Petitions on deposit at Massachusetts State Archives, Numbers 1587/8 and 1587/9.

[15]*Voice of Industry*, December 5 and 19, 1845, July 24, 1846, October 30, 1846, December 4, 1846, and January 8, 1847. The press for the *Voice* was owned by the Lowell Female Labor Reform Association and the first president of the Association, Sarah Bagley, was an editor.

[16]Dublin, "Women at Work," Table 18, p. 122.

[17]*Voice of Industry*, December 4, 1846.

[18]Boston Evening *Transcript*, February 17, 1834.

[19]Boston Daily *Times*, October 6, 1836.

[20]*Tremont-Suffolk Mills Records*, unbound letters, vol. FN-1, October 10, 1836 in Baker Library, Harvard Business School.

[21]Boston Evening *Transcript*, February 17, 1834.

[22]*Voice of Industry*, March 13, 1846.

[23]*Lowell Directory*, 1836, pp. 7-9; *Seventh Census of the United States* (Washington, D.C.: G. P.O., 1850), Manufacturing Schedule for Lowell.

[24]Dublin, "Women at Work,' Table 20, p. 149.

[25]Op. cit., Table 23, p. 153.

[26]Ibid., p. 145.

[27]Ibid., Table 27, p. 159. Female operatives not living with their families included women in company and private boarding houses. These women were somewhat older than those living at home, averaging 24 years of age compared to 20. In company boarding houses, Yankee women predominated while in the private boarding houses, the majority were immigrant. Preliminary findings suggest that female operatives residing in boarding houses had been working somewhat longer than family members and were concentrated in the better-paying jobs in the mills.

[28]For further discussion of the findings and methodology of the study of family relations of female millhands see Dublin, "Women at Work," chapter 10 and appendix 7. Much of the data presented in this article is based on analysis of the female millhand sample since the completion of the dissertation.

[29]In this regard, it is interesting that the autobiographies of female operatives—those of Harriet Robinson and Lucy Larcom—document the experiences of women who came to Lowell as children with their widowed mothers in the 1830s.

[30]Family relationships have been inferred from census listings as they were not recorded by enumerators until the census of 1880. Female millhands living at home other than children of household heads included household heads (10%), spouses (7%) and siblings of household heads (6%). Women in these other groups were decidedly older than those living with their parents. Women who headed households and worked in the mills generally had one child or less. Husbands of female millhands generally were also operatives, and these families averaged two children, both under ten years old. Data on families with older children indicate that wives generally quit work when their children were old enough to enter the mills.

[31]These data underestimate the number of children and the age spread among them since the figures are based on only those children living in the household at the date of the census enumeration, excluding children who had already left the home and those unborn.

[32]Dublin, "Women at Work," Table 40, p. 187.

[33]These findings are based on a separate study made by the author of the annual earnings of laborers employed by the proprietors of Locks and Canals, the major employer of unskilled day laborers in Lowell. Similar yearly earnings were computed for mill operatives in Hamilton. It was evident that laborers did somewhat better than female operatives in the best years and considerably worse in periods of depression.

WOMEN, WORK, AND PROTEST IN THE EARLY LOWELL MILLS: "THE OPPRESSING HAND OF AVARICE WOULD ENSLAVE US"

By THOMAS DUBLIN

In the years before 1850 the textile mills of Lowell, Massachusetts were a celebrated economic and cultural attraction. Foreign visitors invariably included them on their American tours. Interest was prompted by the massive scale of these mills, the astonishing productivity of the power-driven machinery, and the fact that women comprised most of the workforce. Visitors were struck by the newness of both mills and city as well as by the culture of the female operatives. The scene stood in sharp contrast to the gloomy mill towns of the English industrial revolution.

Lowell, was, in fact, an impressive accomplishment. In 1820, there had been no city at all—only a dozen family farms along the Merrimack River in East Chelmsford. In 1821, however, a group of Boston capitalists purchased land and water rights along the river and a nearby canal, and began to build a major textile manufacturing center. Opening two years later, the first factory employed Yankee women recruited from the nearby countryside. Additional mills were constructed until, by 1840, ten textile corporations with thirty-two mills valued at more than ten million dollars lined the banks of the river and nearby canals.[1] Adjacent to the mills were rows of company boarding houses and tenements which accommodated most of the eight thousand factory operatives.

As Lowell expanded, and became the nation's largest textile manufacturing center, the experiences of women operatives changed as well. The increasing number of firms in Lowell and in the other mill towns brought

[1] *Statistics of Lowell Manufactures*, January 1, 1840. Broadside available in the Manuscripts Division, Baker Library, Harvard Business School.

the pressure of competition. Overproduction became a problem and the prices of finished cloth decreased. The high profits of the early years declined and so, too, did conditions for the mill operatives. Wages were reduced and the pace of work within the mills was stepped up. Women operatives did not accept these changes without protest. In 1834 and 1836 they went on strike to protest wage cuts, and between 1843 and 1848 they mounted petition campaigns aimed at reducing the hours of labor in the mills.

These labor protests in early Lowell contribute to our understanding of the response of workers to the growth of industrial capitalism in the first half of the nineteenth century. They indicate the importance of values and attitudes dating back to an earlier period and also the transformation of these values in a new setting.

The major factor in the rise of a new consciousness among operatives in Lowell was the development of a close-knit community among women working in the mills. The structure of work and the nature of housing contributed to the growth of this community. The existence of community among woman, in turn, was an important element in the repeated labor protests of the period.

The organization of this paper derives from the logic of the above argument. It will examine the basis of community in the experiences of women operatives and then the contribution that the community of women made to the labor protests in these years as well as the nature of the new consciousness expressed by these protests.

The pre-conditions for the labor unrest in Lowell before 1850 may be found in the study of the daily worklife of its operatives. In their everyday, relatively conflict-free lives, mill women created the mutual bonds which made possible united action in times of crisis. The existence of a tight-knit community among them was the most important element in determining the collective, as opposed to individual, nature of this response.

Before examining the basis of community among women operatives in early Lowell, it may be helpful to indicate in what sense "community" is being used. The women are considered a "community" because of the development of bonds of mutual dependence among them. In this period they came to depend upon one another and upon the larger group of operatives in very important ways. Their experiences were not simply similar or parallel to one another, but were inextricably intertwined. Furthermore, they were conscious of the existence of community, expressing it very clearly in their writings and in labor protests. "Community" for them had objective and subjective dimensions and both were important in their experience of women in the mills.

The mutual dependence among women in early Lowell was rooted in the structure of mill work itself. Newcomers to the mills were particularly dependent on their fellow operatives, but even experienced hands relied on one another for considerable support.

New operatives generally found their first experiences difficult, even harrowing, though they may have already done considerable hand-spinning and weaving in their own homes. The initiation of one of them is described in fiction in the *Lowell Offering:*

> The next morning she went into the Mill; and at first the sight of so many bands, and wheels, and springs in constant motion, was very frightful. She felt afraid to touch the loom, and she was almost sure she could never learn to weave . . . the shuttle flew out, and made a new bump on her head; and the first time she tried to spring the lathe, she broke out a quarter of the treads.[2]

While other accounts present a somewhat less difficult picture, most indicate that women only became proficient and felt satisfaction in their work after several months in the mills.[3]

The textile corporations made provisions to ease the adjustment of new operatives. Newcomers were not immediately expected to fit into the mill's regular work routine. They were at first assigned work as sparehands and were paid a daily wage independent of the quantity of work they turned out. As a sparehand, the newcomer worked with an experienced hand who instructed her in the intricacies of the job. The sparehand spelled her partner for short stretches of time, and occasionally took the place of an absentee. One woman described the learning process in a letter reprinted in the *Offering:*

> Well, I went into the mill, and was put to learn with a very patient girl. . . . You cannot think how odd everything seems. . . . They set me to threading shuttles, and tying weaver's knots, and such things, and now I have improved so that I can take care of one loom. I could take care of two if only I had eyes in the back part of my head. . . .[4]

After the passage of some weeks or months, when she could handle the normal complement of machinery—two looms for weavers during the

[2] *Lowell Offering,* I, 169.
[3] *Ibid.,* IV, 145-148, 169-172, 237-240, 257-259.
[4] *Offering,* IV, p. 170.

1830s—and when a regular operative departed, leaving an opening, the sparehand moved into a regular job.

Through this system of job training, the textile corporations contributed to the development of community among female operatives. During the most difficult period in an operative's career, the first months in the mill, she relied upon other women workers for training and support. And for every sparehand whose adjustment to mill work was aided in this process, there was an experienced operative whose work was also affected. Women were relating to one another during the work process and not simply tending their machinery. Given the high rate of turnover in the mill workforce, a large proportion of women operatives worked in pairs. At the Hamilton Company in July 1836, for example, more than a fifth of all females on the Company payroll were sparehands.[5] Consequently, over forty per cent of the females employed there in this month worked with one another. Nor was this interaction surreptitious, carried out only when the overseer looked elsewhere; rather it was formally organized and sanctioned by the textile corporations themselves.

In addition to the integration of sparehands, informal sharing of work often went on among regular operatives. A woman would occasionally take off a half or full day from work either to enjoy a brief vacation or to recover from illness, and fellow operatives would each take an extra loom or side of spindles so that she might continue to earn wages during her absence.[6] Women were generally paid on a piece rate basis, their wages being determined by the total output of the machinery they tended during the payroll period. With friends helping out during her absence, making sure that her looms kept running, an operative could earn almost a full wage even though she was not physically present. Such informal work-sharing was another way in which mutual dependence developed among women operatives during their working hours.

Living conditions also contributed to the development of community among female operatives. Most women working in the Lowell mills of these years were housed in company boarding houses. In July 1836, for example, more than 73 percent of females employed by the Hamilton Company resided in company housing adjacent to the mills.[7] Almost

[5] These statistics are drawn from the author's dissertation, "Women at Work: The Transformation of Work and Community in Lowell, Mass., 1826-1860 (Columbia Univ., 1975).

[6] Harriet Hanson Robinson, *Loom and Spindle, Or Life Among the Early Mill Girls*, (New York, 1898), 91.

[7] "Women at Work," Chapter 4. Statistics are based on linkage between company payrolls and register books of the Hamilton Manufacturing Company. The register books were alphabetically organized volumes in which operatives were signed into and out of the

three-fourths of them, therefore, lived and worked with each other. Furthermore, the work schedule was such that women had little opportunity to interact with those not living in company dwellings. They worked, in these years, an average of 73 hours a week. Their work day ended at 7:00 or 7:30 P.M., and in the hours between supper and the 10:00 curfew imposed by management on residents of company boarding houses there was little time to spend with friends living "off the corporation."

Women in the boarding houses lived in close quarters, a factor that also played a role in the growth of community. A typical boarding house accommodated twenty-five young women, generally crowded four to eight in a bedroom.[8] There was little possibility of privacy within the dwelling, and pressure to conform to group standards was very strong (as will be discussed below). The community of operatives which developed in the mills it follows, carried over into life at home as well.

The boarding house became a central institution in the lives of Lowell's female operatives in these years, but it was particularly important in the initial integration of newcomers into urban industrial life. Upon first leaving her rural home for work in Lowell, a woman entered a setting very different from anything she had previously known. One operative, writing in the *Offering,* described the feelings of a fictional character: ". . . the first entrance into a factory boarding house seemed something dreadful. The room looked strange and comfortless, and the women cold and heartless; and when she sat down to the supper table, where among more than twenty girls, all but one were strangers, she could not eat a mouthful."[9]

In the boarding house, the newcomer took the first steps in the process which transformed her from an "outsider" into an accepted member of the community of women operatives.

Recruitment of newcomers into the mills and their initial hiring was mediated through the boarding house system. Women generally did not travel to Lowell for the first time entirely on their own. They usually came because they knew someone—an older sister, cousin, or friend—who had already worked in Lowell.[10] The scene described above was a

mills. They gave the nativity and local residence of operatives as well as additional data. For a detailed discussion of the linkage methods used see the appendices of "Women at Work."

[8] "Women at Work," Chapter 5. Statistics based on on analysis of federal manuscript census listings of Hamilton boarding houses in 1830 and 1840.

[9] *Offering,* I, 169.

[10] *Ibid.,* II, 145-155; I, 2-7, 74-78.

lonely one — but the newcomer did know at least one boarder among the twenty seated around the supper table. The Hamilton Company Register Books indicate that numerous pairs of operatives, having the same surname and coming from the same town in northern New England, lived in the same boarding houses.[11] If the newcomer was not accompanied by a friend or relative, she was usually directed to "Number 20, Hamilton Company," or to a similar address of one of the other corporations where her acquaintance lived. Her first contact with fellow operatives generally came in the boarding houses and not in the mills. Given the personal nature of recruitment in this period, therefore, newcomers usually had the company and support of a friend or relative in their first adjustment to Lowell.

Like recruitment, the initial hiring was a personal process. Once settled in the boarding house a newcomer had to find a job. She would generally go to the mills with her friend or with the boarding house keeper who would introduce her to an overseer in one of the rooms. If he had an opening, she might start work immediately. More likely, the overseer would know of an opening elsewhere in the mill, or would suggest that something would probably develop within a few days. In one story in the *Offering*, a newcomer worked on some quilts for her house keeper, thereby earning her board while she waited for a job opening.[12]

Upon entering the boarding house, the newcomer came under pressure to conform with the standards of the community of operatives. Stories in the *Offering* indicate that newcomers at first stood out from the group in terms of their speech and dress. Over time, they dropped the peculiar "twang" in their speech which so amused experienced hands. Similarly, they purchased clothing more in keeping with urban than rural styles. It was an unusual and strongwilled individual who could work and live among her fellow operatives and not conform, at least outwardly, to the customs and values of this larger community.[13]

The boarding houses were the centers of social life for women operatives after their long days in the mills. There they ate their meals, rested, talked, sewed, wrote letters, read books and magazines. From among fellow workers and boarders they found friends who accompanied them to shops, to Lyceum lectures, to church and church-sponsored events. On

[11] *Hamilton Manufacturing Company Records*, Volume 283, *passim*. This volume, along with all the other company records cited in this article are located in the Manuscript Division of Baker Library, Harvard Business School.

[12] *Offering*, IV, 145-148.

[13] *Ibid.*, I, 5; IV, 148.

Sundays or holidays, they often took walks along the canals or out into the nearby countryside. The community of women operatives, in sum, developed in a setting where women worked and lived together, twenty-four hours a day.

Given the all-pervasiveness of this community, one would expect it to exert strong pressures on those who did not conform to group standards. Such appears to have been the case. The community influenced newcomers to adopt its patterns of speech and dress as described above. In addition, it enforced an unwritten code of moral conduct. Henry Miles, a minister in Lowell, described the way in which the community pressured those who deviated from accepted moral conduct:

> A girl, suspected of immoralities, or serious improprieties, at once loses caste. Her fellow boarders will at once leave the house, if the keeper does not dismiss the offender. In self-protection, therefore, the patron is obliged to put the offender away. Nor will her former companions walk with her, or work with her; till at length, finding herself everywhere talked about, and pointed at, and shunned, she is obliged to relieve her fellow-operatives of a presence which they feel brings disgrace.[14]

The power of the peer group described by Miles may seem extreme, but there is evidence in the writing of women operatives to corroborate his account. Such group pressure is illustrated by a story (in the *Offering*) — in which, operatives in a company boarding house begin to harbor suspicions about a fellow boarder, Hannah, who received repeated evening visits from a man whom she does not introduce to the other residents. Two boarders declare that they will leave if she is allowed to remain in the household. The house keeper finally informed Hannah that she must either depart or not see the man again. She does not accept the ultimatum, but is promptly discharged after the overseer is informed, by one of the boarders, about her conduct. And, only one of Hannah's former friends continues to remain on cordial terms.[15]

One should not conclude, however, that women always enforced a moral code agreeable to Lowell's clergy, or to the mill agents and overseers for that matter. After all, the kind of peer pressure imposed on Hannah could be brought to bear on women in 1834 and 1836 who on their own would not have protested wage cuts. It was much harder to

[14] Henry A. Miles, *Lowell As It Was And As It is* (Lowell, 1845), 144-145.

[15] *Offering,* IV, 14-23. Like so many of the stories in the *Offering,* this one has a dramatic reversal at its conclusion. We learn at the end that Hannah's visitor has been her brother, whose identity could not be revealed because he was afraid that the woman he was courting might learn that his sister was an operative.

go to work when one's roommates were marching about town, attending rallies, circulating strike petitions. Similarly, the ten-hour petitions of the 1840s were certainly aided by the fact of a tight-knit community of operatives living in a dense neighborhood of boarding houses. To the extent that women could not have completely private lives in the boarding houses, they probably had to conform to group norms, whether these involved speech, clothing, relations with men, or attitudes toward the ten-hour day. Group pressure to conform, so important to the community of women in early Lowell, played a significant role in the collective response of women to changing conditions in the mills.

In addition to the structure of work and housing in Lowell, a third factor, the homogeneity of the mill workforce, contributed to the development of community among female operatives. In this period the mill workforce was homogeneous in terms of sex, nativity, and age. Payroll and other records of the Hamilton Company reveal that more than 85 per cent of those employed in July, 1836, were women and that over 96 per cent were native-born.[16] Furthermore, over 80 per cent of the female workforce was between the ages of 15 and 30 years old; and only ten per cent was under 15 or over 40.[17]

Workforce homogeneity takes on particular significance in the context of work structure and the nature of worker housing. These three factors combined meant that women operatives had little interaction with men during their daily lives. Men and women did not perform the same work in the mills, and generally did not even labor in the same rooms. Men worked in the picking and initial carding processes, in the repair shop and on the watchforce, and filled all supervisory positions in the mills. Women held all sparehand and regular operative jobs in drawing, speeding, spinning, weaving and dressing. A typical room in the mill employed eighty women tending machinery, with two men overseeing the work and two boys assisting them. Women had little contact with men other than their supervisors in the course of the working day. After work, women returned to their boarding houses, where once again there were few men. Women, then, worked and lived in a predominantly female setting.

Ethnically the workforce was also homogeneous. Immigrants formed

[16] These statistics are based on the linkage of payroll and register books of the Hamilton Company as were the data on residence presented above. See Chapter 4 and Appendices of "Women at Work."

[17] These data are based on an analysis of the age distribution of females residing in Hamilton company boarding houses as recorded in the federal manuscript censuses of 1830 and 1840. See Chapter 4, "Women at Work."

only 3.4 per cent of those employed at Hamilton in July, 1836. In addition, they comprised only 3 per cent of residents in Hamilton company housing.[18] The community of women operatives was composed of women of New England stock drawn from the hill-country farms surrounding Lowell. Consequently, when experienced hands made fun of the speech and dress of newcomers, it was understood that they, too, had been "rusty" or "rustic" upon first coming to Lowell. This common background was another element shared by women workers in early Lowell.

The work structure, the workers' housing, and workforce homogeneity were the major elements which contributed to the growth of community among Lowell's women operatives. To best understand the larger implications of community it is necessary to examine the labor protests of this period. For in these struggles, the new values and attitudes which developed in the community of women operatives are most visible.

II

In February, 1834, 800 of Lowell's women operatives "turned-out"— went on strike — to protest a proposed reduction in their wages. They marched to numerous mills in an effort to induce others to join them; and, at an outdoor rally, they petitioned others to "discontinue their labors until terms of reconciliation are made. Their petition concluded:

> Resolved, That we will not go back into the mills to work unless our wages are continued . . . as they have been.
>
> Resolved, That none of us will go back, unless they receive us all as one.
>
> Resolved, That if any have not money enough to carry them home, they shall be supplied.[19]

The strike proved to be brief and failed to reverse the proposed wage reductions. Turning-out on a Friday, the striking women were paid their back wages on Saturday, and by the middle of the next week had returned to work or left town. Within a week of the turn-out, the mills were running near capacity.[20]

This first strike in Lowell, is important not because it failed or succeeded, but simply because it took place. In an era in which women had to overcome opposition simply to work in the mills, it is remarkable that they would further overstep the accepted middle-class bounds of female propriety by participating in a public protest. The agents of the

18 Federal Manuscript Census of Lowell, 1830.
19 Boston *Evening Transcript*, February 18, 1834.
20 *Lawrence Manufacturing Company Records*, Correspondence, Vol. MAB-1, March 4 and March 9, 1834.

textile mills certainly considered the turn-out unfeminine. William Austin, agent of the Lawrence Company, described the operatives' procession as an "amizonian [sic] display." He wrote further, in a letter to his company treasurer in Boston: "This afternoon we have paid off several of these Amazons & presume that they will leave town on Monday."[21] The turn-out was particularly offensive to the agents because of the relationship they thought they had with their operatives. William Austin probably expressed the feelings of other agents when he wrote: ". . . notwithstanding the friendly and disinterested advice which has been on all proper occassions [sic] communicated to the girls of the Lawrence mills a spirit of evil omen . . . has prevailed, and overcome the judgement and discretion of too many, and this morning a general turn-out from most of the rooms has been the consequence."[22]

Mill agents assumed an attitude of benevolent paternalism toward their female operatives, and found it particularly disturbing that the women paid such little heed to their advice. The strikers were not merely unfeminine, they were ungrateful as well.

Such attitudes not withstanding, women chose to turn-out. They did so for two principal reasons. First, the wage cuts undermined the sense of dignity and social equality which was an important element in their Yankee heritage. Second, these wage cuts were seen as an attack on their economic independence.

Certainly a prime motive for the strike was outrage at the social implications of the wage cuts. In a statement of principles accompanying the petition which was circulated among operatives, women expressed well the sense of themselves which prompted their protest of these wage cuts:

UNION IS POWER

> Our present object if to have union and exertion, and we remain in possession of our unquestionable rights. We circulate this paper wishing to obtain the names of all who imbibe the spirit of our Patriotic Ancestors, who preferred privation to bondage, and parted with all that renders life desirable — and even life itself — to procure independence for their children. The oppressing hand of avarice would enslave us, and to gain their object, they gravely tell us of the pressure of the time, this we are already sensible of, and deplore it. If any are in want of assistance, the Ladies will be compassionate and assist them; but we prefer to have the disposing of our charities in our

[21] *Ibid.*, February 15, 1834.
[22] *Ibid.*, February 14, 1834.

> own hands; and as we are free, we would remain in possession of what kind Providence has bestowed upon us; and remain daughters of freemen still.[23]

At several points in the proclamation the women drew on their Yankee heritage. Connecting their turn-out with the efforts of their "Patriotic Ancestors" to secure independence from England, they interpreted the wage cuts as an effort to "enslave" them — to deprive them of their independent status as "daughters of freemen."

Though very general and rhetorical, the statement of these women does suggest their sense of self, of their own worth and dignity. Elsewhere, they expressed the conviction that they were the social equals of the overseers, indeed of the millowners themselves.[24] The wage cuts, however struck at this assertion of social equality. These reductions made it clear that the operatives were subordinate to their employers, rather than equal partners in a contract binding on both parties. By turning-out the women emphatically denied that they were subordinates; but by returning to work the next week, they demonstrated that in economic terms they were no match for their corporate superiors.

In point of fact, these Yankee operatives were subordinate in early Lowell's social and economic order, but they never consciously accepted this status. Their refusal to do so became evident whenever the mill owners attempted to exercise the power they possessed. This fundamental contradiction between the objective status of operatives and their consciousness of it was at the root of the 1834 turn-out and of subsequent labor protests in Lowell before 1850. The corporations could build mills, create thousands of jobs, and recruit women to fill them. Nevertheless, they bought only the workers' labor power, and then only for as long as these workers chose to stay. Women could always return to their rural homes, and they had a sense of their own worth and dignity, factors limiting the actions of management.

Women operatives viewed the wage cuts as a threat to their economic independence. This independence had two related dimensions. First, the women were self-supporting while they worked in the mills and, consequently, were independent of their families back home. Second, they were able to save out of their monthly earnings and could then leave the mills for the old homestead whenever they so desired. In effect, they were not totally dependent upon mill work. Their inde-

---

[23] Boston *Evening Transcript*, February 18, 1834.

[24] Harriet Robinson, *Loom and Spindle*, 72; *Offering*, February, 1841, p. 45. For an interesting account of conflict between an operative and an overseer, see Robinson, 57.

pendence was based largely on the high level of wages in the mills. They could support themselves and still save enough to return home periodically. The wage cuts threatened to deny them this outlet, substituting instead the prospect of total dependence on mill work. Small wonder, then, there was alarm that "the oppressing hand of avarice would enslave us." To be forced, out of economic necessity, to lifelong labor in the mills would have indeed seemed like slavery.[25] The Yankee operatives spoke directly to the fear of a dependency based on impoverishment when offering to assist any women workers who "have not money enough to carry them home." Wage reductions, however, offered only the *prospect* of a future dependence on mill employment. By striking, the women asserted their actual economic independence of the mills and their determination to remain "daughters of freemen still."

While the women's traditional conception of themselves as independent daughters of freemen played a major role in the turn-out, this factor acting alone would not necessarily have triggered the 1834 strike. It would have led women as individuals to quit work and return to their rural homes. But the turn-out was a collective protest. When it was announced that wage reductions were being considered, women began to hold meetings in the mills during meal breaks in order tc assess tactical possibilities. Their turn-out began at one mill when the agent discharged a woman who had presided at such a meeting. Their procession through the streets passed by other mills, expressing a conscious effort to enlist as much support as possible for their cause. At a mass meeting, the women drew up a resolution which insisted that none be discharged for their participation in the turn-out. This strike, then, was a collective response to the proposed wage cuts — made possible because women had come to form a "community" of operatives in the mill, rather than simply a group of individual workers. The existence of such a tight-knit community turned individual opposition of the wage cuts into a collective protest.

In October, 1836, women again went on strike. This second turn-out was similar to the first in several respects. Its immediate cause was also

[25] The wage cuts, in still another way, might have been seen as threatening to "enslave." Such decreases would be enacted by reductions in the piece rates paid women. If women were to maintain their overall earnings, given the wage cuts, they would have to speed up their work or accept additional machinery, both of which would result in making them work harder for the same pay. Opposition to the speed-up and the stretch-out were strong during the Ten Hour Movement in the 1840s, and although I have found no direct evidence, such feeling may have played a part in the turn-outs of the 1830s as well.

a wage reduction; marches and a large outdoor rally were organized; again, like the earlier protest, the basic goal was not achieved; the corporations refused to restore wages; and operatives either left Lowell or returned to work at the new rates.

Despite these surface similarities between the turn-outs, there were some real differences. One involved scale: over 1500 operatives turned out in 1836, compared to only 800 earlier.[26] Moreover, the second strike lasted much longer than the first. In 1834 operatives stayed out for only a few days; in 1836, the mills ran far below capacity for several months. Two weeks after the second turn-out began, a mill agent reported that only a fifth of the strikers had returned to work: "The rest manifest *good 'spunk'* as they call it."[27] Several days later he described the impact of the continuing strike on operations in his mills: "we must be feeble for months to come as probably not less than 250 of our former scanty supply of help have left town."[28] These lines read in sharp contrast to the optimistic reports of agents following the turnout in February, 1834.

Differences between the two turn-outs were not limited to the increased scale and duration of the later one. Women displayed a much higher degree of organization in 1836 than earlier. To co-ordinate strike activities, they formed a Factory Girls' Association. According to one historian, membership in the short-lived association reached 2500 at its height.[29] The larger organization among women was reflected in the tactics employed. Strikers, according to one mill agent, were able to halt production to a greater extent than numbers alone could explain; and, he complained, although some operatives were willing to work, "it has been impossible to give employment to many who remained." He attributed this difficulty to the strikers' tactics: "This was in many instances no doubt the result of calculation and contrivance. After the original turn-out they, [the operatives] would assail a particular room — as for instance, all the warpers, or all the warp spinners, or all the speeder and stretcher girls, and this would close the mill as effectually as if all the girls in the mill had left."[30]

Now giving more thought than they had in 1834 to the specific tactics of the turn-out, the women made a deliberate effort to shut down the

---

26 Harriett Robinson, p. 83; Boston *Evening Transcripts,* October 4 and 6, 1836.
27 *Tremont-Suffolk Mills Records,* unbound Letters, Volume FN-1, October 14, 1836.
28 *Ibid.,* October 17, 1836.
29 Hannah Josephson, *The Golden Treads: New England's Mill Girls and Magnates* (New York, 1949), 238.
30 *Tremont-Suffolk Mills Records,* Unbound Letters, Volume FN-1, October 10, 1836.

mills in order to win their demands. They attempted to persuade less committed operatives, concentrating on those in crucial departments within the mill. Such tactics anticipated those of skilled mulespinners and loomfixers who went out on strike in the 1880s and 1890s.

In their organization of a Factory Girl's Association and in their efforts to shut down the mills, the female operatives revealed that they had been changed by their industrial experience. Increasingly, they acted not simply as "daughters of freemen" offended by the impositions of the textile corporations, but also as industrial workers intent on improving their position within the mills.

There was a decline in protest among women in the Lowell mills following these early strike defeats. During the 1837-1843 depression, textile corporations twice reduced wages without evoking a collective response from operatives.[31] Because of the frequency of production cutbacks and lay-offs in these years, workers probably accepted the mill agents' contention that they had to reduce wages or close entirely. But with the return of prosperity and the expansion of production in the mid-1840's, there were renewal labor protests among women. Their actions paralleled those of working men and reflected fluctuations in the business cycle. Prosperity itself did not prompt turn-outs, but it evidently facilitated collective actions by women operatives.

In contrast to the protests of the previous decade, the struggles now were primarily political. Women did not turn-out in the 1840s; rather, they mounted annual petition campaigns calling on the State legislature to limit the hours of labor within the mills. These campaigns reached their height in 1845 and 1846, when 2,000 and 5,000 operatives respectively signed petitions. Unable to curb the wage cuts, or the speed-up and stretch-out imposed by mill owners, operatives sought to mitigate the consequences of these changes by reducing the length of the working day. Having been defeated earlier in economic struggles, they now sought to achieve their new goal through political action. The Ten Hour Movement, seen in these terms, was a logical outgrowth of the unsuccessful turn-outs of the previous decade. Like the earlier struggles, the Ten Hour Movement was an assertion of the dignity of operatives and an attempt to maintain that dignity under the changing conditions of industrial capitalism.

The growth of relatively permanent labor organizations and institu-

31 *Hamilton Manufacturing Company Records*, Volume 670, Correspondence of Treasurer, March 14, 1840; Lowell *Advertiser*, June 6, 1845 gives data on 1842 wage cuts.

tions among women was a distinguishing feature of the Ten Hour Movement of the 1840s. The Lowell Female Labor Reform Association was organized in 1845 by women operatives, It became Lowell's leading organization over the next three years, organizing the city's female operatives and helping to set up branches in other mill towns. The Association was affiliated with the New England Workingmen's Association and sent delegates to its meetings. It acted in concert with similar male groups, and yet maintained its own autonomy. Women elected their own officers, held their own meetings, testified before a state legislative committee, and published a series of "Factory Tracts" which exposed conditions within the mills and argued for the ten-hour day.

An important educational and organizing tool of the Lowell Female Labor Reform Association was the *Voice of Industry*, a labor weekly published in Lowell between 1845 and 1848 by the New England Workingmen's Association. Female operatives were involved in every aspect of its publication and used the *Voice* to further the Ten Hour Movement among women. Their Association owned the press on which the *Voice* was printed. Sarah Bagley, the Association president, was a member of the three-person publishing committee of the *Voice* and for a time served as editor. Other women were employed by the paper as travelling editors. They wrote articles about the Ten Hour Movement in other mill towns, in an effort to give ten-hour supporters a sense of the larger cause of which they were a part. Furthermore, they raised money for the *Voice* and increased its circulation by selling subscriptions to the paper in their travels about New England. Finally, women used the *Voice* to appeal directly to their fellow operatives. They edited a separate "Female Department," which published letters and articles by and about women in the mills.

Another aspect of the Ten Hour Movement which distinguished it from the earlier labor struggles in Lowell was that it involved both men and women. At the same time that women in Lowell formed the Female Labor Reform Association, a male mechanics' and laborers' association was also organized. Both groups worked to secure the passage of legislation setting ten hours as the length of the working day. Both groups circulated petitions to this end and when the legislative committee came to Lowell to hear testimony, both men and women testified in favor of the ten-hour day.[32]

[32] Massachusetts *House Document* No. 50, 1845. Quoted in full in John R. Commons *et al. A Documentary History of American Industrial Society*, (Cleveland, 1910), III, 133-151.

The two groups, then, worked together, and each made an important contribution to the movement in Lowell. Women had the numbers, comprising as they did over eighty per cent of the mill workforce. Men, on the other hand, had the votes, and since the Ten Hour Movement was a political struggle, they played a crucial part. After the State committee reported unfavorably on the ten-hour petitions, the Female Labor Reform Association denounced the committee chairman, a State representative from Lowell, as a corporation "tool." Working for his defeat at the polls, they did so successfully and then passed the following post-election resolution: "*Resolved,* That the members of this Association tender their grateful acknowledgements to the voters of Lowell, for consigning William Schouler to the obscurity he so justly deserves . . . ."[33] Women took a more prominent part in the Ten Hour Movement in Lowell than did men, but they obviously remained dependent on male voters and legislators for the ultimate success of their movement.

Although co-ordinating their efforts with those of working men, women operatives organized independently within the Ten Hour Movement. For instance, in 1845 two important petitions were sent from Lowell to the State legislature. Almost ninety per cent of the signers of one petition were females, and more than two-thirds of the signers of the second were males.[34] Clearly the separation of men and women in their daily lives was reflected in the Ten Hour petitions of these years.

The way in which the Ten Hour Movement was carried from Lowell to other mill towns also illustrated the independent organizing of women within the larger movement. For example, at a spirited meeting in Manchester, New Hampshire in December, 1845 — one presided over by Lowell operatives — more than a thousand workers, two-thirds of them women, passed resolutions calling for the ten-hour day. Later, those in attendance divided along male-female lines each meeting separately to set up parallel organizations. Sixty women joined the Manchester Female Labor Reform Association that evening, and by the following summer it claimed over three hundred members. Female operatives met in company boarding houses to involve new women in the movement. In their first year of organizing, Manchester workers obtained more than 4,000 signatures on ten-hour petitions.[35] While men and women were both

[33] *Voice of Industry,* November 28, 1845.
[34] Based on author's examination of Ten Hour Petitions at Massachusetts States Archives, 1845, 1587/8 and 1587/9.
[35] *Voices of Industry,* December 5 and 19, 1845, July 24, 1846, October 30, 1846, December 4, 1846, January 8, 1847.

active in the movement, they worked through separate institutional structures from the outset.

The division of men and women within the Ten Hour Movement also reflected their separate daily lives in Lowell and in other mill towns. To repeat, they held different jobs in the mills and had little contact apart from the formal, structured overseer-operative relation. Outside the mill, we have noted, women tended to live in female boarding houses provided by the corporations and were isolated from men, Consequently, the experiences of women in 'these early' mill towns were different from those of men, and in the course of their daily lives they came to form a close-knit community. It was logical that women's participation in the Ten Hour Movement mirrored this basic fact.

The women's Ten Hour Movement, like the earlier turnouts, was based in part on the participants' sense of their own worth and dignity as daughters of freemen. At the same time, however, also indicated the growth of a new consciousness. It reflected a mounting, feeling of community among women operatives and a realization that their interests and those of their employers were not identical, that they had to rely on themselves and not on corporate benevolence to achieve a reduction in the hours of labor. One woman, in an open letter to a State legislator, expressed this rejection of middle-class paternalism: "Bad as is the condition of so many women, it would be much worse if they had nothing but your boasted protection to rely upon; but they have at last learnt the lesson which a bitter experience teaches, that not to those who style themselves their "natural protectors" are they to look for the needful help, but to the strong and resolute of their own sex.[36] Such an attitude, underlying the self-organizing of women in the ten-hour petition campaigns, was clearly the product of the industrial experience in Lowell.

Both the early turn-outs and the Ten Hour Movement were, as noted above, in large measure dependent upon the existence of a close-knit community of women operatives. Such a community was based on the work structure, the nature of worker housing, and workforce homogeneity. Women were drawn together by the initial job training of newcomers; by the informal work sharing among experienced hands, by living in company boarding houses, by sharing religious, educational, and social activities in their leisure hours. Working and living in a new and alien setting, they came to rely upon one another for friendship and support. Understandably, a community feeling developed among them.

[36] *Voice of Industry*, March 13, 1846.

This evolving community as well as the common cultural traditions which Yankee women carried into Lowell were major elements that governed their response to changing mill conditions. The pre-industrial tradition of independence and self-respect made them particularly sensitive to management labor policies. The sense of community enabled them to transform their individual opposition to wage cuts and to the increasing pace of work into public protest. In these labor struggles women operatives expressed a new consciousness of their rights both as workers and as women. Such a consciousness, like the community of women itself, was one product of Lowell's industrial revolution.

The experiences of Lowell women before 1850 present a fascinating picture of the contradictory impact of industrial capitalism. Repeated labor protests reveal that female operatives felt the demands of mill employment to be oppressive. At the same time, however, the mills, provided women with work outside of the home and family, thereby offering them an unprecedented. That they came to challenge employer paternalism was a direct consequence of the increasing opportunities offered them in these years. The Lowell mills both exploited and liberated women in ways unknown to the pre-industrial political economy.

Mary H. Blewett

WORK, GENDER AND THE ARTISAN TRADITION IN NEW ENGLAND SHOEMAKING, 1780-1860

In the 1970s American labor history was transformed into a new labor history by the influential work of British historians, especially Edward P. Thompson. Following Thompson's model of examining the cultural expressions of working-class experience, American scholars looked at artisan life in the pre-industrial cities and towns of the Eastern seaboard and located a major source of resistance to early capitalism in artisan culture. Seventies historiography was also challenged by the development of women's history as a distinct field in social history, but many labor historians who were swift to study worker culture concentrated on the cultural, religious and political activities of male artisans, generally assuming that the experience of other family members was subsumed under male experience or was indistinguishable from it.[1] These historians need to borrow the analysis of gender relations in the family and at work from women's history to fully realize the meaning of worker culture and, in the case of pre-industrial artisan life, understand the limitations which the gender perceptions of artisan ideology placed on labor protest. The work of Thomas Dublin on the Lowell mill operatives best combined the new labor history with women's history to analyze the work experience and culture of women in early industrial capitalism.[2] Dublin's work, however, located the ideological source of labor protest among the textile operatives, not in artisan culture, but in the ideology of the Yankee freehold farmer.

This essay examines the relationship between gender and work in the shoe industry in Essex County, Massachusetts before the Civil War. Large numbers of men and women were employed in the putting-out system of domestic production as the boot and shoe industry of New England expanded prior to 1860. Pre-industrial methods of shoemaking involved an initially close relationship between work and family, production and the home, in which the interrelationships of gender and work can be observed. Men and women shared the work and traditions of artisan life in the family, but each gender experienced work, culture and consciousness in different ways. What were the attitudes of male artisans toward women who worked in shoe production and how did these attitudes shape artisan ideology? Did the cultural traditions and ideology of artisan life reflect or serve the interests of pre-industrial women workers who were drawn into production in the early nineteenth century? How did the differences in gender and work affect the ability of artisans to protest the rise of industrialization?

The pre-industrial phase of New England shoe production was a golden age of artisan life, and shoemakers were central to the rise of worker protest against early industrial capitalism. The group experience of training and work in the apprentice system and its traditions of mutual obligation defined artisan culture. Its locus was the shoe shop where the craft was learned and practiced. Decentralized production allowed groups of male artisans significant control over the process of work and fostered a strong tradition of militant resistance to the reorganization of production by employers. Its mechanics' ideology, analyzed by Paul Faler for the shoemakers of Lynn, Massachusetts, rested on the labor theory of value and republicanism as a political heritage from the American Revolution. Alan Dawley has seen this "equal rights" ideology as central to the activities of protesting shoemakers throughout most of the nineteenth century.[3] The ideology of artisan culture also included perceptions of gender relationships in the family and at work which defined and separated the roles of men and women and based collective action on the craftsman and householder.

For women workers, the pre-industrial period was a time of submersion in the family and in the family wage economy. The sexual division of labor placed them outside of the vitality of life, politics and work which centered in the artisan shop.[4] While male artisans defended their craft and its traditions before 1860, women workers experienced the cutting edge of change in the reorganization of work after 1780: a sexual division of labor which denied them craft status, the disassociation of their work from the family labor system, the increasingly direct contact of the individual worker with the employer, the isolation and vulnerability of the outworker and the mechanization and centralization of work in the factory. These changes in women's work affected artisan shoemakers. They faced a loss of control over the coordination of production and a loss of wages for the family economy. In the 1850s mechanization and centralization of women's work altered the size and composition of the male work force, a factor which helped precipitate in 1860 the largest pre-Civil War demonstration of labor protest. However, for many women workers in factory production, the artisan tradition of collective resistance represented neither their work nor their cultural experience. This new generation of female factory workers came into conflict with the striking shoemakers of Lynn over the objectives and strategy of the regional strike in 1860. This division of interests weakened labor protest in 1860 and pointed to the conflict between ideology and reality in the gender perceptions of New England artisans. Women shared the work in shoe production with men, but after 1860 they would need to create an ideology to justify labor protest based on their distinct experience. To understand this experience before 1860 will enrich the meaning of worker culture in early industrialization. The submersion of women's work experience within artisan culture has obscured the penetration of home-life and the work process by early capitalism and has sustained the illusion of the early nineteenth family as a refuge from the market place. The failure of artisans to perceive and accommodate the interests of women as workers weakened their ability to challenge the reorganization of work by early industrial capitalism.

How did women come to share the work of artisans? There is no evidence in primary or secondary sources of any female participation in colonial shoemaking. Men's work was either itinerant or custom work. In the 1750s higher standards for the production of women's shoes based on the European artisan model were introduced in Lynn by John Dagyr, and the master-journeyman-apprentice system was expanded to teach and practice a more refined craft. This system spread throughout Essex County, Massachusetts and was also common in New York, Pennsylvania and New Jersey.[5] Before the expansion of the artisan system, shoemakers had worked alone in the kitchens of their houses (or other people's houses), in an el or an attached shed. This was a domestic setting for work where shared family labor might have evolved as in hosiery making or spinning and weaving in England. However, with the expansion of the artisan system and an increase in production, shoemaking required its own work space to accomodate several men and boys on various levels of the craft. A small out-building called a "ten footer" began to appear in Essex County by the 1780s as a self-contained work area for men.[6] Many wives must have been pleased to rid their kitchens of the clutter, dirt and smell of the shoemaker's paraphenalia.

In the 1780s with the rise of tariff protection, the decline of English imports and the development of a potentially large domestic market, merchant capitalists began to expand production of shoes for a ready-to-wear market. John R. Commons analyzed the evolution of production in the industry and saw the crucial factors as new markets and the influence of competitive forces acting to stimulate the investment of capital and labor in shoemaking. Paul Faler also emphasized the expansion of markets in the transformation of production. Dawley focused on the primary role of the merchant capitalist who supplied the artisan shoemaker with leather, paid him wages and sought out new markets for shoes. Commons, Faler and Dawley ignored the implications of the introduction of the sexual division of labor into shoemaking as a craft. They do, however, point to the rough division of labor in the shoe shop in the 1780s: the separation of the major steps of shoemaking into cutting, sewing and making.[7] The shoemaker continued to be trained as an apprentice to make the entire shoe. When the division of men's work did not fill the demands of production, a solution was found within the shoemaking family.

The motive for the recruitment of women in shoemaking families to new work appears to have been made in the context of a shift in the control of profits as production expanded between 1780 and 1810. Production was expanded by merchant capitalists who bought leather and provided it to shoemakers. The merchant capitalist owned the shoes and marketed them. This control over raw materials meant control of profits as all cordwainers knew, and master shoemakers borrowed capital if they could to purchase leather.[8] Those shoemakers who owned no leather and who accepted work from capitalists had only their labor from which to profit. They divided up the work among the men in their shops and augmented their wage income from labor by recruiting additional family members for work: their women. The male head of the shoemaking family disciplined and controlled women's work in the home. The merchant capitalist, who had no control over the assignment of work in the artisan shop or family, welcomed the new potential for production. As entrepreneurs, they paid no wages directly to women workers and did not need to supervise their work. By adapting to the new work, women added their traditional household labor to their family's income in ways which continued to permit them to combine family and work roles.[9]

Why didn't the apprentices do the sewing of uppers to meet the needs of expanded production? They had learned the skill as part of their apprenticeship, and some did sew uppers whenever bottlenecks in production occurred. Specialization in sewing uppers, however, would have disrupted the apprenticeship system as an orientation to the male world of the artisan and to its work, rituals and hierarchy of subordination and dominance, as well as limiting the various services apprentices provided for the master and journeymen. To use apprentices would not have solved the labor shortage in an expanding market, for in a few years apprentices would become journeymen, no longer available to sew seams. Some more dependable source of new labor was needed, one which the capitalist would accept in the interests of expanded production, yet would not have to pay wages or supervise. The utilization of women in shoemaking families was a solution that would avoid changes in the apprentice system, meet the needs of both capitalist and artisan and threaten no alteration in the traditional patterns of gender formation. The origins of the sexual division of labor in the shoemaking craft was a conscious decision made by artisans and accepted by merchant capitalists to expand production.

Historians of the New England shoe industry have regarded the recruitment of female labor in the late eighteenth century as the natural evolution or inevitable outgrowth of women's involvement in household work or as the fitting of an excess female population in Essex County into a work process which drew on their abilities as needleworkers.[10] The recruitment of women in shoemaking families was instead a carefully controlled assignment of work designed to fit the role of women and to maintain gender relationships in the family, while preserving the artisan training system in its social as well as its craft aspect. Women were recruited to only a small part of the work, the sewing of the upper part of the shoe, and not to the craft itself. They were barred from apprenticeships and group work and isolated from the center of artisan life: the shoe shop. The artisan shop has come to be seen by historians as the center of pre-industrial political and cultural life for New England shoemakers and the source of the ideology and consciousness which many regard as representing the origins of the American working class. It was a world of men and boys.

The introduction of the sexual division of labor into an artisan craft represented a major change in the mode of production. Work was redefined and relocated, new words were coined and new procedures devised for supervision. The work assigned to women took on social meanings appropriate to their gender. Female family members adapted their traditional needle skills to hand sew the leather uppers of shoes in their kitchens without disrupting their domestic duties or their child care tasks. Needle work on leather uppers, a relatively clean part of the job, was accompanied by a new tool designed exclusively for women's work: the shoe clamp. The woman shoeworker would not have to straddle a shoemaker's bench, but would use a long, flexible wooden clamp which rested on the floor and which she held between her knees, holding the pieces of shoe upper together and freeing her hands to ply her needle. Her work was given a new name: shoebinding, which became a major category of women's work in the early nineteenth century.[11]

Binders in shoemaking families earned no wages between the 1780s and the 1810s, but they did contribute their labor to family production and to the wage it commanded. The emergence of shoebinding testified to the adaptibility and persistence of women's labor in household production. At this time, women in Essex County had few alternatives to hard, seasonal agricultural work or barter to add income to their families. The introduction of the sexual division of labor into an artisan craft was carefully controlled, guaranteeing the subordinate role of women by separating the work of shoebinding from any knowledge of the other various skills of the craft and by maintaining separate work places for men and women.[12] These patterns survived the transformation of the industry into the factory system and, therefore, constituted a fundamental social dimension of work.

Although shoebinders worked in their kitchens where domestic tasks and child care continued, the artisan shop and its demands for work intruded. No work in the shop could proceed without a few pairs of sewn uppers. The binder's work in her kitchen was essential to the timing and pace of production in the shop, and she had to keep ahead of the requirements of the shop workers with a ready supply of sewn uppers.[13] Her kitchen was transformed into a workplace where external demands from the ten footer shaped her time and tasks. The collective nature of men's work in the shoe shop, the locus of artisan culture, supported a militant tradition of resistance to the reorganization of production. This tradition did not mirror the experience of women workers who had no craft status and did not share in the political and religious discussions in the shop. The relationship of binders to this tradition was limited by their isolation from group production and mediated through their role in the family.

There were, however, limits to the capacity of female members of shoemaking families to fulfill the needs of the shoe shop for sewn uppers. Increasing numbers of shoes per lot strained the family labor system. Around 1800, ten to fourteen pairs of shoes made up a unit of production. By 1820 fifty, sixty and seventy pairs per lot were common, as most capitalists had organized cutting operations into central shops. Because shoebinding was typically combined with domestic work, the capacity of the binder who was both wife and mother to complete work on large lots had limits. In a pinch for more labor, shoemakers recruited the wives and daughters of neighbors, but this required some kind of a payment.[14] Gradually after 1810, shoebinding, while still performed in the home, shifted to work paid first in goods (often factory-made textiles) and later in wages, provided to the worker by the shoe boss, and increasingly disassociated from the family labor system.[15]

The surviving account books of storekeepers and shoe bosses in Essex and neighboring Middlesex Counties between 1810 and 1830 illustrate the slow development of what would become a widespread practice of giving out work to shoebinders who then returned it to the central shop before it was given out to the makers.[16] By the 1820s homework for women in textiles had shifted decisively into the factory, and those women who wished to contribute income to their families but who also needed or wanted to remain at home had few alternatives: outwork in straw and palm leaf hat making, sewing coats and shirts and, increasingly in Essex County, binding shoes.[17] According to calculations based on the untitled stock book of one Lynn manufacturer (1830-1831), less than 20% of the work put-out by this shoe boss was given to shoemakers and their wives or daughters to make and bind as a family work unit. The rest of the work was given out in separate lots to individual shoemakers and shoebinders whose work was coordinated by the boss in the central shop.[18]

By the 1830s shoe manufacturers had assumed much of the responsibility for hiring binders for wages and replaced husbands and fathers as employers. Even if her husband made shoes, a binder might work on uppers for ladies' boots while her spouse made coarse work shoes for Southern slaves. This disassociation of women's work from the family labor system affected the ability of the shoemaker to coordinate the work process. The shoe boss assumed responsibility not only for hiring female workers, often from non-shoemaking families, but also directed and coordinated the work process from his central shop. The shoemaker had to wait, sometimes for hours, for the shoe boss to provide him with bound uppers.[19] The shift in the coordination of the work of binding and making to the central shop represented a decline in the power of artisans to exert control over the work process.

The disassociation of shoebinding and shoemaking, the direct payment of wages to the binder and the increasing control of women's work by the shoe boss made it essential for binders to organize themselves in order to protest against their employers.[20] Two outbreaks of early labor protest occurred in Eastern Massachusetts shoe towns in the early 1830s over persistent low wages for shoebinding despite a rising market for shoes. Although these women sought and received the support of organized shoemakers especially in Lynn, the shoebinders created separate societies to represent their interests and acted independently. They did not challenge the sexual division of labor, but saw themselves as women workers unjustly treated by their employers and organized to demand a response to their grievances. They also attempted to utilize the mechanics' ideology in new ways to justify their protest and argue for new rights for women.

The shoebinders of Reading and the surrounding towns in Essex and Middlesex Counties formed a society of two to three hundred members in the summer of 1831 to protest low wages and to obtain a uniform wage scale for binding various kinds of work. The objective of the society was to encourage binders to cooperate in resisting individual wage bargains with their shoe bosses, so that inexperienced women would not "work for nothing and find themselves [furnish their labor free]."

Five shoe bosses in the Reading area rejected the demands of the binders' society for increases in wages which they claimed had been customary for ten years. The shoe manufacturers maintained that ". . . we are unacquainted with this new mode of doing business, and firmly protest against it, but are willing to employ them [the binders of the Reading society] on fair and honorable terms as heretofore."[21] Although nothing more was published about the activities of the Reading society, these shoebinders in 1831 were conscious of the vulnerability of the individual woman worker outside of the family labor system. Drawing on their cultural identification with the dignity and independence of artisan life, they expressed expectations of fairness and good treatment from the shoe bosses and were critical of the unwillingness of employers to share the profits of a rising shoe market. Perhaps the most impressive aspect of this early case of collective resistance by shoebinders was the ability of women workers living in different towns to establish a network of protest.

Two years later shoebinders in Lynn organized more resistance. By 1833 there were about 1,500 women in Lynn who earned wages as shoebinders. A wage cut prompted over half of them to organize the "Female Society of Lynn and vicinity for the protection and promotion of Female Industry." In their public statements, the shoebinders voiced the mechanics' ideology, blending it with expressions of their grievances as wage earners and using it as a defense of the worth of their labor as female members of artisan families. Most important, however, was their claim to new rights: the right to public action as women and the right to support themselves respectably and independently on their wages, independently in the sense of making a significant contribution to the family wage economy.[22]

The Lynn binders who organized the Female Society met at the Friends' Meetinghouse on December 30, 1833 where, as the *Lynn Record* noted, women as well as men could speak freely in public. They were joined a few days later by 125 binders who met at the Methodist church in neighboring Saugus and adopted the same objectives, ideology and constitution.[23] In the preamble to the society's constitution, the Lynn binders pointed to ". . . a manifest error, a want of justice, and reasonable compensation to the females; which calls imperiously for redress. While the prices of their labour have been reduced, the business of their *employers* has appeared to be improving, and prosperous, enabling them to increase their wealth. *These things ought not so to be*!" Their demand for higher wages was based on the labor theory of value. As workers, they believed they were not earning a just compensation; their independence and respectability was threatened. Furthermore, this economic injustice enriched the shoe boss. This was a violation of the dignity of their labor and a "moral outrage."

To redress their grievances, the shoebinders of Lynn demanded an extension of the equal rights doctrine of the artisan tradition to women. "Equal rights should be extended to all — to the weaker sex as well as the stronger." Many of the women who attended the society's first meeting on December 30, 1833, the preamble claimed, either supported themselves or their families on their earnings as binders and had become dependent on their wage labor. The disadvantages that women experienced "by nature and custom" should not be aggravated by "unnecessary and unjust" treatment as workers. The preamble expressed the belief that ". . . women as well as men, have certain inalienable rights, among which is the right at all times of 'peaceably assembling to consult upon the common good.'" In this, the Lynn binders were responding to criticism that they were forming a combination against the manufacturers which endangered the town's prosperity. They replied that the shoe bosses combined together themselves to hold down wages and to pay the binders in store orders for goods. The women in the Lynn society equated their interests as workers with the interests of the community, regarding the welfare of the town as consisting, ". . . not in the aggrandizement of a few individuals, but in the general prosperity and welfare of the industrious and laboring classes."

The preamble went on to criticize the recent reduction in wages for shoebinding which prevented them from obtaining "a comfortable support." This concept represented the shoebinders' claim to a just wage, a feminine version of the "competency" sought by artisans, an income sufficient to support their families and permit a little savings for old age.[24] However, in computing the wage which would earn them their comfortable support, the shoebinders used as a measure — not their work in production — but their duties and responsibilities as female members of artisan families. The shoebinders used their gender roles as the wives, daughters and widows of New England mechanics to insist upon a wage level that would confer dignity and independence on them. They calculated the price of the household services that a wife performed as a seamstress, washwoman, nurse and maid and demanded a wage high enough to cover these expenses. By extending the analogy of wage work into their domestic sphere, the wives of mechanics who bound shoes were bridging over the gap between work and domesticity. For a daughter, wages should be high enough to cover room, board and personal upkeep so as not to constitute a drain upon her father's income nor induce her to leave home for factory work. As for a mechanic's widow with dependents, her wage level should ensure a livelihood without the necessity of applying to the town for poor relief.[25]

To be effective the Lynn shoebinders' society had to organize all working women in the local industry, whatever their attachment to the mechanic's family or dependence on their earnings. However, the ideology which the society's members borrowed from the artisan tradition and which they reshaped to their experiences of gender hierarchy within the family betrayed a contradiction between their demands for equal rights for men and women workers and the calculations of a just wage for women. Equal rights for women as workers suggested the primacy of work; wages computed on the expenses of household services indicated that, in family terms, domestic duties were primary for women. For the Lynn shoebinders, their gender role in the family and in artisan ideology transformed the labor theory of value into a measure of their domestic work.

The artisan shoemakers of Lynn promptly offered their support to the Female Society in early 1834, voting as a group to refuse to take work from any manufacturer not agreeing to the wages demanded by the binders. When the Lynn shoemakers had organized a Society of Journeymen Cordwainers in 1830 to defend the wages and privileges of the craft, they regarded the low wages paid to the shoebinders as an injury to themselves as male heads of families. "Look and see how they [the shoe bosses] have depressed the price of female labor, and reduced it down to almost nothing! This has an effect on us as husbands, as fathers, and as brothers."[26] They perceived the grievances of the binders strictly in family terms.

The mechanics and the wives, daughters and widows of mechanics found cooperation easy enough based on the sharing of cultural and work traditions in the family, but the public demand of the binders for a wage sufficient to make a reasonable contribution to family income and their use of the mechanics' ideology as their justification was an explicit claim to new rights for women. The leadership of the society demanded a new moral role for women which involved public activity on behalf of new rights, and some of the leaders of the binders' society would continue this activity on behalf of public morality in the Lynn Female Anti-Slavery Society in 1836.[27] The shift of women's work out of the family labor system had carried with it implications for change in gender relationships. In the typology of traditionalist, loyalist and rebel developed by Paul Faler and Alan Dawley, the shoebinders of Lynn and Saugus in 1834 were early rebels. They saw their interests as workers opposed to those of their employers and regarded collective action as the only means to secure accustomed living standards and independence.[28] They added, importantly, the dimension of gender to the expression of their consciousness as workers.

By the summer of 1834 the Lynn shoebinders' society was in trouble; three-fourths of its members were working for wages below the society's scale or had not paid their dues. One of the society's leaders, probably the President Mary A. Russell, used the *Lynn Record* of June 18 to urge the lagging membership to become "a band of sisters, each considering the welfare of the society as her own peculiar interest." She referred to the example of ". . . that liberty which other females have, that of setting their own prices upon their work." In what appeared to have been a reference to the March 1834 turnouts of the Lowell textile operatives, the writer urged a similar firmness and determination from the binders to become "equally free from oppression." Plans to divide work, share wages during dull times, start a manufacturing cooperative and exhortations to "think seriously, make exertions, be not discouraged" produced little response.[29] The society fell apart as the Reading society had in 1831.

In her study of middle-class New England women from 1780 to 1835, Nancy Cott analyzed the emergence of women's sphere as a vocation based on gender after production and male workers had left the home. A cult of domesticity defined this sphere and encouraged the development of a group consciousness with a positive social role expressed as sisterhood. Cott argued that this sense of sisterhood was a pre-condition to nineteenth century feminism.[30] Working women in New England shoe production also experienced a sense of consciousness as a gender, defined not only by domesticity but also by their work for wages. Shoebinders did not face a shift of production out of the home, but an assignment of new work for women in the home and its intensification in the outwork system. The sexual division of labor in shoe production reinforced the idea of a separate sphere for women and provided a class basis for the cult of domesticity among working women. By the 1830's, however, the family labor system had given way to the employment of women directly by the shoe boss in the outwork system. Sharing the bonds of womanhood both in work and in their domestic sphere, shoebinders in 1834 tried to organize themselves in terms of a female community of workers committed to self improvement and the improvement of society. Mary Russell actively sought to extend the idea of sisterhood as an organizing principle, but the shoebinders of Lynn could only respond hesitantly. The conditions under which many shoebinders labored — isolated from each other, employed by the shoe boss outside a group labor system and combining wage work with domestic responsibilities — discouraged collective activity. The tensions between their relationship to the artisan system and its equal rights ideology and their subordinate role as females in the family were exposed by their arguments for a just wage for women. Neither the social relations of the artisan family nor the realities of working as a woman for a shoe boss encouraged the shoebinder of Lynn to identify with her working sister in the Lowell mills or conceive of herself as a worker capable of supporting herself who could unite with her peers to protest mistreatment.

The efforts of the Lynn Female Society had limited success in 1834. Payments in store orders were temporarily suspended, but wages for binding shoes never even approached the wages offered to women workers in textile factories. Instead of raising wages to local shoebinders, shoe bosses in Eastern Massachusetts built networks of rural outworkers throughout the region extending into New Hampshire and Maine. By 1837, more women (15,366) were involved in shoe production in Massachusetts than female workers (14,759) in cotton textile factories.[31] The decline in the importance of the shoemaking family as a work unit left wives increasingly dependent on their shoemaker husbands for economic support. As the shoe bosses became more important to the coordination of production and the recruitment of binders, the relationship between the shoemaker and his employer changed. The shoemaker was regarded less and less as a middle-man in the recruitment of outwork for the boss, who now ran the central shop and directed the work of both binder and maker. This change in the relationship between shoeworker and shoe boss plus the pressure on the family wage economy may be underlying reasons for the outbursts of collective activity among Essex County shoemakers in the 1840s.

The decade of the 1840s represented a high point of activism among shoemakers in Eastern Massachusetts, who organized on a regional basis and held conventions with other working men and women. The Cordwainers' Mutual Benefit Society of Lynn began to publish a labor paper, *The Awl*, in 1844 and tried to summon support for the society among women including shoebinders.[32] In the first issue of the *Awl* on July 17, 1844, the editors developed a constituency and a set of objectives which limited and subordinated women's relationship to their organization. Oblivious to the implications for women of the disassociation of shoebinding from the family labor system and into a vulnerable isolation from group work and artisan ideology, the shoemakers' society in the 1840s perceived women as persons whose lives were defined primarily by family and morality. The origins of these attitudes may lie in the adjustment of shoemakers to the new industrial morality developing in Lynn as described by Paul Faler or in the claim of Lynn women to the right to act publicly on behalf of moral causes such as the binders' society in 1834 and the anti-slavery society in 1936-38.[33] Women's activities in local temperance groups in Essex County and especially in Lynn in 1841-43 indicated a fervent dedication by female members of shoemaking families to the total abstinence cause of the Washingtonian societies of Lynn. The Washingtonians of Lynn were close to the cordwainer's society and emphasized the special moral role of females and their dedication to family interests.[34] The editors of the *Awl* vigorously sought the support of women, but the circumscribed position for women in the society offered most shoebinders no ideological or strategic foothold with which to associate themselves as workers with the society.

In the first issue, the clearest statement of the aims of the society was contained in a draft circular to "all brothers of the craft" throughout New England.[35] The organization was seeking uniform wages for shoemaking in all New England shoe towns in order to restore the economic and social status of shoemakers in a society which they perceived as rapidly developing invidious class distinctions. The denial of a competency or reasonable income which would support an artisan's family comfortably and supply for old age threatened the equality and rights which freemen had won in the American Revolution. The society of cordwainers was especially sensitive to the declining status of those whose only wealth lay in the useful pursuit of a trade. The *Awl* championed the fundamental values of manly labor and linked its interests with all mechanics and artisans, as well as with the female operatives in the textile mills of New England, and with all working people, male or female, free or slave, who could not live decently and respectably in the economy of the 1840s.

At a meeting of the society on June 29, 1844, the members agreed to urge "the ladies" to lend their support and influence to the men's organization. Membership in the society was, however, defined by craft. The sexual division of labor prevented women from becoming members by learning the craft, although the society did accept as members three women trained as cordwainers: Mrs. Eliza Tuttle and two female apprentices.[36] The appeal for the presence of the ladies at the society's meetings became a persistent theme in the *Awl* during its year and a half of publication. The presence of these ladies, like the membership of Mrs. Tuttle, was to be used for its exemplary and, more importantly, for its moral influence. These requests for women to attend the society's meetings every Saturday night at the Town Hall were predicated not on their status as wage-earners or their work as shoebinders, but on their abilities as wives, mothers and sweethearts to persuade other shoemakers in Lynn to join.[37] The economic interests of most women in the objectives of the society were assumed to be familial: by bettering the wages of men — be they husbands, fathers or sons — women's own interests would be served.

In the December 21 issue of the *Awl*, the editors published under the title, "Woman," a special appeal for female support which illustrated how they viewed the nature of women and the limits this view placed on women's involvement in the activities of the society. Women were perceived as moral beings and were called upon to "hallow and enoble" the objectives of the society. The appeal to them was based on their capacity for self-sacrifice. The editors sought to enlist their energies to serve the interests of others; "the poor and down-trodden" and "her lovely sisters toiling . . . to gain a scanty subsistence."[38] Earlier, the *Awl* had reassured women that it was as moral for them to meet with the cordwainers every Saturday night as to attend church on Sunday. Indeed, their presence at these meetings would guarantee their propriety.[39] The *Awl* regarded women's power as moral, unselfish and spiritual, not as material, self-interested or political. These attitudes seemed to blind the cordwainers' society to the vulnerability and isolation of shoebinders.

The appeal of the *Awl* for female participation was deeply ambivalent. If women were seen as essentially moral and spiritual, characteristics that suggested gentility and the pious, private virtues that historians have identified as the cult of true womanhood, the ideology of the cordwainers' society pointedly rejected the values of the genteel, non-working classes who by their unearned wealth and leisured lives threatened the basic values of artisan culture. This side of their attitudes toward women revealed a fear of genteel or middle-class social behavior in females within their own families which would unfit them for the useful life of a mechanic's wife. These attitudes are best illustrated in several moral tales published in the *Awl* which explore this issue.

One story, reprinted from *The Family Visitor*, entitled "Old Fudge of an Uncle," demonstrated the triumph of a shoebinder over the "demon" of gentility.[40] Mary Burchstead was the niece of Mr. Goodrich, a shoemaker who had rescued her from childhood poverty by teaching her to make her own living binding shoes. Since her marriage to a sea captain, Mrs. Burchstead had fallen victim to gentility, altering at great expense the house which her husband had bought her, acquiring fine, new furniture and placing her husband deeply in debt. At the beginning of the story, Mary Burchstead puzzles over why her uncle has sent her — a lady — shoes to bind, but feels ashamed over her ingratitude and her neglect of relatives:

> "But," she argued, "If a captain's wife bound shoes, what would people think?"

As she glances into her mirror, she finds that her displeasure had marred the beauty which the serenity found in binding shoes had once placed on her face:

> "Mercy!" cried Mrs. Burchstead, "I look like a fright! . . . I must dress and call on uncle Goodrich, and expostulate, or, he will send a bundle of *cowhide brogans* next. I do wish the old man could know a little of gentility, or what belongs to it."

Stung by the incivility of her relatives, Mary visits her uncle and aunt. She is told that her husband has mortgaged their house to pay for the alterations and new furnishings and that, because of a general business depression, the voyage he is on may bankrupt him. Mary blames herself and sets to work, spurns the visitors who look down their noses at her occupation, rents the house and sells the furniture. Her husband returns, overjoyed at his wife's change of heart and her decisions which have cleared him of debt. In admiration of Mary's determination, his employer says to him:

> Now you may congratulate yourself, not only for being in good circumstances, but for having a wife who has dared to sacrifice herself, as I may say, for she has defied gentility by binding shoes.

This story was chosen by the editors of the *Awl* for its criticism of the false social values which Mary Burchstead had chosen over the virtues of hard work and plain living. Her gentility as demonstrated by her rejection of shoebinding as unfitting for a captain's wife was symptomatic of the growing class divisions in American life and a betrayal of the equal rights ideology of Lynn mechanics.

In the February 22, 1845 issue, the editors made their views more explicit by publishing an original story, "Charles-Do-Well," written by one of the *Awl's* frequent contributors, "Noggs." "Charles-Do-Well" is a moral tale set in Lynn about the contest between the social virtues of the mechanic and the false values of the merchant class. The story begins as a young woman tries to decide whom she should marry:

> It is no use talking mother said the pert though somewhat handsome Eliza D______, as I am determined I will never no *never* marry a *mechanic*.

Eliza's father was a merchant, and she believes that it is up to a daughter to "keep up the dignity of [her] father's house," by marrying in the same class. Her inclination to marry a merchant is encouraged not by her kindly, sensible mother, but by the vapid Sarah Amelia Sudora Norton who objects to her friend Eliza's visits with shoebinders and rejects Charles Do-Well, the shoemaker, because "he smells of wax so." On the other hand, Eliza thinks, as she ponders her decision, Charles is handsome, well-informed and very interesting, even ". . . if he does make shoes." Her other suitor is Mr. Cheatem, a merchant who is received in all the best houses, but who has a reputation among working people as a liar and a "tricky trader." She wonders:

> But some how or other it seems strange to me that a man because he sells tape and buckram, small beer and ginger bread should be any more respectable than he who makes shoes . . . !

Charles has opened Eliza's eyes to the changing prospects of the mechanics of Lynn. He has told her that the:

> . . . times were fast altering, that things were beginning to be called by their right names; he says the common people are better informed than they used to be, now, and that it is beginning to be considered no disgrace to get a living honestly.

Thrillingly, this vision of change seems to include Eliza:

> Women too, he says, are beginning to be acknowledged as responsible creatures, as beings who have souls as well as hearts, who were born equal with the man, and who by every right, human and divine, are entitled to a voice in our councils, and are deserving of an equal recompense for their labors.

In contrast, Eliza reflects on Cheatem's philosophy:

> . . . that some people were born to be drawers of water, and hewers of wood, for his part he didn't see what the reformers wanted to make such a d____d fuss about the "niggers" and the poor folkes for.

Eliza observes:

> Oh how ugly he did look, as he with his sneering laugh uttered the above. I could not help contrasting him with the Charles Do-Well, who always takes sides with the oppressed. . . .

She is awakened from her reveries by her mother, and Eliza announces that she is done with girlish dreaming and that she is:

> . . . determined, henceforth, to be a woman, and see if I can't do something for a living. I will go immediately and join the "shoe binders' society of mutual improvement," and what is more I mean to bind shoes myself, for I have come to the conclusion that if we would be good members of society we must be useful.

Sarah Amelia is horrified to find Eliza binding shoes and drops her socially, saying she never did "keep company with the working class," but Charles Do-Well is enchanted to find Eliza binding shoes and dares to hope that his influence on her has produced her reformation. He has always thought that under her surface vanity and frivolity was "strong good sense." Some day, he believes, "she would dare be herself, a sensible, intelligent, *useful* woman." Eliza married Charles and Sarah Amelia married Cheatem. Six months later, Sarah Amelia is a deserted wife with a child left in poverty by her unscrupulous husband. She is wretched when Eliza calls on her, but otherwise much improved by her disastrous fate:

> She [Sarah Amelia] was not now ashamed herself, to bind shoes, aye was thankful, that there was so respectable and easy way for a poor stricken widow [?] to support herself and her child.

Eliza's story was a vehicle for the social criticism implicit in the mechanics' ideology, but when Charles explains to her the new conception of woman as an equal partner in the moral struggle against the merchant class, it becomes clear that the new fields opening to females are designed to permit them only to be sensible, intelligent and, most of all, useful family members: the paradigm of a mechanic's wife.[41] "Noggs" portrayed shoebinding as essential for the useful woman. Ignoring the objective conditions of the shoebinders whose work, if respectable, was never easy, the writer regarded binding shoes as appropriate, necessary and even chastening work for idle women. The useful woman is a much more flattering vision than the images of the shallow, materialistic women of the genteel class, but it is neither self-interested nor does it spring from the aspirations or dilemmas of working women themselves. In contrast to the energetic appeals in the *Awl* for female participation were the constant laments in its pages over the lack of response to these appeals. However, the explanation for this lack of response may lie less in the *Awl's* ambivalence over woman's nature or its fear of genteel values lurking within female members and more in the failure of the cordwainers' society to offer a solution for the vulnerable position of the female outworker in the structure of shoe manufacturing.

The cordwainers' society claimed benefit to shoebinders who associated with the organization, but the advice offered by the society suggests that the cordwainers refused to confront the implications of the isolated situation of most shoebinders in comparison with the collective nature of their own work. The folklore of artisan life in the 1840s and 1850s reflected the growing tensions between the shoemakers and the shoe boss over the quality of work turned into the central shop. Some shoe bosses treated their artisans with careful courtesy, while others did not. Shoemakers expressed resentment against hard bosses like Christopher Robinson of Lynn who tried in the late 1840s to alter the standards of work. Attempts to limit supplies or inspect work still in the shop were stoutly resisted.[42] The cordwainers of Essex County were better able than the individual shoebinder to resist attempts by the shoe boss to control and discipline the work process.

In an early appeal for female participation in the September 11, 1844 issue, the shoebinders were exhorted by the editors of the *Awl* to come to the society's meetings and identify any shoe boss in Lynn who had cheated women by the order system. The order system was an arrangement by which wages were paid in goods rather than in cash, a profitable convenience for merchants and shoes bosses and, according to the *Awl*, one of the greatest evils of the system of production. Widows with dependents were urged to point out the manufacturers who discounted their wages by 10% if they insisted on cash. Name the boss, the appeal went on, so that the world will know him. The strategy of publicly humiliating shoe bosses by focusing the moral power of indignant women on their oppressors did not persuade any shoebinders to come forward.

In addition to this advice, one of the editors, E.C. Darlin, championed a Lynn binder whose wage accounts he had examined and who, he charged, had been cheated by shoe manufacturer, Nathan D. Chase.[43] The case of Mrs. Jane Atherton illustrates the futility of the *Awl's* strategy for helping the shoebinders confront their employers. Darlin charged that Mrs. Atherton had been defrauded by Chase when he did not make it clear to her, when she began binding shoes for his firm in 1840, that the wages were paid 4 cents in cash or 5 cents in store orders. Although she played no direct role in the controversy, Mrs. Atherton had felt surprised and disappointed at the differential between cash and goods, and later thought the arrangements were rather hard, but worked for Chase for the next three years. During the controversy, Chase insisted that Mrs. Atherton had never said she had been defrauded. Darlin pointed out the injustices of the differential between goods and cash, whether Mrs. Atherton had agreed to it or not. He noted that Mrs. Atherton had not known the wage terms until after she had begun to work and referred to her "weakness" in relation to the shoe boss, but failed to analyze how her vulnerability influenced her behavior during the controversy. Mrs. Atherton, whose husband was away from Lynn during early 1845, was probably horrified that the *Awl* had chosen her wage record as the issue with which to attack the practices of the shoe bosses. Her chances for work as a binder were contingent on the good will of the shoe manufacturers whom she placated with reticence and meekness during the interviews which she had with them. Interestingly, as the controversy over the treatment of Mrs. Atherton developed between January 4 and February 22, shoebinders at last began to contribute letters and poetry to the *Awl*, but none of them even alluded to the Atherton case.[44] On the whole, the cordwainers' society of Lynn received little support from shoebinders. Its ideology implied a limited and subordinated role for most women. Its strategy to threaten the shoe bosses with public shame made the individual shoebinder even less likely to make an issue of mistreatment, fearing a stratagem which would focus the combined anger of Lynn shoe manufacturers on her and deprive her of work.

In the 1840s and 1850s the number of women working as shoebinders in Massachusetts grew rapidly, and by 1855, 32,826 women were recorded as employed in the boot and shoe industry in comparison with 22,850 employed in cotton textiles.[45] The number of women employed by Essex County shoe bosses grew from 7,027 in 1837 to 12,395 in 1855, an increase of 76%. By 1855 shoe manufacturing in Essex County had developed four major centers of outwork: Danvers and South Danvers, Haverhill (located near the New Hampshire boarder), Lynn and its neighbor Marblehead. These four centers of production accounted for 51% of all females in Massachusetts who worked in shoe production, and Lynn manufacturers who listed 11,021 women workers in 1855 had developed an extensive outwork system which reached beyond Eastern Massachusetts into Southern New Hampshire and Maine.

Low wages, irregular employment and low productivity plagued both the shoebinder and the shoe boss in the outwork system. Binding shoes was often characterized by intensive periods of effort over several weeks' duration followed by long periods of no shoebinding at all. The account books of John and Charles P. Preston of Danvers (1824-1845) and of James P. Hutchinson also of Danvers (1846-1860) indicate that the shoe bosses came to rely on a relatively small group of steady binders for most production, while employing a widespread and numerous group of casual binders whose work was conducted at irregular intervals. Account books from the 1840s also illustrate a further division of labor within the tasks which the binders performed which limited their earnings. A woman might be assigned only part of the work on uppers, for example, only the most poorly paid work of "closing" or sewing up side seams rather than "fitting" or seaming cloth linings into the upper which earned better pay. The debit side of the account books revealed the continuation of the custom of "furnishing" by which the binder assumed the costs of thread, needles and lining material, thereby further reducing her wages.[46] Much of women's work on shoes continued to be conducted separate from the family labor system by the wives and daughters of non-shoemaking families: farmers, other artisans, mariners and laborers.[47] Work had not yet left the home, but the home setting of women's work was less and less likely to revere the traditions and values of the shoemakers' craft.

With the invention of the sewing machine for leather in 1852 and the subsequent introduction of the factory system, the wages and the work available to shoebinders began to decline. But the adaptation of the sewing machine for cloth to stitch leather uppers did not immediately separate home and work for shoebinders. Neither did mechanization of women's work create a large scale factory system. Over the decade between 1855 and 1865, the process of shoe production slowly evolved toward the steam-powered factory, but the work process retained many features of pre-industrial production, including the sexual division of labor. John B. Nichols, who had succeeded in converting the I.M.

Singer sewing machine to stitch light leather, went to Lynn in 1852 in the employ of Singer who had sold exclusive rights to lease his new machines in Essex County to three Lynn manufacturers. Nichols organized stitching rooms for them and instructed young women in the use of the leather sewing machine. By 1855 several other sewing machine companies: Grover & Baker, Wheeler & Wilson and Nichols & Bliss, were producing and selling machines for work on leather uppers.[48] Shoebinding as women's needle work in the home seemed to face oblivion.

In the shoe centers of Lynn and Haverhill, the shoebinders organized to resist the introduction of the machines. A.S. Moore, one of Singer's agents in Essex County and the employer of machine operatives in Lynn, faced a committee of angry binders in 1852 who tried to pressure Moore and the women operatives to abandon the machines. In Haverhill shoebinders and shoemakers expressed bitterness at Isaac Harding who had brought the first stitching machines into town in 1853. Some of the women shook their fists in the face of Daniel Goodrich, Harding's partner. The binders were convinced that the machine would destroy their work. Many must have realized that centralized machine operations would force them to choose between their domestic duties and their ability to earn wages. Contributing to their distress was their unfamiliarity with the sewing machine for cloth. The marketing strategy of the early sewing machine companies concentrated on the use of the machines for the manufacture of clothing and shoes, ignoring the potential they would later realize in the domestic market for family sewing. Several experienced Haverhill binders who worked for the firm of Sawyer & Wheeler tried the new machines without success and gave up in despair.[49]

Although the binders were correct to fear mechanization, the system of household production accommodated itself to the introduction of the leather stitching machine. Not all work on uppers was mechanized. Suspicions regarding customer acceptance of machine stitched shoes somewhat retarded mechanization. But if hand work was still available in the home, the wages for shoebinding fell rapidly as the productivity of machine work rose and labor costs declined. In 1860 the piece rate for machine sewing was estimated at one quarter the price of hand work, while the operative earned nearly three times as much as the binder.[50] The shoebinder faced an uncertain future, working more intensively if she could obtain the work and at a severe wage reduction. Some binders rented or purchased leather stitching machines with hand cranks or foot treadles for use at home. Estimates differ on the extent of home use of stitching machines. They were expensive; in the mid-1850s the price ranged between $75 to $125. The most widespread use of home operated machines was apparently in Lynn, Salem and Marblehead where manufacturers rented machines to be used at home. Home use of a machine allowed women workers to continue to combine domestic duties with wage work and escape the discipline and long hours of centralized production.[51] Until the introduction of steam power and the invention of a pegging machine to mechanize the work of shoemakers, followed in 1862 by the McKay stitcher, home operations by foot power provided work for many women in their homes.

Some of the shoe manufacturers centralized stitching operations by adding a story to central shops where the leather was cut out or had two story buildings constructed to contain the activities of the central shop on the ground floor and the stitching room on the second floor. Stitching was also sub-contracted by the central shop owners to shops like that of John B. Nichols of Lynn which specialized in stitching uppers.[52] The pre-industrial isolation of the female shoeworker from other operations in production was thereby maintained despite centralization. The work force in these little shops of thirty to fifty workers were "girls," that is, young, unmarried women who left their homes to work all day at stitching machines. *The Lynn News* estimated in 1855 that there were 1,500 to 1,800 sewing machines in operation and that most of them were run in shops by young women who earned an average weekly wage of about $6.00.[53] Many of these young women were members of local families, but by 1860 a sizeable portion of them had left their homes in the towns of Eastern Massachusetts, New Hampshire, Maine and the Maritime Provinces of Canada to board with families in Lynn and Haverhill and work for the attractive wages in the shoe shops. In the 1850s native-born, young New England women were abandoning work in the textile mills in the Merrimack Valley for employment in the shoe shops of Essex County.[54]

The depression years of the late 1850s created a crisis in the rapidly changing New England shoe industry. The crisis involved a collapse in the pre-industrial wage patterns of the family economy as shoe manufacturing moved toward mechanization, centralization and the factory system. In the early 1850s an expanding market for boots and shoes in the developing West had drawn additional male workers into the process of bottoming: the attachment by hand of machine or hand-sewn uppers to soles. Heeling and finishing operations were reorganized and performed separately along with cutting operations in the central shops. Groups of workmen in the surrounding towns of Essex County served by a network of teamsters bottomed shoes for Lynn and Haverhill shoe bosses, but an even more extensive rural outwork system, reaching into Central New Hampshire and Southern Maine and served by railroad, supplied additional male workers for bottoming.[55]

Machine productivity by female factory operatives increased the demand for bottomers, and Irish and German immigrants as well as migrants from New England came to the shoe towns of Massachusetts, crowding the local labor market. While the numbers of men who worked as bottomers increased, stimulated by machine productivity, the sex ratio of male to female shoeworker sharply reversed. The numbers of women employed in Massachusetts shoe production dropped off steadily in the 1850s. In Lynn the number of females employed on shoes shrank sharply by 41% between 1850 and 1860. The mechanization of women's work intensified the hard conditions of labor for both men and women involved in outwork in Essex County. The productivity of the new machine stitchers had stimulated the demand for bottomers, while cutting the demand for shoebinders. By contemporary estimates, one factory girl at her stitching machine could supply enough work for twenty bottomers, while replacing eleven binders. The woman who operated a sewing machine at home still faced the custom of "furnishing," that is, providing thread, needles and lining materials. A considerable gap developed after 1855 between the wages of factory operatives and the wages of women working at home whether by hand or by machine.[56]

Downward pressure on wages during the hard times after 1857 cut sharply into the shoemaker's family wage and helped precipitate the largest American demonstration of labor protest prior to the Civil War. A regional strike, beginning in February 1860 and spearheaded by activities in Natick and Lynn, disrupted production.[57] The values and patterns of the pre-industrial family economy confronted the emerging factory system. This confrontation divided not only the workers and their employers, but also divided the strikers into groups promoting the family wage economy through the artisan tradition and groups of female factory operatives whose place in centralized production and whose status as temporary residents of the shoe city created a different set of interests in the 1860 strike.

The strikers in Lynn, led by the bottomers, hoped to organize the country shoemakers to refuse outwork, while they simultaneously halted production in the Lynn shops. Important to this strategy was the interruption of teamster activities which carried sewn uppers and cut soles to country workshops. Significantly, the first serious conflict in Lynn involved express teams which carried shoe uppers machine-sewn by female factory workers to Marblehead bottomers for the John Wooldredge Company.[58] Wooldredge had pioneered both the adoption of the Singer sewing machine in 1852 and the introduction of steam power in 1858 for heeling and stitching operations. His firm symbolized the emerging factory system.

The strike leadership in Lynn had been considering the organization of the 3,000 shoebinders and stitchers as an auxiliary force to encourage community support and boycott uncooperative shoe bosses. Their decision to organize women workers was made after a violent incident on February 23 between strikers and expressmen which provoked widespread regional criticism in the press, precipitated the arrival of outside police forces and threatened to undermine the crucial support of shoemakers in the neighboring towns of Essex County for the strike.[59] In 1860 the Lynn strike committee attempted to utilize the moral stature of women for the same family and community purposes as had the Lynn cordwainers' society in the 1840s. Women's participation would restore morality to the strike, help generate community support in Lynn and throughout Essex County and mitigate criticism. The involvement of local women would erase the images of violence and disorder and emphasize the nature of the strike as a defense of the New England family.

The strike committee in Lynn was not, however, prepared to acknowledge or represent the interests of the female factory operatives whose leaders quickly seized control of the women's meetings. The interests of these women workers, who were nearly 40% of the female work force in Lynn by 1860, conflicted with artisan conception of the family wage economy.[60] The factory operatives disagreed with the advancement of the wages of male shoeworkers as the only objective in the strike and convinced the women workers of Lynn to strike for higher wages as binders and stitchers. They also began to organize women workers in the neighboring towns of Danvers, Newburyport and Marblehead.[61] Realizing the importance of their strategic position to stop work in centralized production, the factory girls in Lynn proposed a coalition with female homeworkers to raise wages in both categories of work: homework for wives and mothers and factory work for single girls. This alliance of gender represented a bridge between the pre-industrial patterns of women's work and the developing factory system. Unity as a gender would protect the wages of the married and the unmarried, the homeworkers and the shop girls, by linking the cause of working women to the new sources of wages and power in factory work. Mechanization and centralization of women's work had meant higher wages for factory workers, but reduced the numbers of women employed, relegated wives and mothers to homework and depressed the wages of outworkers. For homeworkers, an alliance with the young factory girls represented a real chance in 1860 for women working at home to make a valuable connection with the new industrial workers. In return, factory girls could anticipate marriage and a chance to work at home for decent wages. The family wage economy would be protected by a coalition of women workers acting together on behalf of their own interests.

The factory girls, led by twenty-one year old Clara Brown, a native of Massachusetts, who boarded in Lynn with a shoemaker's family, won several crucial votes on raising women's wages in the strike meetings held by Lynn women. They challenged the male strike committee for leadership of the women workers and to articulation of their interests. The factory girls identified with other women in the industry as workers and as a gender, not unlike the brothers of the craft. The ideology of artisan life did not figure in their vision of an alliance of women workers at home and in the shops, nor did they identify with the bottomers on familial or on ideological grounds. Conscious of the power of factory stitchers in this alliance whose productivity could shut down production in the industry and halt outwork, Clara Brown declared: "Girls of Lynn, . . . strike at once . . . Don't work your machines; let them lie still until we get all we ask." At a later meeting she challenged: ". . . we've got the bosses where we can do as we please with 'em. If we don't take the work, what can the bosses do?"[62]

The male strike committee quickly moved to oppose this unwelcome development. The committee members failed, however, to persuade the women at a meeting on February 28 to reconsider the list of wage demands which had been adopted the night before, a wage list which in the eyes of the striking shoemakers overvalued factory stitching and jeopardized homework. They feared that if the women's wages were raised, all stitching of uppers would be centralized in factories and homework eliminated. For the bottomers, the best protection for the family wage lay in obtaining higher wages for men's work and maintaining homework for women. In a bold move, the strike committee and its supporters among the women homeworkers ignored the high wage list adopted by votes taken at several of the women's meetings and substituted a lower list of wages which they circulated as the official wage list for the women workers of Lynn to sign.[63] On March 2 the supporters of the men's strike committee and the factory girls confronted each other at a tumultuous meeting. James Dillon, representing the bottomers, pleaded for the support of the women as wives and mothers of shoemakers and appealed to them not to alienate the bosses of the stitching shops by demanding an "unfair" increase in wages.[64] Other speakers dismissed the shop girls as interested only in money and in "the right to switch a long-tailed skirt [extravagant dress]."[65] Wage decisions, it was argued at the March 2 meeting, should be made by "sober, and discreet women" and not by "laughing" and "thoughtless girls."[66] Clara Brown countered by insisting that the machine girls of Lynn had the power to protect homeworkers, but that the factory girls would only strike for "something worth having." She pointed out that the low wage list prepared by the homeworkers actually cut wages on factory work. Despite her warnings, representatives of the bottomers' committee persuaded the majority of the women at the meeting to reject the high wage list and the factory girls, accept their recommendations on behalf of the family and community in Lynn and join the striking men in great show of community support for the strike.[67]

The legendary parade of striking women on a snowy March day through the streets of Lynn represented a great victory for the defenders of decentralized production and for the artisan tradition in Lynn. The images of the women's procession printed in the pages of *Frank Leslie's Illustrated Newspaper* have come to epitomize the involvement of women in the 1860 strike, but these sketches obscured the battle which took place over the relationship of women workers to the strike. The political stance of the majority of the women workers who rejected the strategy of the factory girls and supported the bottomers was reflected in the familial values on one of their banners:

> Weak in physical strength but strong in moral courage, we dare to battle for the right, shoulder to shoulder with our fathers, husbands and brothers.[68]

The decision of the homeworkers to support the men's strike committee was taken at the risk of ignoring the implications of mechanization, the factory system and the potential of the shop girls who, as workers in centralized production, represented the reorganization of industrial life in Lynn. Many Lynn women continued to support the bottomers until the strike slowly fell apart in late March, while the factory girls who boarded in Lynn returned to work or to their homes.[69]

The bottomers of Lynn had fought in 1860 to maintain the traditions and ideology of decentralized production, including women's work in the home. The artisan ideology had operated successfully to unite the heterogeneous work force of male workers — rural migrants, Irish, Germans and shoemakers in country shops and shoe towns — in the 1850s, but cut off the new female factory workers from contributing to labor protest. The leaders of the Lynn strike failed to perceive or respond to the strategic potential of female machine operators in centralized production and had ignored and opposed their articulated interests. The perceptions which shoemaking artisans had developed of work and gender made it difficult for them to regard women as fellow-workers outside of family relationships, to include them in the ideology and politics built on artisan life or see in the experience of working women what awaited all workers as capitalism in the New England shoe industry moved toward the factory system.

Historiography in the 1970s on women's work was dominated by a lively debate on the impact of economic change on women and their relationship to the family. Two major interpretations emerged. Joan Scott, Louise Tilly, Jane Humphries and Leslie Tentler emphasized the limitations of changes in women's lives as a result of industrialization, and they regarded the family as primary in defining the work and social roles of women employed at home or in the factory. Edward Shorter, Patricia Branca, Thomas Dublin and Heidi Hartmann have argued for a variety of levels of change in women's lives as a result of new work. All acknowledge the sexual division of labor as a fundamental condition of women's work in the nineteenth century.

This overview of changes in women's work in New England shoe production and the relationship of women shoeworkers to the artisan tradition suggests that tension between women workers and the family values of artisan culture remained constant and unresolved as work reorganized during the shift toward industrialization from 1780 to 1860. Contradictions between perceptions of the proper gender role for women in the family and their consciousness as workers in production prolonged these tensions for women workers into the early factory system and the 1860 strike. This struggle, most visible during moments of labor protest, had been initiated by the recruitment of women into production in the artisan system and maintained by the differences in the location of work and the exposure of the individual worker to the increasing control of the work process by the employer. For the most part, women shoeworkers negotiated those tensions between family and work within the value system of artisan ideology, but in doing so they built limits into their consciousness as workers and into their ability to act together as women to defend their interests or claim new rights. The gender perceptions of artisan ideology as articulated by male shoeworkers in ante bellum New England defined the role of women primarily as family members and as moral agents in society. Gender-based ideology and work experience cut women off from the most vital tradition of collective resistance in the early nineteenth century.

University of Lowell Mary H. Blewett

FOOTNOTES

I would like to thank Helena Wright, Tom Dublin, Milton Cantor, Carole Turbin, Paul Faler and Bruce Laurie for their useful suggestions, helpful criticism and support as this essay developed. The research and writing were aided by grants from the Andrew W. Mellon Foundation and the National Endowment for the Humanities. An earlier and shorter version of this paper was read at the Social Science History Association Conference, November 1982.

1. Edward P. Thompson, *The Making of the English Working Class* (New York, 1966); David Brody, "The Old Labor History and The New: In Search of an American Working Class," *Labor History* 20 (1979): 111-126; Herbert Gutman, *Work, Culture and Society in Industrializing America* (New York, 1976); David Montgomery, "The Working Classes of the Pre-Industrial American City, 1780-1830," *Labor History* 9 (1968): 3-22; Paul G. Faler, *Mechanics and Manufacturers in the Early Industrial Revolution: Lynn, Massachusetts, 1780-1860* (Albany, 1981); Alan Dawley, *Class and Community: The Industrial Revolution in Lynn* (Cambridge, 1976); Bruce Laurie, *The Working People of Philadelphia, 1800-1850* (Philadelphia, 1980); Susan E. Hirsch, *Roots of the American Working Class: The Industrialization of Newark, 1800-1860* (Philadelphia, 1978) and Howard B. Rock, *Artisans of the New Republic: The Tradesmen of New York City in the Age of Jefferson* (New York, 1979). For overviews, see Sean Wilentz, "Artisan Origins of the American Working Class," *International Labor and Working Class History*. 19 (1981): 1-22 and Jim Green, "Culture, Politics and Workers' Response to Industrialization in the U.S." *Radical America* 16 (Jan.-April, 1982): 101-128. Bruce Laurie provided a succinct definition of the new conception of class consciousness: ". . . culture and consciousness are made and remade by the interplay of living and working conditions and by what individuals bring to communities and workshops from prior experience," p. 27. Laurie, however, refrained from examining the experience of women's involvement in worker culture in pre-industrial Philadelphia despite the evidence he located on their participation in work, temperance groups and religious activities, pp. 12-13, 30-34, 43, 49-51. Hirsch explored women's involvement in pre-industrial work in Newark and its connections with family life, but she viewed the male artisan as the typical worker and the industrialization of male crafts as the touch-stone of economic change from 1800-1860. Her definition of status included ethnicity but not gender. In their review articles, Wilentz and Green call for more work on early industrialization from the perspective of rearrangements in gender relations as well as the relations of production. My research on women's relationship to the pre-industrial artisan tradition has been influenced by a workshop on "Family History: A Critique," at the Women and Power Conference, University of Maryland, 1977, later published as Rayna Rapp, Ellen Ross and Renate Bridenthal, "Examining Family History," *Feminist Studies* 5 (Spring, 1979): 174-200; by the work of Thomas Dublin on the Lowell textile operatives and by the work of Heidi Hartmann, especially "The Family as the Locus of Gender, Class, and Political Struggle," *Signs* 6 (Spring, 1981): 366-394.

2. Thomas Dublin, *Women At Work: The Transformation of Work and Community in Lowell, Massachusetts, 1826-1860* (New York, 1979).

3. Faler, *Mechanics*, chapter 3, 9 and Dawley, *Class and Community, passim*. For a critique of Faler and Dawley, see Friedrich Lenger, "Class, Culture and Class Consciousness in Ante Bellum Lynn: A Critique of Alan Dawley and Paul Faler," *Social History* 6 (1981): 317-332.

4. Mary Blewett, "Shared But Different: The Experience of Women Workers in the Nineteenth Century Work Force of the New England Shoe Industry," in *Essays from the Lowell Conference on Industrial History, 1980 and 1981* (Lowell, 1981): 77-85.

5. Faler, *Mechanics*, pp. 11-12. For the patterns of pre-industrial shoemaking in Eastern Massachusetts, Blanche Hazard, *The Organization of the Boot and Shoe Industry in Massachusetts Before 1875* (Cambridge, 1921); David Newhall Johnson, *Sketches of Lynn or the Changes of Fifty Years* (Lynn, 1880) and John Philip Hall, "The Gentle Craft: A Narrative of Yankee Shoemakers," (Ph.D. diss., Columbia University, 1953).

6. Alonzo Lewis and James R. Newhall, *History of Lynn* (Boston, 1865): 50-65.

7. John R. Commons, "American Shoemaking, 1648-1895: A Sketch of Industrial Evolution," *Quarterly Journal of Economics* 24 (1909): 39-83. Commons pointedly dismissed Marxian analysis of changes in the mode of production and ignored the introduction of the sexual division of labor. Dawley, *Class and Community* chapter 1 and Faler, *Mechanics*, chapter 2.

8. Dawley, *Class and Community*, pp. 16-25.

9. Johnson, *Sketches of Lynn*, pp. 336-340; Hazard, *Boot and Shoe Industry*, pp. 4-53; Dawley, *Class and Community* pp. 16-25; Philip C. Swett, "History of Shoemaking in Haverhill," unpublished reminiscences; William Stone, "Lynn and Its Old-Time Shoemakers' Shops," *Lynn Historical Society Register*, (1900): 49-100; Hall, "The Gentle Craft," pp. 49-145; Helen L. Sumner, *History of Women in Industry in the United States*, vol. 9 of*Report on Condition of Woman and Child Wage-Earners in the United States* (Washington, D.C., 1910): 167-170; Edith Abbott, "Women In Industry: The Manufacture of Boots and Shoes," *American Journal of Sociology* 15 (1909): 335-360. In his discussion of Philadelphia shoemaking, Laurie argued that the division of labor did not uniformly reduce craft work to semi-skilled jobs, but created a new hierarchy of occupations at the bottom of which was shoebinding, p. 22.

10. Dawley noted, but does explain the origins of the involvement of women in shoe production, pp. 17-18. Faler discussed the importance of the assignment of work to women in shoemaking, pp. 19-27, but he moved too fast in his argument to speculate on the social dynamics of this decision within the shoemaking family. In attempting to account for the origins of the sexual division of labor (a term which he does not employ), Faler used a circular argument, stating that although women did not participate in shoemaking before the 1780s, the basis of their involvement in production ". . . was an outgrowth of the domestic system of manufacture in which the entire family of a cordwainer, working in the home participated in the productive process," p. 24. He cited the "muted growth" of powerful craft customs in Lynn in comparison with Philadelphia to explain the recruitment of women, but did not explain why women were recruited only to binding and were not admitted into the shoe shop, p. 24. Faler cited evidence on the surplus of females in Essex County, 1790 to 1810, as a labor pool for the ladies' shoe industry, but noted that these women probably resided in non-shoemaking families of seafarers and fishermen, p. 25. This surplus of females in Essex County would indeed be tapped by shoe bosses, but not until *after* the shoemaking family ceased to be the locus of combined production. Faler saw no implications for the mechanics' ideology or the artisan community in the physical and social separation of the workplaces of shoebinders and shoemakers, although he did identify the beginnings of class division in a similar separation between the workplaces of the journeymen in the ten footer and the master, later the shoe boss, in the central shop, pp. 23, 27, 167. On the whole, although he acknowledged the importance of the division of labor, Faler assumed that there were no important changes in women's work until mechanization in 1852. Anna Davin

discussed the neglect of the sexual division of labor as both an object of study and as a tool of analysis in "Feminism and Labour History," *People's History and Socialist Theory*, Raphael Samuel, editor (London, 1981): 178. For two discussions of the involvement of the sexual division of labor in the female experience of work and labor protest, see Louise Tilly, "Paths of Proletarianization: Organization of Production, Sexual Division of Labor and Women's Collective Action," *Signs* 7 (Winter, 1981): 400-417 and Temma Kaplan, "Female Consciousness and Collective Action: The Case of Barcelona, 1910-1918," *Signs* 7 (1982): 545-566.

11. On mechanization, the sexual division of labor and the social uses of technology, see Judith A. McGraw, "Women and the History of American Technology," *Signs* 7 (1982): 798-828. For a general interpretation of the sexual division of labor and capitalist development, Julie A. Matthaei, *An Economic History of Women in America* (New York, 1982).

12. In her study of French women and the artisan system of production in sixteenth century Lyon, Natalie Zemon Davis argued that the work identity of female workers was subordinated to their gender roles in the family, "Women in the Crafts in Sixteenth-Century Lyon," *Feminist Studies* 8 (1982): 45-80. For the separation of men and women in the artisan experience of London, Gareth Stedman-Jones, "Working-Class Culture and Working-Class Politics in London, 1870-1900; Notes on the Remaking of a Working Class," *Journal of Social History* 7 (1974): 485, and Sally Alexander, "Women's Work in Nineteenth Century London: A Study of the Years 1820-1850," in Juliet Mitchell and Ann Oakley, *The Rights and Wrongs of Women*, (New York, 1976): 59-111.

13. For a compelling image of the family labor system, see Johnson, *Sketches of Lynn*, pp. 337-338. In a critique of E.P. Thompson's concept of task and time labor, Lise Vogel pointed to the necessity of combining both task and time labor in a pre-industrial but capitalist productive system. The shoebinders' work, even as a contribution of unwaged labor performed in their kitchens, began to assume a timed and, therefore, industrial character, "Rummaging Through the Primitive Past: A Note on Family, Industrialization, and Capitalism," *The Newberry Papers in Family and Community History* (Nov. 1976): 19-26.

14. For example, see the correspondence between William Richardson, a shoe boss of Stoneham, Massachusetts, with shoemakers, Jesse Reed of New Ipswich, New Hampshire and William Cooke of Bedford, Massachusetts, Richardson Papers, Baker Library, Harvard University.

15. The accounts of Israel Buffum (1806-1847) and Aaron Breed (1805-1817) Lynn Historical Society. John Goodwin Accounts (1810-1834) of Reading, Massachusetts, Mrs. C. Nelson Bishop, Reading.

16. Among the account books which illustrate the shift of binders' work out of the family labor system are Jonathan Boyce (1793-1813) Lynn Historical Society; John Burrell (1819-1820) Lynn Historical Society; Samuel Bacheller Papers (1795-1845) Vol. 2, Sturbridge Village Archives; Untitled Ledger, Lynn (1790-1820) Lynn Historical Society; James Coburn, Boxford (1804-1821); Robert Brown, West Newburyport (1813-1828); Caleb Eames, Wilmington (1819-1825) Sturbridge Village Archives.

17. Percy Bidwell, "The Agricultural Revolution in New England," *American Historical Review* 25 (1921): 685-702. For statistics on the putting-out system in Essex County, Secretary of the Treasury, *Documents Relative to the Manufacturers in the United States, 1832* (Reprint, New York, 1969), Vol. 2, pp. 590-610 and Commonwealth of Massachusetts, *Statistical Information Relating to Certain Branches of Industry in Massachusetts, for the year 1837* (Boston, 1837). For a quantitative analysis of the early Massachusetts censuses, Claudia Goldin and Kenneth Sokoloff, "Women, Children, and Industrialization in the Early Republic: Evidence from the Manufacturing Censuses," *Journal of Economic History* 42 (1982): 741-774.

18. Unidentified Shoe Manufacturer's Stock Book, Lynn (1830-1831) Lynn Historical Society. Based on the figures of cut stock given out to workers in March 1830 and in March 1831, the annual production of this shoe manufacturer was about 30,000 pairs in 1830 and 70,000 pairs in 1831. According to the 1832 report of the Treasury or the McLane Report, only the eleven largest shoe manufacturers in Lynn had this capacity for production. *Documents Relating to Manufacturers, 1832*, Vol. 1, pp. 224-235.

19. See the Journal of Joseph P. Lye, Jr. of Lynn (1819-1830) Lynn Historical Society and the Diaries of Isaac W. Merrill of Haverhill (1828-1878) Haverhill Public Library. For worker control as crucial to class struggle in nineteenth century America, David Montgomery, *Workers' Control in America* (Cambridge, 1976).

20. In the early 1830s there was evidence of widespread collective resistance by shoebinders in Essex and Middlesex Counties in Massachusetts as well as in Philadelphia, New York City and Newark. John B. Andrews and W.D.P. Bliss, *History of Women in Trade Unions* (Reprint, New York, 1974): 41-45 and Augusta Emile Galster, *The Labor Movement in the Shoe Industry: With Special Reference to Philadelphia* (New York, 1924): 22-28. Hirsch in *Roots of the American Working Class* noted shoebinders' activity in Newark in 1836 and observed that "[t]he existence of a separate union for women . . . suggests that the days of domestic manufacture were long gone in shoemaking. The women binders and fitters hired out as individuals and were not wives and daughters helping craftsmen who worked within households," pp. 28-29. See also, Keith Melder, "Women in the Shoe Industry: The Evidence From Lynn," *Essex Institute Historical Collections* 115 (1979): 272-273.

21. The issues of *The New England Christian Herald* (printed briefly in Boston under this name, later *Zion's Herald*) are lost for 1831, but Hall quoted from them at length in his dissertation, pp. 152-154. In the August 12 issue of the *Christian Herald*, the binders' society challenged the figures of the shoe bosses, criticized payment in goods and insisted it represented 227 shoebinders. See also the *Lynn Mirror*, Aug. 6, 1831.

22. "Preamble to the Constitution of the Female Society of Lynn and vicinity for the protection and promotion of Female Industry," *Lynn Record*, January 1, 1834 and "Address of the Shoebinders of Lynn" by Chairman Mary Russell, *Lynn Record*, Jan. 8, 1834. All quotes are from the *Lynn Record*. Andrews and Bliss, *Women in Trade Unions*, quoted the Constitution of the Female Society, but not the preamble, pp. 42-43.

23. Based on the 1837 statistics of manufacturing in Massachusetts, the women of Saugus who met to affiliate with the Lynn Society represented almost the entire work force of binders in town.

24. Faler, *Mechanics*, pp. 172-173.

25. "Address," *Lynn Record*, Jan. 8, 1834. The association of fear and shame with the poorhouse was one of the products of a new industrial morality skillfully described by Faler, *Mechanics*, pp. 110-116.

26. Faler mistakenly dated the Female Society as organized in 1830, p. 198. Although the cordwainers listed the low wages of shoebinders in the 1830 grievances as a society, the Female Society did not appear until 1833 under its own leadership, *Lynn Mirror*, Aug. 14, Sept. 4, 1830. Although the leadership of the Lynn societies did not represent an association of family or kin, the two groups worked together closely in 1834.

27. Lynn Female Anti-Slavery Society, Minutes, 1836-1838, Lynn Historical Society.

28. In this typology developed by Dawley and Faler in "Working Class Culture and Politics in the Industrial Revolution: Sources of Loyalism and Rebellion," *Journal of Social History* 9 (1976): 466-471, gender was not explored. Lenger, "Class, Culture and Class Consciousness," is critical of Dawley and Faler's typology, but not on gender analysis, pp. 325-329.

29. *Lynn Record*, June 18, 1834. Mary Russell greatly exaggerated the results of the 1834 Lowell turnouts which failed to prevent a wage cut or even create an organization such as the binders' society in Lynn, Dublin, *Women At Work*, pp. 89-98.

30. Nancy F. Cott, *The Bonds of Womanhood: "Women's Sphere" in New England, 1780-1835* (New Haven, 1977).

31. Massachusetts, *Statistics of Manufacturing, 1837.*

32. Faler regarded the *Awl* as the most influential labor paper published by shoemakers, its circulation in Lynn probably reaching most of them, *Mechanics*, p. 200.

33. In his fascinating discussion of the impact of a new industrial morality on the social customs and attitudes of Lynn society, Faler analyzed attempts by moral reformers after 1826 to undermine the relaxed morality of the eighteenth century by imposing discipline on sexual practices, such as bundling, on public social occasions, on school yard behavior and on sexual conduct in general, *Mechanics*, pp. 109-138. Whether this new social morality also produced new working-class attitudes on the nature of women as purified, moral beings is a tantalizing question. Faler and Dawley have argued elsewhere that the "rebels" who identified with *Awl* utilized the new industrial morality for purposes of working-class resistance, see "Working Class Culture and Politics." The same argument may apply to the *Awl*'s attempt to utilize women as moral agents in support of working-class objectives in the 1840s and later in the strike of 1860. The concept of women as moral agents in society is crucial to women's history in the early nineteenth century and underlies the public activities of organized middle-class women, see for example, Carroll Smith-Rosenberg, "Beauty, the Beast, and the Militant Woman: A Case Study in Sex Roles and Social Stress in Jacksonian America," *American Quarterly* 23 (1971): 562-584.

34. *Essex County Washingtonian*, Dec. 29, 1842, Jan. 5, 26, 1843 calls attention to the temperance activities of women in the Woodend section of Lynn, the home of a large portion of Lynn's journeymen. On Woodend and temperance activities in Lynn, see Faler, *Mechanics*, pp. 197, 104, 130-136, 206-210. The activity of these women may also indicate their economic dependence on their families as a result of low wages for shoebinding.

35. *The Awl*, July 17, 1844.

36. The training of women as shoemakers in Essex County was not entirely unknown, but reflected the tradition of a widow or daughter carrying on the trade of a husband or father. On Mrs. Tuttle, *The Awl*, Aug. 28, 1844.

37. For appeals for female participation, *The Awl*, Sept. 11, 18, Dec. 7, 1844. For laments over lack of response, Dec. 14, 17, 21, 1844.

38. *The Awl*, Dec. 21, 1844.

39. "Letter to the Editor from Centre Street," *The Awl*, Sept. 18, 1844.

40. *The Awl*, Sept. 11, 1844.

41. "Mechanics' Wives," *The Awl*, June 18, 1845. See also "Frank Russell or the Village Blacksmith," an original story published in the September 4, 1844 issue which argued that the natural and acquired virtues of a mechanic's life could overcome and harmonize class divisions.

42. Stone, "Lynn," pp. 87-93. Faler argued that Robinson was a "good boss" during the 1840s as compared to the "grinders" who were regarded as highly exploitative by the journeymen, *Mechanics*, pp. 177-178. Robinson, however, introduced higher standards of

quality for work, issued printed directives to both makers and binders about how the work should be performed and inspected the work personally. He also apparently paid good wages in return for tighter discipline over work. For Danvers, William L. Hyde, "Reminiscences of Danvers in the Forties and Fifties," *Historical Collections of the Danvers Historical Society* 5 (1917): 1-20 and Edwin Mudge, "The Shoe Trade of Danvers," in Charles B. Rice, *Proceedings at the celebration of two hundredth anniversary of the first parish at Salem Village, now Danvers* (Boston, 1874): 235-243.

43. In 1845 the *Awl* announced an advanced position on women's rights and supported equal compensation for women workers and an absolute equality of rights, including the right to subscribe to a free press. *The Awl*, Jan. 4, 1845. Nathan D. Chase was regarded as a "grinder" by Lynn shoemakers, Faler, *Mechanics*, p. 178.

44. For the manufacturers' side, *The Awl*, Jan. 25, Feb. 22, 1845; for Darlin's side, Feb. 22, 1845. For the shoebinders' contributions, *The Awl*, Feb. 1, 22, 1845. For a complaint by one woman about being subordinated while participating in the activities of the cordwainers' society, see Constance, "On the Art of Shoemaking," *The Awl*, Feb. 22, 1845. The *Awl* supported labor activist Sarah Bagley and *The Voice of Industry*, defended the factory girls of Lowell and the seamstresses of Boston, but did not perceive shoebinders in terms of their vulnerability and isolation.

45. Commonwealth of Massachusetts, *Statistical Information Relating to Certain Branches of Industry in Massachusetts, for the year, 1855* (Boston, 1856).

46. Surviving accounts from the 1830s, the 1840s and 1850s on the outwork system in Essex County are rare. See the accounts of Jeremiah Chapman (1839-1849) Danvers and James P. Hutchinson (1836-1860) Danvers, Essex Institute, Salem, Massachusetts, the accounts of Bartlett Gage (1829-1834) Haverhill and John Tappan (1827-1843) Bradford, Haverhill Public Library and the personal accounts of Edward Poor (1828-1869) Georgetown, Essex Institute.

47. Mary H. Blewett, "'I Am Doom to Disapointment': The Diaries of a Beverly, Massachusetts, Shoebinder, Sarah E. Trask, 1849-1851," *Essex Institute Historical Collections* 117 (1981): 192-212. Trask and her fellow binders had fathers who were laborers, carpenters, mariners and shoemakers. These young women formed female networks with little connection to shoemaking artisans. The Preston accounts of Danvers, Essex Institute, revealed the employment of eleven shoebinders who formed the core of productive workers between 1836 and 1845 of which four were the wives or daughters of farmers. William Mulligan saw the shoemaking family as a harmonious work unit in operation from 1780 to 1850 and analyzed the impact of the close connections between work and family on the fertility of shoemaking families in the Lynn census of 1850. He found that shoemaking families had a fertility rate lower than other skilled workers and produced children in a more concentrated period of their lives. Mulligan contended that the role of women in shoemaking families as workers in family labor units was economically valuable and this valued economic role explains the fertility patterns of the shoemaking family in 1850. See William Mulligan, "The Family as Factory: Shoemaking in the North Shore District of Massachusetts, 1750-1850," paper presented to the American Historical Association, December, 1980. However, the census of population of 1850 does not give information on the occupations of women. The evidence in this essay on the disassociation of women workers from the family work unit suggests that the 1850 fertility patterns of the shoemaking families might better be explained by the penetration of the family by the putting-out system which divided women's work from a family labor context. Lower fertility, possibly evidence of domestic feminism, might reflect the breakdown rather than the continuity of families as work units. The family was still an economic unit, a family wage economy, but no longer a family labor economy. This useful distinction is explored in Joan Scott and Louise Tilly, *Women, Work, and Family* (New York, 1978).

48. Ross David Thomson, "The Origins of Modern Industry in the United States: The Mechanization of Shoe and Sewing Machine Production," (Ph.D. diss., Yale University, Economics, 1976): 245-250; *The Lynn Item*, (Reminiscences of John B. Nichols and Obituary) Nov. 10, 1903, Aug. 30 and Sept. 8, 1913.

49. Swett, "Haverhill," pp. 16-17; (Reminiscences of Charles Buffum) *The Lynn Item*, Oct. 5, 1901; *Lynn Weekly Reporter*, Feb. 28, 1863; "First Introduction of the Sewing Machine into the Shoe Business," *Shoe and Leather Reporter*, Dec. 12, 1867 and Thomson, "Origins of Modern Industry," pp. 247-261.

50. Thomas P. Kettel, "Manufacturers," in *Eighty Years' Progress of the United States* (New York, 1864): 428. See also the wages of Maria Poor in the account book of Edward Poor of Georgetown. Her wages rose in the 1850s just before mechanization and fell in the early 1860s to levels reminiscent of the 1830s as a result of the introduction of the factory system.

51. An examination of the Lynn Tax Assessments in 1860 and the schedules of the United States Census of Manufacture revealed no information on sewing machines owned by manufacturers or individuals. For impressions of the extent of their use in the home, see Johnson, *Sketches of Lynn*, p. 340; Hazard, *Boot and Shoe Industry*, pp. 95-96; *Eighty Years*, p. 428 and Thomson, "Origins of Modern Industry," pp. 69-70.

52. *Lynn Item*, Jan. 1, 1897 and Thomson, "Origins of Modern Industry," pp. 69-71, 138.

53. *Lynn News*, July 20, 1855. The Massachusetts state census of population for 1855 does not list the occupations of women.

54. On the decline of Yankee women as textile workers, Dublin, *Women at Work*, pp. 201-207. Calculations based on the federal manuscript census of population in Lynn for 1860 indicate that 52% of the total number of the 371 female machine operatives (stitchers) boarded in Lynn with private families or in small boarding houses. Of the boarding stitchers, 31% were natives of other states, principally New Hampshire and Maine and 19% were foreign-born, principally in Nova Scotia (7% were Irish natives). The remaining 48% of the boarding stitchers were natives of towns and cities of Massachusetts, assuming that Lynn natives were living with their families or kin.

55. Local observers noted a drop of one third in shoemakers' wages between 1857 and 1860. *Lynn Weekly Reporter*, Mar. 31, Apr. 16, 1860 and the *Salem Observer*, Mar. 3, 1860. Sumner, *Women in Industry*, p. 172, commented on the high productivity of the machine girls in relation to the bottomers after the introduction of the sewing machine. Also see, *Lynn Reporter*, Mar. 31, Apr. 21, 1860; *Marblehead Ledger*, Feb. 29, 1860.

56. See the comments of James Haines, a Boston shoemaker in the *New York Herald*, Mar. 22, 1860 on the relationship of machine stitchers to bottomers in terms of productivity in 1860. Also see letters deploring the development of two wage scales for women, *Tri-Weekly Publisher* (Haverhill), Mar. 3, 10, 1860. For the custom of furnishing by homeworkers, see the testimony of women at the Lynn strike meetings, *Boston Journal*, Feb. 28, 1860.

57. The regional shoe strike of 1860 was the largest demonstration of labor protest before the Civil War and as such has had some attention from historians, but little systematic analysis. The most detailed examination appeared in Philip S. Foner, *Women and the American Labor Movement: From Colonial Times to the Eve of World War I* (New York, 1979): 90-97. Foner emphasized the heroic and exemplary aspects of the strike, especially women's militancy and the unity between working-class men and women, but he dismissed the dissension over strike objectives as "some discussion," pp. 92-93. See also Norman Ware, *The Industrial Worker, 1840-1860* (New York, 1964): 47 and Andrews and Bliss, *Women in Trade Unions*, p. 108. Dawley analyzed the strike, *Class and Community*, pp. 79-90, as a product of mechanization and declining wages, but doesn't pick up the conflict between

women workers and the strike committee. He did, however, note the subordination of women in the ideology and rhetoric of the shoemakers' resistance. Faler saw the strike as marking the end of a community of interest in Lynn and as the beginning of class conflict, but he emphasized the role of the mechanics and overlooked the conflict within the women's organization, see *Mechanics*, chapter 11. Overreliance by Dawley and Faler on local newspaper reporting, especially in the pro-strike (Lynn) *Bay State* whose editor, Lewis Josselyn, acted as an advisor to the bottomers' strike committee and smoothed over evidence of conflicts within the strike, gave them an overly harmonious view of strike events. The preponderance of evidence from the out-of-town press, which sent reporters to Lynn to cover events in detail as eye-witnesses reveals the conflict between the homeworkers and factory girls, especially in the coverage of the women's strike meetings. See the lengthy, eye-witness accounts in the *Boston Herald*, the *New York Times*, the *New York Herald*, the *Boston Post*, the *Boston Journal*, and the *Boston Advertiser*. The *Bay State* and the other Lynn newspapers covered the women's meetings only briefly. Patricia Branca has suggested that women's experience with work has differed significantly from men's experience in ways which must be taken into account in assessing the motivations and behavior of women at work, in strike situations and in unions, *Women in Europe Since 1750* (New York, 1978): 45-46.

58. The *Bay State*, Feb. 23, Mar. 1, 1860.

59. The timing of the involvement of the women in the strike after the outbreak of violence on February 23 is crucial to understanding the motives of the strike committee. Alonzo Draper of the committee issued a call for the first meeting of women on the night of February 23 by urging crowds of striking men to send their wives and sweethearts to a public meeting. Later in a dispute among strike committee members in April 1860 reported in the *Lynn Reporter*, Apr. 14, 1860, a member of the Executive Board of the strike committee, John R. Parrott said: ". . . there was not a word said about the running of machines, or of the women striking, for some time after we struck."

60. Comparisons between data on women workers in Lynn in the United States Census of Manufacture for 1860 and newspaper estimates of women participating in the strike as homeworkers suggest that about 60% of the approximately 3,000 female shoeworkers in Lynn supported the strike committee. The remaining 40% represented the boarding shop girls, a minority of the total work force in Lynn, seasonally employed, but who, as full-time machine operatives in centralized production, were capable of crippling the industry.

61. See the Feb. 28, 29, 1860 issues of the *Boston Journal*, the *Boston Post*, the *Boston Herald*, and the *New York Herald*. For organizational work by the women, the *Boston Herald*, Mar. 6, 12, 1860 and the *Boston Traveler*, Mar. 2, 1860.

62. The *New York Times*, Feb. 29, Mar. 6, 1860.

63. The *New York Times*, Mar. 6, 1860.

64. The *New York Times*, Mar. 6, 1860; the *New York Herald*, Mar. 5, 1860 and the *Boston Journal*, Mar. 3, 1860.

65. The *New York Times*, Mar. 6, 1860.

66. The *Boston Herald*, Mar. 3, 1860.

67. The *New York Times*, Mar. 6, 1860; the *Boston Herald*, Mar. 3, 1860 and the *Boston Journal*, Mar. 3, 1860. Marxist-feminists have recently debated whether the family wage served the interests of patriarchy or served the ability of working-class families to resist exploitation by employers. See Heidi Hartmann, "The Unhappy Marriage of Marxism and Feminism: Towards a More Progressive Union," *Capital and Class* (Summer, 1979): 1-43

and Jane Humphries, "Class Struggle and the Persistence of the Working-Class Family," *Cambridge Journal of Economics* I (1979): 241-258. Both the Hartmann and the Humphries model appear to have operated in the Lynn strike in 1860. The family wage as a strike objective meant that homeworkers defended an increase in men's wages and wanted work in the home to be preserved in the interests of family income. They accepted the male strike committee's strategy. The factory girls led by Clara Brown seemed unconsciously to challenge patriarchal control in the family and in the strike by offering an alliance with the homeworkers based on gender and the sexual division of labor. They were defeated in the Lynn strike by the actions and rhetoric of the male strike committee and outnumbered by those who responded to the ideology of the bottomers' family wage argument. In mid-March, however, the bottomers demonstrated their willingness to jeopardize even homework to win their increases. The *New York Herald* Mar. 19, 1860; the *Boston Journal*, Mar. 20, 1860.

68. The *Bay State*, Mar. 8, 1860.

69. The *Lynn Reporter* denied that by the end of March the women's strike was having any effect at all on the manufacturers, March 21, 1860. To test whether the boarding stitchers who came from other communities to work in Lynn formed attachments to local men and, therefore, might identify with the bottomers' interests in the strike, the 192 boarding stitchers were linked to the Massachusetts marriage records between 1860 and 1870. Forty-five or 23% of the boarding stitchers did marry in Lynn, but only 29 or 15% married between 1860 and 1865 and might be said to have had sweethearts during the 1860 strike. Another sixteen of the 45 boarding stitchers who married in Lynn did so between 1865 and 1870. Three-fourths of the boarding stitchers did not marry in Lynn. Maris Vinovskis warned, however, that migration can affect and distort the evidence of marriage registers. Marriages may be performed in the town where the bride lived, yet the new couple may reside in the community where the groom lived and worked, *Fertility in Massachusetts from the Revolution to the Civil War* (New York, 1981): 49-50.

SEXUAL HARASSMENT AT THE WORKPLACE

Historical Notes

Mary Bularzik

INTRODUCTION: WHAT IS SEXUAL HARASSMENT?

In 1908 *Harper's Bazaar* printed a series of letters in which working women wrote of their experiences of city life. (1) A typical experience was reported by G.E.D., a New York stenographer:

"I purchased several papers, and plodded faithfully through their multitude of 'ads.' I took the addresses of some I intended to call upon... The first 'ad' I answered the second day was that of a doctor who desired a stenographer at once, good wages paid. It sounded rather well, I thought, and I felt that this time I would meet a gentleman. The doctor was very kind and seemed to like my appearance and references; as to salary, he offered me $15 a week, with a speedy prospect of more. As I was leaving his office, feeling that at last I was launched safely upon the road to a good living, he said casually, 'I have an auto; and as my wife doesn't care for that sort of thing, I shall expect you to accompany me frequently on pleasure trips.' That settled the doctor; I never appeared. After that experience I was ill for two weeks; a result of my hard work, suffering and discouragement." (2)

The incident illustrates a common occupational hazard of women in the labor force: sexual harassment. Sexual harassment, defined as any unwanted pressure for sexual activity, includes verbal innuendos and suggestive comments, leering, gestures, unwanted physical contact (touching, pinching, etc.), rape and attempted rape. It is a form of harassment mainly perpetrated by men against women. As in many other forms of violence against women, the assertion of power and dominance is often more important than the sexual interaction. Sexual demands in the workplace, especially between boss and employee, become even more coercive because a woman's economic livelihood may be at stake.

Sexual harassment of women in the workplace is one manifestation of the wider issue of the oppression of women. Violence is central to that oppression, an essential part of establishing and maintaining the patriarchal family.

Until recently violence has only been studied psychologically, as an aberration, not as a norm. When violence occurs in the nuclear family, it is treated as the occasional act of a deviant rather than a prevalent and socially sanctioned way of enforcing the status quo. Statistical evidence shows violence to be pervasive, yet this is ignored. Rape, for example, despite repeated studies showing it is extremely common in many social settings, is still often described as the isolated act of a stranger. Wife-beating was treated as a similar infrequent (though regrettable) event.

Sexual harassment at the workplace is, I would argue, an analogous problem. It is consistent, systematic, and pervasive, not a set of random isolated acts. The license to harass women workers, which many men feel they have, stems from notions that there is a "woman's place" which women in the labor force have left, thus leaving behind their personal integrity.

I would like to propose a model which sees violence, and more specifically the threat of violence, as a mechanism of social control. It is used to control women's access to certain jobs; to limit job success and mobility; and to compensate men for powerlessness in their own lives. It functions on two levels: the group control of women by men, and personal control of individual workers by bosses and co-workers. Violence is used to support and preserve the institutions which guarantee the dominance of one group over others. Sexual harassment is one form. The threat of lynching hanging over Blacks in the South at the turn of the century was another such instance of the use of violence. So is rape. In neither case are the perpetrators of the "crime" totally condemned by society; though there are laws on the books against such behavior, it is clear to the victims that it may be dangerous to bring charges; and the victim is "marked" by the crime (or dead) while the attacker is considered "normal". Both "crimes" serve as warnings to certain groups not to walk the streets alone at night.

Words, gestures, comments can be used as threats of violence and to express dominance. Harassment often depends on this underlying violence — violence is implied as the ultimate response. Harassment is "little rape," an invasion of a person, by suggestion, by intimidation, by confronting a woman with her helplessness. It is an interaction in which one person purposefully seeks to discomfort another person. This discomfort serves to remind women of their helplessness in the face of male violence. To offer such a model is to suggest that it is not simply an individual interaction but a social one; not an act of deviance but a societally condoned mode of behavior that functions to preserve male dominance in the world of work.

The economic aspect of sexual harassment in the workplace differentiates it from other forms of violence against women. A rationalized capitalist economic order tended to separate spheres of sexual power (in the family) and economic power (in the workplace). Sexual coercion in the workplace reasserts the connection between the two. While the women involved did not see sexual favors as a right of their employers and male co-workers, their fear of losing jobs often stifled effective protest.

II

This paper will consider the historical conditions of sexual harassment and focus on white urban working women, primarily in Northern cities, and primarily in working class jobs. Most of the evidence concerns single women, who predominated in the female labor force before the 1940s. (The entrance of many more married women into the labor force during and after World War II added another dimension to the problem which will not be considered here.)

Sexual harassment was a problem faced by paid women workers in the United States from colonial days. Violence and sexual coercion did not originate with industrialization. However, the dynamics of these issues were different in a paid labor force than in a pre-industrial economy. The family setting of work in colonial days makes the incidents of sexual violence part of the history of violence in the family. In a capitalist industrial society, sexual harassment often became an interaction between strangers, not relatives or neighbors, which changed the psychological framework of the sexual violence.

There are scattered instances of women in colonial times protesting violence by male employers against women workers. In the January 28, 1734 issue of the N.Y. Weekly Journal, a group of women servants published a notice saying, "...we think it reasonable we should not be beat by our Mistresses Husband(s), they being too strong and perhaps may do tender women mischief." (3) Court records reveal many instances of servants being seduced by their employers. Since the status of domestic servants is complicated and little historical research has been done on their working conditions, I am not further considering them in this paper.

Much male public opinion didn't distinguish between women workers, prostitutes, the destitute, and the criminal classes in the industrializing stages of the economy. This was due to a complex of factors such as the necessity for women from poor families to be in the labor force, the unusualness of women working outside the family, the analogy between the prostitute and the paid women worker, both in some sense "escaping" from male control, and both "unprotected" and thus fair game for male lust. More thoughtful observers saw that low wages and poor working conditions in factories might make the temptations of the better-paying job of prostitute too much for some working girls to resist (or a logical choice from an economic point of view). As early as 1829, Matthew Carey offered a prize for the best essay on "the inadequacy of the wages generally paid to seamstresses, spoolers, spinners, shoe binders, etc., to procure food, raiment, and lodging; on the effects of that inadequacy upon the happiness and morals of those females and their families, when they have any; and on the probability that those low wages frequently forced poor women to the choice between dishonor and absolute want of common necessaries." (4) Thus from the early 19th century on, we have a series of studies and investigations of the connections between low wages and vice, culminating in the "Purity Crusade" of the Progressive era. The concern for the working girl shown by the middle class reformers who conducted these studies was double-edged; working women often saw it as condescension, and resented the implication that they were morally weak.(5)

The experience of the women workers in the Lowell mills is an example of the assumed connection between the working woman who sold her labor power and the prostitute who sold herself. The idea that factory girls had loose morals was a commonplace in England,(6) and this concept was also prevalent in the United States. Current work on the Lowell mills emphasizes the "protection" offered by the boarding house system, and implies a concern for the moral welfare of their employees by the owners. However, some contemporary accounts indicate public concern about the behavior of the women in the mills. Newspapers carried accounts by physicians and other prominent citizens of immoral activities:

There used to be in Lowell an association of young men called the "Old Line" who had an understanding with a great many of the factory girls and who used to introduce young men of their acquaintance, visitors to the place, to the girls for immoral purposes. Balls were held at various places attended mostly by these young men and girls, with some others who did not know the object of the association, and after the dancing was over the girls were taken to infamous places of resort in Lowell and the vicinity, and were not returned to their homes until daylight. (7)

While these stories often were not verifiable (and were attacked by the women as lies), they do indicate an identification of the single working woman with the prostitute, and a refusal on the part of some men to distinguish the woman willing to sell her labor power with the woman willing to sell herself.

Other material shows evidence of sexual exploitation by supervisors. An article in the *Voice of Industry* told of a factory girl rumored to have saved $3,000 from her work who purchased a farm for herself and son (a favorite Cinderella theme of the management.) The women's paper declared not only that the worker in question had less than half the sum, but that half of this "it was strongly suspected, was obtained as hush money of a prominent factory man who had been intimate with her and was the father of the boy now living in the country." (8)

Contrary to the view of the mill owners as concerned for the morality of the decent girls they hired, the reality may be that they "consciously fostered the idea that the operatives were 'bad' women. Their advertisements carried special pleas for 'respectable young women.' In fact, so prevalent did this idea become that the girls themselves issued a statement (which included) 'we beseech them not to asperse our characters or stigmatise us as disorderly persons!" (9)

A theme in the study of sexual harassment begins to emerge here. The 19th century ideal of True Womanhood required women to be the guardians of purity; if a sexual episode occurred, it was the woman's fault, and she was "ruined for life." In practical terms, this meant she might be thrown out of her job and house. "Ladies" were not to know even of the existence of sexual passion. To admit that sexual contact, even conversation, occurred, was to be blamed for it. Thus the double bind — while women workers were often at the mercy of male supervisors, the repercussions of admitting incidents happened were often as bad as the original event. This conflict between the "lady" or "good girl" who is above sexuality, and the "bad girl" or "whore" who is involved with it, is a major theme in the history of sexual harassment. (10)

Another dilemma for working women was the conflict between labor force participation and the pressure to stay in the home. The way in which industry was organized required a source of cheap labor; in many cases this was furnished by women workers. But traditional masculine control in the family was threatened by waged women; thus the social pressure for women to stay in the home intensified along with early industrialization. The social pressure to stay home was strongest for middle class women as the ideology of the Home emerged as a companion ideology to True Womanhood in the mid 19th century. The economic pressure to work, on the other hand, was strongest for working-class women, and of this group, for single, divorced, widowed women (ie., those not tied in marriage to an individual man.) Women were conflicted about being in the labor force; however, for working-class women, this conflict was not simply competing "attitudes" about their place, but in many situations a "choice" between starvation if unemployed and attempted rape on the job.

Sexual harassment served to reinforce those attitudes pushing women out of the labor force. Yet this was an untenable goal in an industrializing economy. A fall-back function of sexual harassment, then, was to reinforce women's feelings of powerlessness at work.

Again, if sexual harassment was completely effective at driving women out of the workforce, it would work against the interests of management and capitalists as a whole; for an industrialized economy needs women as a source of cheap labor. According to this line of reasoning, one would expect to find some support by management for measures to reduce sexual harassment by supervisors against working women if it threatens the efficiency of the labor force. The individual benefits accruing to males from sexual harassment (personal power) are thus not identical with, and at times contradict, benefits to the capitalist class (of controlling the workforce). At other times these benefits reinforce each other, as it may be cheaper for companies to allow executives the "free" benefit of harassing their secretaries than to give them a raise.

In the late 19th and early 20th century, the increasing participation of women in the labor force went along with a pattern of segregation into low-paying jobs. If, as previously argued, women's occupational mobility was checked by sexual harassment, one would expect to find many instances of sexual harassment in this period. And indeed we do.

The most common description of the harassment victim at that time was — young, single, immigrant, uneducated, and unskilled.(11) This is of course also the description of the typical woman worker. Thus it suggests only that *most* women were harassed, not any particular type of women.

Furthermore, harassment victims could be found in a wide range of occupations. Not only waitresses and domestic servants, but also elevated railway cashiers, union organizers, garment workers, white-goods workers, home workers, doctors, dressmakers, shopgirls, laundry workers, models, office workers, cotton mill workers, cannery workers, broom factory workers, assistant foremen (sic), stenographers and typists, soap factory workers, hop-pickers, shoeshine girls, barmaids, legal secretaries, actresses, sales demonstrators, art students, and would-be workers at employment interviews.

The severity of abuse ranged from verbal suggestions, threats and insults, to staring, touching, attempted rape and rape. Women were propositioned; promised money, jobs and automobiles (!); and then threatened with loss of jobs and blacklisting.

Harassment certainly crossed ethnic lines. Jewish, Italian, WASP, Southern White and black women were all harassed. Black women, however, often interpreted sexual harassment as racism, not sexism. Two Atlanta women talked about their experience in the 1930s:

Isabel: Some of the girls wanted to work downtown as waitresses, you know, and I asked my daddy if I could — to earn extra money. Daddy said, 'You will never work downtown. Not the way white men think about black women.'

Eva: Yes, a black woman was fair prey, you know.

Isabel: You see, a white man that might not dare accost a white girl is safe in his advances on a black girl. Why? Because in court her papa or brothers or any black man — even a black lawyer — wouldn't dare stand up against one white man.
Eva: The answer to all that was to protect us from it ever happening.

While this is both a middle-class and male-identified solution, the message is clear. As Eva pointed out, "the idea was that if you were a black girl outside your area, and a white man decided to insult you... nothing could be done."(12)

The reactions of women to the workplace hazard of sexual harassment can be divided into individual and group responses. There are several components of this problem. Women may have seen sexual harassment primarily as a social problem, or primarily an individual problem (i.e., one's personal bad luck to have a lecherous boss). Seeing it as a social problem led to group responses (unions, protective associations, settlement house organizations), and was a motivation for organizing. Another possible response was legal action. The joining of the group response with the attempt to achieve legal protection in the drive for protective legislation had as one motivating factor, the protection of women from sexual harassment.

The initial move for protective legislation came before the Civil War. However, these laws were overturned, and a second wave of agitation for protective legislation for women began in the 1870s. Not until the *Muller v. Oregon* decision of 1908, though, was the principle of legislative limitation of women's hours upheld by the Supreme Court.

What were the motivations of those pushing this legislation? The weakness of the woman worker was the main reason often given —

weaker in terms of physical strength, in terms of bargaining power, because of having other drains on their energy (housework), and having more to fear from factory employment.

Threats to morals were prominent among these "dangers" of employment to women. The general opinion was that women workers were subject to harassment of supervisors, and thus should be prohibited from certain occupations, and night work, for their own protection. Smuts, in *Women and Work in America,* writes:

Disrespect for the working girl sometimes led to sexual advances by supervisors or male workers. Girls complained of stolen embraces, pinches and vulgar remarks. It was widely believed that many prostitutes were former working girls, first corrupted by supervisors who had threatened to fire or promised to promote them. (13)

Current studies found it an issue of concern for Jewish garment workers and Italian cannery workers. (14)

Many of the "participant-observer" investigations of working women, as well as early sociological analyses, reached the same conclusion. Maud Nathan writes of salesclerks:

"Floor-walkers in the old days were veritable tsars; they often ruled with a rod of iron. Only the girls who were 'free-and-easy' with them, who consented to lunch or dine with them, who permitted certain liberties, were allowed any freedom of action or felt secure in their positions." (15)

Individual reactions of victims of sexual harassment encompassed a wide range of emotions. Many women felt guilt. S.H., a clerk in a store in Los Angeles wrote of this:

"I don't think there was one evening during that

time when I worked in that store that I went home unmolested. I have walked block after block through the business part of the city with a man at my side questioning me as to where I lived, and if I would not like to go to dinner, how I was going to spend the evening, etc. I never answered, except to threaten to speak to the police. That I was ashamed to do, thinking it must be my own fault in some way, and that I ought to possess dignity enough to make men understand they were mistaken." (16)

American Woolen Company, Boston, 1912.

And some women who had "made it" blamed those who didn't. M.C.P., a government worker in Washington, D.C., who made $1,200 a year in 1908, commented:

"Referring to the moral dangers of city life, of course there are many dangers, but it largely depends on the girl, in my opinion, whether she is led into temptation or not." (17)

Fear was another dominant reaction. Elizabeth Hasanovitch was so afraid of her boss after he attempted to rape her, that she never returned to collect her pay.

"I felt what that glance in his eyes meant. It was quiet in the shop, everybody had left, even the

foreman. There in the office I sat on a chair, the boss stood near me with my pay in his hand, speaking to me in a velvety, soft voice. Alas! Nobody around. I sat trembling with fear."

But looking for a new job was agony for her:

"The thought of a new job made me so uneasy that I could hardly sleep. My bitter experience with my last shop pictured me all the bosses as vulgar and rude as the one from whom I ran away on Saturday."(18)

Rose Cohen was too stunned at thirteen to respond effectively to her boss' proposition:

"After a moment or so he said quite abruptly, 'Come, Ruth, sit down here. He motioned to his knee. I felt my face flush. I backed away towards the door and stood staring at him." (19)

A Russian Jewish shopgirl wrote to the Jewish Daily Foreward in 1907 after she had lost her job because she refused the foreman's "vulgar advances:"

"The girls in the shop were very upset over the foreman's vulgarity but they didn't want him to throw them out, so they are afraid to be witnesses against him. What can be done about this?" (20)

Sometimes their fear was replaced by anger. Elizabeth Hasanovitch expressed her rage:

"If only I could discredit that man so that he would never dare to insult a working girl again! If only I could complain of him in court!" [21]

But more often the major reaction was confusion: guilt, anger, fear, and a feeling that attention paid to one as a sexual being was supposed to be appreciated, all intermingled.

Even organizers were torn in their reactions. When her supervisor talked to her and asked her to be his girl, a young organizer in a garment shop laughed at him. But he persisted:

"He went on 'You know it's a rule not to pay the girls the first week, but I like you, and I'm going to pay you the first week.' When I came home from work I told my sister about it and said, 'I don't know if I should feel flattered or insulted'." (22)

A Cleveland manicurist reported an experience comparable to a 19th century potboiler. Alone in the city and propositioned by a friend of a friend to whom she has applied for a job, she was totally traumatized:

"How I ever got out of the building I do not know. I was so blinded with confusion and shame. I did not take the elevator, but reached the street somehow by the long stairways, with the last words of this man ringing in my ears: 'You will be glad to take up with my offer, after you have searched elsewhere'."

Her subsequent failure to get work led her to plan suicide. On her way to drown herself in the harbor a young man whom she met at a restaurant offered her aid, lent her $5 and

Lynn, Massachusetts, 1895. Photo by Frances B. Johnson

encouraged, she went back to the city and found a job.

"Later I married the young man who gave me a helping hand." (23)

While most reactions were not as melodramatic as this (and marriage as an escape from sexual harassment may be questionable), the problem of sexual harassment was a serious threat to the health and well-being of women workers. Power and domination outweighed the sensual or sexual aspect of these incidents in women's working lives.

Sexual harassment was addressed in *Life and Labor*, the publication of the National Women's Trade Union League. In a 1911 editorial on the clothing trade, a section on "The Tyranny of Foreman" claims that:

Abusive and insulting language is frequently used by those in authority in the shops. This is especially intolerable to the girls, who should have the right to work without surrendering their self-respect. No women should be subjected by fear of loss of her job to unwarranted insults. (24)

Stories of harassed women workers were published in the magazine. While these may be composite stories, they do indicate the range of harassment, the results, and the anger of women at being sexually as well as economically exploited on the job. An example is "Rosie's story", the account of a seventeen year old worker in the needle trades.

"The boss from the shop was always fresh with the girls. He liked to see us blush, so we made a society, called "The Young Ladies Educational Society," and we was not to stand the freshness of the boss. But we was afraid of him, and so we

couldn't help each other. Once he touched me, very fresh like, and I cried, and he said, "Lets be good friends, Rosie, and to show you how good I means it, you take supper mit me in a swell hotel, with music and flowers, see?" And I says, "So! Supper mit you — swell hotel! Well I ask my ma," and he said, "Don't do it. You say you going to sleep at a friend's house" and I was trembling so I couldn't nearly do my work, and when my ma sees me, she says, "What's the matter, Rosie?" and I says, "Nothing," because she's sad, my ma is, 'cause I have to work so hard and can't have no education, and she says, "Rosie, you got to tell your ma what's wrong," and we both cried together, and so the next day I went to another shop, and I told the first lie I ever told in my life. *I told the boss I come from another city. I liked this new boss; he was not so fresh and I had a seat by a window, and my ma and me, we was so happy we laughed when I told her about the nice shop and fresh air, and then the next day the boss he come to me and he says, "I'm sorry, Rosie, we like your work, but your other boss he telephoned he no discharged you and so we can't keep you here."* (25)

As did Rosie, many women reacted on an individual level. But Rosie and her friends also saw that this problem wasn't something they were asking for, and did try to meet it on a group level; they formed a "Young Ladies Educational Society" with the purpose of resisting the boss' harassment. The fact that their boss was a habitual harasser, and recognized as such by the group, was not that uncommon a situation. Dorothy Richardson in *The Long Day* (her account of how women workers were exploited at the turn of the century) wrote that after her boss approached her ("...in a moment he had grasped my bare arm and given it a rude pinch"), "...the rest of my companions repeated divers terrible tales of moral ruin and betrayal,... wherein the boss was inevitably the villain." (26) S.R., a saleswoman, suffered repeated harassment and propositioning on a new job before she discovered that she was not the only one:

"I never heard the other girls complain, so supposed for some time that they were not bothered; but when I knew them better I found they had the same trouble..." (27)

There were other instances of groups being formed. In some cases these were more successful than the attempt of Rosie and her friends. Alice Woodbridge, the "moving force and guiding spirit of the Working Women's Society" (the forerunner of the WTUL), was politicized as the result of such experiences,

"She had held at various times positions in offices; these positions had promised to be lucrative, but because of insulting proposals from employers she had been obliged to give them up; she had been buffeted about for many a year, trying to earn an honest living and trying to live on the low wages offered her."

Protection of working women from unwanted sexual advances was a major aim of the Society.

"...it was her purpose to endeavor to shield other working girls from the hideous experiences which had been hers, in her efforts to lead an honest, upright, independent life." (28)

But what could be done to stop sexual harassment? The sisterly support of Rosie's group ("we was not to stand the freshness of the boss") had its obvious limits. The women were afraid of the power of the boss, and with good reason; even more than today, he had the power to fire them at will. As in Rosie's case, he could force them into a position where they felt if they didn't quit they'd be raped. Alice Woodbridge was forced to leave many jobs. When Dorothy Richardson's boss returned and "after looking me over thoughtfully, informed me that I was supposed to be promoted Monday morning to the wrappers' counter," she feared for her own safety and quit. Elizabeth Hasanovitch was so afraid of her former boss after his attempted rape that she never returned to collect her week's wages, although she was at that point almost penniless.(29) But groups to combat harassment were not common, which suggests that women had little faith in their power to change their own lives.

In the short run, less politicized women looked for ways to protect their individual personal safety. This is not to say that they denied the group aspects of the problem, for they often tried to share such knowledge. Their coping strategies included warning other women about "fresh" bosses and supervisors, quitting, finding new jobs, sharing verbal ways to reject passes, staying out of empty offices, and giving in to keep a job. In her first job in a garment shop at the age of twelve, Rose Cohen often felt uncomfortable because the men told dirty jokes.

"I could never keep my face from turning red. One day when Atta (the only other woman worker) and I were alone at our table she said: 'It is too bad that you have a tell-tale face. You better learn to hide your feelings. What you hear in this shop is nothing compared with what you will hear in other shops. Look at me."

Atta was an expert at dodging the boss and threatening him with her needle when he tried to grab her. The first English sentence Rosa learned from her was:

"Keep your hands off please." (30)

A social worker posing as a cannery worker to investigate working conditions for the New York State Factory Investigating Commission (1912), was warned by sister workers to stay away from the men:

"... an Italian girl told me that one must be careful not to get fresh with the Italian boys, because they were dangerous.

She herself was offered an opportunity to make

"two or three dollars on the side any time, if you come up here to work at night, we can go for a stroll. That was the timekeeper and his name was Gillette."

The other workers corroborated her experiences.

"A great many girls told me he was fresh, and he was boss, and it was best to keep away from him." (31)

Occasionally women took harassers to court. In 1908, Grace Abbott and Sophonisba Breckinridge took a saloon-keeper to court in behalf of Bozena, a young Bohemian Immigrant. Her employer had "abused her shamefully and then turned her out when he found that she was to become the mother of his illegitimate child." They lost the case, "because the charge was a penitentiary offense, and the judge was lenient." Not surprisingly, the judge empathized with the defendant rather than the victim.

Grace Abbott had such cases in mind when she started immigrant protection associations in Chicago. Protecting immigrant girls from lecherous bosses was, again, a major theme in organizing. (32) In this case it was because of the middle-class social workers' intervention that Bozena's case was taken to court at all; most women, feeling less able to cope with the male-dominated legal system, would hesitate to bring their case to court. And even the feminist solidarity of the Hull House activists with Bozena did not win her case.

Working women themselves wanted to resist. Elizabeth Hasanovitch's fear was replaced by anger:

"If I could only discredit that man so that he would never dare to insult a working-girl again! If only I could complain of him in court! But I had no witnesses to testify the truth: with my broken English I could give very little explanation. Besides that, if I were working in a shop and were called to court, the firm might suspect some evil in me and send me away." (33)

Her confrontation with this dilemma led her to the conclusion that working women must organize; this seems to have been one of her personal motivations for joining the Waist and Dressmakers Union. As an individual member of a union in a basically non-unionized industry, a woman might not immediately improve her own conditions. Elizabeth Hasanovitch's new foreman, who had previously treated her in a friendly if condescending manner and called her "little daughter" (though she adds he's "too young to be my father") began to criticize her work and harass her until she got terrible headaches and ultimately quit. Unions, then, did not always protect women workers. But the issue of women in unions is complex, and needs to be looked at specifically.

III

UNIONS AND SEXUAL HARASSMENT FROM CO-WORKERS

Looking at unions' role in combatting sexual harassment will also focus our attention on the relation of co-workers to sexual harassment.

Sexual harassment was not simply a boss-employee interaction, but in many cases an interaction between co-workers. Here, of course, the dynamic was somewhat different, as co-workers do not have the power to fire a woman or offer promotions. However, sexual harassment by co-workers can make a job unbearable for a woman; if she publicly complained, she was as likely to be blamed as the harasser, for "leading him on." To the extent a woman internalized the socially conditioned guilt of being responsible for controlling sexuality (while males were allowed to initiate it), she was vulnerable to this kind of manipulation. And real consequences ensue; Brodsky's study of workers victimized at work showed that employers tended to lay them off:

"Employers are not disturbed by the fact that their female employees have been spoiled or contaminated, but they are concerned that this employee might make for further "trouble." Employers want peace. They do not want workers who disturb the tranquility of the organization in any way, not even as a result of bad luck. Employers whose workers are raped would like to have the victim disappear and not disturb the smooth functioning of their organization." (34)

Because of this tendency to "blame the victim," co-workers do have power over women's jobs and economic security. This division in the workforce, like any division, can also benefit employers.

Unions' position on women workers have been contradictory. On the one hand, unions have tried to keep women out of their occupations, or struck to avoid working with women. On the other hand, some male union organizers have been aware of the danger to workers' solidarity in ignoring women as potentially organizable workers, and have attempted to organize them. Gompers and the AFL held officially (at times) to this second position, but in practice did the opposite — ignored women workers, denied women's locals charters, or sought to exclude women from men's locals by complex rules. (35)

Union members harassed women potential members in various ways which preyed upon their anxieties and kept them home. One example was union meetings. Mary Anderson, later head of the U.S. Women's Bureau, wrote of early union meetings:

"The men met in halls that were often in back of a saloon, or in questionable districts, dirty and not well kept. I remember the so-called labor temples that were anything but temples. The girls would not go to meetings in these places and we could not ask them to go under the circumstances. Then, when it came to paying dues at the headquarters of the union, the girls found it very distasteful to go where there were large groups of men playing cards and hanging about. . . " (36)

This is a good instance of the implied threat of violence operating as a social control mechanism. It also shows the connection of workplace-union-street violence in women's actual experience.

Women organizers "realistically" evaluated the ways in which they themselves were treated by their co-workers (ie., male union officials). After a dispute with the male leadership of the ILG in Cleveland, over the issue of equal pay for women organizers, Pauline Newman described the women that John Dyche (the unions' executive secretary) selected to replace her: "Well they are not too bad looking and one is rather liberal with her body. That is more than enough for Dyche." (37)

She, like other women organizers, also tried to

solve problems of sexual harassment outside the union grievance structure. Faced with a complaint that a factory owner's son and his superintendent had taken liberties with female employees, she argued:

"There is not a factory today where the same immoral conditions [do] not exist. . . this to my mind can be done away with by educating the girls instead of attacking the company." (38)

Rose Schneiderman, however, tried to use the unions to fight sexual harassment. Having organized the Aptheker shop she received a complaint from the chairwoman.

She said that Mr. Aptheker had a habit of pinching the girls whenever he passed them and they wanted it stopped. I went to see him, and in the presence of the chairwoman told him that this business of pinching the girls in the rear was not nice, that the girls resented it, and would he please stop it. He was a rather earthy man and looking at me in great amazement, he said, "Why Miss Schneiderman, these girls are like my children.' The chairwoman without a blink answered, 'Mre. Aptheker we'd rather be orphans.' Of course it was stopped." (39)

Mary Anderson also wrote of a strike in a broom factory in which sexual harassment of the workers by the foreman was a major issue. Since the foreman was one who "did not stop at anything," some of the women carried knives to protect themselves. She went to talk with the employer:

"I told him that I had heard stories about one of his foremen, not only of his brutality in dealing with the women, but also that he was immoral and that immoral conditions existed in the plant because of him. The employer said he knew this

was so... finally the strike was settled, the foreman was fired, and the wages raised a little." (40)

Unions, then, have at times provided protection from sexual harassment for women. However, they have also been simply additional places where women experienced sexual harassment. This is one reason why women turned from strategies of group action to protective legislation to protect their interests at work.

CLASS DIFFERENCES AND WOMEN'S CULTURE

What type of women are harassed? The simplest answer is all types of women. No sociodemographic characteristic saved a woman in a sexist society from the possibility of sexual harassment, and the implicit threat of violence. However, there is evidence that the specific forms of sexual harassment did vary according to occupation and social class. All women were subject to at least the subtler forms of sexual harassment (verbal suggestive remarks, dress codes) but physical violence was more common and expected by women in menial jobs.

An examination of the kind of sexual harassment faced by early women doctors shows a pattern of harassment used to force women out of privileged, male-defined jobs. Women's role as professionals in the healing professions had been systematically eliminated by the mid 19th century.

The first women to attempt to become licensed physicians in the United States faced much harassment — psychological, verbal and physical. Most of it came from male co-students (with the tacit approval of their supervisors?), an example of the power co-workers have over a woman's job. Alice Hamilton, an early pioneer in industrial health, suffered from similar treatment as a sex object. (41)

Emily Barringer, the first woman doctor to with an appointment to the staff of Gouvernor Hospital, the downtown branch of Bellevue (N.Y.) found her appointment was resented and opposed by the male appointees:

"But it came to me as a sickening realization that the real opposition I was to meet was to come from my own peers, educated brothers with medical degrees."

An intense campaign of psychological and verbal harassment ensued. For example, other male co-workers discussed graphic details of rape cases at the dinner table, with obvious enjoyment at her discomfort. What she wrote of this experience is revealing of the differences between the experiences of a middle-class professional and an immigrant worker in withstanding sexual harassment. She didn't expect physical violence, a reality to immigrant workers; yet her life was constrained and controlled by this harassment:

"Yes, I could and would endure any taunts or gibes or outrageous insults that these ingenious young men could think of. No matter how degrading their onslaught was, I would stand for it. But if ever in their machinations they should as much as lay a finger on me physically, there would be an immediate reckoning. They knew this perfectly well and always kept completely within bounds. I was as safe in their midst as if I had been surrounded by the strongest iron cage."

Despite this 'confidence,' she kept her door locked nights, and wouldn't open it to any "fellow" male students. (42)

The weight of the evidence indicates that women in working-class jobs, on the bottom of the workplace hierarchy, and also on the bottom of the social hierarchy, were the most likely victims of harassment. While this is plausible, the way the evidence is recorded also biases the sample. Much of the recorded instances of harassment are reported by middle-class observers, who would, because of the consequences and implications, be less likely to report their own similar experiences. During this period, middle-class women were ladies who were considered "above" sexuality, and thus would be "tainted" by being involved in incidents of sexual harassment. To the extent that they accepted the idea that women were responsible for controlling sexuality, they would have trouble recognizing and dealing with such incidents in their own lives.

The language used by many women in reporting such incidents in the late 19th century and early 20th century indicates the inability of Victorian society to deal directly with sexuality. Women reported their boss' and co-workers' conduct as "vulgar remarks," "shameful behavior," "unspeakable suggestions," "things no lady should bear." When Grace Abbott and Sophonisba Breckinridge accompanied Bozena to court, they transgressed these bounds of ladylike behavior:

"...a young lawyer on the State's Attorney's

staff who had known Miss Breckinridge at the University rushed over to her and said, 'Oh, Miss Breckinridge, you and Miss Abbott must not stay here. This just isn't a fit place for women like you. It's a terrible case for you to hear." (43)

This inability of women to speak directly of their experiences had several implications. It led to sexual harassment being greatly under-reported along with other instances of sexual violence, as rape. Women felt guilt rather than anger after such incidents; and fear, not without reason, that the stigma resulting from public association with sexual issues would outweigh any "justice" they might get by reporting the incident. If they had been friendly to the male involved, they would be accused of complicity; when a more likely explanation of what was going on was that the women were looking for husbands, and were responded to as prostitutes. This leaves us with the problem of interpreting vague accounts of behavior, and occasionally makes it hard to determine whether a specific incident really is "unspeakable behavior" or an off-hand vulgar remark.

The other issue this raises is whether women were over-reacting to typical male language. If women and men in the 19th century were raised in separate spheres — in homosocial networks — with different customs, ways of interaction, speech patterns, and expectations, then such a response on the part of women to men's "normal" behavior seems plausible. For immigrant women to respond to the more open social mores of the United States in the same horrified manner is also plausible. This explanation implies that much of what is considered "harassment" behavior by women is simply "teasing" or "humor" or "informality" on the part of men. (44) While this may occasionally be true, this explanation fails to account for the majority of cases; doesn't account for the overtones of terror, force, domination and violence felt by the women in such situations; and doesn't account for the many cases in which severe reprisals (firing, blacklisting, refused promotions, attempted rape, rape) were perpetrated on women who refused to accept such "teasing" as part of the job. It is also clear that sexual harassment is basically a man-against-woman interaction; there are few reported cases of either men-against-men or women-against-men harassment. Although men "tease" other men in the workplace, and use non-sexual types of harassment against each other, neither historically nor currently is there evidence that sex is a common component of this harassment.(45)

The major function of sexual harassment is to preserve the dominance of patriarchy. The use of sexual harassment to push women out of specific jobs may well be a new version of an old phenomenon. Even for older societies which accepted a "men's sphere" and a "women's sphere" as both equally necessary to the survival of the community, there is evidence that women were sexually harassed to keep them from stepping out of line in other ways.

Sexual harassment is a phenomenon that crosses class lines, though it does have a class dimension. It cannot be reduced to bosses exploiting workers, because the problem of harassment by co-workers is so extensive. In addition, harassment by supervisors and co-workers does not necessarily support the needs of a rationalized, profit-oriented production system, and may even work at cross-purposes to it. Furthermore, for many men, sexuality and domination were not entirely separate; thus social control and sexuality are not totally distinct phenomena. And for many women, being defined as sexual beings meant that sexual harassment posed both a "compliment" and a threat to their autonomy and safety.

This suggests that to understand the problems of sexual harassment we must analyze both the organization of capitalism and the organization of male dominance.

I would like to thank Roslyn Feldberg, Susan Forbes, Alexander Keyssar and the members of the Alliance Against Sexual Coercion for their helpful criticism and discussion of the ideas presented in this paper; and Elizabeth Pleck and Judith Smith for supplying references and supporting my interest in this topic.

MARY BULARZIK writes and teaches women's history in Boston. She works with the Alliance Against Sexual Coercion.

NOTES

1. "The Girl Who Comes to the City, A Symposium," *Harper's Bazar*, March 1908, p. 277.
2. Sources for this topic are scattered yet cumulatively persuasive. They include autobiographies, letters, social worker's reports, state investigating commissions, labor newspapers, women's magazines, oral histories, surveys of women's work, studies of women in history, studies of women in ethnic communities. Future sources include union records, personnel records, workmen's compensation claims and legal records. All require vast amounts of reading for small bits of evidence.

I also looked at works on protective legislation and prostitution to make connections between sexual morality, economics, and violence in society. I investigated incidents as case studies in the dynamic of sexual harassment, in order to develop a theory of sexual harassment as a mechanism of social control, which theory can be tested by further historical research.
3. Phillip Foner, *History of the Labor Movement in The United States* (New York: International Publishers, 1975), V. 1, 26.
4. Frank Carlton, "Crusade To Improve Working Conditions," *Life & Labor*, Vol. 4 No. 4, 108-9.
5. Leonora O'Reilly resigned from the WTUL in 1905-7 over such a dispute. See Lieberman, "Their Sisters' Keepers: The Women's Hours and Wages Movement in the U.S., 1890-1925," Ph.D. diss., Columbia, 1971, pp. 87-88. Also see Rosen, ed; *The Maimie Papers* (New York: The Feminist Press, 1977), Introduction.
6. Neff, *Victorian Working Women* (New York: Columbia University, 1929), pp. 54-5.
7. Boston *Daily Times*, Jan. 16, 1839. There were other articles in the *Times*, the Boston *Quarterly Review*, and The Lowell *Courier* similar to this. Norman Ware, *The Industrial Worker* (Chicago: Quadrangle Books, 1964), p. 81.
8. "Vox Populi," *Voice of Industry*, Sept. 11, 1845. Norman Ware, *The Industrial Worker*.
9. Theresa Wolfson, *Women Workers & Trade Unions*, p. 103.

10. For discussion of the "Nice Girl" construct and social control, see Greer Litton Fox, "Nice Girl: Social Control of Women Through a Value Construct," *Signs* V. 2 No. 4, pp. 805-817, especially pp. 805 & 809.
11. See, for example, Rose Cohen, *Out of the Shadow* (New York: George Dovan, 1918), Elizabeth Hasanovitch, *One of Them* (Boston: Houghton Mifflin, 1918), Helen Campbell, *Prisoners of Poverty* (Boston: Little, Brown, 1900), Mrs. John & Marie Von Vorst, *The Woman Who Toils* (New York: Doubleday, Page & Co., 1904).
12. Jeanne Westin, *Making Do* (Chicago: Follett Publishing Company, 1976), p. 96.
13. Robert Smuts, *Women and Work in America* (New York: Schocken Books, 1971), p. 88.
14. Virginia Yans-McLaughlin, *Family and Community* (Ithaca: Cornell University, 1977), p. 199 and Alice Kessler-Harris, "Organizing the Unorganizable", *Labor History* V. 17 No. 1: 5-23.
15. Maud Nathan, *The Story Of An Epoch-Making Movement* (New York: Doubleday, 1926), . 7.
16. *Harper's Bazar,* July 1908, p. 693. Also see *One of Them,* pp. 108-110, and *Out Of The Shadow, pp.* 127-9.
17. *Harper's Bazaar,* November 1908, p. 1141.
18. *One of Them,* pp. 108-10-11.
19. *Out Of The Shadow,* pp. 127-9.
20. Isaac Metzger, ed. *A Bintel Brief, Sixty Years of Letters from the Lower East Side to the Jewish Daily Forward* (New York: Doubleday, 1971), p. 72.
21. *One of Them,* p. 110.
22. Andria Hourwich, ed., *I Am A Woman Worker* (New York: Affiliated Schools For Workers, 1930s(?)), p. 86.
23. *Ibid,* December 1908, pp. 1230.
24. *Life and Labor,* Vol. 1 No. 1, January 1911, p. 14.
25. *Ibid.,* Vol. 4 No. 8, August 1914, p. 242.
26. Dorothy Richardson, *The Long Day,* p. 260.
27. *Harper's Bazaar,* July 1908, p. 693.
28. Maud Nathan, *Epoch-Making Movement,* pp. 15-16.
29. Dorothy Richardson, *The Long Day,* p. 263; Elizabeth Hasanovitch, *One of Them,* p. 110.

30. Rose Cohen, *Out Of The Shadow*, p. 851.
31. *New York State Factory Investigating Comm.*, 2nd Report, Vol. 3, 1913, ·Testimony of Mary Chamberlain, pp. 1016, 1004.
32. Edith Abbott, *Unpublished Biography of Grace Abbott*, Chapter Two, "Lost Immigrant Girls", The Abbott Papers, University of Chicago, Box 1, Folder 16, Addenda 2.
33. Elizabeth Hasanovitch, *One Of Them*, p. 110.
34. Carroll Brodsky, "Rape At Work," in Walker, *Sexual Assault*, (Lexington: DC Heath & Co., 1976), p. 48.
35. Lieberman, p. 84. Also, for example, See Gompers, S., "Don't Sacrifice Womanhood," *American Federationist* 4:186-187 October 1897 and "Female Labor Arouses Hostility And Apprehension in Union Ranks," *Current Opinion*, 64: 292-4, April 1910.
36. Mary Anderson, *Woman At Work* (Minneapolis: U. of Minn., 1951) p. 66. Also see, *Life & Labor* V. 3 No. 4, p. 103 and Theresa Wolfson, *Woman Worker and Trade Unions*, p. 55.
37. P.N. to R.S. Nov. 14, 1911. R.S., A 94 quoted in Harris, *Labor History* article.
38. P.N. to R.S., July 11, 1912, R.S. A 94.
39. Rose Schneiderman, *All For One* (New York: Paul S. Erikson, 1967), p. 86.
40. Mary Anderson, *Woman At Work*, p. 56, incident about 1915.
41. Alice Hamilton, *Exploring The Dangerous Trades*.
42. Emily Dunning Barringer, M.D., *Bowery To Bellevue* (New York: Norton, 1950), p. 184.
43. "Lost Immigrant Girls", *Abbott Papers*, pp. 2-3.
44. On homosocial networks and sisterhood, see Carroll Smith-Rosenberg, "The Female World of Love and Ritual," and Nancy Cott, *The Bonds of Womanhood*. For differing perceptions of harasser and victim, see Carroll Brodsky, *The Harassed Worker*.
45. On current conditions, Brodsky, *The Harassed Worker*, and interview with members of the Alliance Against Sexual Coercion, a Boston group working on this issue. Prison may be a significant exception to this as a situation in which men are frequently subjected to sexual harassment. See, for example, the interviews with prisoners in the film *Rape Culture* (Cambridge Documentary Films).

Social Change and Women's Work and Family Experience in Ireland and the United States

EDWARD L. KAIN & NIALL BOLGER

THIS PAPER EXAMINES the changing nature of the female labor force in Ireland and the United States. Data from the two countries are used to illustrate both similarities and variations in the Western experience of women during the period of rapid change in work and family life since the late nineteenth century.

A central facet of how Western families have been transformed during the past century has involved the increased participation of women in the paid labor force, and in the most recent decades, a dramatic rise in the labor force participation of married women. In his classic work, *World Revolution and Family Patterns*, Goode suggests that the increase in female participation in the non-agricultural labor force was clearly evident in Western countries but was not dramatic during the first half of this century (1963: 59–60). Since 1950, however, increases in the economic activity of women have occurred throughout the West. For example, using data from Scandinavian countries, Haavio-Mannila and Kari (1980) document the increased economic activity of women

Edward L. Kain is an assistant professor in the Department of Human Development and Family Studies, Cornell University, Ithaca, NY 14853-4401. Niall Bolger is a Ph.D. candidate at the same university.

An earlier version of this paper was presented at the International section of the 1984 annual meetings of the National Council on Family Relations, San Francisco, October, 1984.

Social Science History 10:2 (Summer 1986).

Table 1 Demographic data on selected Western countries

Country	Year	Marriage* rate	Divorce rate	Crude birth rate	Fertility rate
Australia	1980	7.3	2.6	15.3	62.5
Belgium	1980	6.7	1.5	12.7	51.9
Canada	1979	7.9	2.5	15.5	58.6
Denmark	1980	5.2	2.6	11.2	49.0
Finland	1980	6.2	2.0	13.1	52.8
France	1980	6.2	1.6	14.8	59.6
West Germany	1980	5.9	0.5	10.0	38.8
Ireland	1979	6.2	not allowed	21.5	99.2
Italy	1980	5.7	0.2	11.2	55.1
Norway	1980	5.5	1.6	12.5	56.4
Sweden	1980	4.5	2.4	11.7	51.1
Switzerland	1980	5.6	1.6	11.6	45.1
England & Wales	1980	7.4	3.0	13.3	56.3
United States	1980	9.7	5.2	15.8	61.1

Source: United Nations, 1982.
*Marriage, Divorce, and Crude Birth Rates are per 1,000 mid-year population. Fertility Rate is births per 1,000 females age 15–49.

throughout this century, the transformation of the economies of Scandinavia from an agricultural to an industrial base, and the rapid increase in labor force participation of married women since 1950.

Work rates of women in the United States have been increasing since the nineteenth century, with the most rapid change occurring since the second World War. While the nature of the growth and change of the female labor force in this country has been well documented (Oppenheimer, 1970; Masnick and Bane, 1980), very little work has attempted to place this experience within the broader context of changes in the work and family lives of women in other Western countries. Until the experiences of women in different countries are compared, it is impossible to determine which aspects of the American experience are unique and which reflect more general relationships between industrialization and urbanization and the ways in which women organize their roles in terms of work and the family.

Ireland provides an excellent comparison to the United States in examining broad changes in women's labor force participation in the West. Although both Ireland and the United States are

Table 2 Data on communication and industrialization in selected Western countries

Country	Telephones per 100 inhabitants (most recent available year)	Per capita national income in U.S. dollars (most recent available year)	Per capita energy consumption in Kilograms of coal (most recent available year)
Australia	44.0	6,540	6,032
Belgium	33.2	9,025	6,037
Canada	64.8	7,572	10,241
Denmark	56.9	9,869	5,224
Finland	44.7	6,090	5,135
France	37.2	7,908	4,351
West Germany	40.4	9,278	7,408
Ireland	17.2	2,711	2,955
Italy	30.1	3,076	3,318
Norway	40.2	7,949	6,437
Sweden	74.4	9,274	5,269
Switzerland	67.7	12,408	3,708
United Kingdom	41.5	4,955	4,942
United States	77.0	8,612	10,410

Source: United Nations, 1981.

Western, industrialization and urbanization began much earlier in the United States. Indeed in many ways Ireland and the United States present the widest contrast possible within the West on both family and economic variables. Demographers have long noted that Ireland has consistently had one of the highest ages at marriage in the world, while the age at marriage in the United States is much lower. Ireland and the United States also stand at near opposite poles in terms of percentage of the population remaining never-married. Among Western countries, the United States has the highest marriage and divorce rates, while in Ireland marriage rates are much lower, and divorce is not allowed by law. Ireland also has the highest crude birth rate and highest fertility rate in the West (see Table 1). In the economic realm, indicators such as number of telephones, per capita national income, and energy consumption also find Ireland and the United States at opposite ends of the spectrum (see Table 2).

Given this contrast between the two countries, the paper is organized around three issues. First, we address the importance of the social and historical contexts in shaping family life in the two countries. The general relationships between industrialization and family change are outlined, and the different experience of industrialization and urbanization in the two countries is reviewed. In addition, differences in the culture and history of the two nations are briefly discussed.

With this background in place, the paper turns to an examination of national data on changes in the female labor force of both countries. In particular, increases in the size of the female labor force, shifts in its marital status distribution, and changes in the occupational structure are explored. These changes are linked to processes of industrialization and urbanization.

The concluding section of the paper begins to develop theoretical propositions concerning linkages between the worlds of work and family, and suggests ways in which these propositions might be used to predict future trends in married women's work force participation in both Ireland and the United States.

Before examining the historical patterning of women's labor force participation in the two countries, it is important to lay out clearly a general model linking the social and historical context to families and to note the differences between the culture and history of Ireland and the United States.

IMPORTANCE OF SOCIAL AND HISTORICAL CONTEXTS IN SHAPING FAMILY LIFE

At the most basic level, the general model which guides our analysis specifies the technological base of a society as the major force which shapes work and family life, including the participation of women in the labor force. We are interested, in particular, in the transition from an agricultural to an industrial base. The work of William F. Ogburn (1928, 1935, 1955) laid the foundation for such a macro-analytic model which was later expanded to include more careful examination of the importance of other variables in addition to technology. In particular, population, organization, environment, and technology have come to be called the "ecological complex" of variables (Duncan, 1959; Hawley, 1950; Lenski and Lenski, 1982). As Berry and Kasarda (1977) note in their book on urban ecology, these four broad variables are reciprocally causal, and depending upon the research question, any of the four may serve as a dependent variable. Our focus in this paper is particularly upon one aspect of economic and family organization—females in the labor force, and how it has changed during the transition from one technological base to another. Thus, in comparing Ireland and the United States with respect to technological change and family organization, the other factors in the ecological complex, i.e., environmental and population characteristics, need to be considered. These we will discuss presently.

In addition to the ecological complex of variables, any model of family change must take into consideration cultural differences, as embodied in values, attitudes, and social institutions. Goode (1963) convincingly argues that values play a part, independent of technology, in shaping family life. As a result, we also discuss in this section the cultural differences between Ireland and the United States as we examine the patterning of women's work.

Finally, any model of social change must include an understanding of the unique historical background of different countries. We conclude this section by briefly addressing the unique historical circumstances of Ireland and the United States.

Environment and population

A comparison of Ireland and the United States in terms of environment and population reveals profound differences. Ireland is less than one hundredth of the size of the United States, being an island roughly two hundred and twenty miles long by one hundred and ten miles wide. Its population of 3.5 million is barely 1.5% that of the United States. The population density is one quarter that of the United States.

Unlike the United States, Ireland has few mineral and hydrocarbon resources. No major deposits of iron, coal, or oil have been found (although there is growing optimism with regard to the last of these in recent years). This lack of natural resources is important in understanding the low level of industrialization in Ireland compared with the United States. There was less basis for an Industrial Revolution in the nineteenth century in Ireland than in other countries, notably Great Britain (Cullen, 1972).

Table 3 Percentage distribution of the Irish and U.S. labor forces by sector of economic activity

	United States			Ireland			
	Agriculture	Industry	Services	Agriculture	Industry	Services	
				51.3	29.3	19.4	1841
1850	45.6	23.8	30.6				
1860	41.2	24.7	34.1				
1870	46.5	21.6	31.9				
1880	43.2	21.7	35.1				
1890	37.5	24.3	38.2	44.4	20.4	35.2	1891
1900	37.5	35.8	26.7				
1910	30.9	38.2	30.9				
1920	27.0	40.2	32.8				
1930	21.2	39.6	39.2	53.4	13.0	33.6	1926
1940	17.4	39.8	42.8	48.4	14.9	36.7	1936
1950	11.8	41.1	47.1	40.5	19.1	40.4	1951
1960	6.3	39.7	54.0	35.7	23.7	40.6	1961
1970	3.1	36.3	60.6	26.3	28.4	45.3	1971
1980	2.8	31.7	65.6	15.8	29.5	54.7	1981

Irish data for 1841, 1891 are from Daly (1981). Irish data for 1926–1981 are derived from the *Census of Population of Ireland 1926, 1936, 1951, 1961, 1971, 1981*; the 1981 figure is based on a 5% sample of the census.
U.S. data for 1850–1890 are calculated from pp. civ-cviii of the *Report on Population of the United States at the Eleventh Census: 1890, Part II.* Washington, D.C.: Government Printing Office, 1897. Data for 1900–1970 are calculated from series D 182-232, p. 139 of *The Historical Statistics of the United States*, United States Bureau of the Census, 1975.
U.S. data for 1980 are calculated from Table No. 693, p. 417 of *The Statistical Abstract of the U.S., 1984.*

The size and population of the United States together with its many natural resources, make its economy a relatively "closed" one in comparison with Ireland's. That is, many goods and services which are domestically produced in the United States must be imported in Ireland. Furthermore, an analysis of the sectoral composition of both economies illustrates the large differences in industrialization alluded to above. Table 3 shows the percentage of the labor force engaged in agriculture, industry, and services in both countries. It can readily be seen that, proportionately speaking, Ireland has five times as many people in agriculture, the U.S. one-fifth more in service occupations.

Culture, values and institutions

In contrast to the cultural diversity of the United States, Ireland shows relative homogeneity. Over 95% of the Irish are Catholic, the remainder mainly Protestant. Consequently a traditional Catholic ethos has been evident in the attitudes, values, and institutions in Ireland (Chubb, 1982; Whyte, 1980). Moreover, there is some evidence that these have influenced the participation of married females in the labor force. For example, the Constitution of Ireland contains a special section devoted to the family in which it guarantees that mothers will be protected from economic pressures to work. In addition, other Irish institutions have served to discourage the employment of married females. Up to 1972, women employed in public service in Ireland were required to retire upon marrying (McCarthy, 1978).

Historic Events

Historical events also influence the participation of women in a country's work force. We will illustrate the influence of the Great Famine upon population decline and women's changing work.

The Great Famine is a major landmark in Irish history. Prior to its occurrence the population stood at over six million. By the time of the partition of the country and foundation of the state in 1922, the population had declined to less than two million. This was due to the large-scale emigration and industrial decline which followed the event. High levels of emigration continued until the 1960s when a change in domestic economic policy, coupled with a favorable world economic climate, resulted in a high rate of industrialization and economic growth.

The Famine was devastating for the work role of women in Ireland because of the large-scale change from tillage to livestock which occurred in its wake (Lyons, 1973). Under the tillage system wives took an equal share with their husbands in farm work. After the Famine, women's work became more restricted when livestock replaced crops as Ireland's principal export.

Although the general model used in our analysis is at the macro-analytic level, we do not mean to imply that the processes involved in historical change in women's labor force participation in Ireland and the United States can be fully understood by examining macro variables alone. The individual and family decisions made about female employment take place at the micro level.

One example of the linkage between macro and micro levels is provided by the Famine in Ireland. At the macro level, the Famine caused a series of major economic and social changes which are discussed below. These resulted in transformations at the micro level. There were shifts in both the resources and options available to families, as well as in their personal economic situation. This type of micro-analytic model has been applied effectively in examinations of the effect of the Great Depression in the United States (e.g., Elder, 1974) and is more fully developed elsewhere (Moen, Kain, and Elder, 1983). In this paper, however, we concentrate upon the macro-level in order to lay a broad foundation for comparative purposes.

We thus see that Ireland and the United States differ in their environmental and population characteristics, as well as in cultural and historical contexts. Having noted these differences, we now turn to the patterning of women's participation in the labor force in the two countries.

CHANGING PATTERNS OF WOMEN'S WORK

Three variables are important to consider in discussing sociohistorical change and women's work: the overall level of labor force participation, the distribution of the female labor force by marital status, and changes in the occupational structure. Historical change in these three variables will be examined for both the United States and Ireland (Data are not always available for comparable years, and the Irish census materials prior to 1926 are less complete). On this basis, differences and similarities in the patterning of the variables over time will then be linked to differential urbanization and industrialization in the two countries.

Level of participation

In the United States both female participation rate and the percentage of females as a proportion of the total labor force have increased consistently since 1890. Historical events such as the Great Depression and the two World Wars have affected the rate of increase, but the general directional trend has not been altered. The most significant increases have occurred since World War II (see Table 4).

Table 4 Female labor force participation rate and women as percentage of total labor force, United States and Ireland

Year	Female labor force as % of female population		Females as % of total labor force		Year
	U.S.	Ireland	U.S.	Ireland	
1890	18.9		17.0		
		—		—	—
1900	20.6		18.1		
		—		—	—
1910	25.4*		NA		
		—		—	—
1920	23.7		20.4		
		23.5		26.3	1926
1930	24.8		21.9		
		24.3		26.2	1936
1940	25.8		24.6		
		22.9		25.8	1946
1950	29.0		27.8		
		22.3		25.5	1951
1960	34.5		32.1		
		20.4		25.9	1961
1970	41.6		37.2		
		27.3		25.7	1971
1980	51.1		41.9		
		29.7		28.3	1981

*The data for this year are not comparable with earlier or later censuses because of a difference in the basis of enumeration. In the printed instructions for the enumerators in 1910 there was a note on the importance of reporting "the occupation, if any, followed by a child of any age or by a woman." This was not emphasized in any other census years, and it is felt that enumerators may have included many women as gainful workers who would not have been included in other censuses—particularly in the case of agricultural workers.

U.S. data for the decades through 1970 are adapted from Series D 49-62 and Series D 29-41, pp. 132–133 in *The Statistical History of the United States From Colonial Times to the Present*. New York: Basic Books, 1976. Data for 1980 are from the *Statistical Abstract of the United States 1982–83*. United States Department of Commerce, Bureau of the Census, 1982.

Irish data are from the *Census of Population of Ireland, 1926, 1936, 1946, 1951, 1961, 1971, 1981*. Dublin, Ireland: The Stationery Office. 1981 figures are based on a random 5% sample of the total census.

Relevant census data for Ireland are not available until 1926. Evidence on the pre-Famine era, however, suggests that many women were outworkers in domestic industries such as weaving and spinning. In fact, available data suggest that at that time women accounted for more than one-half of the total non-agricultural labor force (Lee, 1978). Similarly, in terms of agricultural labor, the role of women was extremely important. Under the tillage system, they engaged in the same manual work at planting and harvesting as did men (O'Tuathaigh, 1978).

Post-Famine changes led to a major decline in the female labor force in Ireland. First, due to foreign competition, the numbers employed in the domestic spinning industry fell by 75% between 1841 and 1851 (Lee, 1978). Second, as alluded to earlier, the dominant mode of agriculture shifted from tillage to livestock, thereby decreasing the labor intensiveness of farm work and hence the work role of women. A further point to note is that in the absence of an Industrial Revolution, there was no significant separation of work and family in nineteenth-century Ireland such as occurred in the United States.

What of the evolution of the female labor force in twentieth-century Ireland? Once again one finds a marked contrast with the United States. As Table 4 indicates, there was no substantial increase in the female share of the Irish labor force. The overall proportion hovered around 26% for half a century, although there has been a noticeable increase in the period 1970–1980. Over the same time period the participation of women has not shown any dramatic changes, with the exception of a seven-point increase between 1961 and 1971, a time of rapid economic development.

In broad terms, these figures accurately reflect the divergence between the two countries. Whereas, we observe a more or less steady increase in the American female labor force from the late nineteenth century onward, in Ireland the female labor force was roughly halved between 1841 and 1921 and remained relatively static in size until the most recent decade.

Marital status distribution

Clear shifts can also be seen in the linkage between the marital and work status of women in both countries. In the late nineteenth century the female labor force in the United States contained predominantly single women (see Table 5), and single

Table 5 Percentage distribution of civilian female labor force by marital status: United States and Ireland

United States				Ireland			
Year	Single	Married	Widowed or divorced	Year	Single	Married	Widowed
1890	68.2	13.9	17.9				
1900	66.2	15.4	18.4				
1910	60.2	24.7	15.0				
1920	77.0*	23.0	*				
				1926	76.9	7.0	16.1
1930	53.9	28.9	17.2				
				1936	79.0	6.8	14.2
1940	49.0	35.9	15.0				
				1946	80.4	6.8	12.9
1950	31.9	52.2	16.0				
				1951	81.5	6.8	11.7
1960	23.6	60.7	15.7				
				1961	80.0	8.5	11.5
1970	22.5	62.3	15.0				
				1971	77.7	13.6	8.7
1980	25.0	59.7	15.3				
				1981	64.0	31.5	4.5

* During this year, the figures for the single category include the widowed and divorced. 1960 is the first year for which figures include information on Alaska and Hawaii.

U.S. data for the decades through 1970 are from the decennial census and are taken from Series D 49–62, *The Statistical History of the United States From Colonial Times to the Present*. New York: Basic Books, 1976, p. 133. Data for 1980 are from the *Statistical Abstract of the United States 1982–83*. United States Department of Commerce, Bureau of the Census, 1982.

Irish data are from the *Census of Population of Ireland, 1926, 1936, 1946, 1951, 1961, 1971, 1981*. Dublin, Ireland: The Stationery Office. 1981 figures are based on a random 5% sample of the total census.

women were nine times as likely to be employed as their married counterparts (see Table 6). The proportion of the female labor force which was composed of married women increased each decade so that since 1950, over half of the working women in the United States have been married. The probability of a woman's working continues to be affected by marital status (see Table 6), but the marital status differentials have declined over time.

Disaggregating the Irish female labor force by marital status

Table 6 Female labor force as percent of female population by marital status: United States and Ireland

United States				Ireland			
Year	Single	Married	Widowed or divorced	Year	Single	Married	Widowed
1890	40.5	4.6	29.9				
1900	43.5	5.6	32.5				
1910	51.1*	10.7*	34.1*				
1920	46.4*	9.0**	**				
				1926	51.0	5.7	41.1
1930	50.5	11.7	34.4				
				1936	53.3	5.6	39.3
1940	45.5	15.6	30.2				
				1946	53.9	5.0	32.9
1950	46.3	23.0	32.7				
				1951	56.5	5.0	29.5
1960	42.9	31.7	36.1				
				1961	56.4	5.2	26.2
1970	53.0	41.4	36.2				
				1971	55.5	7.5	19.3
1980	61.2	50.7	41.4				
				1981	54.9	17.4	

*These data are not comparable to the other census data. See note for Table IV.
**In this year the single category includes the widowed and divorced.
For U.S. data, the two sources for this table are Series D 42-48, *The Statistical History of the United States From Colonial Times to the Present*. New York: Basic Books, 1975, p. 133, and the *Statistical Abstract of the United States 1982–83*, United States Department of Commerce, Bureau of the Census, 1982, p. 388, No. 652.
Irish data are from the *Census of Population of Ireland, 1926, 1936, 1946, 1951, 1961, 1971, 1981*. Dublin, Ireland: The Stationery Office. 1981 data are based on a random 5% sample of the total census.

also reveals notable differences. The post-famine economic decline affected married women more than it did single women. Following the collapse of the weaving and spinning industries and the contraction of available farm work, the remaining female occupation in late nineteenth-century Ireland was domestic service. Daly (1981) cites that in 1891, 255,000 women worked as domestic servants while another 139,000, all unmarried, worked without pay for brothers or parents. The majority of all domestic servants were unmarried.

By the twentieth century, we find very low levels of labor force participation on the part of married women. Those in the labor force were mostly engaged in farm work. This situation remained unchanged until the 1960s as can be seen from Tables 5 and 6. Starting from a low base (i.e., 5.2% in 1961) the participation rate for married women more than tripled over the following two decades, reaching a level of 17.4% by 1981. Similarly, married women as a proportion of the total labor force almost quadrupled over the same period. Taking a broader timespan, we can see that the proportion of working women who were married increased from 1 in 15 in 1926 to 1 in 3 in 1981.

With regard to other marital states, it can be seen that the participation of widowed women has decreased substantially thus far this century (i.e., by a factor of four between 1926 and 1981) while that of single women has remained relatively static. However, the proportion of the female labor force composed of single women has declined, the decline being partially offset by the rise in the share attributable to those married.

These more recent trends in labor force composition are still poorly understood; however, a number of commentators have attempted an interpretation. Writing in 1973, Walsh and O'Toole suggest that a rising marriage rate and increased female participation in post-primary education led to a smaller pool of single female labor and hence a greater demand for the work of married women. More recently, emphasis has been placed on the relaxing of institutional constraints (anti-discrimination and equal pay legislation, the removal of the marriage bar in the public service sector) and on the increase in job opportunities in the services sector (Bolger, 1984; Blackwell, 1982).

Occupational structure

The final variable of interest involves the types of jobs which women occupy when they enter the labor force. As the United States has moved increasingly from an agricultural to an industrial economy, the proportion of women employed in agriculture has declined dramatically. This development has been accompanied by an even more rapid decline in the proportion of women

Table 7 Distribution of the U.S. female labor force in selected occupations 1900–1980 (14 years and older)

Year	Total # (in thousands)	% Clerical and kindred workers	% Sales workers	% Operatives & kindred workers	% Private household workers	% Farm workers	% Professional, technical & kindred workers
1900	5,319	4.0	4.3	23.8	28.7	18.9	8.2
1910	7,445	9.2	5.1	22.9	24	15.8	9.7
1920	8,637	18.7	6.3	20.2	15.7	13.5	11.7
1930	10,752	20.9	6.8	17.4	17.7	8.4	13.8
1940	12,574	21.5	7.4	19.5	18.1	4	12.8
1950	16,445	27.4	8.6	20	8.9	3.6	12.2
1960	22,304	29	7.8	16.2	7.9	1.7	12.5
1970	30,601	32.4	6.8	13.8	3.6	.7	14.4
1980*	42,117	35.1	6.8	10.0	3.3	1.2	16.8

Data for 1900–1970 are calculated from Series D 182-232, p. 140 of *The Historical Statistics of United States.* U.S. Department of Commerce, Bureau of the Census. Washington, D.C., 1975. 1980 data are from p. 390 of *The Statistical Abstract of the United States 82/83.* Washington, D.C. 1982.

*1980 data are women 16 years and older.

employed in domestic service as well as by decreases in the proportion of the female labor force found as operatives and kindred workers. The most striking change has been the continued growth of the number of women clerical workers (see Table 7).

This distribution of women in various sectors of the labor market is closely linked to cultural values about the types of work which are appropriate for women. In nineteenth-century United States only a few jobs were considered appropriate for women, notably domestic work, work as operatives in the textile mills, and schoolteaching (see Bernard and Vinovskis, 1977; Brumberg and Tomes, 1982; Dublin, 1975; Dudden, 1983). In addition, most of these jobs were limited largely to single women. Many regions had laws prohibiting married women from teaching school (Punke, 1940), and cultural norms dictating that a woman's sphere was in the home (Welter, 1966) meant that most other female occupations were dominated by single women.

Rotella (1981) suggests that the first decade of the twentieth century was most important in terms of women's movement into the labor force, while the next decade was a period of redistribution within the female occupational structure—particularly the decline in domestic and agricultural work and a rapid increase in clerical occupations. She also notes an increase in the number of married women who are in the clerical sector each decade. Successive cohorts of women not only faced a different labor market in terms of the types of jobs which existed, they also worked within different sets of cultural values which defined what types of work were available to women in different marital states.

There is also evidence of change in the availability and appropriateness of various occupations for women in Ireland. Table 8 provides information on changes in the occupations of working women in Ireland over the period 1926–1979. The occupations have been chosen to reflect the major work options of women in the post-Famine era (i.e., farm work and domestic service) and also the areas of rapid expansion over recent decades (i.e., the professions and clerical work).

The most dramatic change has occurred in the numbers working in agriculture: The largest occupational category in 1926, it now ranks among the smaller ones, having declined by a factor of 15 over the intervening period. Although the numbers engaged in agriculture have been falling overall, note that the comparable decline for men (not included) was by a factor of 2. Similarly, the

Table 8 Occupational distribution of the Irish female labor force 1926–1979

Year	Agricultural occupations #	Agricultural occupations %	Textile workers #	Textile workers %	Professionals #	Professionals %	Domestics #	Domestics %	Clerks & typists #	Clerks & typists %	Other #	Other %	Total #	Total %
1926	121,957	35.5	23,362	6.8	29,505	8.6	87,553	25.5	12,801	3.7	68,716	20.0	343,894	100.1
1936	106,723	30.4	27,632	7.9	32,937	9.4	86,102	24.5	19,254	5.5	78,719	22.4	351,367	100.1
1946	81,526	24.3	25,910	7.7	36,806	11.0	78,522	23.4	23,898	7.1	88,200	26.3	334,862	99.8
1951	67,718	20.8	30,313	9.3	38,847	12.0	57,589	17.7	30,763	9.5	99,618	30.7	324,848	100.0
1961	42,111	14.7	24,859	8.7	44,176	14.4	31,101	10.9	46,284	16.2	101,048	35.3	286,579	100.2
1971	25,319	8.8	24,606	8.6	50,702	17.6	20,543	7.1	67,127	23.3	99,570	34.6	287,867	100.0
1981	8,100	2.4	—	—	77,400	23.1	—	—	97,200	29.0	—	—	335,300	—

Data are from the *Census of Population of Ireland, 1926, 1936, 1946, 1951, 1961, 1971,* and *1981*. Dublin, Ireland: The Stationery Office. The 1981 figures are based on a 5% sample of the census.

numbers of women working as domestic servants has fallen considerably, especially since World War II.

In contrast, the number of female clerks and typists has increased almost eightfold over the same period so that 3 out of every 10 working women were engaged in clerical work by 1981. Along with this increase in the numbers of female clerical workers has been an increasing "feminization" of such work. In 1926 male clerks outnumbered females by over 7 to 2; by 1974 there were 34% more female clerks than male clerks. Over all years, the vast majority of typists have been female.

Another occupational group showing considerable female expansion is the professions. In 1926 fewer than 1 in 10 working women were engaged in professional work, whereas by 1979, the proportion has increased to almost 1 in 4. Professional work now stands as the second largest source of female employment. Although there has been an increase in the number of female professionals, the continuity in the types of professional work carried out by females is striking. In 1926, 9 out of 10 female professionals were either nurses, teachers, or nuns. In 1971 (the latest date for which disaggregated data are available), these three occupations accounted for the same proportion of all female professionals.

DISCUSSION

Our analysis of changes in women's work and family experience is rooted in the historic change from a rural agricultural to an urban industrial economy. We view this economic transition as the essential motor for changes in the work experience of women. However, as our data have shown, there is considerable variability in the manner in which this change occurred in Ireland and the United States. This variability is explained in terms of the unique features of both countries: economic, social, and geographical.

Our aims in this section are threefold. First, we will summarize the similarities and differences between Ireland and the United States in terms of the work and family experience of women. Second, we will develop a number of general propositions regarding the determinants of female labor force participation. Finally, we will apply these propositions to the Irish and American cases and make predictions regarding future participation by women in the work force.

Despite the many contrasts between Ireland and the United

Table 9 Urbanization in Ireland and the United States

Ireland	1841	1861	1881	1901	1926	1946	1966	1971
towns	16.8	22.4	24.1	28.3	32.3	39.3	49.2	52.1
rural	83.2	77.6	75.9	71.7	67.7	60.7	50.8	47.9
U.S.	**1840**	**1860**	**1880**	**1900**	**1920**	**1940**	**1960**	**1970**
urban	10.8	19.8	28.2	39.7	51.2	56.5	69.9	73.5
rural	89.2	80.2	71.8	60.3	48.8	43.5	30.1	26.5

In the U.S. data, urban is defined as areas with 2500 or more population. For Irish data the town population includes all persons living in towns with 1500 or more.

States discussed earlier, we observe in our data evidence of a common trajectory of development in the female labor force. This is particularly so with respect to changes in the marital status of working women and with respect to the types of jobs available to women. In both countries there has been a considerable rise in the proportions of married women working and also a switch from agriculture and domestic service to clerical and professional work as main areas of female employment.

These commonalities are also evident in more general indicators of modernization and economic development. Table 9 provides comparative data on urbanization from the mid-nineteenth century to the present, and reference back to Table 3 illustrates change in industrialization at the same period. Both countries have a history of continuous decrease in the rural population over this period. Similarly, twentieth-century economic changes in Ireland are broadly similar in direction to those in the United States as evidenced by a decreasing agricultural labor force and a rise in the numbers employed in industry and services. The later increase in services is also evident in both countries.

Some major dissimilarities between Ireland and the United States concern the considerable lag in industrialization in Ireland and also the small increase in its overall level of female employment during the twentieth century. The first of these can be explained in part by the devastation of the Great Famine, subsequent emigration, and industrial failure through competition with Britain (Lyons, 1973). In the first half of the nineteenth century, indices of economic development show both countries at similar levels (see Tables 9 & 3). Toward the end of that century and into the next, we observe dramatic urbanization and industrialization in the United States, whereas the Irish figures show slow urbanization and industrial decline. It is not until recent decades that pronounced economic development has been evident in Ireland.

The lack of increase in overall female employment in Ireland may reflect an unfavorable balance between the decline in agricultural work and the slow emergence of clerical and professional work. For example, in the period 1926–1979 the agricultural sector of the economy declined by a greater amount than the services sector expanded (by a 1.8:1 ratio). It is not until the 1960s that a pronounced rise in clerical and professional work is evident. It is noteworthy that subsequent to this rise, increases in female participation have occurred.

We are now in a position to consider the theoretical implications of our comparative work. Perhaps the strongest generalization to emerge concerns the connection between the development of the service sector of the economy and the rise in female employment. We observe this association for both countries, albeit at different times. It is also noteworthy that a major portion of the service sector, e.g., clerical work, shows a high degree of sex segregation in both countries (for example, Irish figures for 1971 indicate that 99.7% of all typists were female).

An issue related to the development of the service sector concerns the availability of part-time work. The service sector is perhaps the most flexible in this regard and may help to explain why its growth has been strongly associated with the rise in participation by married women in the labor force (in the post World War II era in the United States and in the 1960s and 1970s in Ireland). In Ireland in 1979, 1 in 3 employed married women worked part-time, whereas only 1 in 20 employed single women did so.

We have not directly examined societal attitudes toward female employment (due to lack of sufficient Irish data), yet we propose that these have played an important role in influencing behavior. The exact nature of this role is, most likely, complex. For example, there is evidence that attitudes toward female employment actually respond positively to increasing participation (Molm, 1978). However, societal unfavorability is also a constraint on participation, as it has traditionally been for all but the poorest married women. The most plausible situation is that economic and societal exigencies (e.g., World War II in the United States) cause changes in labor force behavior which produce more favorable attitudes. These attitudes, in turn, influence subsequent behavior.

The transition from an agricultural to an industrial economy has also been associated with increased levels of education. More recently, opportunities for advanced education have been widening for females. For example, in Ireland, between 1960 and 1979 the number of females attending universities increased by 129%; the comparable figure for males is 10% (Blackwell, 1982). Our contention is that the higher the level of education and training a woman receives, the more likely it is that she will use these skills in the labor market.

What are the likely future trends in the work and family experience of women? To answer this question we must consider both countries separately. In the case of Ireland, it is highly likely that female participation will increase. We argue so for a variety of reasons. First, given the intermediate level of economic development in Ireland, further declines in the agricultural sector and increases in the service sectors of the economy appear likely. Consequently we envision an expansion of job opportunities for women. Second, the growth of part-time work in service industries will in all probability continue especially in light of the "information revolution" of computer technology and will allow more married women to combine employment and childrearing. Third, the impact of increasing levels of education among females will become evident in higher rates of participation in future years. A related feature is the fall in fertility which tends to accompany increased education, increasing the likelihood of female employment. Finally institutional changes which occurred in Ireland in the late 1970s (equal pay, anti-discrimination laws, and tax changes favoring married women) are having positive effects on female participation which are not yet fully evident.

Our forecast regarding participation rates in the United States is similar in that we expect these to continue rising. Underlying this prediction is our expectation that employment in services will continue to increase. At present, despite two major recessions in recent decades, an underlying rising trend is evident (see Table 6).

As in the Irish case, the number of highly educated females in the United States has been increasing. Given the enhanced job prospects accruing to highly educated persons and the fact that such persons tend to enter the work force, we predict that this trend will serve to increase the number of gainfully employed women.

Similarly, United States attitude surveys indicate increased acceptance of women's working. On the assumption that this change affects women's work decisions controlling for other variables, further increases in participation are likely.

In view of our emphasis on the differences between Ireland and the United States in the timing of female labor force participation, we now consider the likelihood of a slowing down in the rate of growth of the women's work force in the United States as some "ceiling" is approached. We have found no evidence for this proposition. The data in Table 4 are consistent with the converse, i.e., that since the 1930s increases in female participation have been accelerating. In addition, projections for 1990 given by Masnick and Bane (1980) indicate a constant or increasing rate of increase in participation.

CONCLUSIONS

In this paper we have examined the proposition that the major social and family change of increased participation by women in gainful employment has its basis in the change from an agricultural to an industrial economy. In doing so we have chosen two strategically different societies as examples in order to ascertain the proposition's cross-cultural validity. Our findings indicate considerable cross-national similarity with respect to the evolution of the female labor force, its marital status composition, and the types of jobs available to women. In tandem with these similarities we observe important differences attributable to the unique historical circumstances of each country, e.g., the major deceleration of industrialization due to the Famine in Ireland.

The scope of our analysis has been constrained by a lack of comparable measures across the two countries (e.g., on social attitudes) and by a lack of data over all years of interest. Nonetheless, our findings show that key features of women's work and family change are similar in both countries and are indicative of general as opposed to country-specific processes. As such they form a modest contribution toward a genuinely cross-cultural theory of social and family change.

REFERENCES

Bernard, R. M., and M. A. Vinovskis (1977) "The Female School Teacher in Ante-Bellum Massachusetts." Journal of Social History 10 (3): 332–345.

Berry, B. J. L., and J. D. Kasarda (1977) Contemporary Urban Ecology. New York: Macmillan.

Blackwell, J. (1982) Digest of Statistics on Women in the Labor Force and Related Subjects. Dublin: The Employment Equality Agency.

Bolger, N. (1984) "Labor Force Participation of Married Women in Ireland: Models of Current Behavior and Future Plans." M.S. thesis, Cornell University.

Brumberg, J. J., and N. Tomes (1982) "Women in the Professions: A Research Agenda for American Historians." Reviews in American History (June): 275–296.

Chubb, B. (1982) The Government and Politics of Ireland. Stanford, CA: Stanford University Press.

Cullen, L. M. (1972) An Economic History of Ireland since 1660. London: Batsford.

Daly, M. E. (1981) Social and Economic History of Ireland since 1800. Dublin: The Educational Company.

Dublin, T. (1975) "Women, Work, and the Family: Female Operatives in the Lowell Mills, 1830–1860." Feminist Studies 3 (1/2): 30–39.

Dudden, F. (1983) Serving Women: Household Service in 19th Century America. Middletown, Connecticut: Wesleyan University Press.

Duncan, O. D. (1959) "Human Ecology and Population Studies," in P. M. Hauser and O. D. Duncan (eds.) The Study of Population. Chicago: The University of Chicago Press: 678–716.

Elder, G. H. Jr. (1974) Children of the Great Depression. Chicago: University of Chicago Press.

Goode, W. J. (1963) World Revolution and Family Patterns. New York: The Free Press.

Haavio-Mannila, E., and K. Kari (1980) "Changes in the Life Patterns of Families in the Nordic Countries," in Yearbook of Population Research, XVIII. Helsinki: 7–34.

Hawley, A. (1950) Human Ecology: A Theory of Community Structure. New York: The Ronald Press Company.

Ireland: Central Statistics Office (1926–1981) Census of Population of Ireland, 1926, 1936, 1946, 1951, 1961, 1971, 1981. Dublin, Ireland: The Stationery Office.

Lee, J. J. (1978) "Women and the Church since the Famine," in Women in Irish Society: The Historical Dimension. Dublin: Arlen House.

Lenski, G., and J. Lenski (1982) Human Societies. New York: McGraw-Hill.

Lyons, F. S. L. (1973) Ireland Since the Famine. London: Fontana.

Masnick, G., and M. J. Bane (1980) The Nation's Families: 1960–1990. Boston: Auburn Publishing.

McCarthy, E. (1978) "Women and Work in Ireland," in Women in Irish Society: The Historical Dimension. Dublin: Arlen House.

Moen, P., E. L. Kain, and G. H. Elder, Jr. (1983) "Economic Conditions and

Family Life: Contemporary and Historical Perspectives," in R. R. Nelson and F. Skidmore [eds.] American Families and the Economy: The High Costs of Living. Washington, D.C. National Academy Press: 213–254.
Molm, L. D. (1978) "Sex Role Attitudes and the Employment of Married Women: The Direction of Causality." The Sociological Quarterly 19: 522–533.
Ogburn, W. F. (1935) "Recent Changes in Marriage," American Journal of Sociology, XLI: 285–98.
Ogburn, W. F. and E. R. Groves (1928) American Marriage and Family Relationships. New York: Henry Holt and Co.
Ogburn, W. F. and M. F. Nimkoff (1955) Technology and the Changing Family. Boston: Houghton Mifflin Co.
Oppenheimer, V. K. (1970) The Female Labor Force in the United States. Berkeley: Institute of International Studies, University of California.
O'Tuathaigh, G. (1978) "The Role of Women in Ireland Under the New English Order," in Women in Irish Society: The Historical Dimension. Dublin: Arlen House.
Punke, H. H. (1940) "Marriage Rate Among Women Teachers." American Sociological Review 5 (4): 505–511.
Rotella, E. J. (1981) From Home to Office: U.S. Women at Work, 1870–1930. Ann Arbor, Michigan: UMI Research Press.
United Nations (1981) Statistical Yearbook 1979/1980. New York: Statistical Office of the United Nations.
______(1982) United Nations Demographic Yearbook, 1980. New York: Statistical Office of the United Nations.
United States Bureau of the Census (1897) Report on Population of the United States at the Eleventh Census: 1890, Part II. Washington, D.C.: Government Printing Office.
______(1975) Historical Statistics of the United States from Colonial Times to 1970. Washington, D.C.: United States Government Printing Office.
______(1982) Statistical Abstract of the United States 1982–83. Washington, D.C.
______(1984) Statistical Abstract of the United States 1984. Washington, D.C.
Walsh, B. M., and A. O'Toole (1973) Women and Employment in Ireland: Results of a National Survey. Dublin: The Economic and Social Research Institute, Paper No. 69.
Welter, B. (1966) "The Cult of True Womanhood: 1820–1860. American Quarterly 18: 151–74.
Whyte, J. (1980) Church and State in Modern Ireland. London: Gill & Macmillan.

WORKING-CLASS IMMIGRANT WOMEN IN MID-NINETEENTH-CENTURY NEW YORK
The Irish Woman's Experience

CAROL GRONEMAN
New York Council for the Humanities

The beginnings of mass immigration in the pre-Civil War decade would profoundly affect both American society and the men and women who came here. The transition of America from a pre-modern to an industrializing nation in this and later decades coincided with the entrance of a predominantly preindustrial agrarian peoples of diverse European backgrounds. While physically "uprooted," these immigrants brought with them distinct patterns of behavior of work, family, and leisure which continued to mold their responses and adaptations to the circumstances of their new life.

American social historians have only recently begun the difficult task of reconstructing the diverse and complex historical experiences of these groups and the interaction of these experiences with the changing American society they entered.[1]

Author's Note: *My thanks to Barbara and Gilbert Millstein for their generosity in lending me their prints of the Fi Points.*

JOURNAL OF URBAN HISTORY, Vol. 4 No. 3, May 1978

Much work needs to be done. Only through numerous detailed studies of particular groups at particular times in our history will we be able to know the "many pasts" of America. By focusing on Irish women's experiences in pre-Civil War New York City, we will look in more detail at some of these cultural continuities—namely, work, leisure patterns, and family life—which added coherence to their lives in an alien and changing world.

Let us look at the Irish lassie in mid-nineteenth-century New York, at least how she was viewed by an upper-class contemporary: the attire of "Lize," the wife or sweetheart of a Bowery b'hoy,

> was a cheap but exaggerated copy of the prevailing Broadway mode; her skirt was shorter and fuller, bodice longer and lower; hat more gaudily trimmed; handkerchief more ample and flauntingly carried; corkscrew curls thinner, longer and stiffer; her gait and swing were studied imitations of her lord and master.[2]

Who were these Irish young women who came here in such great numbers during this period? Why had they come? What were their expectations? How did their past experiences affect the choices they made both in Ireland and in America?

The story begins not here but in Ireland. The backdrop for the tragedy of rural Ireland was painted in the late eighteenth and early nineteenth centuries when several factors converged: increased use of land for tillage rather than pasture because of higher grain prices, a consequent break up of large pastures into small farms, an increased reliance by the peasants on the potato as the only source of food, the decline of the domestic industries, and a phenomenal growth in population. Because there was simply no other way to feed one's family in rural Ireland for most of the peasantry, land on which to grow potatoes was an absolute necessity. Holdings had been increasingly subdivided over generations so that by 1841 the majority of the rural population held, but did not own, fewer than five acres.[3] Contemporary reports indicated that many of these small holders lived in wretched poverty, existing mainly on potatoes, and desperately in need of work to pay their rent. Seasonal migration to harvest crops in the English and Scottish countryside became traditional for many men and some women during this period.[4]

The impulse toward permanent emigration to British Canada or America was already present in the early nineteenth century among the small farmers, weavers in the declining linen and wool industry, servant girls, and city workres in general who could save the money necessary for passage. The one million Irish who emigrated to the United States between 1815 and 1845 would provide the possibility for the much greater emigration following the Great Famine of 1846-1849. Even in this early emigration, and particularly after 1830, women formed a higher proportion of those leaving Ireland compared to migrants from other European countries, a trend that would continue throughout the nineteenth and early twentieth centuries. By 1845 one-half of the total emigrants were women, partly because laborers left in family groups, but also because a growing number of single young women emigrated.[5]

This eagerness to leave their beloved country can be accounted for in several ways. Marriage age in Ireland had continued to fall throughout this period. The subsistence level at which peasants lived encouraged them "to seek a partner to share their misery," for all a young couple needed to start life together was a tiny plot of land on which to grow potatoes and a mud hut which could be built with little difficulty. In a land where professional matchmaking was important only to the small class of peasants who owned land and had the money for a dowry for their daughters, most Irish girls had little hope that marriage would provide anything more than subsistence existence.[6] As one young emigrant girl wrote to her parents from New York in 1850, "Oh how happy I feel . . . that it was not . . . destined for me to get married to some Loammum or another at home that after a few months he and I may be an Incumberance upon you or perhaps in the poor house."[7]

The high proportion of female emigrants continued throughout the nineteenth and early twentieth centuries; in some years females even exceeded males. Robert E. Kennedy, in his demographic study of Ireland, has suggested that Irish women, relative to Irish men, had more to gain by emigrating. The freedom and independence promised by a paying job in a distant city were more attractive than the subordinate role of unpaid helper in her own family, he concluded, and convinced many young women to make the difficult break from home and family. Furthermore, young women were more certain of obtaining immediate employment and were particularly faithful in sending remittances to their families. It is possible that families, especially after the Famine, chose to send their daughters rather than their sons to the New World as the hope for insuring the family's future.[8]

The work experience of women in an agricultural society like Ireland included the usual domestic chores connected with very small farms. As one Cork correspondent reported upon seeing a group of women preparing for departure to America, "the women could not have been capable of anything more than to churn, to feed pigs, work in dairies, or mind children."[9] But his report was not completely accurate. Over one-fourth of the adult women in Ireland had some skill as spinners, weavers, seamstresses, and other cloth workers, predominantly in the cottage industries of the north and east of Ireland. As the woolen and cotton domestic industries declined in the early nineteenth century, some of these women migrated to Belfast and Dublin, to the industrializing cities of Scotland and England, or to the United States and Canada.[10]

Approximately one-quarter of a million women (one-tenth of the adult female population) worked as domestic servants in the 1840s. These women came from laborers' or the very poorest cottiers' families. As one farmer's wife commented:

> I would be glad to get my little girl into a house where she could learn something and earn something; but sure, as for three or four pounds a year, she can earn that at home, and more, in the fields, at the wheel, the needle or the straw plait, and Mrs. Mullin's [the local gentry] food isn't much better than our own.[11]

Domestic servants were relatively better off economically than those women who remained with their families since they received wages and lived in the houses of the gentry or substantial farmers. Even so, in the spring, when they received their wages and the emigrant ships left port, some took advantage of the possibility of going to America or Canada.[12]

In general, women did not hire out as agricultural laborers, although approximately 8,000 migrated yearly in the early 1840s to Scotland and England for the harvest. Whole families immigrated to the industrializing towns and cities of Scotland and England. Some 60,000 Irish-born women lived in Scotland in the early 1840s, and the labor force in the Scottish cotton mills was composed chiefly of Irish girls. In England, Irish women could be found working in the mills, as domestic servants, as pedlars, hucksters, and lodging-house keepers.[13]

Over half of the 300,000 adult women who emigrated from Ireland between 1851 and 1855 listed an occupation with British government officials. Approximately 10,000 indicated that they were spinners, weavers, or other cloth workers; 22,000 had been domestic servants; and over 120,000 said they were agricultural workers. The latter figure was predominantly women who worked on their families' small plots of land, as well as the increasing number of women hiring out as agricultural laborers after the Famine.[14] While most of these women would not work on farms in America, many of them would perform work somewhat similar to their work in Ireland as domestic servants, pedlars, or boarding-house keepers. Work in the textile mills of Belfast and Glasgow may have prepared some women for work in the textile mills of New England, but most of their experience as spinner and weavers in their family homes would not be comparable to the piece-work and sweating system of the Boston and New York City tenements,

Upon arrival in America, most immigrants sought out relatives or fellow country folk with whom to stay. A job had to be found within a few days because few women came with any surplus cash and most had families who were counting on their remittances. Irish women worked in a variety of occupations, including umbrella, paper box, and flower makers, book binders, printers, pedlars, store keepers, and in the needle trades, but the majority were domestic servants. Given the increasing demand for servants in expanding middle-class households and in the hotels and boarding-houses of the growing city, it is not surprising that Irish girls chose this kind of work. Over 25% of the Irish working population of the city were domestic servants, compared to less than 15% of German, Welsh, Scottish, French, and Swiss workers. I use the word "chose" cautiously because of the limited opportunities in other fields. However, factory work in the clothing industry of the city had been developing since the 1830s, and the amount of skill required would not have been prohibitive. But domestic service offered a greater possibility of saving the few dollars a month one earned because room and board were supplied in addition to the four to $8.00 per month wages. These few dollars were absolutely crucial as remittances to their familes in Ireland, either to help pay the rent on the few acres of potatoes or to bring other members of the family to America. Out of the meager wages of servants and other Irish workers in the city, over $20 million was remitted to Ireland in the decade following the Famine.[15]

About one-third of Irish women under 30 years of age worked in the needle trades. Some had probably learned the rudiments of the trade in Ireland, and the Irish tailor and tailoress teams in New York City were possibly the children of the Irish weavers and spinners of the early nineteenth century. The 1853 investigation by the New York *Tribune* vividly described the appalling conditions of the "Needlewomen of New York" and the shops which paid them about 8¢ to make a shirt. Since finishing three shirts was a hard day's labor, the *Tribune* estimated that a woman needle worker, taking into consideration the time expended to obtain and return the goods and other journeys to secure her pay, could conceivably receive 50¢ for an entire week's labor. "Though some thousands of females in different callings—milliners, dressmakers, shop-assistants—make between $3.50 and $6.00 a week which could be considered a living wage," stated the *Tribune*, "there are hundreds of women tailoresses and seamstresses who have an average yearly income, if fully employed, of only $91."[16] Obviously, needle trade workers paid this nonliving wage either had several members of their family working or turned to other means of support: help from friends and relatives, the very limited funds from charitable agencies, or prostitution.

Of the 2,000 prostitutes questioned by Willian Sanger in 1855, over one-third were Irish-born, almost half had been prostitutes for less than one year, about 40% were married or widowed, and almost half had children. Most listed their former occupation as domestic service or needle trades. As Sanger himself suggests, prostitutes were working women who moved into the trade when faced with periods of unemployment. "Those who follow an employment at intervals," he stated, "are mostly women whose trades are uncertain, and who are liable at certain seasons of the year to be without employment. Then real necessity forces them on the town until a return of business provides them with work." A prostitute put it more succinctly when asked why she followed the profession: M. T. answered, "I had no work, no money, and no home." S. F., a widow with three children, stated that she could earn only $2.00 weekly at cap-making, but could not get steady employment even at those prices.[17] One might assume, particularly since almost half had been prostitutes for less than one year, that the opportunity for other employment might find prostitutes moving out of the trade and returning to their former work. As Judith and Daniel Walkowitz have shown in their study of prostitution in nineteenth-century England, "[Prostitutes] were not dehumanized vagabonds. . . . They were very much part of a lower-class community, and their general social and economic profile did not differ significantly from that of the rest of the poor in those districts."[18] A look at the most notorious slum in nineteenth-century America, New York City's predominantly Irish Five Points, supports their conclusions.

One middle-class reporter believed that in the Five Points "nearly every house and cellar is a groggery below and a brothel above. . . . In the doors and windows may be seen, at any hour of the afternoon or evening, scores of sluttishly-dressed women, in whose faces drunkenness and debauchery have destroyed every vestige of humanity."[19] A social and economic profile, however, indicates that single young women living alone or in groups, who might have been prostitutes, shared the streets of the Five Points with a variety of working-class families, mainly laborers, but including some artisans and the usual assortment of grocery/liquor stores, pawn shops, and old-clothing stores found in poor neighborhoods. Neither the age distribution, the marital status, nor the household and family composition of these women was peculiarly deviant compared to available statistics on the city and on other poor neighborhoods.[20]

While the occupational experience of single young women can tell us much about that segment of the community, we must also look at the experiences of their married sisters. In a study of one mid-nineteenth-century immigrant community, New York City's Sixth Ward, evidence from the census manuscripts indicates that almost one-half of Irish households had at least one other member of the household, most often working wives, contributing to the family income. The major occupation of these married women, one which has often been overlooked by historians relying on the compiled census statistics, was taking boarders into their households. Fully 25% of Sixth Ward married women supplemented family income in this manner.[21]

It is interesting to speculate on the amount of possible income these women sacrificed by working in the home. The Sixth Ward factories, for example, paid an average of $5.50 per week to women workers. Certainly lack of skills might have had some influence on the limited number of married women working outside the home. Many industrial trades, however, were easily learned with a few weeks' apprenticeship. The lower wards also offered the greatest number of industrial jobs, and many single women worked in the local factories, hotels, and laundries. Thus, we might hypothesize that the work Sixth Ward married women performed reflected more than limited opportunities—namely, an element of conscious choice. Women may have chosen this particular occupation because it allowed them to continue to function in their role as housewife and mother while also contributing to the family's support.[22]

This is not an insignificant suggestion. A considerable body of historical literature insists that immigration and the alienation of the large city led to disruption and breakdown of the family.

The evidence from a poor working-class area like New York City's Sixth Ward is all the more revealing because its residents, many of whom had fled the Irish famine, would have been particularly vulnerable to the processes of family disintegration. These traditionally family-centered Irish peasant women adapted to the economic pressures of urban life by combining their economic activity with the functions of childrearing and housekeeping. The sheer magnitude of the Sixth Ward married women engaged in the occupation of taking boarders would suggest that this was a central means of coping with the multiple demands placed upon immigrant women in America. Even when forced by necessity to work, they did so in ways which would reinforce, rather than disrupt, their traditional familial values.

The long hours of work in the 1850s consumed a major portion of the day, but what did these women, recently arrived from the Irish countryside, do during their free time? Life in the urban slum was lived mainly on the streets, to escape the cramped, uncomfortable tenements. On a warm June Saturday night in the 1850s, crowds gathered in and around the little triangular park, rather winningly called Paradise Square, in the heart of the Five Points. Threading their way through the crowd in front of the notorious Old Brewery across from the park might be Mary O'Neill and her sister Margaret returning home to Mulberry Street from work as umbrella makers in a local factory. They would probably have changed to dresses reserved for the Saturday night promenade along the Bowery. The center of working-class night life, parts of the Five Points on a Saturday night must have resembled a county fair in their home villages[23]

On Centre Street they would have passed by the apple stands, quoit games, pedlars, weighing machines, lung testers, and other penny catchers going full tilt. The rows of booths on each side of the street, the colorfully-dressed women busy making their purchases or chatting and laughing, and the hearty kiss given when people met all describe both a fair in Killala, County Mayo in the 1840s as well as the heart of the working-class district in urban America in the 1850s. The Connaught lass, described by C. Otway in a journey through Ireland in the early 1840s, could have been the O'Neills' older sister:

I see her there coquetting most intensely, with Pat on one side, and he's a clean, comely broad shouldered, light limbed, springy fellow. He could run to Sligo and never draw breath, hurl or fight till the cows come home. On the other side of her is a sailor. . . . Sally, the deceiver, is dividing her smiles between her two admirers, and an old wrinkled body (Sally's aunt no doubt) is standing behind and watching the colleen. Paddy with his bit of ground and decent cabin would do better for her Sally.[24]

Margaret and Mary's New York City beaux were probably laborers or building-trades workers, not farmers, but most likely they came from the same county as the O'Neills, for County Sligo men and women tended to live on the upper part of Mulberry Street, while Corkonians settled on the lower half and Kerryonians on parts of Baxter Street.[25]

A night on the town for the O'Neills and their boyfriends would include a visit to a saloon like D. Brennan's on the park or to the oyster cellars of Canal Street where for 6¢ they would consume vast quantities of oysters and beer. This might be followed by a visit to the Bowery or Olympic Theaters to see "A Glance at New York," a play featuring the John Bunyan-like character, Mose, modeled after a New York City fireman. They would have shared their gallery seats with "butcher boys... the mechanic with his family, the bhoy in red flannel shirt sleeves, the chop woman, the sewing girl, the straw braider, the type rubber, the paper box and flower maker, with a liberal sprinkling of undercrust blacklegs and fancy men." Foot-stomping, clapping, hissing, shouts of encouragement greeted the "blood and thunder plays"—audience participation was a much a part of the show as the performance on the stage.[26]

There was other entertainment: Kit Burn's Sportsmen's Hall, where these sons of rural Ireland watched waterfront rats being pitted against a terrier; variety acts in the concert saloons, some including women pugilists; or, for the more bizarre, McGlory's Armory Hall where waiter girls were joined by a bevy of lithe-limbed waiter boys, both outfitted in short skirts and high red boots.[27]

The evening would end with a visit to Harry Hill's or one of the many dance halls in the neighborhood. A room about 25 feet square, its whitewashed walls garnished with wooden benches, a bar at one end and a raised platform for the musicians, usually several fiddlers and a tambourine man, provided dancing room for about one-dozen couples. The corners of the room filled with onlookers, paying 10¢ admission and 3¢ for a glass of whiskey, waiting for their chance to enter the smiling, foot-stomping throng.[28] As Charles Dickens recorded in an 1840s visit to a Five Points dance hall,

> [as the couples take the floor] instantly the fiddler grins, and goes at it tooth and nail, there is new energy in the tambourine; new laughter in the dancers. Single shuffle, double shuffle, cut and cross-cut, snaping his fingers, rolling his eyes, turning in his knees, presenting the backs of his legs in front, spinning about on his toes and heels like nothing but the man's fingers on the tambourine, . . . having danced his partner off her feet, and himself, too, he finishes by leaping gloriously on the bar-counter, and calling for something to drink.[29]

The "breakdowns" described in the Five Points dance halls sound much like the description of rural Irish weddings in the years before the Famine. "First single parties dance reels, jigs, and doubles . . . the male partner 'shows off,' and the best idea we can give of it," commented Mr. and Mrs. Hall on an Irish wedding party in 1841, "is that it consists in striking the ground very rapidly with the heel and toe, or with the toes of each foot alternately. . . . A stranger, not hearing the music, and seeing only the dancer, would be sure to imagine he was killing a rat; nor would it be very safe to have this dance performed by a stout fellow in a frail loft."[30] These young people had brought their dances and music with them to America.

Just as in Ireland, young single women in America had relatively more independence than married women. Care of children was completely in the hands of the mother, but more than that, Irish recreation tended to be separated along sex lines, particularly after marriage.[31] While all members of a family, in America as in Ireland, attended crucial family events such as weddings, christenings, and wakes, the everyday recreation, visiting bars, theaters, dance halls, or the races, tended to be male only or single males and their girlfriends. The traditional function of such customs as dances and saints' festivals was matchmaking, and thus single girls were more likely to be in attendance. A young Irish man in the 1850s had more organized forms of recreation than did the women in his household. He might have been a member of the Sixth Ward Democratic Club, the Kenmare Hurlers, the semisocial and political clubs of the Five Points, like the Plug Uglies or the Dead Rabbits, the Lady Washington Engine Company or a militia unit.

Sabina Conway Devlin of 213 Mulberry Street, 27 years old, married to an Irishman from County Sligo, her home county, and the mother of two children, belonged to no clubs or organizations. She had lived in America for nine years, and like many of her fellow countrywomen she married a few years later in America than girls in Ireland. She would have between three and four children, probably one of whom would not reach adolescence. She faced the real possibility of being widowed young since her husband, James, a laborer, was subject to what the City Inspector called a "high rate of deaths among the young male laboring population due to industrial accidents." More than one-quarter of her countrywomen in New York City over the age of 50 headed their own households. The possibility for remarriage was lessened for Sabina, compared to other immigrant women in the city, because of the higher proportion of Irish women to men in all age groups.[32]

Like most Irish peasant women, Sabina was used to a life of hard work and insecurity. Employment for day laborers was irregular and seasonal, and perhaps her husband spend several months a year away from his family working on the railroad gangs in upstate New York. These separations, although difficult, had been traditional in County Sligo, where she was born, and her father might have gone to harvest crops each year in England or Scotland. The irregularity of employment and the low wages meant that she would have to take in washing or sewing, and although there were not boarders in her house, her 18 year old brother probably contributed his wages to the family income.

What effect did the tensions and strains of the immigration process, the new and alien urban world, and the developing industrialization of America have on the families of the Sabina Conways of mid-nineteenth-century New York? Did the massive exodus from the Great Famine encourage a sundering of family ties? After settling in New York City, did the Irish—traditionally family-oriented, and in the pre-Famine period organized into nuclear family households[33]—constitute a mass of disorganized, unattached individuals in the "alienating" atmosphere of a large port city like New York? We have one further fragment of historical evidence on Sabina Conway: when her second son, James, was christened in 1855, the godparents included her brother, Patrick Conway, and her husband's sister, Elizabeth Devlin.[34] Although thousands of miles from their Irish homeland, the families of Sabina Conway and James Devlin continued to fill their traditional roles. While family ties were strained by immigration and tensions were created by the movement into an urban industrializing world, the Irish brought with them and maintained enduring cultural patterns and family and kin relationships.

Elsewhere, I have looked in greater detail at the endurance of these family ties and the stability of family structure in an Irish neighborhood in mid-nineteenth-century New York City.[35] An analysis of the census manuscript schedules of this area indicates that almost three-quarters of this Irish population came to America either in family groups or by the process of "one-bringing-another"; 86% of the population lived with at least one person related by blood or by marriage; the great majority of the population (93%) lived in households headed by a nuclear family, with only a small proportion living alone or with unrelated adults; large masses of unattached young Irish men and women did not create a separate class living outside organized family since only 5% lived in boarding-houses rather than boarding with a family; and 75% of the Irish over 60 years of age lived with relatives, indicating that the strong bonds of duty and affection toward parents were not broken by imigration.[36] These statistics take on even more significance because they describe one of the poorest areas of New York City, home to the disreputable Five Points slum.

Let us turn from a consideration of numbers to a much more eloquent state of what these figures show. Margaret McCarthy, a young Irish immigrant, wrote to her "Dear Father Mother Brothers and Sisters" in 1850:

> Come you all Together Couragiously and bid adieu to that lovely land of our Birth, that place where the young and old joined Together in one Common Union, both night and day Engaged in Innocent Amusement. But alas, I am now Told its the gulf of Misersry oppression Degradetion and Ruin of evry Discription which I am Sorry to hear of so Doleful a History to Be told of our Dr. Country. This my Dr. Father induces me to Remit to you in this Letter 20 Dollars . . . until you might Be Clearing away from that place all together and the Sooner the Better for Beleive me I could not Express how great would be my joy at seeing you all here Together where you would never be at a loss for a good Breakfast and Dinner.[37]

She continues by giving them suggestions about what tools and clothing to bring, advising her sisters not to worry, for she has clothes to fit them, but to "Bring Flannels and do not form it at home as the way Flannel at home and here is quite different . . . with the exception of whatever Quantity of Drawers you have you can make them at home. But make them Roomly Enough But Make No Jackets." She defers to her father's authority and better judgment by telling him that "Thade Houlehan wrote to me Saying that if I wished to go up the Country that he would send me money but I declined so doing until you Come and then after you Comeing if you think it may be Better for us to remain here or go west it will be for you to judge but until then I will Remain here." Obviously in touch with family friends in America, she recounts their belief that her father, sisters, and brothers will have no trouble securing work. She continues:

> I have Evry Reason to Believe that we will all do well Together So as that I am sure its not for Slavery I want you to Come here

> no its for affording My Brothers and Sisters An I an oppertunity of Showing our Kindness and Gratitude and Comeing on you Seniour days that we would be placed in that possision that you my Dr. Father and Mother could walk about Lesuirly and Indepenly without Requireing your Labour an object which I am Sure will not fail even by Myself if I was oblidged to do it without the assistance of Brother or Sister for my Dr. Father and Mother.

She suggests that "when you are Comeing here if you Possibly can Bring My Uncle Con I would Be Glad that you would and I am sure he would be of the greatest acquisision to you and also Tell Mary Keefe that if her Child died that I will pay her passage véry Shortly." She includes a list of family and friends to be remembered to:

> you will give Mr and Mrs Boyan my best love and respect And let me know how they and family are as they would or will not Be ever Better than I would wish them to be also Mrs Milton and Charles Mr and Mrs Roche and family Mr and Mrs Day and family Mr Walsh and as for his family I am sure are all well Mr and Mrs Sullivan and family Mrs OBrien Con Sheehan wife and family own Sullivan of Carriganes and family Darby Guinee and family John Calleghan and family Timothy Calleghan and family Timothy Sheehan and Mother.

She closes by saying, "I am in Raptures of joy when I think of one day Seeing you all at the dock in New York and if I do not have a good Bottle of Brandy for you Awaiting your arrival its a Causion."

Margaret McCarthy was only one of the millions of Irish immigrant women to come to America throughout the nineteenth century, but her response to her experiences was far from unique. Strong ties of duty and affection continued to endure in spite of the immigrant process. It might be said that the Irish were hardly breaking family ties by leaving Ireland—over five million Irish men and women emigrated during this period—they simply went to live with other members of their families or eventually managed to bring those temporarily left behind to join them in America.

Patterns of behavior of work, leisure, and family brought with them from Ireland continued to influence these immigrant women in mid-nineteenth-century New York. Their experience in Ireland as farm laborers, domestic servants, seamstresses, hawkers, pedlars, and factory hands provided some preparation for their work experience in America. Family and kinship ties, while strained by emigration, continued to endure. Music, dance, and leisure patterns, while transformed on the streets of American cities, provided ties with their Old World experience. Uprooted physically from the land of their birth, their cultural roots continued to shape their responses and adaptation to their new environment. This process was true for the millions of immigrants and migrants to America's urban centers throughout the nineteenth and twentieth centuries. Only by studying the complex interaction between the culture they brought with them and the society which they entered can we begin to understand the "many pasts" of America.

NOTES

1. See, in particular, Herbert G. Gutman, "Work, Culture and Society in Industrializing America, 1815-1919," American Historical Review, 78 (June 1973), 531-588. On immigrant women, see, for example, Virginia Yans-McLaughlin, *Family and Community: Italian Immigrants in Buffalo, 1880-1930* (Ithaca, N.Y., 1977), ch. 7; and Daniel J. Walkowitz, *Worker City: Company Town* (Urbana, Ill., forthcoming), chs. 2, 4.

2. Quoted in Abram C. Dayton, *The Last Days of Knickerbocker Life in New York* (New York, 1897), 218.

3. Thomas W. Freeman, *Pre-Famine Ireland: A Study in Historical Geography* (Manchester, England, 1957), 54-58; Kenneth H. Connell, *The Population of Ireland, 1750-1845* (Oxford, England, 1950), 163-165, and Connell, "The Colonization of Waste Lands in Ireland, 1780-1845, "Economic History Review (2nd ser., 3; 1950-1951), 49; George O'Brien, *The Economic History of Ireland from the Union to the Famine* (London, 1921), 105; E. B. McDowell, "Ireland on the Eve of the Famine," in R. Dudley Edwards and T. Desmond Williams, *The Great Famine* (New York, 1957), 9; see, for the contemporary view, J. G. Kohl, *Travels in Ireland* (London, 1844), 25-26.

4. James Edmund Handley, *The Irish in Scotland, 1798-1845* (Cork, 1945), 37; Kohl, 34; Henry D. Inglis, *A Journey Throughout Ireland* (London, 1846), 373.

5. William Forbes Adams, *Ireland and the Irish Emigration to the New World from 1815 to the Famine* (New Haven, 1932), 66, 223; Robert E. Kennedy, *The Irish: Emigration, Marriage and Fertility* (Los Angeles, 1973), 84; Inglis, 103; G.R.C. Keep, "The Irish Migration to North America" (Ph.D. dissertation, University of Dublin, 1951), 22.

6. Connell, *The Population of Ireland*, 46-85; McDowell, 5; Freeman, 16; Edith Abbott, *Immigration* (Chicago, 1924), 85; Arthur Young, *A Tour in Ireland in 1776, 77, 8, 9* (3 vols.; Dublin, 1780) Vol. 2, 86-87; *Parliamentary Papers, 1830*. First, Second, and Third Reports of Evidence from the Select Committee on the Sate of the Poor in Ireland (London, 1831), Vol. 7, 34; Adams, 32; George Potter, *To the Golden Door* (Boston, 1960), 38; Inglis, 26; see, for the present day, Conrad Arensberg and Solon T. Kimball, *Family and Community in Ireland* (Cambridge, Mass., 1940), 150.

7. Diarmond OMuirithe, *A Seat Behind the Coachman: Travellers in Ireland, 1800-1900* (Dublin, 1972), 140.

8. Kennedy, 7, 84; Keep, 148.

9. Quoted in Franklin Fitzpatrick, "Irish Immigration into New York from 1865-1880" (M.A. thesis, Catholic University, 1948).

10. Computed from *Parliamentary Papers*. Report of the Commissioners to take the Census of Ireland for the Year 1841 (Dublin, 1843), Vol. 24, 440-446; *Parliamentary Papers*. Reports from Commissioners: The Census of Ireland for the Year 1851 (Dublin, 1856), Vol. 31, 634-636. For a comparison with other countries, see Joan W. Scott and Louis A. Tilly, "Women's Work in Nineteenth-Century Europe," Comparative Studies (1975), 36-64.

11. Mr. and Mrs. S. C. Hall, *Ireland: Its Scenery and Characters*, (3 vols.; London, 1843), Vol. 2, 320.

12. Adams, 59.

13. Keep, 25; Inglis, 389; Arthur Redford, *Labour Migration in England, 1800-1850* (New York, 1968), 150-164; Handley, 90-92.

14. *Parliamentary Papers*. Reports from Commissioners: 1851, Vol. 31, xcii-ci; Redford, 157.

15. *Irish American* (New York), February 11, 1860.

16. *New York Tribune*, June 8, 1853; Adams, op. cit. 49-53; Rober Ernst, *Immigrant Life in New York City, 1825-1863* (New York, 1949), 68-69.

17. William Sanger, *The History of Prostitution* (New York, 1859), 491, 523.

18. Judith R. Walkowitz and Daniel J. Walkowitz, "'We are not Beasts of the Field.' Prostitution and the Poor in Plymouth and Southampton Under the Contagious Diseases Act," in Mary S. Hartman and Lois Banner, eds., *Clio's Consciousness Raised: New Perspectives on the History of Women* (New York, 1974), 193.

19. George G. Foster, *New York in Slices: By an Experienced Carver* (New York, 1849), 22.

20. See my Ph.D. dissertation, " 'The Bloody Ould Sixth': A Social Analysis of a Mid-Nineteenth-Century New York City Working-Class Community" (University of Rochester, 1973), and "The Five Points Revisited: A Social Analysis of a New York City Slum" (article in progress).

21. Boarders paid an average of $1.25 per week according to the New York *Tribune*, March 7, 1845.

22. For further discussion, see my article, " 'She earns as a child, she pays as a man': Women Workers in Mid-Nineteenth-Century New York," in Milton Cantor and Bruce Laurie, eds., *Sex and the Woman Worker* (Westport, Conn., 1977).

23. Names and other information from the manuscript schedules of the New York State Census for 1855, located at the County Clerk's Office, New York City. *Monthly Records of the Five Points House of Industry*, 1 (January 1858), 233; contemporary descriptions of Irish fairs can be found in Otway, 1966; Inglis, 54; Kohl, 43, 195.

24. Otway, 166.

25. Marriage Records of the Church of the Transfiguration, 1853-1860, located at 23 Mott Street, New York City.

26. Quoted in Michael and Ariane Batterberry, *On the Town in New York From 1776 to the Present* (New York, 1958), 96; see also David Grimsted, *Melodrama Unveiled: American Theater and Culture, 1800-1850* (Chicago, 1968), 46-75; John Thornbury, "Players and Play-Goers Twenty Five Years Ago," The Galaxy, 21 (May, 1876), 171, 582-586; George C. D. Odell, *Annals of the New York Stage, 1843-1850* (New York, 1931), vol. 5, 108, 373; Arthur H. Quinn, *A History of the American Drama From the Beginning to the Civil War* (2nd ed.; New York, 1943), 305; Bernard Hewitt, *Theatre U.S.A., 1668 to 1957* (New York, 1959), 116, 121-122, 145-147.

27. Batterberry and Batterberry, 104.

28. *Monthly Record of the Five Points House of Industry*, 1 (1857), 147-149; Junius Henri Browne, *The Great Metropolis: A Mirror of New York* (Hartford, Conn., 1869), 278-279; George G. Foster, *New York By Gaslight* (New York, 1849), 72-81; William M. Bobo, *Glimpses of New York* (New York, 1852), 96-97; Samuel I. Prime, *Life in New York* (New York, 1847), 174-176; Alvin F. Harlow, *Old Bowery Days: The Chronicles of a Famous Street* (New York, 1931), 272-277; Willis L. Turner, "City Low-Life on the American Stage to 1900" (Ph.D. dissertation, University of Illinois, 1956), 121.

29. Charles Dickens, *American Notes* (London, 1842), 99.

30. OMuirithe, 64; see also Inglis, 225-232.

31. See Arensberg and Kimball, 36-39, for present-day examples.

32. All examples are from the 1855 New York State Census and the Marriage Records of the Church of the Transfiguration, cited above. Quote cited in the *Annual Report of the City Inspector of the Number of Deaths and Interments in the City of New York for the Year 1851* (New York, 1852), 448-450.

33. The Parliamentary studies of the poor in Ireland in the 1830s and 1840s suggest that a son usually set up a separate household, often near his parents, when he married. See also Connell, *The Population of Ireland*, 56.

34. The Marriage Records of the Church of the Transfiguration, cited above.

35. See my Ph.D. dissertation, ch. 3.

36. In Michael Anderson's study, *Family Structure in Nineteenth-Century Lancashire* (Cambridge, England, 1971), 139-140, about 86% of old people lived with relatives. Since almost half of his sample was Preston-born, and the majority of the non-Preston-born emigrated from less than 30 miles away, the similarity in his findings with that of New York City is highly significant.

37. Quoted in OMuirithe, 138-142. Original spelling, punctuation, and capitalization retained.

Female Labor Force Participation: The Origin of Black and White Differences, 1870 and 1880

Claudia Goldin

THE participation rate of women in the American labor force increased dramatically over the period 1890 to 1970, and the jump from 18.9 percent to 42.6 percent indicated to one observer "a genuine revolution, not only in the lives of women, but in the American economy and the American family as well."[1] Aggregate figures such as these, however, disguise important underlying changes within various racial and marital groups. (See Table 1.) Although the extensive participation of white women is a recent phenomenon, the same is not true of their black counterparts. The labor force participation for white women more than doubled between 1890 and 1960, increasing from 16.3 percent to 33.7 percent, while that for non-white women remained almost constant (39.7 percent to 41.7 percent). The most impressive labor market gains during this period were achieved by married white women, who increased their participation rate by over ten times. Although married non-white women also entered the labor force over these years, single non-white women exited as they increasingly were able to afford education and to enjoy the leisure of youth. Therefore the revolutionary increase in the participation of women in the labor force mainly involved whites. Black women had been abundantly represented in the labor market as slaves and had remained so as freed persons.

Many of the reasons for the dissimilar historical experiences of married black and white women are evident. Throughout this period black husbands have had lower labor income and higher unemployment than white husbands, and non-labor income for blacks has also been less than that for whites. Black male mortality has been higher

Journal of Economic History, Vol. XXXVII, No. 1 (March 1977).

The author gratefully acknowledges the help of her colleagues Roger Gordon and Harvey Rosen. Stanley Engerman, Joseph Reid, Hugh Rockoff, Richard Sutch and Harold Woodman commented on an earlier version. Peter Greenhalgh and Hope Reisman laboriously copied and coded information from the census manuscripts, Linda Johnson provided expert research assistance, and Brian Carney helped with the programming. National Science Foundation grant No. SOC75-13630 supported this work by providing funds for research and computation.

[1] Robert W. Smuts, *Women and Work in America* (New York: Columbia University Press, 1959), p. 1.

TABLE 1
FEMALE LABOR FORCE PARTICIPATION RATES BY MARITAL STATUS, RACE, AND NATIVITY, 1890 TO 1970

	(1)	(2)	(3)	(4)	(5)	(6)	(7)	(8)	(9)
	≥ 16 Years Old					≥ 15 Years Old		≥	≥ 16
	1890	1900	1910[a]	1920	1930	1940	1950	1960	1970
Total	18.9	20.6	25.4	23.7	24.8	25.8	29.0	34.5	42.6
Married	4.6	5.6	10.7	9.0	11.7	13.8	21.6	30.7	40.8
Single	40.5	43.5	51.1	46.4	50.5	45.5	46.3	42.9	53.0
White	16.3	17.8		21.6	23.7	24.5	28.1	33.7	41.9
Married	2.5	3.2		6.5	9.8	12.5	20.7	29.8	39.7
Single	38.4	41.5		45.0	48.7	45.9	47.5	43.9	54.5
Nonwhite	39.7	43.2		43.1	43.3	37.6	37.1	41.7	48.5
Married	22.5	26.0		32.5	33.2	27.3	31.8	40.6	52.5
Single	59.5	60.5		58.8	52.1	41.9	36.1	35.8	43.6
Foreign Born	19.8				19.1				
Married	3.0				8.5				
Single	70.8				73.8				

[a] The 1910 labor force figures are too high relative to those for other years because the census reported certain women employed in agriculture as in the labor force rather than at home.

Notes:

Definition of Labor Force: The precise definition of the labor force changed over the period 1890 to 1970. Gertrude Bancroft discusses some of these problems in Appendix C, "Some Problems of Concepts and Measurement," in *The American Labor Force: Its Growth and Changing Composition* (N.Y.: John Wiley and Sons, 1958).

The largest bias entering this table probably relates to the time period during which the respondent could be at work and still be considered in the labor force. The 1890 to 1930 data will overcount the labor force, in relation to the 1940 to 1970 data, to the extent that people enter and leave the labor force during the year. The former figures will include anyone in the labor force during the *year* preceding the census, whereas the latter will include those in the labor force during the *week* preceding the census. However, a mitigating influence is that the 1890 to 1930 figures will not include an unemployed person in the labor force unless that person specifically listed an occupation.

Marital Status: Definition of married in columns (1), (2), (3), (4), and (5) is married, spouse present or absent. That for (6), (7), (8), and (9) is married, spouse present. Definition of single in columns (1), (2), (3), and (5) is single and unknown. That for (4) is single, widowed, divorced, and unknown, and that for (6), (7), (8), and (9) is just single.

Race: White refers to all white, including foreign born, except for (5) where it excludes foreign born. Nonwhite includes Chinese, Japanese, and "civilized Indians" for (1), (6), (7), (8), and (9).

Sources: (1) *Eleventh Census of the U.S.: 1890, Parts I and II* (Washington: G.P.O., 1897).

(2) *Twelfth Census of the U.S.: 1900, Supplementary Analysis and Derivative Tables* (Washington: G.P.O., 1906).

(2), (3), (5) *Fifteenth Census of the U.S.: 1930, Occupational Statistics, Abstract Summary for the U.S.* (Washington: G.P.O., 1932).

(4) *Fourteenth Census of the U.S.: 1920, Vol. IV, Occupations* (Washington: G.P.O., 1933).

(5) *Fifteenth Census of the U.S.: 1930, Population, Vol. V, General Report on Occupations* (Washington: G.P.O., 1933).

(6), (7) *Special Reports: Employment and Personal Characteristics, U.S. Census of Population: 1950* (Washington: G.P.O., 1963).

(8) *Subject Reports: Employment Status and Work Experience, U.S. Census of Population: 1960* (Washington: G.P.O., 1963).

(9) U.S. Dept. of Labor, Bureau of Labor Statistics, *Special Labor Force Report No. 129: Employment and Unemployment in 1970* (Washington: G.P.O., 1971).

than that for whites, and, for other reasons as well, the female-headed family has been more prevalent among blacks.

Much has been learned about the determinants of female labor force participation from research using contemporary (post-1940) data. The presence of preschool children, a woman's education and training, the level of non-labor income, and the husband's unemployment experience have emerged as primary factors. Most importantly, almost all studies have found striking differences between the responses of black and white women to the same environmental and family variables. Black women participate more than whites even when sharing the same characteristics. Differences in family life cycles, discrimination in the housing and labor markets, and measurement problems in valuing part-time labor are among the suggested explanations for this intriguing finding.[2] Data constraints have unfortunately prevented a thorough study of the historical antecedents to these contemporary racial differences.[3] Without extensive research in primary sources, we can record women's labor history only from 1890 to the present and can analyze it extensively only for the period beginning in 1940.[4]

[2] William G. Bowen and T. Aldrich Finegan, *The Economics of Labor Force Participation* (Princeton: Princeton University Press, 1969) is a very comprehensive study which includes an examination of black and white female labor. Bowen and Finegan emphasize differences in marital stability and the problem of part-time service labor in explaining why black women work more than whites even after accounting for age, schooling, other family income, children, and the employment status of the husband. Glen G. Cain, *Married Women in the Labor Force: An Economic Analysis* (Chicago: University of Chicago Press, 1966) finds that black and white women respond differently in their labor force participation to the presence of preschoolers but that this might be explained by both the greater availability of other family members and different living situations. James A. Sweet, *Women in the Labor Force* (N.Y.: Seminar Press, 1973) suggests discrimination in both the housing and male job markets as well as differences in family stability as explanations for the diverse labor force experiences of black and white women in his sample. Duran Bell, "Why Participation Rates of Black and White Wives Differ," *Journal of Human Resources*, 9 (Fall 1974), 465-79, uses more recent data than Bowen and Finegan and gets somewhat different results. Bell still finds that "if black wives had white characteristics, they would work more, not less" than whites (p. 478), but attributes some of the difference to discrimination in the "high-status employment" of white women. Robert E. Hall, "Wages, Income, and Hours of Work in the U.S. Labor Force," Chapter 3 in G. Cain and H. Watts, eds., *Income Maintenance and Labor Supply* (Chicago: Rand McNally, 1973) summarizes many of the theoretical problems in estimating labor supply functions, particularly that of determining wages for persons who are out of the labor force. Hall also finds that black women respond differently than whites to family, economic, and environmental factors. There are many other excellent articles on labor supply in general and the participation of black and white women—by Boskin, Kosters, Ashenfelter, Mincer and H. Rosen—but the above list includes those that are most germane to this work.

[3] Studies which have attempted to explain the change in female labor force participation through time include Clarence D. Long, *The Labor Force Under Changing Income and Employment* (Princeton: Princeton University Press for the National Bureau of Economic Research, 1958), and John Durand, *The Labor Force in the U.S., 1890 to 1960* (N.Y.: Social Science Research Council, 1948).

[4] There are several recent papers dealing with female labor force participation and family

In the present essay I attempt to push back these frontiers; my hope is that research on the labor force experience of black women directly following their emancipation will reveal both slavery's effect on racial differences at that time and its impact through time. It is possible that the differences in socialization between antebellum southern black and white women are reflected in their late-nineteenth-century labor experiences. The results of these differing socialization processes may have been dissipated through time as succeeding generations of black and white women became more removed from the experiences of their ancestors. Social factors serving to stigmatize work can, however, be resistant to change and could have lingered for many years.[5] Furthermore, higher participation rates for black women could have influenced both the structure of the black family and migration patterns, thereby reinforcing the initial labor force differences. Although the black family during the twentieth century may have been changed by the urban setting, the black response to urbanization itself may have been conditioned by the slave experience—more precisely by the greater willingness of black

structure in the late nineteenth century, almost all relying heavily on the manuscripts of the Federal Population Census. Elizabeth Pleck, "A Mother's Wages: A Comparison of Income Earning Among Urban Black and Italian Wives, 1896-1911," in Milton Cantor, *History of American Working Women* (forthcoming) examines why the labor force participation of black and Italian wives differed and suggests many variables, but employs no rigorous tests. Pleck finds an unexplained differential in Italian and black labor force participation and concludes that "cultural norms, economic pressures, and demographic conditions all played a part in determining the choice between work and family for Italian and black wives in American cities. For black women cultural attitudes favored responding to the family's economic need and the offer of higher wage rates, while for Italian wives cultural values took precedence over economic need except under circumstances of high wage rates for female labor." Herbert Gutman, "Persistent Myths About the American Negro Family," *Journal of Interdisciplinary History*, 6 (Autumn 1975), 181-210, concludes that "slavery and quasi-freedom imposed countless burdens upon American blacks, but the high proportion of two-parent households found among them between 1855 and 1880 tells how little is yet known about the slave family structure, its relationship to the dominant white family structure, and the ways in which freedmen and freedwomen adapted, transformed, retained, or rejected older forms of family life." Frank Furstenberg et al., "The Origins of the Female-Headed Black Family: The Destructive Impact of the Urban Experience," *Journal of Interdisciplinary History*, 6 (Autumn 1975), 211-34, use data from Philadelphia to evaluate whether "slavery resulted in a permanent deterioration of the black family structure" and whether "family structure accounts for economic disadvantage." John Blassingame, "Before the Ghetto: The Making of the Black Community in Savannah, Georgia, 1865-1880," *Journal of Social History*, 6 (Summer 1973) gives a general social history of blacks and whites in Reconstruction Savannah. His *Black New Orleans 1860-1880* (Chicago: University of Chicago Press, 1973), Chapter 4 explores some data on female-headed families and female labor force participation. Michael R. Haines, "Industrial Work and the Family Cycle, 1889-1890," (mimeo, April 1976) analyzes the labor force participation of the wives and children of industrial workers using the records of the commissioner of labor.

[5] Valerie Kincade Oppenheimer, *The Female Labor Force in the U.S.: Demographic and Economic Factors Governing Its Growth and Changing Composition*, Population Monograph Series, No. 5 (University of California, Berkeley, 1969) discusses the social stigmatization of women's work in the twentieth century.

women to work for pay. These are bold conjectures, but they point to the importance of studying the post-emancipation black and white woman. In the present essay I examine the labor record of black and white women in 1870 and 1880 both to extend our historical knowledge of this subject and to develop explanations for the long-run differences between these two groups.

THE SAMPLE

General description

In order to compute the labor force participation of women in 1870 and 1880 the manuscripts of the United States Population Census have been sampled and to enable an analysis of these data to be made, economic and demographic variables have been coded. Although the compilers of the 1870 and 1880 Federal Population Censuses collected data on occupation and family structure by race and by sex, they did not analyze this information. Fortunately the original data are preserved in the census manuscript collection of the National Archives, and this paper is based on research using these documents. Only cities have been sampled for this study because such data allow a richer analysis than those for rural areas.[6] Families or households from seven southern cities—Atlanta, Charleston, Richmond, Mobile, New Orleans, Norfolk, and Savannah—were randomly selected.[7] Information on sex, age, race, marital status (for 1880), health, literacy, occupation, months unemployed (for 1880), wealth (for 1870), nativity, parents' nativity, and the presence of boarders and servants was coded for each selected individual. In total, 5,130 persons were sampled in 1870 and 5,314 in 1880, with blacks comprising 45 percent

[6] It would be very difficult to explain the divergent labor market experiences of black and white women in agriculture whose husbands all listed the identical occupation of "farmer." A future study will analyze similar data from rural counties to enable broader conclusions to be drawn and correct for possible biases in this regionally sampled data set.

[7] One in fifty pages from the census manuscripts were sampled for all cities except New Orleans, for which one in two hundred were used. All persons, though, have been weighted equally in the analysis. This weighting procedure was used because New Orleans was a disproportionately large city, accounting for 20 percent of the total southern urban population (excluding Kentucky, Missouri, and Maryland) in 1880. Weighting by this factor reduced to 19 percent the percentage of the population accounted for by New Orleans in 1880. Complete households were taken even if they ran over to a succeeding page. This eliminated the bias toward small households inherent in a strict page sampling procedure.

Because information on sex and age was not compiled for cities in the Federal Population Censuses for 1870 and 1880 one cannot determine the biases in these sampled data. I plan to expand this sample and also use those collected by others to ascertain this important information. The more expanded data set will sample more heavily from the non-seaboard urban South.

in 1870 and 41 percent in 1880. Information on 792 families with both spouses present in 1870 and 813 in 1880 is contained in this sample.

There were, in 1860, nearly four million slaves in the South and over one-quarter million free blacks. Barely 5 percent of all slaves resided in cities and towns of over 2,500 persons, although about one-third of the free blacks had urban residences.[8] By 1870 8.8 percent of all southern blacks lived in cities and most southern cities had become almost one-half black. Blacks had migrated within the South during and directly following the Civil War—many following Union troops for protection and rations; some reuniting with friends and family; and others using their new freedom to escape the rigor of the farm, at least for a while. Some southern cities grew enormously during the period from 1860 to 1870, and almost every large city increased its proportion of black persons. (See Table 2.) Atlanta, for example, doubled in population over these ten years mainly because its black populace quintupled. The migration of freedmen at the close of the war did not continue long beyond 1870, and the growth of the urban black population moderated considerably during the next ten years. Although blacks migrated within the South, barely a trickle entered the North before 1900 and over 90 percent of all blacks in both 1870 and 1880 resided in the South.

The migration of blacks from the farm to the cities was probably selective. Those who had the desire to work for wages left the countryside and entered towns. Women, especially those who were single, divorced, and widowed, went to the cities to seek employment because they were effectively prohibited from renting farm land. This movement of labor indicates that some information in this sample is particular to the cities. Unmarried females are, for example, overrepresented, and thus one cannot make simplistic comparisons of family structure between the city and the countryside. This is one problem inherent in any regionally sampled data set.

The variables suggested by contemporary labor force studies are used in this paper to analyze the participation of married black and white women during 1870 and 1880. These variables include both economic characteristics, such as family labor income and wealth, and demographic data, such as the wife's age, and the presence of young children. (See Table 3.) These variables are described below for the individuals and families in the sample, and, in the analysis which follows, their interrelationships will become more apparent.

[8] See Claudia Goldin, *Urban Slavery in the American South* (Chicago: University of Chicago Press, 1976), Table 1, p. 12.

TABLE 2
BLACK AND WHITE POPULATIONS IN SEVEN SOUTHERN CITIES, 1860-1890

	1860			*1870*			*1880*			*1890*		
	White	*Percentage Black*	*Black*	*White*	*Percentage Black*	*Black*	*White*	*Percentage Black*	*Black*	*White*	*Percentage Black*	*Black*
Atlanta	7,615	20 percent	1,939	11,860	46 percent	9,929	21,079	44 percent	16,330	37,416	43 percent	28,117
Charleston	23,376	42 percent	17,146	22,749	53 percent	26,173	22,699	55 percent	27,276	23,919	56 percent	31,036
Mobile	20,854	29 percent	8,404	18,115	43 percent	13,919	16,885	42 percent	12,240	17,429	44 percent	13,647
New Orleans	144,601	14 percent	24,074	140,923	26 percent	50,456	158,367	27 percent	57,617	177,376	27 percent	64,663
Norfolk	10,290	30 percent	4,330	10,462	46 percent	8,766	11,808	46 percent	10,068	18,617	47 percent	16,254
Richmond	23,635	38 percent	14,275	27,928	45 percent	23,110	35,765	44 percent	27,832	49,034	40 percent	32,354
Savannah	13,875	38 percent	8,417	15,166	46 percent	13,068	15,041	51 percent	15,654	20,211	53 percent	22,978

Sources: C.D. Goldin, *Urban Slavery in the American South* (Chicago, 1976), pp. 52-53; *Statistics of the Population of the U.S. at the Tenth Census* (Washington, 1883), p. 416; *Eleventh Census of the U.S., 1890, Part II* (Washington, 1897), Table 118.

TABLE 3
AGE DISTRIBUTION BY RACE AND SEX, 1870 AND 1880
(for seven southern cities)

Age	*Black*		*White*	
1870	*Female*	*Male*	*Female*	*Male*
0-4	9.4 percent	13.2 percent	12.0 percent	13.2 percent
5-9	9.5	10.7	11.0	9.9
10-14	12.4	13.0	10.8	10.8
15-19	10.2	9.5	10.6	10.4
20-29	21.4	18.2	20.7	19.1
30-39	13.7	15.0	13.8	13.8
40-49	11.2	10.5	10.9	12.0
50-64	8.2	7.1	8.0	8.9
over 64	3.9	2.8	2.2	1.8
No. in sample	1,292	1,030	1,476	1,332
1880				
0-4	9.8	13.2	9.9	10.8
5-9	10.2	14.0	10.8	11.4
10-14	10.2	11.9	10.1	10.4
15-19	9.3	8.5	11.3	9.1
20-29	21.9	14.6[a]	20.6	20.4
30-39	16.0	14.4	13.8	14.0
40-49	8.9	13.2	10.5	11.8
50-64	10.0	7.9	9.8	9.4
over 64	3.8	2.4	3.3	2.7
No. in sample	1,226	958	1,643	1,487

[a] Even though age distributions by sex were not substantially different for blacks and whites in 1870, they had become considerably altered by 1880. Black males between the ages of 20 to 29 comprised only 14.6 percent of their group, whereas 20.4 percent of white males were between these ages. This short-fall in the number of black males was so high that black women in this age category outnumbered black men by almost two to one. Although it is possible that this imbalance was caused by the selective migration of single black women, it is also possible that there was an undercount of single black men in that age category.

Source: Manuscripts of the U.S. Population Census. See text for a complete description of the sampling procedure.

Economic variables

The most striking differences between blacks and whites in these data involve economic variables. Black women participated in the labor force on average three times more than did white women, and married black women averaged almost six times the rate of married white females. (See Table 4.) Single black women across all age categories labored more in 1880 than in 1870, and by 1880 their participation rate was 73.3 percent, an increase in that decade of ten percentage points. The rate for single white women was about the same for the two years. Both married black women and married white women participated more in 1880 than in 1870 (the figure for the

TABLE 4
FEMALE LABOR FORCE PARTICIPATION BY RACE, MARITAL STATUS, AND AGE, 1870 AND 1880
(for seven southern cities)

	Single		*Married*		*Other*[a]		*All Marital Groups*	
Age	*Black*	*White*	*Black*	*White*	*Black*	*White*	*Black*	*White*
1870								
15-19	51.8 percent	17.4 percent	13.3 percent	0.0[c] percent	33.3[c] percent	0.0[c] percent	47.0 percent	16.6 percent
20-29	74.4	37.8	27.2	3.0	76.7	25.0	55.2	18.4
30-39	42.9	12.5	38.6	4.0	72.5	46.4	52.0	18.7
40-49	—[b]	33.3	34.5	4.0	65.6	29.1	47.6	13.2
50-64	—[b]	0.0[c]	19.4	10.3	54.7	16.7	44.3	14.4
over 64	—[b]	—[b]	28.6[c]	0.0[c]	34.1	12.0	33.3	9.7
All ages	63.4	26.4	31.0	4.0	60.3	27.9	49.5	16.5
1880								
15-19	58.7	17.5	33.3	13.3	100.0[c]	—[b]	57.0	17.2
20-29	80.7	28.7	32.3	5.5	78.1	48.3	57.5	20.5
30-39	80.6	28.2	38.8	8.3	78.0	53.5	55.3	20.3
40-49	90.5	35.3	33.3	8.2	81.3	26.3	58.9	17.0
50-64	87.5[c]	8.3	38.8	7.5	51.5	22.1	48.8	16.3
over 64	—[b]	33.3[c]	28.6[c]	0.0[c]	46.2	2.4[c]	43.5	5.6
All ages	73.3	23.8	35.4	7.3	65.0	27.9	55.1	18.1

[a] Includes married spouse absent, divorced, widowed, and all ambiguous cases for 1870. The 1870 manuscripts did not contain marital status, and it had to be inferred from information on last name, age, and the presence of other family members.
[b] Empty cells
[c] Less than ten persons in the cell
Source: Manuscripts of the U.S. Population Census. See text for a complete description of the sampling procedure.

latter group rose from 4.0 percent to 7.3 percent). Widowed and divorced black women also increased their rate of participation, although white women in this group did not.

The impressive change in the participation by single black women in these seven cities between 1870 and 1880 can be explained conjecturally by two very different theories. The increase might have reflected a migration to the cities of those desiring work. These women might have become live-in domestics for urban white families, although the occupational data in this sample do not substantiate this thesis.[9] A second possibility is that this increase in participation indicates a change in the work habits of those already in the city. Black women may have withdrawn their labor directly following emancipation but then reentered the labor force after a short period of adjustment.[10]

Black women as a group labored more intensively than whites but occupied lower paying positions. (See Table 5.) They were abundantly represented in the ranks of the unskilled. About 10 to 15 percent of those over nine years old were laundresses—women who generally worked at home, taking in clothes and working by the piece—and between 19 to 23 percent were servants, 70 to 75 percent of whom lived in the home of their employer. Cooks, nurses, and seamstresses were also among the more common occupations. Few black women were proprietors and clerical workers, and variety in employment for black women was limited, in part due to the lack of a large manufacturing sector in the urban South.

Black men were also more prevalent in the labor force in comparison with whites. Only 4.8 percent of all black males over 14 years old stated that they were not working, whereas 8.5 percent of white males declared no occupation. Black males were, however, subject to more unemployment, on average 3 weeks per year as compared to 1.6 weeks for whites who listed an occupation. Black men also had lower paying occupations than whites. They were abundantly represented in the unskilled category but few appear in professional, clerical, and proprietary employments. They were, though, about equally represented in the skilled trades, which included carpentry, masonry,

[9] Data on servants show a decrease from 1870 to 1880 in the percentage of black women who were live-in domestics.

[10] Roger Ransom and Richard Sutch, *One Kind of Freedom, The Economic Consequences of Emancipation* (New York: Cambridge University Press, forthcoming) discuss the withdrawal of black female and child labor directly after emancipation and claim that the period of readjustment was over by 1868.

TABLE 5
FEMALE OCCUPATIONAL DISTRIBUTION
(percentage over nine years old in seven southern cities)

	Black		White	
	1870	*1880*	*1870*	*1880*
No occupation[a]	18.8 percent	16.2 percent	26.0 percent	26.4 percent
At home	36.4	33.8	59.6	58.1
Servant	23.3	18.8	5.7	3.5
Laundress	10.5	14.7	0.4[f]	0.6
Cook	2.4	5.5	0.2[f]	0.5
Unskilled[b]	3.4	3.6	0.4[f]	0.6
Prostitute	0.1[f]	—[e]	0.1[f]	0.7
Nurse	1.8	2.1	0.1[f]	0.2
Seamstress, milliner	3.1	3.7	5.4	6.1
Semiskilled[c]	0.1[f]	—[e]	—[e]	0.2[f]
Skilled[d]	—[e]	0.4[f]	0.2[f]	—[e]
Clerical, teacher	0.1[f]	0.7	0.4[f]	2.1
Proprietor, boardinghouse keeper	—[e]	0.4[f]	1.6	1.1

[a] "No occupation" and "at home" differ only slightly in interpretation. "At home" was listed as the occupation for persons the census taker believed were old enough to have an occupation. "No occupation" was listed for those who were very young or very old, and a blank was given for those who were young.

[b] Includes laborers, packers, porters, janitors, milkwomen, agricultural laborers, peddlers, and so on.

[c] Includes manufacturing workers giving a precise occupation (not "laborer"), and hairdressers.

[d] Includes apprentices, painters, and bookbinders.

[e] Empty cell

[f] Less than five persons in a cell

Source: Manuscripts of the U.S. Population Census. See text for a complete description of the sampling procedure.

cabinet making, painting, and so on. This "legacy of slavery" was especially pronounced in Charleston, where most artisans, even by 1890, were black.[11] On balance, however, slavery's legacy was to weight occupations toward the lower end of the wage and class spectrum; on net, black men and women swelled the ranks of the lesser skilled.

Family labor income is determined by two variables—the potential wage of family members and their labor force participation.[12] Blacks had much higher rates of participation than whites but lower occupational skills, and thus black family labor incomes were considerably less than those for whites. Blacks had 57.8 percent of white family

[11] Claudia Goldin, *Urban Slavery in the American South* discusses the extensive use of slave artisans in antebellum cities. The Epilogue of that book summarizes what became of these skills after 1865.

[12] A family is defined here as consisting of at least a husband and a wife. The term "labor income" is used because income from property is, for the most part, excluded.

TABLE 6
MEAN FAMILY LABOR INCOME BY RACE, 1870 and 1880
(for seven southern cities)

	Total	*Per Capita*	*Mean Family Size*
Black			
1870	558.4	178.6	3.58
1880	547.8 (584)[a]	172.0 (184)	3.78
White			
1870	966.1	259.1	4.17
1880	915.4 (936)	247.2 (254)	4.31

[a] Figures in parentheses are labor income assuming months unemployed equalled zero. This enables comparisons with 1870 for which no unemployment data were available.
Note: Family labor income was computed by assigning monthly wages rates to occupations, multiplying by 12 minus months unemployed, and adding together the husband's, wife's, and children's components. The wage rates used are based on contemporary sources and vary by sex and age, with children under 15 years given half the adult wage for their occupation. These data are available from the author and are in an Appendix: *Wages for Various Occupations, 1870 and 1880*. The absolute value of family income is not necessarily correct. Families are defined here as married persons with both husband and wife present.
Source: Manuscripts of the U.S. Population Census. See text for a complete description of the sampling procedure.

labor income in 1870 and 62.4 percent in 1880. (See Table 6.) On a per capita basis black families fared slightly better, and each family member received 68.9 percent of a white's per capita labor income in 1870 and 74.4 percent in 1880. The mean family wealth of whites in this sample was about $1,500, the median $390 and the distribution was right skewed with 45.5 percent of the families reporting no wealth in excess of $100. Black families, not surprisingly, had very little wealth—far less than their current labor incomes might indicate—with over 85 percent reporting none over $100. The sample mean was $125 and the median only $40, even though fully 6 percent had managed to accumulate over $500. Later censuses do not contain information on wealth, and although the extent of asset accumulation by blacks from 1870 to 1880 could not have been substantial, the percentage of black male proprietors in the sample rose from 6.6 percent to 10.1 percent of the total.

Black and white family income varied differentially over the husband's age and the components of family income also differed by race. The white husband's income tended to peak around the age of 40 to 49 years, and although the average black husband reached a maximum income at approximately the same age, the peak was considerably less pronounced.[13] This pattern could reflect an occupa-

[13] The age-income profile for black males in 1870 is even flatter.

tional structure for blacks that changed less with their age, but it probably indicates that younger cohorts were entering better occupations. Black women contributed to family income over the full lifetime of their husbands, supplementing their lessened earning power in later years. Black children within each age group participated in the labor force more than did white youngsters, but somewhat paradoxically, black children on average worked less than whites—13.4 percent of all black children had occupations in 1880 compared with 17.5 percent for white children. This difference results from the earlier withdrawal of children over twenty years old from the urban black family. The age structure of children living with families therefore accounts for the surprising finding that although black children had high participation rates by age they contributed little to family income.

Demographic variables

Although there is an extensive literature that stresses the demographic contrasts between the black and white family, these data do not reveal many differences.[14] Black and white women were equally represented across the various marital categories. (See Table 7.) The percentage of black families with children which were headed by a female was identical to that for whites in 1880. Approximately 30 percent of all two-parent and female-parent families with at least one child were headed by a female, for both blacks and whites.[15] These data, of course, cannot alone refute the tale of black family instability, because they do not contain information on past marriages. But they

[14] E. Franklin Frazier, *The Negro Family in the U.S.*, rev. ed. (Chicago: University of Chicago Press, 1969), popularized the notion that the twentieth-century matrifocal black urban family was a product of slavery. Gutman, "Persistent Myths About the American Negro Family," and Furstenberg et al., "The Origins of the Female-Headed Black Family," are two excellent reexaminations and challenges to Frazier's work.

[15] A female-headed family is defined as a woman with at least one child, and a two-parent family is one with both husband and wife and at least one child. These distinctions get around the problem of using the census marshal's determination of "head of household," and use, instead, an operational definition. Note that families with only a father or a male head with a child have been excluded. It is difficult to contrast these results with those of Gutman and Furstenberg. See Gutman, "Persistent Myths . . . ," and Furstenberg et al., "The Origins of the Female-Headed Black Family." Both the Gutman and Furstenberg data are grouped by households and not by nuclear families. A widowed mother living with her parents, for example, would not be counted in these data sets. Furthermore Gutman includes as households individuals who live alone and childless couples. Therefore a high proportion of single persons without children or childless couples could distort his findings.

My results appear to indicate a higher percentage of female-headed families in the cities than in rural areas for both blacks and whites. This is not a surprising finding considering the selective migration of such individuals from the countryside to the city in search of jobs and relatives.

TABLE 7
MARITAL STATUS BY SEX AND RACE, 1870 AND 1880
(for seven southern cities)

	Single		*Married*		*Other*[a]	
	White	*Black*	*White*	*Black*	*White*	*Black*
1870						
Female	53.3 percent	50.9 percent	30.2 percent	27.2 percent	16.5 percent	21.8 percent
Male	57.9	57.9	33.3	34.1	8.9	8.1
No. of obs.[b]	787 (771)	658 (596)	446 (443)	352 (351)	243 (118)	282 (83)
1880						
Female	55.8	52.4	28.1	29.5	16.1	18.0
Male	62.9	58.6	31.4	37.4	5.6	4.1
No. of obs.[b]	917 (936)	643 (561)	461 (467)	362 (358)	265 (84)	221 (39)

[a] Includes widowed, divorced, married spouse absent, and any ambiguous cases for 1870. The population census did not report family relationships for 1870 and marital status had to be inferred from other information, such as the similar age of a male and female with identical last names. Marital status was coded as unknown when it was ambiguous, and the unknown category has been grouped with "other" in this table. Black women outnumbered white women in this group, and this reflects part of the transition from slavery to freedom. Directly following the Civil War black women and men reunited and those who had been recently married as freedmen were in the process of changing their last names. By 1880 this process appears to have been completed because all marital groups were equally represented by race.

[b] Number of observations. Figures for males are in parentheses.

Source: Manuscripts of the U.S. Population Census. See text for a complete description of the sampling procedure.

do reveal that urban black children in 1880 experienced the presence of a two-parent family in the same proportion as did white children.

Black urban families in this sample were smaller on average than were white families—there were 1.78 black children per two-parent family in 1880 but 2.31 white.[16] Black fertility, however—measured by children 0 to 4 years old per thousand women 15 to 44—was not correspondingly lower. Black fertility exceeded that for whites in this sample for 1870 (258 versus 213) and equalled it for 1880 (262 versus 261).[17] Although black fertility was somewhat higher, it is compatible with smaller family size because black infant mortality was probably greater and black children exited from their nuclear families at an earlier age than white children. The percentage of all children living at home who were over 19 years old was 17.1 percent for whites but

[16] Note that this is the mean number of children per nuclear family, not per household. Families here can include childless couples but are defined as having both husband and wife present.

[17] This decline in black fertility continued, and by 1910 the white figure considerably exceeded that for blacks in the urban South. See Stanley Engerman, "Changes in Black Fertility, 1880-1940," (mimeo, July 1974) for a description and some analysis of the decline in black fertility after 1880.

only 8.2 percent for blacks. There is no obvious explanation for this difference, but it seems likely that older white children were still at home because they could be more dependent on their parents' income and wealth and had higher rates of school attendance than did their black counterparts.

AN ANALYSIS OF MARRIED WOMEN IN THE LABOR FORCE: RACIAL DIFFERENCES

Married black and white women have had different labor force participation rates throughout American history. The difference during the period up to 1865 can be explained by the institution of slavery, and much after that date can also be attributed to the slave experience. This "legacy of slavery" has been both economic and social, both direct and indirect. Slavery directly affected the labor force participation of newly freed blacks by altering their economic earning power. By lowering the husband's earnings, slavery directly induced black wives to enter the labor force, and lower parents' income meant that more black children worked. The almost total lack of wealth among black families implied that unemployment of the primary worker, usually the husband, was a harsh reality which doubtless forced other family members into the labor force.

The slave experience also had an indirect or social impact. Black women were conditioned by slavery to laboring—work for pay was less socially stigmatizing to them than it was to white women. As Carter G. Woodson, in his article on the Negro washerwoman, cogently observed: "Many poor whites of that day were not any better off than the Negroes, but they were too proud to work."[18] A confirmation of this statement is contained in this study's data. Only 14 percent of white women with low family labor income ($0 to $299) were in the work force in 1880, but over 44 percent of low-income married black women were. In 1870 the comparable figures were 5 percent for whites and 37 percent for blacks. Holding wealth constant at zero does not substantially reduce this difference—40 percent of low-income, zero-wealth blacks and only 7 percent of this category of whites were in the labor force.

There are other variables in addition to family labor income and wealth that can be important determinants of the labor force participation of married women. The presence of young children not in

[18] Carter G. Woodson, "The Negro Washerwoman: A Vanishing Figure," *Journal of Negro History*, 15 (July 1930), 274.

school, the health of a woman, and her income-earning ability, are a few. By holding these factors constant one can observe differences in labor force participation that can be attributed to race. The direct effects of slavery—those that influence earning power, asset accumulation, and family structure—can in this way be separated from the indirect ones. The conventional method employed for such analysis is that of regression, but simple ordinary least squares techniques are not necessarily acceptable procedures when the dependent variable is dichotomous, and one solution is to employ a probit analysis model.[19] This model constructs an index, I, which is a linear function of the independent variables. The value of the standard normal cumulative distribution at I is the probability that a female will be in the labor force, given the vector of characteristics used to construct I. The coefficients of the index are estimated to maximize the probability of reproducing the choices made by those in the sample—that is, to maximize the likelihood of the sample.

The results of the probit analysis (using the sample data) are given in Table 8. The dependent variable is the labor force participation of the wife and is dichotomous—either a women is in the labor force or is not—and the observations are for married women, husband present.[20] The independent variables are all dichotomous except:

Per Capita Y = per capita family labor income divided by 100 (without the wife's contribution);
LnWealth = the log of family real and personal estate;
Husband Unemployed = the number of months the husband was unemployed during the previous year.

The family labor income variable was computed by assigning wage rates to the various occupations, by accounting for months unemployed (for 1880) and differences among men, women, and children, and by summing the contributions of each family member.[21] Regres-

[19] Two problems arise in the case of a dichotomous dependent variable—that of heteroskedasticity and that of specification. The first is not particularly troublesome for very large samples, but the second is serious because the predicted values from ordinary least squares will not be bounded on the unit interval. This creates difficulties in interpreting the results as conditional probabilities of being in the labor force. For a more complete exposition see Arthur Goldberger, *Econometric Theory* (N.Y.: John Wiley and Sons, 1971), pp. 248-51 which discusses qualitative and limited dependent variables, and Henri Theil, *Principles of Econometrics* (N.Y.: John Wiley and Sons, 1971), which has a short section on probit analysis, pp. 630-31.

[20] Sixteen families in 1870 and six in 1880 were listed as having no family member in the labor force and no wealth. These were dropped from the sample as being anomalous. They probably contained a working family member who was not in the nuclear family or not living in the same household.

[21] An appendix to this paper, *Wage Data for Various Occupations in the South, 1870 and 1880*, details the construction of these components and the sources used. It can be obtained by request from the author.

TABLE 8
MARRIED WOMEN IN THE LABOR FORCE, 1870 AND 1880:
PROBIT ANALYSIS MODEL
Dichotomous (0,1) Dependent Variable: Female labor force participation for married women, husband present.

	Maximum Likelihood Estimates		
	1870	*1880*	
Independent Variables	*(1)* $\hat{\beta}$	*(2)* $\hat{\beta}$	*(3)* $\hat{\beta}$
Constant	−0.884	−1.030	−1.176
	(0.300)[a]	(0.240)	(0.247)
Race	0.812	0.954	0.967
	(0.201)	(0.150)	(0.151)
Foreign	−0.243	0.122	0.161
	(0.248)	(0.207)	(0.207)
Child Ten[b]	−0.482	−0.410	−0.375
	(0.147)	(0.131)	(0.133)
Health		−0.452	−0.516
		(0.648)	(0.677)
Age[c] 25-29	0.150	0.282	0.284
	(0.213)	(0.193)	(0.193)
30-34	0.427	−0.029	−0.016
	(0.217)	(0.209)	(0.209)
35-39	0.304	0.481	0.484
	(0.220)	(0.194)	(0.195)
40-49	0.245	0.134	0.121
	(0.196)	(0.200)	(0.201)
50 and over	0.050	0.156	0.123
	(0.255)	(0.210)	(0.211)
Per Capita Y	−0.201	−0.182	−0.133[d]
	(0.074)	(0.059)	(0.059)
Board	−0.306	−0.196	−0.218
	(0.502)	(0.199)	(0.199)
Servant	−0.563	−0.377	−0.376
	(0.332)	(0.264)	(0.263)
Husband Unemployed			0.070
			(0.026)
LnWealth	−0.053		
	(0.026)		
−2 × LLR[e]	148.8	131.1	134.0
Percentage Predicted Correctly	84.1	81.7	81.5
Number of Observations	776	807	807

[a] Standard errors are in parentheses.

[b] Child Ten indicates the presence of at least one child ten years and under who is not in school.

[c] The age group from 15 to 24 years was the omitted dummy variable.

[d] Family income is constructed for this case as a "full income" concept with months unemployed equal to zero.

[e] Minus two times the log likelihood ratio, which has the chi-square distribution with 12 degrees of freedom for regressions (1) and (2) and 13 for (3). The null hypothesis is that all coefficients are zero.

sion (3), for 1880, used the husband's months unemployed as a separate explanatory variable and, for that specification, the income variable assumed no unemployment. The other, all dichotomous, variables describe the wife and are:

Five age dummies:	15 to 24 years old is the omitted dummy.
Race:	0 = white; 1 = black.
Foreign:	0 = native born; 1 = foreign born.
Child Ten:	0 = no children 10 years old or under except those attending school; 1 = presence of children 10 years old or under, not in school.
Health:	0 = no health problem; 1 = some health problem.
Board:	0 = does not have boarders; 1 = has boarders.
Servant:	0 = does not have a servant; 1 = has a servant.

The wealth variable was available only for 1870, unemployment only for 1880, and health status was reported too infrequently in 1870 to be used.[22]

Coefficients are listed for one specification for 1870 and two for 1880.[23] Almost all coefficients have the expected sign. The presence of preschoolers had a negative impact on female labor force participation; less healthy women tended to stay out of the labor force; wives with richer families, as measured by the per capita labor income and wealth, were less likely to be in the labor force; and a husband's unemployment induced his wife to enter the labor force. Boarders and servants were included as proxies for wealth, and both had a negative impact on the index. The foreign-born dummy was negative for 1870 and positive for 1880, although there is no readily available explanation for this result. The age dummies for 1870 rose to 30-34 years and then declined, but they had no clear trend for 1880.

The magnitudes of the coefficients generated by the probit estimating procedure are not by themselves interesting. One cannot directly determine the percentage change in female labor force participation by increasing, for example, income by one percent; this is true

[22] There is no obvious reason why health status was underrecorded in 1870.

[23] Other explanatory variables which were tried include illiteracy and the presence of other non-working family members over 15 years old. The first, measured by the ability both to read and to write, yielded an insignificant coefficient. This indicates, perhaps, that literacy is not a good measure of a women's earning ability for the nineteenth century. The "other family member" variable had the wrong sign, probably due to the method of coding the data. Families having either a wife or a husband with children were coded as separate units even if they were living with another family. Therefore the category "other family members" can only include children and unattached individuals. However, the existence of an aunt living with a family, for example, might indicate that there was, in addition, another complete family in the household. Although the presence of an aunt might enable a wife with a preschooler to work, the presence of other working adults might be an economic deterrent to such behavior.

Specifications which include only blacks appear very similar to those given in Table 8. Regressions for whites only had similar coefficients on Child Ten and Per Capita Y but had much larger standard errors.

because such an elasticity is conditional on the values for all other independent variables. To compute the probability that a woman with a particular vector of characteristics is in the labor force, an index (I) is constructed as in equation (1), conditional on values for all the included variables.

$$\hat{I} = \hat{\beta}_0 + \hat{\beta}_1 X'_1 + \hat{\beta}_2 X'_2 + \ldots + \hat{\beta}_n X'_n. \quad (1)$$

This index is then evaluated using the cumulative standard normal distribution,

$$\hat{y} = F(\hat{I}). \quad (2)$$

Particular variables can then be changed to observe their effects conditional on values for all the other variables.

Table 9 has been constructed to illustrate this procedure and to

TABLE 9
CONDITIONAL PROBABILITIES OF PARTICIPATING IN THE LABOR FORCE

	White		*Black*	
	Child Ten[a]	No Child Ten	Child Ten	No Child Ten
1870				
Wealth = $0		For a married woman, husband present, who is 35 to 39 years old and native born, and has no servants, and no boarders		
Per capita family labor income =				
$218[b]	6.7 percent	15.4 percent	24.5 percent	41.7 percent
$180[c]	7.8	17.4	27.1	44.8
$248[d]	5.9	14.1	22.7	39.4
Wealth = $500				
Per capita family labor income =				
$218	3.4	8.9	15.4	29.5
1880				
		For a married woman, husband present, who is 35 to 39 years old, in good health, and native born, and has no servants, and no boarders		
Per capita family labor income =				
$205[b]	9.2	17.9	35.2	51.2
$165[c]	10.4	19.8	37.8	54.0
$236[d]	8.1	16.1	33.0	48.8

[a] Child Ten indicates the presence of at least one child ten years and under who is not in school.
[b] This is the mean per capital family labor income (without the wife's contribution) for both blacks and whites.
[c] This is the mean for black families.
[d] This is the mean for white families.
Source: Table 8.

analyze the data. The expected labor force participation rate of black and white women between 35 to 39 years old is analyzed by income, wealth, and the presence of young children, assuming all other dummy variables equalled zero. The difference between the black and white probabilities of participation are large, even though several important explanatory variables are held constant. Black and white women with identical family labor income, equal to $218, no wealth, and no young children differ in expected labor force participation by 26 percentage points in 1870 and 33 percentage points in 1880. The presence of a preschooler lowers the probabilities for both black and white women but has a greater percentage impact on white women. The white probability for 1870 is cut by 56 percent and the black by 41 percent. Comparable figures for 1880 are 48 percent and 31 percent. Increasing per capita family labor income reduces the probability of a woman's working. The elasticity around the mean income for 1870 was −0.68 for whites and −0.41 for blacks. Similar results were obtained for 1880.[24] Increasing wealth to $500 reduces the conditional probabilities, and the white response to this change is, again, somewhat larger. The effect of separating the income variable into two components—one a "full time" labor income variable and the other a measure of the husband's unemployment—is revealing. Increasing a husband's unemployment by one month augments the index, equation (1), by 0.07—equivalent to decreasing family labor income by $50. The wife, therefore, was purchasing a substantial insurance policy against her husband's being unemployed because per capita income was, on average, about $200.

The labor force participation of married black women for these southern cities was not enormously high by today's standards and certainly not by the norms of the antebellum period. It was very high, however, by the white standard of the day. Numerous relevant variables have been used in this study to account for the difference, but race appears to have had an effect apart from income, wealth, and demographic characteristics. One possible reason for this result is that there may be important omitted variables which are correlated with race.[25]

[24] Using the current status measure of employment Cain found, for 1960 data, that the white elasticity was −0.45 and the black −0.13. See G. Cain, *Married Women in the Labor Force*, Table 33, p. 107.

[25] Another possibility is that because the wages assigned in the construction of the labor income variable do not differ by race, black labor incomes are too high and black wives appear to be working "too much." If black wages were overstated in the computation of labor income, the residuals would be systematically biased and correlated with race. But occupations were, for the

Contemporary studies on black and white female labor force participation have found results similar to those reported here. Black women with the same economic and demographic characteristics as their white counterparts participate to a greater extent in the labor market. Glen Cain's study, using variables almost identical to those employed in this paper, found that black women between 35 to 39 years old, with 12 years of education, a child under six years old, and family labor income of $5,000, had a probability of being in the labor force almost four times that for a white woman of identical characteristics. Many explanations have been offered for this and similar findings. Some have claimed that the life-cycle marital experiences of black and white women differ. Black women stand a greater chance of being unmarried with dependents and therefore do not exit from the labor force during their married years. They are, in some way, hedging against their having to support children sometime in the future. Discrimination in both the labor market and the housing market has also been suggested as a possible explanation. Black women may be faced with less discrimination in the labor market than their husbands, causing a substitution toward female labor in the family. Black housing might be of lesser quality than desired and its residents may therefore have less incentive to remain in the household. The higher incidence of the extended family structure and a closer community might also be responsible for the smaller response of black women to the presence of young children. All of these suggestions provide possible rationalizations for the recent findings, although none of these hypotheses seems to account fully for the large difference between black and white women observed in this sample.

CONCLUSIONS

This study has found that race is very important in explaining differences in labor force participation among females. Black women in this sample worked more (holding family labor income, wealth, the presence of children, and other characteristics constant). I have suggested that the slave experience might be partially responsible for this residual. Slavery seems to have left an indirect legacy on black and white women. It changed the relative valuations that black and white women had for work—possibly lowering that of whites and

most part, racially segregated and research by Robert Higgs indicates that wages by race were equal for given occupations in 1900. See R. Higgs, "Racial Wage Differentials and Segregation in Competitive Labor Markets: An Empirical Report," University of Washington, Discussion Paper No. 75-8 (Sept. 1975).

raising that of blacks. Somewhat similar developments probably occurred among white women in the North because of the presence of immigrant women. Thus native-born females may have remained out of the labor force, despite their economic position, because woman's work became socially stigmatized.[26]

The role of social forces in determining the labor force participation of women in 1870 and 1880 was dramatized in the literature of the period. Orra Langhorne wrote in 1886 that there is "a very great need for occupations in which white women could support themselves . . . [T]he cigarette factories [in Virginia] were employing three hundred white girls . . . [however] married women were not accepted."[27] Somewhat later Greene and Woodson wrote of the 1870s that ". . . Southern poor whites . . . looked upon domestic service as a 'Negro job' [and therefore] Negroes encountered virtually no opposition" in entering this field.[28] In my own research I have tried to model these statements so that they can be rigorously tested. The results indicate that economic and demographic differences alone cannot entirely explain black and white female labor force participation rates; to me it seems likely that these findings can be attributed to an indirect legacy of slavery.

CLAUDIA GOLDIN, *Princeton University*

[26] This proposition will be tested with the data from the Philadelphia Social History Project.

[27] Quoted in Anne Firor Scott, *The Southern Lady: From Pedestal to Politics, 1830-1930* (Chicago: University of Chicago Press, 1970), p. 122.

[28] Lorenzo J. Greene and Carter G. Woodson, *The Negro Wage Earner* (Washington: The Association for the Study of Negro Life and History, Inc., 1930), p. 31.

Journal of Interdisciplinary History, x:2 (Autumn 1979), 227–248.

Judith A. McGaw

"A Good Place to Work." Industrial Workers and Occupational Choice: The Case of Berkshire Women

In 1848 Mrs. Amy Fuller of Sheffield, Massachusetts, wrote to the owners of a paper mill in Dalton, a town about thirty miles distant, "We have been informed that you are in want of help in your mill and I have heard it was a good place to work." This simple event poses a complex question for students of nineteenth-century American work and workers. Given the somber hues in which historians have sketched the industrial workplace, what could an industrial worker have meant in describing a mill as "a good place to work"? We can make sense of this phrase only by answering two related questions: To what extent did mill operatives have a choice between alternative employments, and, where there is evidence that they exercised choice, on what basis did they choose?[1]

The focus of most previous scholarship has made it difficult to answer the first of these questions. Traditional American labor history was preoccupied with unions and skilled workers, thus bypassing the problems of most industrial workers altogether. More recently, many of the best insights of "the new labor history" are the products of careful studies of individual industries. Such studies look only at workers who have already opted for work in a particular industry and avoid the issue of choice between mills. The "new urban history" which considers the entire range of work available in individual cities has the potential to analyze industrial work choices. However, its preoccupation with tracing workers' movements between broad occupational strata has led it generally to ignore differences between specific industrial jobs.[2]

Judith A. McGaw is Assistant Professor of History at the University of Virginia.

A summer research fellowship from the University of Oklahoma made completion of this article possible. The final version has benefited significantly from the critical comments and suggestions of Robert A. Nye and Robert Asher. Paul W. Glad has been especially helpful on matters of style. I also wish to thank Gary B. Cohen, Norman L. Crockett, Vaughan C. Hennum, Brooke Hindle, Elizabeth Hitz, and Ronald Snell for reading drafts of this article.

1 Crane Museum of Paper Making, Dalton, Mass., Letter File 326, 11/25/1848. Hereinafter file numbers refer to the Crane Museum Letter File.

2 A useful discussion of the changing focus of labor history is David Brody, "The Old

Occupational choice by women workers such as Fuller has not merely been neglected by scholars, it has been presumed not to exist. With the exception of certain transitory and aberrant cases such as Lowell, scholars have pictured women moving passively into their jobs. The presence of father, husband, or son and his ability to earn a living decided whether or not they remained within the home. Beyond its walls, the kind of mill or shop in the immediate vicinity determined their job selection. With some qualifications to account for class and ethnic differences, these have been historians' prevailing assumptions. Recently this emphasis on the passivity of women workers has been somewhat modified by historians of the family. In documenting the importance of the family wage economy among the working classes, they have uncovered the roles of wives, mothers, and daughters in work decisions. Nonetheless, their concern has been almost exclusively with household decisions as to who should work, not with the selection of particular employments by women and their families.[3]

Despite their general neglect of the issue of mill workers' occupational choice, historians have addressed the issue of workers' motives in choosing occupations. Traditional labor historians have followed the unions that they have studied in emphasizing financial rewards. Recent urban historians, because of their concern with social mobility, have also assumed the primacy of the

---

Labor History and the New," paper presented at the Organization of American Historians meeting, 1978 and comments by Mari Jo Buhle, Leon Fink, James O. Morris, and David Montgomery. Brody, *Steelworkers in America: The Nonunion Era* (New York, 1969), is one of the best examples of the single industry studies. A good review of the "new urban history" is James A. Henretta, "The Study of Social Mobility: Ideological Assumptions and Conceptual Bias," *Labor History*, XVIII (1977), 165–178. Clyde Griffen and Sally Griffen, *Natives and Newcomers: The Ordering of Opportunity in Mid-Nineteenth-Century Poughkeepsie* (Cambridge, Mass., 1978), 193–206, is a partial exception to this generalization.

3 The preoccupation of students of women's industrial work with communities dominated by the cotton textile industry and the general neglect of female workers by the new urban history have both contributed substantially to this state of affairs. On the focus on cotton textile work see McGaw, "Technological Change and Women's Work: Mechanization in the Berkshire Paper Industry, 1820–1885," in Martha Moore Trescott (ed.), *Dynamos and Virgins Revisited: Women and Technological Change in History*, forthcoming. On the family and work see Elizabeth H. Pleck, "Two Worlds in One: Work and Family," *Journal of Social History*, X (1976), 178–195; Louise A. Tilly and Joan W. Scott, *Women, Work, and Family* (New York, 1978), esp. 63–145.

money motive, as well as the often related desire for prestige and for opportunity to advance.

Recent labor history has identified another cluster of motives as useful in explaining the behavior of certain groups of workers, especially first generation industrial workers. These workers, early nineteenth-century American-born operatives and late nineteenth-century immigrant laborers, frequently preferred jobs offering independence; control over work; fraternity with fellow workers, especially fellow countrymen; and security. Historians of the family have underscored the degree to which households subordinated all such individual motives to broader assessments of the family's needs.[4]

What follows is an attempt to understand what Fuller meant when she referred to a particular mill as "a good place to work." Did nineteenth-century American industrial workers exercise occupational choice? In the case of Fuller, a female industrial worker living in Berkshire County, Massachusetts, that question entails determining whether women in the region moved about in search of work, whether several kinds of industrial work for women were widely available within the area in which they readily moved, whether different kinds of women ended up in different kinds of mills, and whether these women followed personal preferences or the dictates of their husbands or fathers. Once the alternatives open to these women have been outlined, it is possible to consider realistically why they made particular choices, or, in the case of Fuller, which of the motives historians have suggested best explains why she perceived a particular mill as "a good place to work."

Female industrial workers merit study both because they were the nation's pioneer mill operatives and because they have been neglected by historians. Since studies of industrial workers must rely on census data, female workers also provide a clearer case for study because they were excluded from the skilled trades

4 David Montgomery, "Workers' Control of Machine Production in the Nineteenth Century," *Labor History*, XVII (1976), 485–509; John Bodnar, "Immigration and Modernization: The Case of Slavic Peasants in Industrial America," *Journal of Social History*, X (1976), 44–71; Daniel T. Rodgers, "Tradition, Modernity, and the American Industrial Worker: Reflections and Critique," *Journal of Interdisciplinary History*, VII (1977), 655–681; John Modell, "Patterns of Consumption, Acculturation, and Family Income Strategies in Late Nineteenth-Century America," in Tamara K. Hareven and Maris A. Vinovskis (eds.), *Family and Population in Nineteenth-Century America* (Princeton, 1978), 206–240.

and, therefore, invariably listed the mill in which they worked as their occupation. Male workers sometimes listed the mill, sometimes their trade, making it impossible to identify all male industrial workers. Moreover, since industry confined women to a relatively small number of unskilled or semiskilled tasks, the possible reasons for their occupational choices are easier to enumerate than are those for men.

Berkshire County, Massachusetts, in the second half of the nineteenth century provides a good place to study the occupational choices of women industrial workers. It was a picturesque region dotted with economically declining hill towns and prosperous mill villages scattered along the river valleys. Because it contained only one small city, Berkshire County provides a work setting more representative of the late nineteenth-century American experience than more frequently studied urban areas, since only about one third of the American population in the period lived in towns of 2,500 or more. Unlike previously studied industrial communities where a few large companies and a single industry controlled women's work opportunities, for most of the nineteenth century a variety of smaller mills lined Berkshire's streams and rivers. In 1880, twenty-two woolen mills, twenty-one paper mills, eighteen cotton mills, and seven mixed textile mills operated in the county. All of these industries presented substantial employment opportunities for women, cotton and paper mills generally hiring a preponderance of females, and woolen mills, a substantial minority. In 1880, 751 women reported to the census taker that they worked in woolen mills, 829 identified themselves as paper mill workers, 1,222 claimed employment in cotton factories, and 191 worked for unspecified textile manufacturing concerns. This group of nearly 3,000 female industrial workers and more than 7,000 other individuals who made up their households provides a population that is large enough to ensure meaningful statistical results, but small enough to be studied without sampling.[5]

5 United States Census Office, *Report on the Manufacturing of the United States at the Tenth Census* (Washington, 1883), 255. The figures for numbers of workers and all subsequent quantitative statements, except where otherwise identified, are based on an analysis of all female textile and paper mill workers and members of their households listed in the United States 1880 Manuscript Census Schedules for Berkshire County, Massachusetts. Computer assistance in analysis was made possible through the University of Oklahoma Computer Services and a Research Council Grant from the University. Alice Foister and Ron Schmidt

To what extent did this group of mill operatives have a choice among alternative employments? Clearly no historian can presume to answer this question in any absolute sense, primarily because industrial workers left few records of their thoughts, necessitating deduction from their actions, a risky business at best. Just as clearly, in directing our attention to female mill workers we are considering occupational choice in its narrowest sense. These women worked out of economic necessity and brought only the most limited skills to the marketplace.

Acknowledging these limitations, what follows is a series of perspectives on female mill workers' occupational choices. We begin by arguing that both geographical mobility and mills offering work were common enough that the 3,000 women in our study might have opted for cotton, paper, or woolen mill employment. Then, we present evidence that differences between workers in the various mills cannot be explained as random, but reflect deliberation. Finally, we suggest ways in which family considerations constrained the women's decision-making and adduce reasons for believing that women who chose most freely preferred to work in paper mills.[6]

Were female industrial workers geographically mobile enough to take advantage of work opportunities scattered throughout a county?[7] The evidence suggests that they were. Even in the mid-1800s, when several Berkshire mill owners' relatives ran mills in New York state and eastern Massachusetts,

---

of Computer Services, T. R. Carr of the Bureau of Government Research, and Duncan Aldrich of the department of history provided programming assistance.

Cotton, woolen, and paper mills accounted for virtually all industrially employed women in the county. The only other industry hiring more than fifty women in 1880 was boot and shoe manufacturing, employing 210 women according to the census of manufactures. This much smaller group has not been considered here because its concentration in only four mills meant that women throughout the county could not have chosen to enter this industry with the same freedom as they could the other three.

6 As indicated above, deducing motive from behavior is a dangerous business. The reader should be cautioned at the outset, therefore, that little direct evidence on decision making will be adduced in what follows. Rather, my argument will rest primarily upon a structure of inferences from a quantitative analysis of the traits of mill workers and their families.

7 That women were mobile there is no doubt, but why they were is a question that remains to be answered. Some light is shed on the issue of mobility among male and female paper workers in McGaw, "The Sources and Impact of Mechanization: The Berkshire County, Massachusetts, Paper Industry, 1801–1885, as a Case Study," unpub. Ph.D. diss. (New York Univ., 1977), 372–379.

correspondence between family members frequently discussed the willingness of women employees to move between various mills. In 1846, Z. M. Crane of Dalton received a request from his brother-in-law A. H. Laflin, who lived about seventy miles away in Ware, Massachusetts. "We have plenty of water but want more girls . . . Do you know of any? Please send them along." Six years later, when the future of the family's Ballston Spa, New York, mill was uncertain, L. M. Crane warned his brothers in Dalton that unless some family member could guarantee jobs to currently employed women "they want to look up work some where else."[8]

From 1844 to 1886 women also testified to their willingness to move in search of work by addressing requests for employment to a paper making firm which has preserved letters from workers. Some of these letters came from isolated hill towns, competing paper making communities, and other industrial centers within the county. Women from towns in nearby counties in Massachusetts, Connecticut, Vermont, and New York also wrote asking for jobs. Manufacturers from surrounding counties advertised for women workers in Berkshire newspapers, joining Berkshire mill owners in assuming the willingness of women to respond to offers of employment in other towns. Also, discussions of the Massachusetts law restricting women's work hours routinely assumed that women would leave the state in search of better wages.[9]

To some degree, all women appear to have shared this geographical mobility, for, although single women wrote most of the letters requesting work, others came from married women and men seeking employment with their spouses, from parents looking for work for themselves and their daughters, and from widows hunting for jobs to support their children. Clearly, single women moved more easily than those with families, but the degree of mobility did not follow simply from marital status.[10]

8 Files 741, 3/6/1846; 451, 6/17/1852; 446–448, 450–453, 463, 469, 489–490, 493, 496–497, 741, *passim*.

9 Files 326–335, 498, 12/31/1869. *The Valley Gleaner*, a weekly newspaper published from 1857 in Lee, Massachusetts, the Berkshire paper making center, carried frequent advertisements for women to work in paper mills outside the county. *Valley Gleaner*, March 12, 1874, 2; Massachusetts House Document no. 44, *Reports of Commissioners on the Hours of Labor* (Boston, 1867).

10 On the relationship between geographical mobility and number of offspring for both

If a variety of women were willing to travel considerable distances, sometimes across state lines, in search of work, women probably moved relatively freely between mills in Berkshire County. The most widely separated of the sixty-eight textile and paper mills operating in 1880 were only about forty miles apart, and virtually all county women had a variety of mills within ten miles of their homes. Indeed, most of Berkshire's working women had a choice among paper, woolen, and cotton mill employment without leaving the town where they resided.[11]

In one sense, then, women in Berkshire County had a choice of industrial occupations. Considering their geographical mobility, the distribution of mills within the county offered them a possibility of cotton, paper, and woolen mill work. Although, psychologically, the mere possibility of choice may have been important to workers, we cannot assess its influence on their definition of "a good place to work." For our purposes it is also important to know whether workers acted on their options. One way of answering this question is to look more closely at the characteristics of the women working in the various industries. If they differed significantly from one another, for example, if certain kinds of women tended to be cotton mill workers while others were more prevalent in paper mills, this would indicate that women in Berkshire County did not simply walk into the nearest mill employing women. It would suggest that they exercised a measure of choice.

Women talking to the 1880 census takers reported a number of things about themselves in addition to their occupations. Comparing the distributions of these characteristics among cotton, paper, and woolen mill workers reveals marked differences between women working in the different industries. The most pronounced disparities occurred between women who worked in the two types of textile mills and those who labored for paper making firms. They differed substantially in age, marital status, and relationship to the head of the household in which they resided.

male and female household heads see Michael B. Katz, Michael J. Doucet, and Mark J. Stern, "Migration and the Social Order in Erie County, New York, 1855," *Journal of Interdisciplinary History*, VIII (1978), 687–689.

11 Of the eight towns sending fifty or more women into such mills in 1880, six sent women to all three industries, one offered work in either cotton or woolen mills, and one provided only paper mill employment.

Older women, married and widowed women, women who headed their own households, and women who boarded, more frequently opted for paper mill work. Less marked, but still significant, was the preference of women of native parentage for paper mill employment. The daughters of the foreign born, generally Irish and French Canadian, more frequently worked in the textile industries.[12]

Although less pronounced, differences also existed between cotton and woolen textile workers. Cotton mill workers were significantly more likely to be illiterate and to be the children of the more recently arrived French Canadian immigrants. Cotton mills also hired a greater proportion of women fifteen years old or younger.[13]

Not chance, then, but choice determined the presence of women in particular industries in western Massachusetts. Whose choice, however, remains at issue. These women, their husbands or fathers, and the owners of the mills in which they labored might each have acted to select certain women for textile mill work and others for paper mill work. A full assessment of the extent of these women's occupational choices requires us to consider the influence of their employers and of their families.

The role of Berkshire County employers in determining the character of their work forces was a complex and changing one and its final influence is difficult to assess. Most of the preferences that they expressed were held by all mill owners, however, and would not explain different types of workers being selected for different industries. All mill owners sought workers who were temperate and reliable. All discriminated against the county's black population, virtually excluding blacks from industrial em-

12 Both considerations of space and readability preclude extensive discussion of the statistical tests underlying these statements. However, here, as elsewhere, when a difference is described as "significant" it means that the computation of the chi square (χ^2) statistic revealed a statistically significant relationship at the .001 level: i.e., that the particular characteristic was distributed among various types of mill workers in a way that would occur by chance less than one time in a thousand. When a difference is described as "substantial" it indicates that it has not only met this test of significance, but that the value of lambda (λ) calculated with the occupation variable dependent fell between .14 and .20: i.e., that knowledge of a particular characteristic of a woman would improve the chance of predicting which kind of mill she worked in by 14 to 20 percent. For the kind of data historians generally employ, this is indeed substantial evidence of differences between mill populations.

13 This last difference is only significant at the .01 level.

ployment. Initially, prejudice also impeded the hiring of ethnic minorities, but, at least for the Irish, the years after the Civil War saw a lessening of discrimination. In any case, there is nothing to indicate that such prejudice was stronger in one industry than in another. Also, since women's work in all three types of mills generally required little more than attentiveness to monotonous, routinized tasks, there is no technological reason why certain kinds of women should have been preferred in particular mills.[14]

Although mill owners' prejudice was probably relatively uniform between industries, the preferences of other family members exerted a disproportionate influence on textile mill women. Women who worked in cotton and woolen mills were more likely to have been sent there by their parents or drawn there by their husbands' or fathers' work. By contrast, paper mill women probably took a far more active part in the decisions that sent them into the mills. A closer look both at Berkshire female industrial workers and at their households helps delineate the nature of occupational choice among female industrial workers and establishes female paper workers as more independent decision makers.[15]

All female industrial workers had to consider family relationships and responsibilities when making decisions about work, but textile workers most frequently arrived at their choices of work jointly with other family members. Although fewer than half of the paper mill workers were daughters still living at home, nearly three quarters of the textile mill workers resided with their parents (75.5 percent of the cotton mill workers and 70.1 percent of the woolen mill workers). This fact alone suggests that textile mill operatives were unlikely to have chosen their occupations by themselves. This is particularly true of cotton workers. More than three fifths (61.5 percent) of the women in these mills were

14 McGaw, "Sources and Impact," 279–282, 351–354, 362–364; Griffen and Griffen, *Natives and Newcomers*, 193–206; Donald B. Cole, *Immigrant City: Lawrence, Massachusetts, 1845–1921* (Chapel Hill, 1963), 26–67 *passim*.

15 In what follows, comments about cotton, woolen, or paper mill households refer to all individuals, male and female, living in the same dwelling unit as a woman employed in one of these mills. Virtually no household sent women to more than one industry. The few boarding houses and other households sending only boarders to work in the mills have been excluded from consideration. However, most boarders lived in private households which also sent family members to work in the mills and these boarders have been included in calculations as household members. Where the term families is used instead of households, only those related to the household head have been included in calculations.

younger than twenty-one and nearly a quarter (22 percent) had not celebrated their sixteenth birthday.[16]

In addition, several members of a family generally sought work together in cotton and woolen mills, making the selection of a workplace a family decision. The average cotton or woolen mill household sent three people to work in the mill (2.97 and 2.92 respectively). Even including the larger number of boarders living within them, paper mill women's households averaged only two paper mill employees (2.01). As minor daughters, most textile mill workers probably exerted relatively little influence on such family decisions.[17]

Poverty among cotton mill households appears to have forced parents to send as many children out to work as possible. Daughters working in cotton mills were significantly more likely to come from families headed by unskilled or unemployed men, suggesting that more bitter necessity drove them to work. The two categories included 40 percent of male cotton mill household heads, but only about a quarter of male household heads in woolen and paper mill families (22 percent and 27 percent respectively). A further indication of their families' more precarious circumstances is the large proportion of very young cotton workers, reflecting the larger average size of cotton mill families and their sending a greater proportion of their children to work in the mills.[18]

16 All figures reflecting differences in age, marital status, relationship to head of household, nativity, and nativity of parents have been tested for statistical significance and only significant differences are reported here. Where other differences cited are significant they will be referred to as such. See note 12. Figures presented for textile mill operatives include those in cotton and woolen mills and those who worked in one of these mills but failed to specify which.

17 The dynamics of the family decision-making process in the Manchester, New Hampshire, cotton mills are traced by Hareven, "Family Time and Industrial Time: Family and Work in a Planned Corporation Town, 1900–1924," *Journal of Urban History*, I (1975), 365–389.

18 Designations of fathers' occupations follow the Philadelphia Social History Project vertical code described by Theodore Hershberg and Robert Dockhorn in "Occupational Classification," *Historical Methods Newsletter*, 9 (1976), 59–77. I use the term unskilled as equivalent to Vertical 5, non-manual as equivalent to Vertical 1 and 2, and skilled as equivalent to Vertical 3.

Of households sending daughters into the mills, cotton mill families sent 2.4 children to cotton mills, woolen mill families averaged 2.1 children in woolen mills, and paper mill families sent 1.2 children into paper mills. Paper mill families had 3.6 children on the average, woolen mill women's families had 4.4, and cotton mill women's families had 4.6. Of these children, paper mill families sent 32.7 percent into paper mills, woolen mill

Because the members of these cotton mill families were more ignorant, less familiar with American life, and poorer, they probably made their way to the cotton mill simply because it was the most obvious place of employment for women. Much larger than the average paper mill and employing a greater proportion of women than the woolen mill, it offered more jobs to women than either. Moreover, once cotton mills began employing large numbers of young girls, the practice perpetuated itself. Since Massachusetts law required young workers to attend school three months a year, even with widespread violation of this statute, numbers of young cotton workers would regularly have been leaving their jobs to go to school. For a family in desperate need of employment for its several daughters, then, the cotton mill probably afforded the best prospect.[19]

A different kind of family decision sent daughters into the woolen mill. Like cotton mill women, they frequently accompanied their brothers and sisters to work. But although native-born, English speaking daughters in cotton mill households may have helped their unskilled immigrant fathers choose cotton mill work for them, paternal decisions determined the choices of many woolen mill women. Nearly three fifths (58.9 percent) of the male heads of their households worked in woolen mills.[20]

Although many women woolen mill operatives probably entered the mills because their fathers already worked there, one cannot discount the possibility that the decision was a joint one. At the very least it is likely that prospective employment for daughters entered male woolen mill workers' job selection calculations. These men might have considered not only the larger total family wage such a work choice would make possible, but also the advantage of being present at their daughters' place of employment. Unlike the more desperate fathers of the cotton mill

families sent 48.9 percent into woolen mills, and cotton mill families sent 52.5 percent into cotton mills. In addition to the Hareven study, Thomas Dublin, "Women, Work, and the Family: Female Operatives in the Lowell Mills, 1830–1860," *Feminist Studies*, III (1975), 30–39; Daniel J. Walkowitz, "Working Class Women in the Gilded Age: Factory, Community, and Family Life among Cohoes, New York Cotton Workers," *Journal of Social History*, V (1972), 464–489, suggest broadly comparable characteristics of women cotton workers and their households elsewhere.

19 *Manufactures, Tenth Census*, 255.

20 Only a little over one third (34.1 percent and 34.9 percent) of paper and cotton mill household heads worked in paper and textile mills. This represents a significant difference.

girls, they might avoid sending their daughters into workplaces where they could not follow.

In contrast to women textile workers whose work choices were bounded by various family constraints, paper mill workers were probably able to exercise more independent choice. They had the advantage of maturity. Whereas three fifths (60.2 percent) of the cotton and woolen mill women were twenty years old or younger, three fifths (59.7 percent) of the paper mill women had passed the age of twenty. As this age difference implies, married women and women who headed their own households more frequently chose to work in paper mills. Nearly one third (30 percent) of female paper workers, but only one twelfth (8.5 percent) of textile workers, had achieved the measure of independence such status entailed. In addition, paper mill workers more frequently lived as boarders (15.9 percent versus 11.3 percent for all textile workers), a practice suggesting that they had fewer binding family ties.

Paper mill women possessed other advantages as well. Compared to cotton and woolen workers, they were more than twice as likely (26.1 percent versus 11.3 percent) to be children of native-born parents, assuring them whatever added measure of control over their situation a greater understanding of the American environment permitted. Greater prosperity may also have afforded paper mill women more room for choice. Even when weavers, who often headed textile mill households, are counted as skilled workers, paper mill households were significantly more likely to be headed by non-manual workers, farmers, or skilled workers. More than one third (36 percent) of paper mill women workers living with fathers or husbands came from such families, whereas less than one quarter (23.2 percent) of cotton and woolen mill women did. Female paper workers' families also contained fewer children and sent a smaller percentage of those children into the mills, differences suggesting less dire economic circumstances among paper mill workers.[21]

Women who worked in paper mills not only possessed ad-

21 See note 18. These paper mill family patterns as well as patterns obtained for paper workers for all other variables except marital status show some resemblance to patterns obtained for women teachers and their households as listed in the 1880 census for Berkshire County. Since teachers have been recognized as a middle-class group, such similarities reinforce the suggestion that paper mill households were more prosperous.

vantages indicating greater capacity for choice, but they also more frequently found themselves in situations where they could have made their own decisions. Because fewer lived under parental supervision, their families were probably less likely to intervene. In addition, husbands' career decisions influenced fewer married women paper workers than married woolen or cotton operatives. Just as daughters often entered woolen mills to join their fathers, wives in woolen mills had frequently chosen to work near their husbands. More than two thirds (67.2 percent) of these married women had husbands who also worked in woolen mills. Similarly, over half (52.7 percent) of married women cotton workers had cotton worker spouses. In contrast, closer to one third (36.7 percent) of married paper mill women worked in the same industry as their husbands.[22]

Underlying this difference among the mill workers is the fact that many married textile workers had probably first entered the mills while still children in their parents' households. The high percentage who worked in the mills with their husbands probably resulted from many having met their mates on the job. After marrying, they had simply decided to continue working, at least until the birth of their first children. Evidence that the average married textile worker was younger (33.6 years old as opposed to 38.2 for married paper workers) and more likely to be childless (39.3 percent versus 22.7 percent) lends credence to these assumptions. Such women, despite their adult status, had probably exercised no more choice than the young man who found himself still in the mill or shop where his parents had originally placed him.[23]

As with female textile workers, larger questions of family well-being entered into female paper workers' calculations. Paper mill women, however, more frequently resembled the traditional image of the male worker in their ability to influence or even direct the household's choices. One of the most fundamental of these mill family decisions was whether adult women would

22 Because the census specified only relationships to household heads, making relationships between married boarders and between married children living at home with their spouses unclear on occasion, only those listed as wives of household heads are included here. Very few married women fell into other categories.

23 Michael Anderson, *Family Structure in Nineteenth-Century Lancashire* (Cambridge, 1971), 71–72, found similar patterns among married British textile workers.

work in industry or only at keeping house for the family. Given contemporary values, most adult women probably preferred to remain at home, especially since mill labor did not exempt mothers and wives from housekeeping responsibilities. Although one can hardly characterize wives' and widows' decisions to work outside the home as free choices, such decisions were clearly ones in which these women participated and were most likely to be made where paper mill work was the alternative. Fewer than one third (32.7 percent) of the female heads of paper workers' households selected full-time housekeeping, while three quarters (74.9 percent) of their peers in textile workers' families stayed at home. Similarly, close to seven eighths (85.3 percent) of wives in textile mill households, but only half (51 percent) of households sending women into paper mills, listed "keeping house" as their occupation.

Even more striking, these women paper workers had other alternatives to working in the mills. They could have sent their children to work, but chose instead to enter the mills and permit their children to remain in school. Although reaping some benefits from this decision, their daughters also often worked to aid their brothers. Consequently, as compared to textile mill women's families, women paper workers' households had significantly more sons and slightly more daughters in school. Women paper workers' choices enabled nearly half (49.2 percent) of the sons in their households to attend school, while only one seventh (14.3 percent) entered paper mills. By contrast, both woolen and cotton mill families sent more sons into the mills (41.1 percent and 43.1 percent) than into the schools (38.5 percent and 39.4 percent). Similar, but less pronounced, differences existed between daughters in the different kinds of mill households.[24]

In other communities, ethnic and religious traditions frequently limited the ability of immigrant women to select work outside the home. This was also the case in Berkshire County. Of the three principal ethnic groups, working wives and female household heads were least evident among the most recently arrived mill workers, the French Canadians (11.5 percent), more common among the Irish (13.4 percent), and most common among the native-born (22.5 percent). When French Canadian

24 Differences in frequencies of daughters in school or at work are statistically significant at the .05 level.

and Irish wives and widows broke with tradition and entered the mills, however, they showed an even stronger preference for paper mill work than native-born wives and widows. Although paper mill work was the choice of those most able to choose, it was also most likely to be selected by those whose decision probably required more deliberation.[25]

Women shouldering the greatest family responsibilities, female heads of households, were also drawn disproportionately to the paper industry. They clearly preferred such work not only for themselves, but also for their daughters. Women headed nearly one third (32.1 percent) of female paper workers' households, but less than one quarter (22.2 percent) of women cotton and woolen workers' households. Female household heads moved their families to paper mill neighborhoods primarily in search of jobs for themselves. Nearly two thirds (65.4 percent) of the female heads of paper worker households worked in the mills. Inasmuch as married and widowed paper workers frequently interrupted their careers, many other female heads of paper workers' households were probably former employees using their knowledge of the industry and, perhaps, their acquaintance with foremen, to aid their daughters in obtaining work.[26]

Like male heads of woolen mill households, many female household heads probably worked in the paper industry because it gave them a chance to oversee their children's transition to the mills. For example, Fuller continued her letter, "[I]f you wanted help I would come with two daughters. [O]ne I would like to have work in saul [finishing room] and one in the rag room with myself." Such advance planning appears to have occurred often in the paper industry, where a large proportion (44.9 percent) of female workers who headed households accompanied their children to work. Fewer (32.1 percent) textile mill women heading

25 Virginia Yans-McLaughlin, "Patterns of Work and Family Organization: Buffalo's Italians," *Journal of Interdisciplinary History*, II (1971), 299–314; Laurence A. Glasco, "The Life Cycles and Household Structures of American Ethnic Groups: Irish, Germans, and Native-born Whites in Buffalo, New York, 1855," *Journal of Urban History*, I (1975), 339–364. Since marked differences exist between marginal totals, Goodman and Kruskal's tau (τ) has been used here rather than lamdba. With occupation dependent and relationship to head of household independent, the value of tau (the fraction by which knowledge of household status improves our ability to predict occupation) is .18 for those of French Canadian parentage, .12 for the offspring of the Irish, and .04 for daughters of natives.
26 McGaw, "Sources and Impact," 376–379.

households brought children to the mills with them. Working wives who wanted their daughters to work near them displayed an even stronger preference for paper mill employment.[27]

Clearly, from this evidence both on women industrial workers and on their families, some nineteenth-century women exercised a measure of choice among employment options. Women who worked in cotton and woolen mills had less choice about where they worked. Poverty and ignorance pushed some of them into the most readily available work, whereas others were limited by parental preferences and paternal or husbandly employment. Women who chose most freely were those with the most financial security, the greatest familiarity with America, and the least interference from parents or husbands. They opted for work in the paper industry. What factors influenced this selection? Both the needs of these workers and the conditions of the industry suggest answers.

Money appears to have been a relatively unimportant consideration. Using wages alone as a criterion, cotton mill employment was most desirable and paper mill work least so. According to the state census of 1875, Berkshire female cotton workers averaged $294.19 a year, woolen mill women earned $272.52, and paper mill workers, $238.13, or only about four fifths as much as cotton mill hands. Both textile trades also offered women more opportunities for piecework, where wages were higher, substantially so in cotton. The 1885 Massachusetts figures on weekly wage distributions within the various industries show woolen mill women far more likely to earn the highest wages, indicating that paper mills were not offering the best prospect of financial advancement.[28]

It is hardly surprising that the money motive loomed largest among those with the greatest financial need. Households attempting to maximize their family income by sending large numbers of children to work naturally directed their daughters to the most remunerative mills. But women less driven by financial necessity deemed other aspects of their work more important.

27 File 326, 11/25/1848.

28 Massachusetts, Bureau of Statistics of Labor, *The Census of Massachusetts, 1875, II: Manufactures and Occupations* (Boston, 1877), 443, 530, 577; Massachusetts, Bureau of Statistics of Labor, *The Census of Massachusetts, 1885, II: Manufactures, the Fisheries and Commerce* (Boston, 1888), 1113–1125. These figures are for actual amounts women earned in one year. Paper mill women worked more days per year, but fewer hours per day. These factors probably offset one another.

What they especially valued can best be summarized by the words autonomy and security.

None of the women working in Berkshire industry possessed the measure of autonomy that has been documented among some groups of skilled male industrial workers. The preference of women for paper mill work, however, suggests that women also favored work situations granting them a measure of control. Unlike women in the textile mills, where the undiscriminating day work rate or the often oppressive piecework scale prevailed, most paper mill women worked under a mixed system. They were guaranteed a day's wage for accomplishing a minimum amount of work, but earned "over work" pay if they performed additional work. Also, although most women textile workers were forced to work at the rate of the machines they tended, most women paper workers did not tend machines and those who did worked at individual small finishing machines the pace of which they frequently controlled. Mill owner L. M. Crane referred specifically to these women's machines when he wrote, "As we have our callenders, ruling machines, triming presses, stampers, etc., etc. all in trim & man'd for letter & cut cap[,] if we run on flat cap or ledger papers part of the time these hands won't have more than half employment. Yet some way or another they will manage to get *full time*."[29]

As compared to textile workers, paper workers also had more hours each day away from the mill, an equally important measure of autonomy. In 1865 women in Pittsfield's woolen mills finally refused to report for work at 5 A.M., maintaining that since an eleven-hour day was customary in eastern Massachusetts textile mills, Berkshire mill owners could not continue to require twelve or thirteen hours of labor. Cotton and woolen mill workers in northern and southern Berkshire raised the same demand. By contrast, women in at least one leading Berkshire paper mill had worked an eight-hour day since 1830. Some other paper mills adopted the ten-hour day for women even before state law mandated it in 1874.[30]

More than ten years after passage of this law, Massachusetts

29 Montgomery, "Workers' Control," 485–509; McGaw, "Technological Change"; *idem*, "Sources and Impact," 304–328; File 448, 6/26/1850.

30 *Valley Cleaner*, Sept. 21, 1865, 2; Sept. 28, 1865, 2; United States Census Office, *Report on the Statistics of Wages in Manufacturing Industries* (Washington, D.C., 1886), 276; McGaw, "Sources and Impact," 319.

conducted a statewide survey of 153 cotton mills, 163 woolen mills, and 118 paper mills. It found women working more than ten hours in twelve cotton and thirteen woolen mills and fewer than ten hours in only three textile mills. Because textile mill women tended the industry's principal machines, the mills had to be shut down when they went home. Not surprisingly, textile mill owners kept their female operatives on the job as many hours as they could. Paper making machinery was tended by men and operated around the clock, unaffected by the arrival and departure of women rag processors and paper sorters and finishers. As a result, none of the paper mills employed women for more than ten hours, and one quarter (twenty-nine) of them set women's hours at fewer than ten, generally at eight or nine.[31]

If even the rosy-hued memoirs of Harriet Robinson take on a more somber tone when she recalls the long work hours of her childhood and young womanhood spent in Lowell cotton mills, most women making an informed choice among employments understandably preferred paper mills. For wives and female household heads doing double duty as mill workers and housekeepers, the choice must have been even clearer. Also, those wives and widows with young children returning home from school in the afternoon could work and still provide some supervision for their offspring. This particular benefit must have been especially appealing to a group of women who had chosen to work out of concern for their children's well-being. It also helps explain the stronger preference for paper mill work of immigrant wives and widows, whose cultures underscored the importance of maternal and wifely duties.[32]

Because individual workers were not tied to the pace and hours of other workers or of machines, paper work permitted a flexibility of scheduling which occasionally made for even greater autonomy. In some cases mills listing their hours of work as ten a day scheduled shorter hours in particular departments, especially those employing mothers. If Berkshire mills followed the example of their British competitors in this as in some other respects, the few mothers with infants could interrupt their work schedules to

31 *Mass. Census, 1885*, II, 1131–1137; Constance McLaughlin Green, *Holyoke, Massachusetts: A Case History of the Industrial Revolution and America* (New Haven, 1939), 199–200.
32 Harriet H. Robinson, *Loom and Spindle or Life Among the Early Mill Girls* (Kailua, 1976; orig. ed. 1898), 19–20.

nurse. Also, paper mills allowed absences for occasional brief demands on women's time, such as the need to care for sick friends and family members.[33]

At bottom, this flexibility as well as other elements of autonomy rested on the greater awareness of individual needs possible in the paper industry. Berkshire cotton, woolen, and paper mills all grew in size over the course of the nineteenth century, but paper firms remained the smallest of the three. By 1880 they averaged sixty-seven workers, about half of whom were women. Cotton mills employed an average of 137 workers, about half women. Although only about two fifths of woolen workers were female, the average of 147 workers per factory made the female work group far from small. Merely in planning, then, paper mills had an easier time accommodating individual needs.[34]

While this smaller size permitted the greater flexibility and autonomy that women workers evidently preferred, it also facilitated the more personal relationship with their employers which women workers particularly prized. Also, in contrast to the absentee ownership of many textile mills, local residents owned most paper mills and they managed their mills themselves. Thus, the paternalism of an earlier era persisted longer in the paper industry. Even in the late nineteenth century, women workers in one local mill regularly sat down and ate with the mill owner during the lunch hour while one woman read the newspaper aloud.[35]

Paternalism also lay at the root of the greater security that the paper industry guaranteed its women workers. Men who lived near their employees could better understand their workers' need for continuous income. Paternalistic paper mill employers resolved workers' grievances without the strikes which flared intermittently in local textile mills, another assurance of regular work. Furthermore, because paper making was relatively more

33 McGaw, "Sources and Impact," 319–320, 378–379; B. L. Hutchins, "The Employment of Women in Paper Mills," *Economic Journal*, XIV (1904), 236.

34 *Manufactures, Tenth Census*, 255. United States and Massachusetts censuses throughout the nineteenth century show paper mills consistently preferable in this regard.

35 Theresa M. McBride, "The Long Road Home: Women's Work and Industrilization," in Renate Bridenthal and Claudia Koonz (eds.), *Becoming Visible: Women in European History* (Boston, 1977), 290; Patricia Branca, "A New Perspective on Women's Work: A Comparative Typology," *Journal of Social History*, IX (1975), 141; McGaw, "Sources and Impact," 278–303.

capital intensive and less labor intensive than textile production, paper mill owners had less to gain by shutting down their mills during periods of slack demand. In the early years of Berkshire industry, women paper workers had the added benefit of not being machine tenders, whose work was frequently curtailed by low water and spring freshets.[36]

All of these factors explain the greater regularity of paper mill employment. The Massachusetts Manufacturing Census of 1875 found women paper workers in Berkshire County averaging 300 work days a year, 5.2 percent more than cotton workers and 6.6 percent more than woolen workers. Inasmuch as this figure allows for only a few days beyond Sundays and holidays, most women must have been assured work even during shutdowns to clean and overhaul machines. The smaller group of women classified as pieceworkers probably stayed at home during this time since they averaged eight fewer days, but even they worked more regularly than textile mill women. Breakdowns and power problems in the early part of the century, periodic strikes in the late 1850s, and mill closings for lack of cotton in the early 1860s must have made these differences between industries even more pronounced in the years before 1875.[37]

Paper mill owners writing to one another often noted the greater interest women workers had in regular pay. Rag room workers, those most likely to be wives or widows, expressed particular concern. The greater family responsibilities of these women undoubtedly made job security an especially important reason for their choice of paper mill work.[38]

More fundamental to their decision was that women who worked in paper mills were the kind of women who planned for themselves and their families. They had weighed alternative employments and the expected benefits of different family members working. In writing to mill owner Z. M. Crane in 1850, foreman J. D. Gibbons underscored paper mill women's concern with planning. As he explained, he had told "the rag room girls" that although the present company was ceasing operations "in all

36 *Ibid.*

37 *Mass. Census, 1875*, II, 445, 532, 579; McGaw, "Sources and Impact," 208–218; *Valley Gleaner*, Aug. 26, 1858, 2; Sept. 2, 1858, 2; Jan. 2, 1859, 2; Feb. 3, 1859, 2; Sept. 21, 1865, 2.

38 File 448, 6/5/1850, *passim*.

probability the mill would be run by some one and thay [sic] can have work. . . . [B]ut," he added, "thay don't like to rest on probibility [sic] thay want something decisive [sic]." Such women would be least likely to tolerate unexpected interruptions of work.[39]

The size, technology, and paternalism of paper mills assured women workers of another important kind of security: security of person. Unlike textile women who tended heavy machinery, almost no paper mill women were injured, disabled, or killed in job-related accidents. Most paper mill women worked in groups with other women which, with the added protection of the owners' oversight, prevented unwelcome attention from foremen. Also, paper mill villages were often set apart from the most congested parts of towns, giving women the security of knowing most of those whom they met on the streets as well as most of those with whom they worked in the mills. For victims of drunken husbands and fathers, the ability of mill owners to bar liquor from these smaller communities may also have been an important consideration.[40]

Judging from Berkshire County, then, even for women mill workers "a good place to work" was not an empty phrase. Granted, by 1880 those who came to the factories came there of necessity. Nevertheless, the ability to move and the existence of different kinds of mills guaranteed such women a measure of choice. Family needs and expectations curtailed the range of options for some, but others were both capable of choosing and permitted to do so. For them "a good place to work" meant autonomy and security.

Did these women choose jobs for reasons peculiar to their sex or can their behavior tell us something about the job preferences of all factory operatives? Several recent studies suggest that male mill workers shared the motives of their sisters in industry. The continued ill-starred attempts of men to found their own small businesses, the appeal of the crafts even as they declined, and the attachment of industrial workers to customary work rules provide evidence of the appeal of autonomy. Superficially the

39 File 447, 3/25/1850.

40 McGaw, "Technological Change." For a full discussion of other factors mentioned by women job applicants as reasons for seeking work, including, especially, preference for living in a particular town, see *idem*, "Sources and Impact," 372–376.

peripatetic nineteenth-century industrial worker appears to have been unconcerned about security, but the high rates of worker turnover probably tell us more about the overwhelming uncertainty of industrial employment than about workers' preferences. At least some immigrant workmen placed security high among their reasons for choosing the kinds of work that they did. As was the case for women in Berkshire County, only the most powerless workers in nineteenth-century America probably entered jobs simply because they paid best.[41]

But the case of women workers in Berkshire County does more than suggest some additional motives for mill operatives' job selections. It contributes to an emerging portrait of nineteenth-century workers as active shapers of their world, rather than passive victims of it. That even women industrial workers had employment alternatives reinforces this view, as does the evidence that they weighed these alternatives, making judgments about which mills were "good" places to work. Moreover, in selecting the alternative which offered the greatest autonomy and security, workers not only chose, but they chose to maintain their ability to choose.

41 Griffen and Griffen, *Natives and Newcomers*, 103–192; Rodgers, "Tradition, Modernity," 666–667; Brody, Steelworkers, 96–111, *passim*; Bodnar, "Immigration and Modernization," 53–57.

"Honor Each Noble Maid": Women Workers and the Yonkers Carpet Weavers' Strike of 1885

By SUSAN LEVINE

Though they were accused of being "unwomanly," the young women carpet weavers forced their views upon their employer. Their efforts are noteworthy in the history of labor and of American women. Susan Levine is in the Department of History at Duke University.

STUDIES OF AMERICAN WORKING WOMEN have focused either on early factory experiences, as in the case of the Lowell Mill girls, or on the new immigrants of the Progressive Era, post 1890. The critical period of American industrial expansion, the years between 1850 and 1890 have, by and large, been ignored.[1] Yet those years witnessed the general transformation of manufacturing from skilled hand production to large scale factory operations and the widespread entry of women into certain mechanized industries. One of these industries, carpet manufacture, illustrates the effects of this transition on a new female work force and the special place of working women in an organized late nineteenth-century laboring community.

Skilled hand loom weavers traditionally held considerable reign over the production of carpets. They established laws governing the role and prerogatives of weavers and manufacturers in the shop, and set the price for weaving, while enforcing rules determining who might learn the craft. By the 1880s, however, manufacturers challenged the power and the very existence of the hand loom weavers, introducing new

The author would like to thank Herbert Gutman, Leon Fink, Judy Hilkey and Allis Wolfe for their help and encouragement in preparing this paper.

1. However, see Philip S. Foner, *Women and the American Labor Movement from Colonial Times to the Eve of World War I* (New York and London, 1979), pp. 80–256. Foner discusses the Yonkers strike on pp. 195–96.

power looms worked by semi-skilled young women. But these new power loom weavers continued to demand control of work practices—control assured by their right to belong to a union. A series of long and bitter strikes that focused on union recognition and the women's rights in the shop, marked the industry during the mid 1880s. One of the most protracted strikes occurred in 1885 at the Alexander Smith and Sons Carpet Company in Yonkers, New York, one of the nation's largest mills. Led by the Knights of Labor, this strike revealed many of the sources of conflict between a new, predominantly female work force and an expanding industrial management.[2]

Alexander Smith, son of a prosperous New Jersey farmer and merchant, entered the carpet business with a small mill in West Farms, New York, in 1845. This first venture was unsuccessful, but, financed by his brother, a New York merchant, Smith began production again in 1851 with 100 hand looms. At the time, the majority of carpets used in this country were imported. Domestic production, centered in small Philadelphia hand-loom shops, was slow and very expensive. During the 1850s, Smith hired the "inventor," Halcyon Skinner, who produced the first axminster power loom in 1860. Four years later a fire destroyed all but one of these looms, reportedly leaving only the American flag flying above the mill. Undaunted, Smith moved his works to a brick mill in Yonkers where he began production with 100 hand looms and 30 axminster power looms. Within ten years Skinner's inventions and loom improvements gave Smith a near monopoly on the domestic production of axminster carpets, which were inexpensive and growing in popularity.[3]

2. For general accounts of the carpet industry see Arthur H. Cole and Harold T. Williamson, *The American Carpet Manufacture: A History and an Analysis,* (Cambridge, Mass., 1955) and John S. Ewing and Nancy P. Norton, *Broadlooms and Businessmen: A History of the Bigelow-Sanford Carpet Company,* (Cambridge, Mass., 1955).

3. *Carpet Trade,* December 1878; Yonkers *Statesman,* November 28, 1878; Rev. Charles E. Allison, *The History of Yonkers From Earliest Times to the Present* (New York, 1896), pp. 356-357; and J. Thomas Scharf, *History of Westchester County, New York* (Philadelphia, 1886), pp. 106-107. Erastus Bigelow invented the first carpet power loom in the 1850s. His was for ingrain carpets, a very popular type in the late nineteenth century. Axminsters were a pile carpet originally quite expensive. Smith's axminster power loom mechanized the process and greatly facilitated what had been the slowest and most painstaking carpet to produce by hand. The axminster and a variation, the moquette, quickly became very popular. See Cole and Williamson, *American Carpet Manufacture,* p. 69.

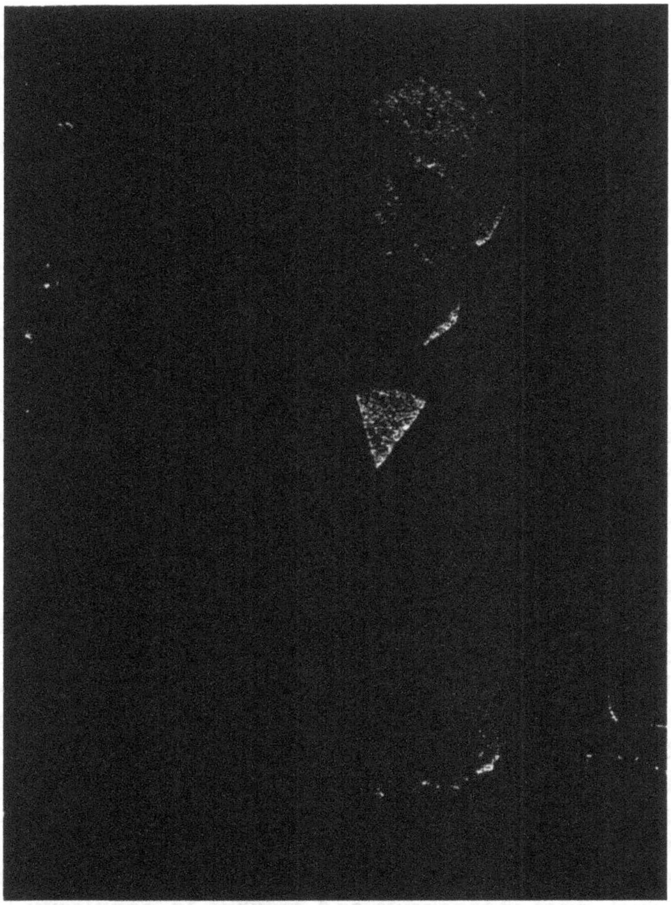

Alexander Smith. From Allison, The History of Yonkers *(1896). Photo by Dick Kennedy, City of Yonkers Office of Public Information. Courtesy of the Yonkers Public Library.*

Carpet power looms such as the one invented by Skinner drastically lowered the cost of production and changed the nature of carpet manufacturing. One historian of textile machinery estimated that the Smith axminster power loom "attended by one competent girl would produce in a day an amount equal to the product of ten English or French hand looms attended by as many men." Not only could the manufacturers now hire women to replace the much costlier labor of skilled men, but the women themselves could attend two or three looms at once. Within ten years of the introduction of power looms, weaving rates fell from thirty to six cents per yard. A census report in 1880 estimated that since 1860 the carpet industry had experienced a 100 percent increase in production accompanied by a decrease of over 50 percent in the cost of production.[4]

When Alexander Smith died in 1878, the Yonkers company was one of the country's major carpet mills, employing over 1500 people. Smith was the largest domestic producer of axminister carpets and second only to John Crossley of Scotland in the world market. Locally, Smith's interest in real estate and building gave additional employment to Yonkers' citizens. His contributions to local charities and hospitals together with his business enterprises prompted a eulogy to Smith as one of Yonkers' "most widely useful and honored citizens." Smith had also been active in local Republican politics, and was elected to Congress only hours before his death. On the afternoon of his funeral, flags in Yonkers flew at half mast and many shops including the carpet mills were closed.[5]

4. John L. Hayes, *American Textile Machinery* (Cambridge, England, 1879), p. 53. United States Census, Tenth Census, 1880, Joseph D. Weeks, *Report on the Statistics of Wages in Manufacturing Industries* (1886), p. 323.

"Duncraggan," the Yonkers home of William F. Cochran. From Scharf, History of Westchester County *(1886).*

William F. Cochran. From Allison, The History of Yonkers *(1896). Photo by Dick Kennedy, City of Yonkers Office of Public Information. Courtesy of the Yonkers Public Library.*

Smith's son, Warren B. Smith, and son-in-law, William Cochran, who inherited the business, set a more aggressive pace than the elder Smith in both plant expansion and labor productivity. Within the year, one of the leading trade journals, *The Carpet Trade,* reported the company's first strike and much discontent in the mills over reduced wages and new shop policies. The journal noted, "There was never a time in the history of the Smith Carpet Company when they have been in a more unsettled condition." However, the company weathered the transition and prospered. By 1885, their output had doubled. In the seven years after Alexander Smith's death, the work force increased to over 3000 and the plant expanded to three mills that housed 600 looms plus all the auxiliary machinery for spinning, printing and finishing. The

5. Yonkers *Statesman,* November 21, 1878 and June 8, 1882. See also Scharf, *Westchester County,* pp. 108-109, and Allison, *History of Yonkers,* pp. 359-61. Sophie Green, "The History and Development of the Carpet Industry in Yonkers" (master's thesis, Columbia University, 1936) has an account of Smith's role in the community; see p. 41.

English poet laureate, John Masefield, who worked in the Smith mills during the early 1890s, described the huge expanse of red brick buildings that covered several acres along the Nepperhan river in Yonkers:

> I crossed the track, went up the wooden steps and through some big green doors into a deafening, roaring, clanging clack in which one had to shout to make oneself heard. We were on the lower weaving floor, where, I suppose, more than one-hundred power looms were in full work. All the floor on each side of the gangway was filled with looms, nearly all in action. The shuttles were stabbing and clacking, the belts were humming, the swords were coming back with a bang, and the appalling ceiling of advancing spools shook and jerked overhead. The noise was like nothing I had ever heard. The air was already filled with wool dust, and sweepers were moving along the gangway with their great brooms to sweep away the coloured dust.[6]

Mill work fell into categories divided by sex and by skill. Women constituted three-quarters of all mill employees, working as loom tenders, setters and winders. Although these were semi-skilled jobs requiring only a short period of training, the hierarchy of wage rates indicates that these were, in fact, the high status jobs for women in the factory. Other women and a few unskilled men cleaned and processed the wool, the dirtiest and lowest paid mill jobs. Here were found, especially among the men, the "greenhorn" immigrants employed in the factory. Most of the men were yarn printers, who operated huge printing drums. The printers along with a number of loom fixers and "boss" weavers made up the mill's skilled work force.[7]

In general, the workers in Smith's mills constituted a very young, immigrant work force, fresh to the factory experience. Of 1025 carpet weavers appearing in the Yonkers census for

6. John Masefield, *In the Mill* (London, 1941), p. 7; *Carpet Trade Review*, September 1879; Scharf, *Westchester County*, pp. 108–109; Allison, *History of Yonkers*, pp. 359–61. For an important discussion of the transition from first generation paternal management to second generation business concerns see Robert Ozanne, *A Century of Labor-Management Relations at McCormick and International Harvester* (Madison, Wisc., 1967).

7. This description of the work divisions has been compiled from the local histories and newspaper accounts of the strike. Some jobs were difficult to identify, notably the pickers who by most accounts were the lowest paid workers, yet they formed their own union. The women loom tenders and setters worked the power machines. The male loom-fixers were probably the most important workers in the mills. They fixed or prepared the looms for weaving and repaired broken looms. It is likely that at least some of the loom-fixers had once been hand-loom weavers. See Cole and Williamson, *American Carpet Manufacture.*

1880, 63 percent were under 21 (86 percent were under 25), 70 percent lived with one or both parents, and 72 percent had been born in Ireland or were the children of Irish immigrants (see table, below). Only 10 percent had fathers whom the census identified specifically as working in an industrial setting. One-quarter were daughters or sons of skilled artisans (carpenters, brick masons, etc.). Another 7 percent derived from families engaged in farming or petty commerce. Fully half of the women and men came from families headed by

AGE, MARITAL STATUS AND NATIVITY OF YONKERS CARPET WEAVERS

		Male (N=380)	Female (N=645)	Total (N=1025)
Age	10–15	24%	14%	18%
	16–20	37%	50%	45%
	21–25	16%	27%	23%
	26–30	6%	6%	6%
	31–40	8%	2%	4%
	41–50	5%	.5%	2%
	over 50	3%	.2%	1%
Marital Status	Married	21%	5%	11%
	with children	17%	2%	8%
	without children	4%	2%	3%
	Single	77%	93%	87%
	living with parent	66%	72%	70%
	living with other relative	3%	7%	6%
	Boarding	8%	15%	12%
	Spouse deceased	1%	2%	2%
Nativity	Native born	65%	76%	72%
	native parent	12%	13%	13%
	Irish parent	41%	50%	47%
	other parent	12%	13%	12%
	Foreign born	35%	24%	28%
	Irish	19%	18%	18%
	British	14%	5%	8%
	Irish parent	5%	4%	4%
	other parent	9%	1%	4%
	Other	2%	1%	2%
	Total number	380	645	1025

Source: United States Census, 10th census, 1880 Population Schedules, Yonkers, New York.

unskilled laborers. At least 18 percent of the latter can be identified specifically in the census as holding such non-factory jobs as gardener or teamster. The rest probably were outdoor construction workers, farm laborers, casual laborers and men who did the hauling, carting and cleaning around the factories. This latter group would slightly increase the number of fathers engaged in an industrial setting but it seems clear that Smith's operatives generally represented the first generation of their families to enter factory work.[8]

This young factory vanguard, however, did not venture into the marketplace or even into the factory alone. Almost half of the Yonkers carpet weavers had at least one brother or sister working with them in the carpet mills. An additional 14 percent had siblings employed elsewhere, often in either the local hat factory or silk mills. These figures suggest that the families of the carpet weavers did not or could not depend on the father's income alone. On the other hand, since the young carpet weavers were not the sole support of their families, they may have been less vulnerable to employer attacks when they formed labor organizations.[9]

In 1884, a severe depression in the carpet industry exacerbated the tense relations between management and carpet weavers. The level of domestic competition had so increased at the beginning of the decade that it first drove imports out of the market and then drastically reduced prices in the home market. Power mills had rapidly forced smaller hand manufacturers to expand production and switch to power looms or drop out of business. Because of the low market price for carpets, the large mills became increasingly anxious to cut costs by reducing the cost of labor and by introducing technological improvements. Wages and work discipline thus became focal points of conflict.[10]

8. The above and following information is taken from data on 1025 people in the 1880 population census manuscript schedules for Yonkers who gave their occupation as "works in carpet mill." This represents all the carpet mill workers in Yonkers for that year.

9. For a discussion of the role of wages for daughters and children in general in working-class families during the nineteenth century, see Joan Scott and Louise Tilly, *Women, Work and Family* (New York, 1978).

10. See Cole and Williamson, *American Carpet Manufacture*, pp. 77–94, and reports in the *Carpet and Upholstery Trade Review* each month for 1882–1885.

In response to the new factory conditions and as part of the general drive of the Knights of Labor, weavers at Smith began secretly to organize a union during early 1884. Encouraged by carpet locals in New York and Philadelphia, the Yonkers weavers formed their own local Knights of Labor assembly (Number 2985) and became part of the Knight's controversial District Assembly Number 49. Union activity centered among the skilled male printers, but in departments where no men worked, women were active and became officers. The setters, for example, elected Maggie McCabe president of their department. By early 1885, about 1500 women "of various ages" (out of 2500 women in the mills) belonged to the local.[11]

The Knights proclaimed an interest in organizing women along with blacks and all unskilled workers as early as 1881. Over the next few years, over 1200 women's locals formed around the country, including housewives and domestic servants as well as factory workers. Women moved into positions of local leadership, particularly during strikes when they served on local executive boards and negotiating committees. Although few women achieved national prominence, the Knights tried to develop a conscious program to address the predicament of women in industry. By the mid 1880s, there were a number of women organizers and in 1886 a national woman's investigator was appointed. In a mill such as Smith's where the vast majority of workers were women, this awareness of the needs and problems of women probably increased the popularity of the Knights.[12]

During 1884, tensions at the Smith mills mounted until both management and the newly organized weavers sought a strategic moment for a showdown. Smith reduced wages twice that year and introduced a new system of shop rules which disrupted the workers' customary social patterns within the mill by restricting conversation and imposing fines for being away from the looms. The second wage cut, in December, was seen by union spokesmen as a calculated provocation. Industry prices had reached record lows during the fall

11. Yonkers *Statesman*, February 27 and May 2, 1885; Yonkers *Gazette*, February 28, 1885 and New York *World*, June 6 and 29, 1885.

12. For a general account of the Knights of Labor see Norman Ware, *The Labor Movement in the United States, 1860–1890* (New York, 1929). See also Gerald N. Grob, *Workers and Utopia*, (Chicago, 1961).

The weaving mills (above) and the spinning and print mills (opposite page) of the Alexander Smith & Sons Carpet Company in Yonkers. From Scharf, History of Westchester County *(1886).*

season and Smith still had a large surplus of carpets on hand in December. This surplus, combined with the high cost of winter operations (increased need for light and heat) meant that a shutdown would not hurt the company.[13]

Union activity during 1884 concentrated on building a benefit fund in preparation for a strike. The weavers did not respond to Smith's wage cuts, apparently waiting until their own position was strengthened. In early February, 1885, however, Smith discovered the union's existence and immediately fired a number of workers including several women he accused of being ringleaders. To defend its very existence the union was forced to call a strike. On February 20, workers in the tapestry mill (the factory's largest department) left their looms at ten o'clock in the morning and paraded in the street in front of the mill. The company quickly informed the other workers that the factory would close at six o'clock and that the "doors would be locked." An hour later, the moquette weavers left their looms and joined the others in the street. Between 800 and 1200 union members began the

13. Yonkers *Statesman,* February 27, 1885, and Yonkers *Gazette,* February 28, 1885. See also *Carpet and Upholstery Trade Review,* March 1, 1885.

strike but by the end of the day, over 3000 people were locked out of Smith's mills.[14]

The following Monday, the pickers' union joined the strike, and by the end of that week the strikers elected an executive committee and issued a public statement detailing their grievances and listing four demands:

> First, the restoration of wages paid before December 1, 1884; Second, a readjustment of the arbitrary and unjust system of docking adopted by the firm; Third, a reinstatement of all employees unjustly discharged and no one to be discharged in the future except for cause assigned; Fourth, NO MORE BOSS OR SUPERINTENDENT TYRANNY.[15]

The strikers' major resentments focused on issues relating to control at the work place. Management had gradually been encroaching on prerogatives of work rhythms and social behavior in the mills. Less than a year before the strike the company had introduced a system of docking which outraged the workers. Calling the new discipline "white slavery," the strikers outlined the new rules:

14. Yonkers *Statesman*, February 27 and March 2, 1885; *Irish World*, March 7 and 9, 1885.

15. Yonkers *Statesman*, February 27, 1885; New York *Times*, February 24, 1885.

If a girl is caught looking out of a window, which in some portions of the mill is only allowed to be raised three inches for ventilation, her loom is stopped and she is sent to the boss to explain, and is very often docked . . . They (the women) are not allowed to talk to one another during working hours or at noon under penalty of being docked or discharged. Several cases are known where girls were discharged for laughing aloud during dinner hour, the time which really belongs to themselves . . . they are not allowed to eat dinner together, even two sisters working in two different departments are not allowed to eat their meals together in the factory, and during the noon hour men are kept walking through the different departments to watch them and prevent them from holding any conversation with one another . . .

If one of us happens to be sick and unable either to attend the factory or send word of our disability, she is discharged . . . One operative narrowly escaped discharge for staying home on the morning of her mother's death she having failed to send a message of the cause of her absence.[16]

The docking system went beyond simple behavior "modification" into the realm of the work process. Women were paid by the "stretch" or length of carpet prepared or woven. Traditionally, the price for weaving had been set by the weavers' association just as the weavers had determined who was taught the trade by regulating "learners." Previously, if a worker made a mistake in production, she was called into the office and required to buy the damaged rug which she could then sell herself. Now, the company set the weaving rate, docked a certain amount from the weaver's pay for damaged goods, and kept the damaged rug. As the women frequently watched each other's looms if they were late or absent, they complained of being penalized for faulty work that was not their own. They further complained of unjust fines and unfair loom assignments.

In cleaning or brushing down their looms which they are compelled to do twice a day, while the machinery is in motion, if a part of it is broken by accident the operative is docked $5; if the brush is broken, 25¢, the brush costing originally 12¢; in drawing out a wire, and by so doing they bend it, which does not in any way injure it, they are docked 50¢, the wiring costing 1¢ when new . . . Girls have been frequently docked for work not done by them, and no satisfaction given when fault was found except to say that "someone had to pay for the flaw and if they did not like it they could leave."

Since the average loom tender earned about $1.48 per day before the December wage cut, fifty cents constituted a severe fine.[17]

16. Yonkers *Statesman*, February 27, March 2, May 2, 1885.

17. Ibid.

Smith's new factory discipline, explained as necessary for "so large a factory," imposed a new mode of behavior and work atmosphere upon the weavers. The young workers who had probably never worked outside the home before had to learn to concentrate on their work in the factory and to make work-time the central organizing principle of their daily lives. The veteran weavers were being asked to give up old privileges and shop rights. Company and union were locked in a battle for control of the conditions and prerogatives of work.[18]

Smith absolutely opposed the union from the start and refused to speak with or recognize any committee of workers. The only person he agreed to see was a reporter from the local Republican newspaper, the *Statesman*, who was authorized to announce that "the strikers are simply individuals who were in our employ and chose to leave it. We shall never take any of them back except at reduced wages." A few days later, the paper added that the company was "convinced it would be better to sell the property than submit to the demands." Reflecting the company's conviction that the union threatened control over its business, the *Statesman* rephrased the strike demands:

> The carpet company must pay not what the market will justify, but what the hands demand. There must be an end to all wholesome discipline found absolutely necessary to the success of every large business, and the proprietors must surrender the privilege of deciding who they will employ and who they will not. In other words, the management of this large capital and these immense works is to be passed over by the proprietors to the control of the union.[19]

Unions in general and the Knights of Labor in particular angered company spokesmen. To the trade's major journal, the *Carpet and Upholstery Trade Review*, as well as to the *Statesman*, the Knights represented a secret and illegal combination meant to "coerce both capital and labor" and "interfere with freedom of contract between employer and employees."[20] The *Carpet and Upholstery Trade Review* believed it an "absolute necessity that manufacturers stamp out at any cost all further connection between their employees and the

18. Yonkers *Gazette*, March 7, 1885. For discussions of work discipline and job control, see Ozanne, *Century of Labor-Management Relations;* Harry Braverman, *Labor and Monopoly Capital* (New York, 1974); and David Montgomery, *Worker's Control in America* (Cambridge, 1979).

19. Yonkers *Statesman*, March 7 and 19, 1885; *Irish World*, March 7, 1885.

Knights of labor." The editor pointed out that the "salient" feature of the strike was not a question of wages, "but an attempt to dictate to the proprietors of mills with regard to management of their business." The success of the union, he wrote, "would have left the Alexander Smith and Sons Carpet Company the nominal owners of the mills, but the practical control of them would have been vested in the Knights of Labor." Both the company and the union recognized that the issues of factory rules, prerogatives over hiring and firing and the right to belong to a union vitally defined their relations with one another.[20]

The Yonkers carpet weavers, in contact with weavers' organizations in other mills, had been preparing for a long battle. During the previous year, they built up a strike fund and a chain of support throughout the carpet industry. One union spokesman reported, "Other locals have been preparing with us . . . for a year past for this struggle." The Yonkers local "was also preparing for the strike by setting aside a small portion of each week's wages so as to have everything arranged for a prolonged siege."[21]

From the outbreak of the strike, the battle of the Yonkers carpet weavers became a *cause célèbre* of organized labor throughout upstate New York and in Philadelphia. *John Swinton's Paper,* the nation's leading labor weekly, demanded, "Brothers, help your sisters!" By the beginning of May, after eleven weeks of lockout and strike, the Yonkers weavers had received over 8000 dollars in support. News of the contest spread across the country. Delegations of Yonkers women carpet weavers appeared at weekly meetings of the New York Central Labor Union (CLU) and other union meetings in the area. In response, the CLU and member unions, including a number of New York City women's unions, sent weekly contributions and held several benefit balls and concerts in support of the strikers.[22]

20. *Carpet and Upholstery Trade Review,* March 1, April 1, 1885; New York *Herald,* March 19, 1885.

21. Yonkers *Statesman,* March 2, 1885.

22. *John Swinton's Paper,* April 19, April 29, May 3, 1885. Reports in this paper and in the New York *Herald* listed contributions and meetings of support. See, for example, New York *Herald,* June 6, 15, 22, 1885. See also New York *World,* June 22, 1885; *Irish World,* May 30, 1885. Newspapers in other carpet centers also reported the events of the Yonkers strike. For examples see Philadelphia *Inquirer,* March 5, 1885, and Amsterdam (New York) *Daily Democrat,* February 27, 1885.

The women carpet-weavers shown here were on strike in Philadelphia at the same time as their Yonkers sisters. From Frank Leslie's Illustrated Newspaper, *February 7, 1885.*

As soon as the strike began, an appointed committee sounded out local Yonkers businessmen for support. Some merchants reported fears of boycotts and threats of closing owing to lack of business, but even the *Statesman* grudgingly admitted that many Yonkers tradesmen sympathized with the striking carpet weavers. A local doctor offered his services free to all strikers, and several "Yonkers gentlemen" sent donations. In addition, the Montgomery Club, the local branch of the Irish nationalist *Clan Na Gael,* contributed 100 dollars to the union benefit fund. The most significant evidence of community support came when the owner of the skating rink, the town's most popular meeting place, donated his premises without charge for a benefit ball. With the help of the CLU, the carpet weavers sold nearly 6000 tickets in both Yonkers and New York City to what the *Statesman* reported as one of the "finest events of the year."[23] And the

23. Yonkers *Statesman,* March 2, March 25, May 2, 1885. The papers often noted the dependence of local merchants on trade from the carpet weavers.

June 6, 1885 issue of *John Swinton's Paper* saluted "each noble maid" with an impassioned poem modelled in metre and emotion upon Tennyson's "Charge of the Light Brigade":

THE YONKERS WOMEN'S STRIKE

"Strike for your rights!" she said,
Wildly her shuttle waved,
While round about the maid,
Machinery thundered.
"Down with your tools!" she cried,
Then they marched side by side,
Eyes flashing honest pride,
Gallant few hundred.
Oh! What a strike they made,
Was there a girl afraid?
E'en though the varlets said,
"Someone has blundered".
Weavers with shuttles deft,
Of every right bereft,
Nothing but strike was left,
So struck the few hundred.

Dailies to right of them,
Weeklies to left of them,
Slander in front of them,
Volleyed and thundered.
Charged at with shot and shell,
(But not a striker fell),
Boldly they stood and well,
Noble few hundred.
Oh! How they struck that day,
Striking to get fair play,
Striking for honest pay,
Their wrongs are unnumbered.
When can their glory fade?
Honor the strike they made,
Honor each noble maid,
Gallant few hundred.

Smith spent the eleven weeks from the beginning of the strike until early May "cleaning and repairing machinery and straightening accounts" and, probably, watching the market. Preparing to reopen on May 5, in time for the spring trade, he announced that those hands who had not walked out could resume work. Despite immediate reports in the *Statesman* of the "music of machines" and droves of workers returning to their jobs, by the highest count less than one-third of the workers actually returned to the mills. On May 15, ten days after the doors reopened, only 50 out of 600 looms were in operation. One woman reported men at "women's work" attending the looms, and another saw "petty bosses" operating the machines. Those who returned did so with the promise of three dollars back pay for each week of the lockout. However, when the first payday arrived, those who had returned the first day received less than half the promised amount. Those who returned the second day received only seven dollars and those who came after that received nothing at all. In response, fifty-two hands, half of all who had gone back to work, walked out and joined the strike. Smith's assertion of authority in the shop only served to strengthen the union's position.[24]

The "lady picketers" of Yonkers became famous. Workers from the mills, including the women, began a mass picket in front of the mill gates as soon as the lockout ended. The women often took the initiative in talking with other workers and publicizing the strike by parading in front of the mills or on the city streets in their "Sunday best," ignoring accusations by local papers of their "unwomanliness." For the first several days, members of the New York City Knights of Labor reinforced their ranks. Committees, mainly of women weavers, made lists of those who crossed their lines and sent delegates to the homes of those workers to convince or cajole them into supporting the strike. The police chief with fifteen of his men (of a force of thirty five) appeared at the mill gates to insure "all those who desire to go to work will be protected in their right to do so." Yet even the police force was not immune to the general current of community feeling. One officer remarked, "I know every one of them [the lady pickets] for years, and know them to be respectable . . . I think it would be a creditable act for Mr. Smith to come out and talk with

24. New York *World*, May 25, 1885; Yonkers *Statesman*, daily reports, May 5-29, 1885. See also Yonkers *Gazette*, March 7, 1885 and *Irish World*, May 23 and June 6, 1885.

the strikers." The *Statesman* condemned this officer for "condoning lawlessness" and recommended he be returned to private life.[25]

The tension mounted daily in front of the Smith mills. The strikers attempted to keep scabs away from the gates and the police protected the "rights of citizens" to work. After a week of confrontation, the officers arrested carpet printers John Welsh and John Devine and charged them with "walking to and fro in front of the drum room of the mill and refusing to disperse when ordered to do so." Another carpet printer, Rudolph Strinnadel, was arrested the next day on the same charges. Despite the arrests, picketing continued in force, and crowds gathered around the mill gates every morning and evening as those working inside came and went. Two days after Strinnadel's arrest, police arrested three women, also for "walking to and fro." The three, Ellen Tracy, Lizzie Wilson and Mary Carey, were taken to the courthouse where the local prosecutor advised them to go home "and never do this again." He refused a motion to dismiss their cases and set bail at fifty dollars each. The union's lawyer paid the bail and the women were conveyed home in a special carriage provided by the court. During their hearing, an "immense crowd" gathered outside the courthouse and loudly applauded the "heroines for a time."[26]

Far from intimidating the striking women, the arrests seemed only to strengthen their resolve. Three days later, Mary Carey was arrested again, this time with her sister Margaret and two other sisters, Bridget and Maggie Flynn. All were described as "well known in Yonkers" and released on bail. Striking workers gathered around the police station to support them.[27]

The arrests in general, but of women in particular, outraged the town. Concerned citizens held a mass meeting the day after the first group of women were taken into custody. The meeting in Getty Square, the city's central plaza, attracted a huge crowd estimated to number 2000 by the *Statesman* and nearer to 10,000 by John Swinton. The YMCA band

25. Yonkers *Statesman*, May 7, 8, 15 and 22, 1885; *Carpet and Upholstery Trade Review*, March 1, 1885; *John Swinton's Paper*, May 24, 1885.

26. Yonkers *Statesman*, May 16–19, 1885.

27. Yonkers *Statesman*, May 22, 1885. See also New York *Herald*, May 22, 1885.

entertained and Edward King of the New York Typographical Union Number Six and leader of the CLU addressed the meeting. Other speakers included J. Shewitz, editor of the German socialist eight-hour paper, *VolkZeitung*, and two Yonkers aldermen whose names the papers neglected to print. The meeting passed resolutions denouncing the police actions as being "despotic and prejudicial to the best interests of the law abiding citizens of our city" and heartily commending the strikers "who have conducted the strike with calmness, moderation and ability." The meeting pledged its "moral support until the strike is ended."[28]

Reaction was equally intense in New York City where the CLU held an "indignation meeting" two weeks later. Over 2000 people attended, described as "women of every craft and men of every trade." One paper reported that representatives of the entire working-class community including wives as well as "every grade of labor, male and female, white and black, native and alien" had come out for the ceremonies. Yonkers' Democratic paper, the *Gazette,* described "five hundred pretty working girls arrayed in attractive spring suits . . . five hundred women of maturer age, and fifteen hundred members of the CLU." Nationally known leaders including Adolph Strasser, John Swinton and Edward King addressed the meeting. There were speeches in English and German, and Henry George and James Redpath sent telegrams of support. Finally, John Swinton announced the formation of a "New Order of Nobility, the Women's Legion of Honor," and presented Mary Carey, Lizzie Wilson and Ellen Tracy with special silver medals of honor.[29]

In presenting the medals, Swinton praised the young women for showing strength and dedication as unionists and commended them for their "self denial in behalf of . . . womanhood." Edward King warned the enemies of labor that they might strike at men, but to beware of "trampling upon the rights and privileges of women." For much of organized labor, the strike came to symbolize the pluck as well as the plight of young women workers. Locally, the three women were honored at later labor gatherings and appeared

28. Yonkers *Statesman*, May 15 and 19, 1885; *John Swintons' Paper*, May 24, 1885.

29. *John Swinton's Paper*, June 6 and 14, 1885; New York *Herald*, May 29, 1885; New York *World*, May 29 and June 8, 1885; Yonkers *Gazette*, June 6, 1885.

Warren B. Smith. From Allison, The History of Yonkers. *Photo by Dick Kennedy. Courtesy of the Yonkers Public Library.*

even after the strike ended in Labor Day parades as far away as Newark, New Jersey.[30]

The strike went on through June into early July. Women continued parading in the streets and holding their positions as pickets despite reports of pressure by local priests on the families of union members and a campaign mounted by the *Statesman* to "let [the women] play amazon no longer." The paper advised the women in vain to "go to Sunday school . . . and be good girls" so that they "may yet get good husbands and become honored members of society." Yet throughout the strike only two or three union women were reported to have deserted the organization.[31]

The arrested strikers were never brought to trial. After turning down the prosecution's motion for a trial without jury, a move probably aimed at avoiding sympathy for the

30. New York *Herald*, May 29, 1885; *Irish World*, July 18, 1885; Yonkers *Gazette*, June 6, 1885; *John Swinton's Paper*, February 14, 1886; *Woman's Journal*, July 11, 1885. The strike prompted one anonymous poet to send to *John Swinton's Paper* "The Yonkers Women's Strike," the poem that appears on p. 168 of this article.

31. Yonkers *Statesman*, May 29, 1885; New York *World*, May 29, June 13, 1885; *Irish World*, May 29, 1885.

women strikers, the district court dismissed all cases on a technicality.

In mid-June, a bomb was found in the drum room of the mill. Smith immediately accused the Knights of Labor of planting it. The Knights, however, denied responsibility for the bomb and implied that Smith himself had arranged the incident. The Knights went so far as to offer a reward for any information relating to the event, but an investigation was never made.[32]

By mid-July, there were several indications that Smith was no longer interested in continuing the strike. His surplus stock had been sold and the time for beginning next season's contracts had already passed. The union, however, sustained by support from all over the east coast, maintained their stance, well aware of the company's weakness. One union spokesman commented that "we keep ourselves as well posted about the carpet world as the bosses do. They must have samples by fall."[33]

On July 16, after a series of secret meetings, the carpet weavers announced a settlement. After five months on strike, the union claimed a victory, "tho not as decisive as hoped for." The agreement did appear to represent a triumph for the strikers. The 10 percent wage cut was restored and another 10 percent advance granted. The company agreed to rehire all union members including those who had been fired originally. More important for the existence of the union in the mills was a guarantee that no one would be dismissed in the future "without cause or for belonging to the union." The company agreed to adjust the docking system and to deal with a union grievance committee. For their part, the carpet weavers' union and the Knights of Labor agreed not to strike without notice and to try to settle by arbitration first.[34]

Because of the importance of Smith's agreement to the industry in general, the company insisted upon keeping the

32. Yonkers *Statesman*, June 16, 22, and 27, 1885; New York *Herald*, June 18, 1885; New York *World*, June 17, 1885; *Irish World*, July 18, 1885.

33. *John Swinton's Paper*, June 21 and 27, 1885; Yonkers *Statesman*, May 29, June 1, 1885; Yonkers *Gazette*, June 6, 1885.

34. Yonkers *Statesman*, July 13, 1885; *Irish World*, July 11, 1885; Cole and Williamson, *American Carpet Manufacture*, p. 247. That the union won the right to a grievance committee was very important as these committees were particularly militant and abhorred by management. See *Carpet and Upholstery Trade Review*, July 15, 1886.

exact provisions secret. The union apparently agreed not to "trumpet victory," and the *Statesman* maintained that "no degrading concessions had been made." The union victory at Smith's, in fact, signaled a general wage raise in the carpet industry. Smith's nearest competitors, Stephen Sanford in Amsterdam, New York and E. S. Higgins in New York City, immediately granted their workers a 10 percent wage increase. By 1890, the United States census reported that carpet weavers received the highest wages of all women employed in the textile industry. In addition, the price of carpets increased, with Smith raising his by five cents per yard as soon as the strike ended.[35]

The carpet weavers' union continued at the Smith mills through the 1880s. In early 1886, six months after the strike was settled, *John Swinton's Paper* carried reports of violations of the strike agreement and of union members, men and women, being discharged and blacklisted. In February 1886, the Central Labor Union called for a boycott of the Smith company, but owing to a dispute between the carpet weavers' local and the national leadership of the Knights of Labor, the Knights never took up this boycott. By the end of 1886, the carpet union became the focus of an internal dispute among the New York Knights of Labor over the competing jurisdiction of mixed and trade assemblies. The local was suspended for refusing to carry out district orders to take back members who had refused to strike. This dispute reflected an increasingly serious problem of authority within the Knights' organization. In 1887, the Yonkers local joined other carpet assemblies in seceding from the district assembly. They formed their own carpet District Assembly, Number 126, and were summarily ousted from the order. The general decline of the Knights after 1886 combined with selectively conciliatory moves by Smith management (they were the first carpet mill to voluntarily grant a Saturday half-holiday during the summer in 1886) weakened the union at Yonkers. By the end of the decade Smith once again maintained an open shop.[36]

35. *Carpet and Upholstery Trade Review*, July 15, 1885; *John Swinton's Paper*, June 7 and 14, 1885; United States Census, 11th Census, 1890, Report on Manufacturing Industries, S.D.N. North, "Wool Manufacture," p. 42.

36. Green, "Carpet Industry in Yonkers," p. 57; Knights of Labor, *Proceedings*

MONOPOLIST—"*What! Laboring people banding together and talking about* their *rights? I must reduce wages!" From* Frank Leslie's Illustrated Newspaper, *September 5, 1885.*

The Yonkers carpet weavers' strike illustrates both the capacity and the limits of a predominantly female and youthful labor force. The fact that most were women gave the weavers an ambivalent strength. Exercising new found independence, the weavers militantly protected their right to organize and to protect themselves at work. In doing so they left the expected domestic sphere of women behind and entered a more public domain. But it cannot be said that they entirely rejected the traditional ideals of feminine virtue and woman's role in the family. In many ways they defended their rights at work in terms of the traditional virtues and privileges of women. It is likely that by 1890 many, if not most, of the women who had participated in the Yonkers strike had married and left the mills.

But the youth and unmarried status of the weavers also provided a source of strength for their organization. Since

---

of the General Assembly, 1885, p. 140; *John Swinton's Paper*, February 14, 1886; Cole and Williamson, *American Carpet Manufacture*, pp. 184–86.

they were in most cases not the sole support of their families, they could afford, although obviously not without sacrifice, to hold out until Smith was forced to settle or lose the spring trade. The weavers' families undoubtedly felt the strain but their main income was not cut off. This strength in their family position in addition to the wide support they received from labor organizations and other community groups gave the power-loom weavers some of the leverage which monoply over skill had given the generation of hand-loom weavers before them. But this very lack of skill and their consequent vulnerability to the blacklist or to technological replacement meant that long term organization was more difficult.

The weavers' strike in both its strengths and weaknesses suggests important elements in the conflicts between a new factory labor force and an expanding industrial management. Each came to the factory with a certain conception of prerogatives and rights governing work and the work place. The relations between management and weavers developed not simply from an inevitable logic of efficiency and profit, but by the constant testing of the legitimacy of their respective standards of authority and power in the mills.

THE UNION OF SEX AND CRAFT IN THE HAVERHILL SHOE STRIKE OF 1895

By MARY H. BLEWETT

Female industrial labor in the late nineteenth century is generally understood to have been unskilled, low-wage, young, unmarried, living with their families and foreign-born or of foreign parentage. This pattern seemed to condemn women workers to passivity and powerlessness. In fact there was a lively tradition of effective group action in the nineteenth century among women factory workers in laundries, garment-making, carpet-weaving, textiles and shoe-making. Indeed women in the shoe industry in eastern Massachusetts, Pennsylvania, and New York established a long history of union and strike activity beginning in the 1830s. The women workers in the shoe industry depended strongly on a linkage between sex and craft to provide a power base for their unions. This link underlay the participation of women workers in a shoe strike in Haverhill, Massachusetts in the winter of 1895.[1]

[1] For a general description of the condition of wage-earning women in the late nineteenth century, see John B. Andrews and W. D. P. Bliss, *History of Women in Trade Unions* (New York: Arno Press, 1974), a reprint of Senate Document No. 645, v. 10 of the *Report on Condition of Woman and Child Wage-Earners in the United States*, 61st Congress, 2nd Session (Washington: Government Printing Office, 1911); Edith Abbott, *Women in Industry: A Study in American Economic History* (New York: D. Appleton and Co., 1910); Alice Henry, *Women and the Labor Movement* (New York: George H. Doran Co., 1923); Robert W. Smuts, *Women and Work in America* (New York: Schocken Books, 1971); Susan Levine, "Then Strive For Your Rights, O, Sisters Dear, The Carpet Weavers' Strike and the Knights of Labor," a paper read at the Berkshire Conference on Women's History, June, 1976 and Meredith Tax, "Conditions of Working Women in the Late 19th and Early 20th Centuries," *Women: A Journal of Liberation*, 2 (1971), 16-20. For female shoeworkers, Augusta E. Galster, *The Labor Movement in the Shoe Industry: With Special Reference to Philadelphia* (New York: The Ronald Press, 1924). For a discussion of the general lack of interest in organizing women workers, James J. Kenneally, "Women and Trade Unions, 1870-1920: The Quandary of the Reformer," *Labor History*, 14 (1973), 42-55.

The Women Stitchers' Union of Haverhill conducted militant strike activity in concert with male workers, supported by the American Federation of Labor and the Socialist Labor Party. Cross-class ties with privileged women outside of Haverhill provided a crucial source of money and respectability for the strikers. The women who led the strike action also led efforts by the community of Haverhill to resist changes in its factory system and in its relationship with the native-born shoe workers. As skilled workers whose class consciousness was stimulated by the bitter depression years of the 1890s, the stitchers exercised real power in the 1895 strike which they used to advance their interests as female workers. Their militant support for an industry-wide federation of crafts was reinforced by an unusual pattern of geographical mobility for a female work force, a mobility shaped by the economic requirements of an extremely seasonal industry. The stitchers of Haverhill and of other Massachusetts shoe cities played a major role in the formation of the Boot and Shoe Workers' Union (B&SWU) in Boston in April 1895. The leader of the Haverhill stitchers' union, socialist Mary A. Nason, became the first woman to represent a constituency of women unionists on the general executive board of a national trade union.[2]

The tradition of organization by female shoeworkers began in 1833 in Lynn, Massachusetts and in 1836 in Philadelphia where female associations of binders organized the women who did the hand work of sewing or binding the upper portions of shoes at home before mechanization and the introduction of the factory system. These associations of binders were not, however, represented in the general trades organizations of either Lynn or Phila-

[2] Nason was followed in this position on the General Executive Board of the BSWU by Emma Steghagen and Mary Anderson. Anderson represented women workers in this capacity from 1905-1919 and also became a national organizer for the Women's Trade Union League in 1910. In 1920 she became the first chief of the Women's Bureau in the Department of Labor. Recent writing on the leadership role of women in the trade union movement includes R. Scharnau, "Elizabeth Morgan, Crusader for Labor Reform," *Labor History*, 14 (1973), 340-351 and Lucille O'Connell, "Women in the Massachusetts Labor Movement: Mary Kenny O'Sullivan," a paper read at the New England Historical Association meeting, May 3, 1975. In an analysis of about sixty, skilled Scottish women weavers in Holyoke, Massachusetts in 1853-1860, Ray Ginger concluded that the mobility of the work force retarded the development of group consciousness and organization because two-thirds of these immigrant workers left the industry after three years. This importation of skilled female workers however filled a short term need for an industry which was rapidly mechanizing to eliminate skilled labor. Ray Ginger, "Labor in a Massachusetts Cotton Mill, 1853-1860," *Business History Review*, 28 (1954), 67-91.

delphia, although male workers, in and out of the shoe trades, supported their strikes and encouraged the organization of women.[3]

In the post-Civil War period, labor activity among female shoe workers continued. The introduction of the sewing machine in 1852 in Lynn began to replace binding by hand with stitching by machine and to remove the workplace from the home to the factory. Civil War orders for boots and shoes stimulated investment and mechanization. Stitching in factories was at first done by men using foot-powered machines, but as the male shoeworkers marched off to the war, women replaced many of them at steam-powered machines. With the encouragement of the National Labor Union Congress in 1868 and the support of the male shoeworkers organized in the Knights of St. Crispin, the Daughters of St. Crispin became the first national trade union for women. The eagerness of the Crispins to organize the female workers as stitchers in 1868 suggests an effort to stabilize competitive wage rates for male and female: one of the demands of the Crispins was equal pay for equal work. During 1869 the Daughters established twenty-four lodges throughout the shoe producing states (fourteen in eastern Massachusetts), but the organization seemingly disappeared during the depression following the Panic of 1873.[4]

---

[3] Similar kinds of activity took place in New York City. The Philadelphia group was called the Female Association of Boot and Shoe Binders (1836) and the Lynn group, the Female Society of Lynn and Vicinity for the Protection and Promotion of Female Industry (Andrews and Bliss, 41-44; Galster, 24-27).

[4] The first stitcher in Lynn in 1852 was Hannah Harris according to Blanche Evans Hazard, *The Organization of the Boot and Shoe Industry in Massachusetts Before 1875* (Cambridge: Harvard Univ. Press, 1921), 78-80 106, 109. Hazard indicates that prior to the Civil War, men stitched uppers by machine in factories in Natick and the female workers remained binding uppers at home. She also notes male stitching of this sort in Lynn in 1857. However the impact of the Civil War in Randolph stimulated the shoemaking industry and recruited soldiers from the shoemaking work force. Both males and females took the place of drafted workers (Hazard, 117). Hazard (140) also includes the report of "Lucy Brown, a Contented Rapid Stitcher" who stitched by foot power in 1861 in North Bridgewater and witnessed men leaving the stitching rooms because they were unable to make satisfactory money at piece work rates. The *Haverhill Directory* lists sixty-eight female stitchers and eleven male stitchers in 1857 and 112 female and thirty male stitchers in 1859. After an initial period of sharing the stitching work on uppers, women came to dominate, while males worked on the heavy welting (Goodyear) and sole stitching (McKay) machines in the bottoming department. See also John Philip Hall, "The Knights of St. Crispin in Massachusetts, 1869-1878," *Journal of Economic History*, 18 (1958), 163, and Don D. Lescohier, *The Knights of St. Crispin, 1867-1874* (New York: Arno Press, 1969), a reprint of the 1910 edition, 17-21. The

Former Crispins, both Knights and Daughters, formed the nucleus of the shoeworkers' assemblies organized by the Knights of Labor in the 1880s. The shoeworkers dominated the Massachusetts assemblies of the Knights. The Garfield Assembly of Philadelphia in 1881 was the first female local in the Knights and sent its delegate, shoeworker Mary Stirling, as an official representative to the General Assembly in 1881. However, the Knights failed to support the Garfield Assembly's first fight with its employers over the discharge of its officers. Only after a bitter struggle by the women to reinstate their leaders and a successful floor fight at the 1884 convention to quash a rival organization, did the Knights of Labor show some sign of support for organizing women workers. Most shoe centers in Massachusetts were organizing assemblies of women workers, and Haverhill's local #3117 was established in early 1884.[5]

The General Assembly of the Knights of Labor in 1885 encouraged the organization of women by designating a special committee of three to gather statistics on women's work. One of the members was shoeworker Mrs. Lizzie Shute of Haverhill who represented District Assembly No. 77 of Essex County, Massachusetts where Lynn was also situated. The committee

---

National Labor Union Congress also recognized and encouraged the work of Miss Kate Mullaney of the Laundry Workers' Union of Troy, New York and made her national organizer of women, the first appointment of this kind. The laundry union in Troy was crushed in a strike in 1869 (Andrews and Bliss, 106-107). Hall (162) and Lescohier (77-78) barely acknowledge the existence of the Daughters of St. Crispin. See also Galster, 42-45; Andrews and Bliss, 108-110.

[5] Norman J. Ware, *The Labor Movement in the United States, 1860-1895: A Study in Democracy* (New York: Appleton, 1929), 200-201 and Gerald N. Grob, *Workers and Utopia: A Study of Ideological Conflict in the American Labor Movement, 1865-1900* (Chicago: Quadrangle Books, 1961), 55, 122-123. Ware argues that Harry F. Skeffington (later organizer of the Boot and Shoe Workers' International Union in 1889) organized the first women's local in the Knights, the Garfield Assembly. As a shoeworker, Skeffington understood the importance of organizing all crafts in the industry and was never comfortable with the Knights' insistence on the mixed assembly of various crafts. Ware also emphasizes the hesitation and ambivalence of the Knights over the question of organizing and integrating women workers into their organization. Levine examines the ambivalence of the Knights toward women workers in the setting of carpetweavers' strikes in 1883 and 1884 (Levine, *passim*). At the first convention of the Knights of Labor in 1878, the following resolution was adopted as one of the principal objectives of the order: "To secure for both sexes equal pay for equal work." This was an attempt to remove women and children as a source of cheap labor in an industrial order which was rapidly mechanizing. The objective was reemphasized at the 1879 convention as an effort to protect the interests of adult male labor. A resolution at this convention to admit women as members was tabled (Andrews and Bliss, 114-132).

found the average working day for women was ten hours and the average wage to be $5.00 a week, except for women stitchers in the shoe industry who earned "a more lucrative" wage. By 1886 there were nineteen assemblies of women shoeworkers and seventy-two female assemblies of other trades in the Knights as well as numbers of women involved in mixed-sex locals.[6]

At the next convention in 1886, Knights of Labor General Master Workman Terence V. Powderly directed all sixteen women delegates to consider the report of the special committee. They immediately organized themselves into a permanent committee to investigate women's work and elected four officers including a Lynn stitcher, Nellie Hardison, as Treasurer and Mrs. Leonora Barry of Amsterdam, New York, as General Investigator. The women delegates then successfully recommended that the General Assembly support the committee's work financially.[7]

For the next three years Barry worked for the Knights, but she was quickly barred from entering factories to gather information and turned her energies to education, organizing women's locals, and testifying for factory reform legislation. The efforts of Barry and the committee on women's work also attracted the attention and support of Frances E. Willard and the Women's Christian Temperance Union. Discouraged after four years of hard work by the social conditioning which kept women workers submissive and unorganized, Barry remarried, ended her work, and dropped out of union activity. In subsequent General Assemblies, women delegates from the shoe industry disappeared, the work to organize women's locals was abandoned, and after 1892 no women delegates participated in a Knights of Labor convention. Defeat of the Knights in the shoe industries of Philadelphia and Cincinnati in 1887-88 also was a factor in the withdrawal of women delegates from the shoe industry.[8]

[6] Andrews and Bliss, 115, 131: Grob, 56. In addition to District No. 77, District No. 30 of Boston and the South Shore had enrolled 6,742 male and 1,847 female shoeworkers by January 1887. The other two members of the special committee on women's work were Mary Stirling and Mary Hannafin of the Garfield Assembly. Grob estimates one in eight members of the Knights were female in 1886, and during the eighteen months prior to January 1887, 13,200 women were admitted to membership in Massachusetts alone.

[7] Andrews and Bliss, 116-132. Among the sixteen women delegates were three stitchers from Massachusetts: Maggie Burk of Marlboro, Nellie Hardison of Lynn, and Annie F. Moran of Natick as well as Lizzie Shute of Haverhill who acted as Grand Venerable Sage of the convention.

[8] Barry found unions for women deterred by "... the ignorant, the apathetic, and

Initiative, militancy, organization by sex and craft, and encouragement from shoe craftsmen had characterized the tradition of female shoe workers' organizations. This tradition was a lively one, but it was also sporadic. None of the female organizations seemed to last. However the Crispin tradition of organizing shoeworkers by sex and craft was advanced by a rebellious shoeworker, Harry F. Skeffington, who had helped organize the Garfield Assembly of female shoeworkers in 1881. Frozen out of the Philadelphia labor market, Skeffington brought his organizational activities to eastern Massachusetts in 1887. However when Powderly openly rebuked him at the 1888 General Assembly for organizing trade districts instead of mixed assemblies, Skeffington left the Knights. He organized the Boot and Shoe Workers' International Union (BSWIU) in 1889 and affiliated with the AFL. Rivalry continued between the Knights and the BSWIU in Haverhill until the depression years of the 1890s. The Haverhill strike of 1895 tested this tradition of organization for male and female shoe workers threatened by further mechanization, severe wage cuts, and changes in the nature of the industry and the community.[9]

The shoe town of Haverhill had adopted mechanization before the Civil War and had expanded rapidly, growing by the 1890s into an industrial city of 30,000 with over 150 shoe factories of various sizes. There were about 8,300 industrial workers in Haverhill in 1895 of which 2,500 or 31% were females.[10] Most of the women workers came to the city from small towns in New

---

the hopeless who, through long years of endurance, have acquired, as a sort of second nature, the habit of submission and acceptance without question of any terms offered them, with the pessimistic view of life in which they see no ray of hope" (Andrews and Bliss, 112). The American Federation of Labor was slow to organize women workers until after 1900 (Andrews and Bliss, 155-157 and Kenneally).

[9] Grob, 123-124; Ware, 208-209; Horace B. Davis, *Shoes: The Workers and the Industry* (New York: International Publishers, 1940), 166-167; John Laslett, *Labor and the Left: A Study of Socialist And Radical Influences in the American Labor Movement, 1881-1924* (New York: Basic Books, 1970), 55-56. In 1889 in the Massachusetts shoe trade there were three separate organizations: The Lasters Protective Union (AFL), the Boot and Shoe Workers' International Union (AFL) and the Knights of Labor trade assemblies for cutters. Although Laslett acknowledges that "... women continued [after the Daughters of St. Crispin] to play an important role in the national unions of the trade ...," he does not examine their role in his chapter on the shoe workers of New England.

[10] The Massachusetts Census of 1895 shows 5,755 males employed in the industry in Haverhill and 2,534 females, representing 31% of the work force. *Census of the*

England and the Maritime Provinces of Canada, drawn by an industry which paid higher wages than those paid in the textile mills of other industrial cities in the Merrimack Valley in northeastern Massachusetts. The women who stitched expected to earn up to ten dollars a week for skilled work. Two thirds of the women working in the shoe shops of Haverhill in 1895 were native-born Americans of Yankee, Irish, and French-Canadian background. The remaining third were foreign-born French and English Canadians.[11]

Most of the female labor force of Haverhill were young and unmarried, but unlike the majority of women factory workers in the late nineteenth century, they had left their families and were living with other women in boardinghouses or in rooms in private homes. This pattern of geographical mobility in the lives of the shoe stitchers of Haverhill appeared at the beginning of mechanization in 1857 and conformed with the shoe-making season.[12]. A marketing system in which shoe salesmen with their

Commonwealth of Massachusetts, 1895, v.I (Boston: Wright and Potter, 1896), 252. The *Boston Advertiser* put the work force in late 1894 at 6,080 and got its information from the *Haverhill Bulletin. Boston Advertiser,* Dec. 31, 1894, 1. The *Haverhill Gazette* placed the number of female shoeworkers in the city at 2,500. *Labor Problems Scrapbook, 1894-1914* (clippings from the *Haverhill Gazette*), n.p., Haverhill Public Library, hereafter cited as *L.P.S.* Haverhill was a medium size city with a narrow industrial base dominated by light industry. Similar to the textile cities, the Haverhill economy had a relatively high proportion of women workers (30-40%). However the occupational structure of the shoe industry, which provided the chance for females to do skilled, sex-typed work, is a major difference. For a full discussion of the methodology of dealing with women in an urban setting, see Susan J. Kleinberg, "The Systematic Study of Urban Women," *Historical Methods Newsletter,* 19 (Dec. 1975).

[11] *Census of Massachusetts, 1895,* v. IV, 38. This information however was gathered late in 1895 during the slack season. The actual percentage of native born women workers was probably somewhat higher. See Introduction to the census in v. I, xi.

[12] Haverhill's town and city directories, 1853-1895, reflect the job structure of the shoe industry. The first directory in 1853 is organized by male heads of households or boarders and listed no women in connection with the industry prior to the introduction of the sewing machine. Presumably the female binders who worked at home were not heads of households or boarders. The male shoeworkers were listed as heads of households and boarders, whether they actually boarded or were related to the head of household as son or nephew. The male workers are also listed by craft but not by marital status. When the female shoeworkers appear in the 1857 directory as a result of the opening of three stitching shops, they were listed like the male workers by residence and craft, but also by marital status. By comparing the addresses of boardinghouses, it is possible to tell how many stitchers boarded together at the same residence.

There is mention in subsequent post-Civil War directories of the difficulties of gathering information on the growing population of Haverhill. Special efforts were made to locate both resident and transient workers. By 1889 the directories provide more information on the city's population including all family members of adult age, even students or those with no occupation. It is there-

sample cases invaded the retail market and obtained the year's orders, intensified the seasonality of the industry in the late nine-

---

fore possible to discover the marital status and residence (house, boardinghouse or rented room) of the stitchers listed in the directory, whether the stitcher is living with a widowed mother, sister, in a male-headed family of father or brother (and whether the males were shoeworkers), with siblings or alone. What is unknown is the number of dependent children at the residence.

For the 1895 strike the major drawback of the 1895 city directory is that it was compiled by the police in early December, 1894, jnst as the busy season began. Therefore many of the stitchers do not appear in the directory. I was able to locate only 154 stitchers out of an estimated 2500 who worked in the city, according to state census of 1895. Forty-four percent of the 154 stitchers listed in the 1895 directory were unmarried and living with no related person. Nineteen percent were married women living alone in rooms or boardinghouses. Twenty-one percent were living in a female-headed household of relatives. In all, eighty-three percent of the stitchers in the 1895 directory were living independently of a male-headed family. This 154 stitchers were probably the most stable population of female shoeworkers as they were counted several weeks before rush season began. Nevertheless they show a striking pattern of personal independence. Can one assume a different pattern from the hundreds more who arrived later but in time for the busy season? In an attempt to corroborate these findings, a search was made for the manuscript census of Massachusetts in 1895, but according to the state archives staff, the schedules have been lost.

The lack of definitive statistical evidence on the striking female stitchers is not surprising, however the evidence from the many newspapers which covered the strike consistently describe the strikers as young, unmarried and living on their own in Haverhill. Indeed the leadership of the stitchers' union, Mary A. Nason, Mary P. Gardner and Margaret C. Barnett, fit the pattern of living alone or with a sister, young and unmarried.

The 1895 Massachusetts state census examined families by size and sex composition but warned its readers of the distortion of family statistics caused by the phenomenon of lodging houses in industrial cities "... in which numerous single persons are employed, who are living in lodging rooms and providing their own meals in their rooms or taking their meals at restaurants. Every such person constitutes, in the Census, an independent family, as they recognize no other family head, and the preponderance of families of this class composed of females over those composed of males is due to the larger employment of single women who live in the manner stated.... The peculiar composition of families of two persons, each of the same sex, also reflects the conditions which we have noted in accounting for the families of one person each, and indicates the combination in single families of males or females, who are thus living together in family relations, although families of this kind composed of females only largely preponderate over those of males only." *Census of Massachusetts, 1895*, v. I, 455. For Haverhill, the state census listed 156 families composed of one female, 174 families of two females, 66 families of three females, etc. totaling 930 females living in lodginghouses or rooms. However many of the 2500 female shoeworkers in the city lived with private families as boarders and therefore were listed as family members in the state census. *Census of Massachusetts, 1895*, v. I, 394-395.

See also John Modell and Tamara Hareven, "Urbanization and the Malleable Household: An Examination of Boarding and Lodging in American Families," *Journal of Marriage and the Family*, 35 (1973), 467-492; Women's Educational and Industrial Union, *The Boot and Shoe Industry in Massachusetts as a Vocation for Women*, v. VI in *Studies in Economic Relations of Women*, United States Department of Labor, Bureau of Labor Statistics, (Washington: Government Printing Office, 1915), 17-25; Joan W. Scott and Louise A. Tilly, "Women's Work and the Family in Nineteenth Century Europe," *Comparative Studies in Society and History*, 17 (Jan. 1975), 36-64; Tamara Hareven, "Modernization and Family History: Perspectives on Social Changes," *Signs: Journal of Women in Culture and Society* 2 (1976), 190-206.

teenth century. Especially in the production of high grade, stylish ladies' shoes, a specialty of Haverhill and Lynn, the busy season began with great intensity in late December—once the styles had been determined—and continued until June when the slack season began. An account in the *Haverhill Gazette* of January 19, 1895 describes the residential patterns and mobility of the stitchers:

> Those who live in the Merrimac street boarding houses, however, constitute but a fraction of the hundreds, yes thousands, who board and room in Haverhill. In fact there is hardly a house in some districts of the city that is not a boarding house to a greater or lesser extent, hardly a family that has not at least one boarder in the house; and it is true of the great bulk of the female population that they live in houses where there is considerable of the home life—1½ and two-story dwellings and cottages—the head of which is an elderly woman who has, perhaps, in her younger days herself worked in the shoe shops. . . . It is in these home boarding houses where the great majority of the girls live. In one boarding house visited there were 25 girls rooming. The proprietor said that when the dull times came about 10 of this number would go away; some to their homes in Maine and New Hampshire, some to Lynn, Brockton or other shoe towns, and others to room with friends, or go off he could not tell where. This was about the average, he claimed, of the number who came and went as the work fluctuated, buffeted about from place to place, but always willing to stay where they could get work.[13]

The residence of many stitchers in "home boarding houses" meant that their lives as workers were well integrated into the community of Haverhill. The close ties between the private homeowner and the worker created strong sympathy for the strike in Haverhill.

By the late nineteenth century the shoe industry in Massachusetts had become highly specialized in its operations. The major steps in shoemaking began with the skilled job of cutting tanned leather into pieces for the upper shoe. These pieces were passed on to the stitching room where they were sewn together into the upper. Meanwhile the sole department cut out and assembled the soles, heels and the internal structures or boxes for the toes. The

[13] *L.P.S.*, Jan. 19, 1895. The *Haverhill Gazette* featured a lengthy story on Jan. 19 on the conditions of the female shoe workers. See also L. C. Bell to the Editor of the *Haverhill Gazette*, Jan. 23, 1895.

lasters then put together the upper, the insole, and the toe box around a last which standardized the size of the shoe. The shoe was then bottomed by having the outer sole and heel attached, shaped, and finished. The stitchers worked at one of the key processes in making shoes, and their skills at top stitching and vamping fancy ladies' shoes were especially valued in an industry dependent on style changes. The ladies' turned shoe industry located in Haverhill (and in Lynn) produced a light weight, high grade product and employed the maximum number of women workers in shoe manufacturing.[14]

The work in the shoe industry was highly sex-typed. No women worked as cutters, lasters, or bottomers; a very few men worked as vampers, attracted by the wages, and a few women worked as finishers, trimmers and packers. On the whole, stitching was women's work, and the rest of the operations were run by men. Stitching had been mechanized prior to the Civil War and with the exception of the introduction of automatic machines for buttons and button-holes, the work had not much changed since then. The work of the skilled male workers, however, underwent continuous mechanical changes in the late nineteenth century which threatened their skills, wages, and status. For example, in the 1890s, the lasters faced the introduction of a lasting machine with mechanical fingers which seemed to whisper as it worked, "I've got your job." The women's work, in contrast, was not only a sex monopoly but was unthreatened by further mechanization.[15]

The depression years of 1893 and 1894 had forced severe wage cuts on all workers, and by the end of 1894 the shoe stitchers' wages had been cut one third. Women workers saw the ten dollar weekly wage disappear, and more so than previously, experienced the rigors of the seasonal nature of the shoe business.

---

[14] Women's Educational and Industrial Union, *The Boot and Shoe Industry in Massachusetts*, 33-41 and Frederick Allen, *The Shoe Industry* (Boston: The Vocation Bureau of Boston, 1916), 163-164, 261. As early as 1857 women shoeworkers self-consciously listed their occupations in the *Haverhill Town Directory* as stitchers to differentiate themselves from the less skilled jobs of other women shoeworkers such as shoe binders, shoe trimmers and shoe pasters. The stitchers were the overwhelming majority of the female workers in the industry. Some of the subdivisions of the stitching operation such as button-hole making and the sewing of cloth linings required much less skill than stitching leather, but the high wages for top stitching and vamping supplied a constant stream of learners for these skills.

[15] Women's Educational and Industrial Union, *The Boot and Shoe Industry in Massachusetts*, 33-40 and Allen, *The Shoe Industry*, 60-61.

Unlike the relatively steady employment in the textile mills of Lawrence and Lowell and of Manchester, New Hampshire, shoe factories operated during a busy season of December to June when the bulk of the work was completed. Work was scarce from June to November which meant the wages earned during one season had to be stretched until the next at a time when women workers could expect only a weekly wage of $5 to $6. Since full-time work was unobtainable during the slack season, wages were further reduced. In 1894 eighty-two out of eighty-five stitchers in one of the better paying shops in Haverhill averaged only $2.58 weekly for the year because of wage cuts and slack time. These skilled native workers now believed that they were no better off than the immigrant textile mill worker. In early 1894, the union shoeworkers of Haverhill had resolved to fight to prevent the introduction of "mill wages and mill customs" into Haverhill.[16]

This intensive pressure on wages had deeply affected the lives of the stitchers. Most needed supplemental work or alternative living arrangements. After a ten-hour day in the factory during the busy season, women sewed or copied letters at night to earn extra money. Others slipped away from the factories a few minutes before noon to serve at tables during the lunch hour in hotels and restaurants crowded with hungry workers. Cooperative living with other women cut the cost of boarding houses. In some instances five women would rent a flat, four would work in the shoe factories and the remaining woman would cook, clean, and launder for the others. Some women arranged to rent single rooms out of their apartments to other workers. Others simply rented unheated rooms and spent the evenings before bedtime in public halls. Slack season during the depression years was a particularly trying time. Boardinghouse keepers reported that female lodgers roomed with friends to save money or simply went off somewhere. Others grudgingly accepted work as domestics. Despite the hardships, there was little evidence of union activity among the stitchers. There were work stoppages at individual shops, but a Lady Stitchers' Union, organized in 1892, had only twenty-eight members. Additional pressure on wages in late

[16] *L.P.S.*, Jan 19, 1895; *Haverhill Gazette*, May 10, 1894, 4.

1894, however, produced an explosion of resistance.[17]

The central issue of the shoe strike, which began in mid-December 1894, was the "ironclad" contract adopted by the three largest factories in Haverhill. The contract required the employee to deposit with the company one dollar per week out of a five dollar weekly wage as a security against the worker leaving without giving two weeks notice. This twenty percent of the weekly wage was subtracted until a deposit of fifty dollars accrued. Failure to give notice by the worker meant forfeiture of the money, a good reason for the worker to avoid strikes and union membership. The deposit was to be repaid annually with seven percent interest, but no receipt was given the worker for the wages kept by the company, and the pay envelope listed the full week's wages. The worker's good behavior was the only assurance of getting the deducted sum. The employer had no requirement in the contract to give notice when terminating a worker, and as a rule, simply broke the contract by discharging the worker for some cause—such as poor work—and then kept the deposit. The ironclad contract shops in Haverhill intended to eliminate all strike action by making the workers pay for it out of their own pockets.[18]

The three big shops which adopted the contract system, the W.W. Spaulding Company, the Spaulding and Swett Company, and the Chick Brothers' Company were all relatively new to Haverhill. Organized in the early 1880s, they had built large modern factories on River Street, a mile west of the central shoe district of the city. Because of the high cost of leather in 1894 and the ensuing pressure on profits reduced during the depression, the owners of these shops adopted the ironclad to lower labor costs.[19]

Haverhill was the national center of the ladies' turned slipper and low-cut shoe industry, and the competitors of the big shops on River Street were the small, long-established factories and

[17] *L.P.S.*, Jan. 19, 1895.

[18] Shoeworkers had fought this kind of a contract, variously called a yellow dog or good behavior contract, since the Crispin strike in Worcester, Massachusetts in 1870 (Hall, 172 and Lescohier, 42-43). *Boston Advertiser*, Jan. 5, 1895, 1; *L.P.S.*, July 23, Jan. 21, 1895; *Boston Globe*, Jan. 2, 1895, 2.

[19] *Lawrence-American*, Jan. 2, 1895, 4; *L.P.S.*, Jan. 2, 1895; *Obituary File*, Everett Swett, Jan. 14, 1905; W.W. Spaulding, Jan. 5, 1929; Lamont Chick, June 11, 1915; William Chick, Jan. 30, 1925 (Haverhill Public Library).

sub-contractors, financed locally and run by old residents of the city. These companies, located in the traditional shoe district in the heart of the city, had accepted craft unions of male shoe-workers and paid higher wages than the big shops.[20]

The general adoption of the ironclad contract by the big shops for all workers would force the smaller shoe factories, by their own admission, to cut wages. The craft unions faced drastic wage cuts and extinction. In mid-December 1894, as the busy season began, the River Street factories and a few of the large shops in the old shoe district began to apply the ironclad contract to all labor, both native and foreign, skilled and unskilled. On December 26 and 31 the women stitchers at Spauldings, Spaulding and Swetts, and Chicks joined the strike called by the craft unions. Numbers of Jewish, Italian, and Armenian men then forfeited their deposits under the ironclad contract and joined in. The Haverhill shoe strike began with a commanding show of unity and militancy.[21]

On January 1, 1895 the strikers held a giant parade through the snowy streets of the city's business and industrial district. At the head of the line of march, four hundred women stitchers led the two thousand strikers. The demonstrators carried banners which included the slogans: "The Women Are With Us" and "Daughters of Hannah Duston", a reference to a local colonial symbol of female strength and fearlessness. This demonstration of mass action by women workers prompted the *Haverhill Gazette* to headline the march as the "Crusade of the Women." [22]

Following the parade, the strikers and their supporters jammed the city's public halls for speeches by Frances Willard, president of the WCTU and by two English temperance and trade union leaders, Lady Henry Somerset and Amy Hicks. The three women were touring the United States in late 1894, speak-

---

[20] *Boston Advertiser*, Dec. 31, 1894, 1.
[21] *L.P.S.*, Dec. 24, 26, 27, 31, 1894.
[22] *L.P.S.*, Jan. 2, 1895. Hannah Duston was a resident of colonial Haverhill who was captured by Indians attacking the village in 1697. She later escaped by killing her captors and brought their scalps back as proof of her deeds. Edward T. James, *et al*, eds., *Notable American Women, 1607-1950: A Biographical Dictionary*, v. I (Cambridge: Harvard Univ. Press, 1971), 535-536. A statue erected in 1879 commemorates her bravery, depicting her as a formidable and threatening figure, hatchet in hand. The statue stood near the City Hall adjacent to the boardinghouse district which surrounded the central manufacturing center. The parades of the strikers often passed it.

ing on the subject of Women and the Labor Movement, when the strike in Haverhill erupted. The strike committee contacted them in Boston and invited them to speak. Willard supported the strikers' demand for a living wage, denounced the contract system, urged unity between women and men workers, and endorsed the eight hour day. In her first public statement on behalf of women strikers, Willard urged the stitchers " . . . to stand as a unit in the struggle which is being fought for the nation, in Haverhill." Somerset and Hicks stressed the need to organize women into trade unions.[23]

The leader of the Lady Stitchers' Union, Mary A. Nason, made the last speech to the crowds. Nason was a skilled worker at the Field-Thayer Company and an organizer for the Boot and Shoe Workers' International Union. She had worked for several years in Haverhill determined to overcome the passivity of the women shoeworkers, conceding even the "Lady" in Lady Stitchers' Union to attract them to membership. She criticized the inept activities of middle class church women in Haverhill who, through the Women's Union for Good Works, had organized a Home for Working Women in 1892 but were charging more rent per week in 1894 than the average wage. Nason had organized a strike at Field-Thayer in the summer of 1894 and had won some support from the men's unions for it. On the night of the parade, she spoke warmly of regaining her faith in the capacity of the women workers of Haverhill to take strike action as a unified body. Acknowledging the three speeches before her, Nason asked if, after listening to these fine women, anyone could now say it was not respectable for women to organize?[24]

The strikers represented a coalition of skilled workers in various craft unions in the industry, including the Lasters' Protective Union, the Knights of Labor cutters, the Lady Stitchers' Union, and the Boot and Shoe Workers International Union (a collection

---

[23] *L.P.S.*, Jan. 2, 1895.

[24] *L.P.S.*, Jan. 2, 1895. The Jan. 7, 1895 *Haverhill Gazette* features a story by Helen Mae Shaw of the *Boston Journal*. No suffragists in Massachusetts interested themselves in the stitchers' strike; the suffrage movement in Haverhill was inactive. Massachusetts was the eastern locus of anti-suffrage sentiment, and the state suffrage groups were conservative and weak until after 1900. Sharon Hartman Strom, "Leadership and Tactics in the American Woman Suffrage Movement: A New Perspective from Massachusetts," *The Journal of American History*, 62 (1975), 296-315.

of heel fixers, bottomers, and other crafts). The lasters had specific grievances concerning mechanization but all agreed to stand together against any further wage cuts. The strike however was not simply a strike of skilled labor. The strike leaders quickly organized and marshaled support from large numbers of unskilled foreign workers, chiefly Jewish, Italian, and Armenian males, who, with training on new machines, threatened the jobs, wages, and status of the strikers. To organize this immigrant work force and feature them in the strike parades was a blow to the strategy of the managers of the large factories.[25]

The strategy of the strike leaders was to confine the strike to the three River Street shops, using the women stitchers' monopoly on skills to close down their production, but to allow their competitors to operate. The shut-down would demonstrate the uselessness of the ironclad contract to prevent strike action and thus result in its abolition. The second strike aim was to end all competition in wages by getting a city-wide agreement to an arbitrated price list. This strategy prevailed from late December until mid-January. It held out the hope of a short strike and a quick victory, manageable financially for the loosely organized unions in Haverhill.[26]

The initial phase of the strike received widespread support from the community led by the small factory owners, the professional class, almost all of the Protestant and Catholic clergy, local businessmen, and retailers. A few of the small factories gave their employees two hours off to participate in the strike parades. The skilled workers' unions had been active in local politics, and the city government was consequently prostrike. The City Council unanimously voted its support for the strike and offered the free use of city-owned halls for meetings of the strikers, and the City Solicitor was put on retainer by the strike committee.[27]

A clear identity of interest between the skilled native shoe worker and the community of Haverhill explains the depth of

[25] Irwin Yellowitz, "Skilled Workers and Mechanization: The Lasters in the 1890s" *Labor History*, 18 (1977), 197-213. See also *Boston Journal*, Jan. 4, 1895, 5; *Boston Globe*, Jan. 24, 1895, 4, January 25, 1895, 3.

[26] *Boston Journal*, Jan. 4, 1895, 4; *Boston Globe*, Jan. 10, 1895, 7; *Lawrence-American*, Jan. 10, 1895, 1; *Lynn Item*, Jan. 1, 1895, 6.

[27] *Boston Advertiser*, Dec. 31, 1894, 1, Jan. 3, 1895, 1, Jan. 4, 1895, 1; *Boston Globe*, Jan. 9, 1895, 7; *Boston Post*, Jan. 3, 1895, 6, Jan. 17, 1895, 1; *Lynn Item*, Jan. 7, 1895, 5, Feb. 11, 1895, 4; *Boston Advertiser*, Jan. 9, 1895, 8; *Boston Herald*, Jan. 2, 1895, 1; *L.P.S.*, Jan. 16, 1895.

local support for the strike. The boardinghouse keepers quickly declared themselves as union houses with the exception of those owned outright by the anti-union factories. There was a frequently expressed fear that if the strikers lost, the character of the city would change, especially if a new and uncontrollable, low-wage foreign work force replaced the native workers. The community stood together against undesirable change.[28]

Two outside factors however disrupted the strategy of the strike and its local support. The Massachusetts State Board of Arbitration investigated the situation in early January and recommended that the strike end and wage arbitration begin in June after the busy season—a proposal totally rejected by the unions. Secondly, the State Superior Court at Salem issued an injunction on January 15 at the request of Chick Brothers to prevent the strike leaders from participating in and directing the strike.[29]

Local events also were a factor. In January the strike widened and affected other companies. One result was that a thousand additional strikers were added to the financial burdens of the strike committee. By January 17 six of the largest shoe factories and their subcontractors had been struck by approximately three thousand workers. Furthermore, the city authorities found themselves responsible for enforcing the court injunction; this diluted the support of the local government for the strike. Retailers, hurting from the loss of sales, appealed for settlement. As a result unity and money became critical to sustaining the strike; the stitchers

[28] *Boston Advertiser*, Jan. 3, 1895, 1. On Jan 26, 1895 the *Advertiser* reported that the *Shoe and Leather Reporter*, which was observing the strike, indicated that the small producers of Haverhill were doing more business than anytime for two years. See also *L.P.S.*, Jan. 25, 1895 and Feb. 2, 1895. In Herbert Gutman's well-known article on strikes in 1877 and 1878 in Paterson, New Jersey, he points to the importance of local community opposition to the power of factory owners. Gutman sees this as a phenomenon of rapidly industrializing cities. In the Haverhill experience in 1895, severe economic depression and major reorganizations of the shoe industry also stimulated local resistence to the economic power of the larger factories. Some of the opposition came from small factory owners themselves, but most came from workers with community power as voters and consumers. The Paterson strike in the mid-1870s and the 1895 shoe strike are quite similar in strategies and community support, but the role of women in the Haverhill situation is different. See Herbert G. Gutman, "Class, Status and Community Power in Nineteenth Century American Industrial Cities —Paterson, New Jersey: A Case Study," Frederic C. Jaher, ed. *The Age of Industrialism in America* (New York: Free Press, 1968).

[29] *L.P.S.*, Jan. 12, 1895, Jan. 15, 1895; *Boston Post*, Jan. 13, 1895, 8; *Boston Globe*, Jan. 12, 1895, 2, Jan. 14, 1895, 1.

and their leader Mary Nason provided both.[30]

Nason's leadership of the stitchers' union was energetic and militant. During the strike she organized parades and meetings and recruited members for the stitchers' union. She addressed shop crews, settled problems, and headed off rumors. She represented the stitchers on the strike committee and attended the meetings of the State Board of Arbitration.[31]

Nason's chief ally on the strike committee was James F. Carey of the BSWIU, a Populist candidate for state representative in 1894 who declared himself a Socialist during the 1895 strike. Carey had no formal role in the Haverhill Stitchers' Union but attended the meetings of the organization and helped organize and rally the female strikers. Carey had four sisters who worked in the shoe shops, and he lived cooperatively with them, his brother, and one brother-in-law. He was a strong supporter of unions for women, and at a meeting of the Brockton Central Labor Union where he appeared with Nason, he endorsed women's suffrage and urged the women shoeworkers of Brockton to organize.[32]

As head of the stitchers' union and a symbol of their strike activity, Nason went on a fund-raising tour of Massachusetts cities, addressing labor meetings. A lucid and persuasive speaker, she was permitted to address the Boston Labor Council on January 20, and in response the council committed itself to raise $1,000 a week for the stitchers. However, Nason sometimes demonstrated frustration and anger as in a speech at Union Hall, Boston on January 14 to the Young Men's Christian Union. In this speech she attacked married women workers who refused to join unions and fight for better wages with their unmarried coworkers. On another occasion she suggested that married women be prohibited from factory work. Occasionally she criticized the unfair treatment of the stitchers' union by men unionists.[33]

Nason also addressed private meetings in Back Bay and Beacon

[30] *L.P.S.*, Jan. 16, 17, 22, 23, 1895; *Lawrence-American*, Jan 31, 1895, 4; *Boston Herald*, Jan. 25, 1895, 1; *Boston Globe*, Jan. 11, 1895, 5; *L.P.S.*, Mar. 4, 1895.

[31] *L.P.S.*, Jan. 7, 25, 1895; *Boston Globe*, Jan. 7, 1895, 5, Jan. 18, 1895, 5.

[32] *L.P.S.*, Jan. 23, 1895. The *Boston Herald*, Feb. 11, 1895, 2, printed a long interview with a socialist shoe worker who describes the way socialism could transform the shoe industry and American society. Also see *Boston Globe*, Jan. 18, 1895, 5; *Boston Journal*, Jan. 21, 1895, 5.

[33] *L.P.S.*, Jan. 21, 28, 1895; *Lynn Item*, Jan. 15, 1895, 5; *Boston Globe*, Jan. 2, 1895, 2, Jan. 21, 1895, 2.

Hill drawing rooms such as the meeting on February 16 at Annette P. Rogers' townhouse at 5 Joy Street, Beacon Hill. She invariably received large donations after the meetings. The primary concern of many at the meetings was that the strike be peaceful, as the violent Pullman strike was still a vivid memory. Secondly, it was considered shocking for *women* to have to strike for a living wage. The financial aid was not so much to organize unions for striking women, but to relieve their suffering. This attitude of chivalry rather than the acceptance of women as unionists also surfaced at the trade union meetings. Nevertheless the news that Nason and the stitchers had tapped the wealth of Brahmin Boston gave the Haverhill women strength and excellent publicity. The upper-class women at these Boston meetings were, moreover, reported in the press as strongly in favor of women's unions.[34]

Nason developed a remarkable set of contacts among women of various classes. Martha Moore Avery, an active, Boston member of the SLP, addressed the stitchers' meetings on at least three occasions during the strike, and she gave advice and support. Willard, Somerset and Hicks continued to advocate unionization of women, notably at a WCTU banquet in Boston on January 3 given for Somerset. On January 14 at Union Hall in Boston, socialite and state factory inspector Mrs. Charles Gorden Ames organized a public discussion of the Haverhill strike. Appearing with her were Willard, Hicks, and Somerset flanked by Nason and T. T. Pomeroy, the chairman of the strike committee. Willard, Hicks, and Somerset also addressed a meeting of the Boston Central Labor Union before they left New England. Josephine Shaw Lowell, a Boston and New York socialite who headed the Consumers' League of New York and energetically contributed to feminist causes, concluded the Parker Memorial lecture series with a speech supporting the strikers. When Josephine Shaw Lowell spoke, even the *Boston Evening Transcript,* the voice of Brahmin Boston, carried her remarks. The expenses of the strike, estimated at $4,000 a week for twelve weeks, were covered by the many sources tapped by these contacts.[35]

The action of the stitchers was the decisive factor in the 1895

[34] *L.P.S.*, Jan. 26, 1895, Feb. 19, 1895; *Lynn Item*, Jan. 26, 1895, 5, Mar. 26, 1895, 5; *Boston Globe*, Feb. 12, 1895, 1, 2, Feb. 16, 1895, 4.

[35] *L.P.S.*, Jan. 16, 18, 25, 1895; *Lawrence-American*, Jan. 4, 1895, 4; *Boston Transcript*, Jan, 14, 1895, 4, Jan. 16, 1895, 12; *Boston Globe*, Jan. 15, 1895, 5.

strike. This was recognized by all: the Haverhill union leaders, the local newspapers, the major newspapers of the state, and the journal of the Massachusetts AFL, *The Labor Leader*—indeed even by the owners of the River Street shops.[36]

The first reaction of Spauldings and Chick Brothers to the great parade of January 1 was to send out their forewomen to visit the stitchers at their boardinghouses to persuade them to come back to work. This failing, all the strikers were warned to return to their jobs at the old wages or face a blacklist. In a few days rumors of a break in the strike swept the city, but a 6:30 a.m. parade of striking women on River Street on January 6 averted a back-to-work move among the stitchers. Such a breakdown in communication never occurred again. The major stitching sub-contractor for Chick Brothers then tried to persuade the women's union to finish the work under contract, but the union refused. The big shops then gave up trying to break down the unity of the stitchers.[37]

Instead they searched for stitchers to come to Haverhill as strike-breakers. Notices of employment at good wages were sent throughout northern New England, and agents seeking stitchers visited Lynn and Brockton. These efforts proved unsuccessful as the busy season had just begun. One group of eight women stitchers from Exeter, New Hampshire did arrive in Haverhill, but no boardinghouse would accommodate them, and their employers had to pay their expenses at a hotel.[38]

The River Street shops also tried to send their unlabeled work to be stitched in other shoe cities. When the unions of Lynn discovered a consignment of Chick Brothers' work in a Lynn shoe shop, they set up a search committee to visit all shops to look for scab work. The Lynn stitchers held indignation meetings and threatened to strike any establishment in Lynn which took Haverhill work. Agents from Haverhill promised Lynn stitchers good wages and jobs for their husbands. These actions outraged the women workers of Lynn, and the local Lady Stitchers' Union increased its membership by 700 in 1895 as a result of the Haverhill strike. The big shops also tried to find stitchers among Arme-

[36] *Labor Leader*, Jan. 26, 1895, 1.
[37] *L.P.S.*, Jan. 7, 1895; *Boston Post*, Jan. 8, 1895, 1; *Boston Globe*, Jan. 2, 1895, 2, Jan. 7, 1895, 5; *Lawrence-American*, Jan. 5, 1895, 1.
[38] *L.P.S.*, Jan. 23, 1895; *Boston Herald*, Jan. 18, 1895, 3.

nian, Jewish, and Italian men who came from cultures where stitching was not female-typed work, but there simply was not enough skilled help to be found.[39]

By mid-January the stitchers faced anger and rough treatment in recognition of their power to end production. The J. H. Winchell Company threatened to discharge any stitchers even discussing the strike. The management at the Gale Shoe Company, which with Winchell's was struck on January 15, locked out eighty female strikers and threw their possessions at them out of the windows. Such actions only strengthened the stitchers' sense of importance and militancy.[40]

The Lady Stitchers' Union changed its name to the Women Stitchers' Union during the course of the strike. Nason wanted this change and had apologized to the press for the word "Lady", explaining that the leadership had accepted the latter word in deference to the younger members who in 1892 still had middle class aspirations. The depression, the wage cuts, and the strike had ended such dreams, and the strikers now accepted their position as workers.[41]

Approximately 500 stitchers had gone out on strike against the three River Street shops and later 300 more in the strikes in mid-January. Attendance at mass meetings ranged between 600 and 800. The strike activity was selective and directed at the largest shops. The strikers were a young group of mixed background. The majority were under thirty years of age. Fifty percent of the 400 members of the Women Stitchers' Union were natives of Yankee and Irish background and the other fifty percent were French-Canadians, both native-born and immigrant. The union leadership was particularly happy with the response of the French women and undertook continuous recruitment during the strike.[42]

The union organized its members into shop crews, distributing $3 to $4 weekly in strike benefits and meeting every other day

---

[39] *L.P.S.*, Jan. 5, 1895; *Lynn Item*, Jan. 5, 1895, 6, Jan. 12, 1895, 5, Jan. 18, 1895, 2, Jan. 19, 1895, 4, Feb. 2, 1895, 7; *Boston Herald*, Jan. 18, 1895, 3. One skilled Jewish male stitcher, Jacob Blastein, was locked up at night by management in the Chicks' factory because if he left, no stitching could be done at all. He was rescued by friends and joined the strike.

[40] *L.P.S.*, Jan. 22, 1895.

[41] *Boston Globe*, Jan. 18, 1895, 5.

[42] *Boston Globe*, Jan. 17, 1895, 4, Jan. 18, 1895, 1, 5; *Brockton Enterprise*, Jan. 17, 1895, 7; *Boston Herald*, Jan. 21, 1895, 7; *Boston Post*, Jan. 18, 1895, 5, Jan. 28, 1895, 2.

during the strike to exchange information. Married stitchers who had children received benefits in accordance with the number of their dependents. The members of the union addressed each other as "sister" in the fraternal parlance of trade unionism and identified themselves resolutely as members of "Chicks crew #1," etc. The words and actions of the women strikers indicated they rejected individualism for collective action.[43]

The stitchers' union demonstrated a strong commitment to sex equality as well as to organization. Special money-raising programs, featuring entertainment and dancing, were organized by the male-dominated strike committee, and these programs often used the stitchers' sex to attract support and attendance. The women's union however worked hard to downplay the attention-getting phenomenon of striking females by an insistence on sex equality in the conduct of the strike. For example, the stitchers refused to accept the idea of special, cheaper tickets for themselves as admission to strike benefit programs. Cheaper tickets suggested that low wages were the lot of a female worker. A differential wage rate for the tiny number of male stitchers in the industry rankled the women, and under pressure from the stitchers' union, the strike committee adopted equal pay for equal work as a principle of unionism. However, the stitchers knew that most male unionists were skeptical of their commitment. The stitchers' leadership and many of the women strikers understand that if they were ever to figure in the trade union movement, women had to prove their militancy in this strike.[44]

---

[43] *Boston Globe*, Jan. 18, 1895, p. 5. One of the strikers expressed this commitment to collective action in a letter to the editor of the *Haverhill Gazette* on Jan. 23, 1895: "So much has been said about the manufacturers being willing to treat with their help individually that perhaps an instance of individual treatment of the wage question may be of interest. Last June in the stitching room in which I was at work a cutdown was proposed. I knew that the price paid was less than was paid for similar work in other factories and demonstrated, and was assured by the superintendent that my employer was willing to pay what others did. I at once secured the figures from two other factories and proved that they were paying from 20 to 100 percent more than we were getting, presenting the figures to the superintendent. The result was only that the cut was prevented, but the promise made to me that the wages should be the same as in other factories was forgotten. It was at the end of the sales. I, as an individual, was at the mercy of the manufacturer and was forced to continue to work at low wages, until as a crew, backed by the union, we struck. The plea of individual agreement sounds well, but the individual is always offered Hobson's choice: Accept my proposition or get out."

[44] *L.P.S.*, Jan. 10, 1895; *Boston Advertiser*, Jan. 4, 1895. 1, Jan. 15, 1895. 8; *Boston Herald*, Jan. 21, 1895, 7; *Boston Globe*, Jan. 16, 1895, 1, Jan. 17, 1895, 4, Jan. 18, 1895, 1, 4, Jan. 21, 1895 2, Feb. 6, 1895, 7, Feb. 8, 1895, 1, Feb. 9, 1895, 1.

Frequent parades of two to four hundred women strikers marched in long skirts and thin boots through streets that were alternatively icy, snowy, slushy, and muddy. Frank Foster, editor of the *Labor Leader* was inspired to recast a Tennyson poem into a celebration of "The Union Girls of Haverhill":

> The "newer women" no longer suppliant meek—
> The moment's fancy or the hour's delight—
> But full equipped, abreast with those who seek
> For those who toil the measure of their right.
>
> Pentucket's streets have seen their columns march,
> Through storm and sleet, upon the entrenched foe—
> What though above them towered no triumph arc
> The foul injunction armed to lay them low?
>
> Barbara Freitches here fast held the UNION flag,
> Grace Darlings braved the fierce industrial sea;
> Their firm demand. "Take off the contract gag,
> For union stitchers must and shall be free!"[45]

The solidarity among the women strikers was severely tested by a blunder committed by Chairman Pomeroy of the strike committee. In a speech in Boston on January 18 he pointed to the relationship between low wages for women and prostitution, declaring that there were 300 women living in Haverhill's central business district whose room rent was "paid by men." This statement exploded across the front pages of the Boston newspapers and immediately called into question the morality of the female strikers. The women workers did not permit the incident to be used by their opponents to divide them or weaken their resolve. The stitcher's union publicly rebuked Pomeroy, and the controversy painfully and slowly subsided.[46]

The strike committee had endorsed women's suffrage as a labor reform on the night of the giant parade of Jan. 1. There were a very small number of men who worked as stitchers in Haverhill, most of them on heavy McKay or Goodrich machinery, but the city directory of 1895 listed about thirty men as stitchers. Presumably they worked also on the turned shoe process wich employed the female stitchers.

45 *Labor Leader*, Jan. 26, 1895, 1.

46 Pomeroy made additional rash statements in the same speech which his opponents used to discredit him (*Boston Herald*, Jan. 19, 1895, 9, Jan. 22, 1895, 7; *Boston Journal*, Jan. 22, 1895, 1). The defense of the female workers voiced by the clergy ranged from reference to a report by the State Bureau of Labor which found it impossible for a woman to work ten to twelve hours a day and then lead a life of "infamy," to the statement of the Reverend George Benedict of the New Union Congregational Church who said, "As with all fellows who

Again and again the stitchers proved to be the most militant group among the strikers. They supported additional strike action against anti-union factories throughout the twelve weeks of conflict. By the first week of March, however, the strike funds were nearly exhausted. On March 10 at the strike committee's recommendation, the remaining strikers voted 239—199 to return to work. The stitchers cast the majority of the votes *against* the motion.[47]

The strike committee argued that the strike had been partly successful. The ironclad was gone at one of the River Street shops, wage cuts were halted, 118 factories had signed the agreement to arbitrate a uniform price list, and the strength of the new stitchers' organization had seriously hurt several of the largest manufacturers in the city. The real hope for improvement of conditions in Haverhill however lay with a national union of all shoe crafts. On March 7 an organizing convention had been called for Boston in April. This convention rang with the spirit of the Haverhill strike.[48]

The Haverhill stitchers played a prominent role in the organization and decisions of the new Boot and Shoe Workers' Union. Women shoeworkers of Haverhill and Marlboro, Massachusetts were active on all of the small organizing committees at the convention. This activity reflected the role that organized stitchers had played in the Haverhill strike and the role that stitchers expected to play in the new federation. The three hundred delegates elected Mary Nason to sit with six male unionists on the decision-making body of the federation, the General Executive Board. This action represented an unprecedented acceptance of women as important to policy-making on the national level of trade unionism.[49] Nason's successors used their position in the union bureaucracy to work with the Women's Trade Union League for

---

have been through college, I know the abandoned class of women by sight and can tell one the moment I see her.... There are prostitutes in Haverhill but they are not shoeworkers" (*Boston Journal*, Jan. 21, 1895, 1, 5). Statements by the City Missionary and the Overseers of the Poor confirmed the opinion of the clergy, and a brakeman at the Boston and Maine Railroad station in Haverhill indicated that he had seen something of life and that the Haverhill girls were "slow" and altogether too strict (*Boston Journal*, Jan. 21, 1895, 5).

[47] *Boston Globe*, Mar. 2, 1896, 5; *Lynn Item*, Mar. 8, 1895, 8; *Boston Herald*, Mar. 11, 1896, 1; *Boston Post*, Feb. 20, 1895, 2.

[48] *Boston Globe*, Mar. 11, 1895, 1.

[49] *Boston Post*, April 11, 1895, 2; *Boston Globe*, April 11, 1895, 4; *Haverhill Gazette*, April 15, 1895, 6.

protective legislation and suffrage.

The Haverhill stitchers and their activities in the 1895 strike and in the formation of the B&SWU realized the tradition of union activity of female shoeworkers in the nineteenth century. Alongside skilled male shoeworkers, they sought to defend their position in a rapidly changing industry through effective union organization. The stitchers used collective action and a sex monopoly on the stitching craft to advance their interests as women workers. Their mobility in the labor force led them to support an industry-wide federation of skilled workers, but they sought to maintain exclusively female locals through which to maximize their interests. They obtained power and representation on the governing board of the new federation.

The position of the stitchers in the job structure of the industry enabled them to succeed where other female factory workers failed. They were first of all skilled workers. They were native-born Americans of different ethnic and religious backgrounds to whom class was more important than parentage in the depression years of the 1890s. The majority of the women workers of Haverhill were unmarried and living independently of their families. These three factors of skill, consciousness as a class, and personal mobility gave the stitchers their ability to organize. Support from the Massachusetts AFL and from upperclass women sustained the strike financially. The SLP encouraged the stitchers' own vision of women participating equally and fully in the labor movement. And the community of Haverhill was far from shocked at the sight of women marching in its streets. The city had seen the strike as an effective defense of community integrity by women who had for years been welcomed into the homes of its residents during the busy season.

The Work and Wages of Single Women, 1870 to 1920

CLAUDIA GOLDIN

Single women dominated the U.S. female labor force from 1870 to 1920. Data on the home life and working conditions of single women in 1888 and 1907 enable the estimation of their earnings functions. Work in the manufacturing sector for these women was task-oriented and payment was frequently by the piece. Earnings rose steeply with experience and peaked early; learning was mainly on-the-job. Occupational segregation by sex was a partial product of the method of payment, and the early termination of human capital investment was a function of the life-cycle labor force participation of these women, although the role of the family was also critical.

IN the history of women's labor market experience in the United States the half-century from about 1870 to 1920 was the era of single women.[1] Fully 75 percent of the white female labor force in 1890 and 1900 were single; fewer than 10 percent were married. But by the late 1920s married women comprised over 25 percent of the female work force. Even though the participation rate of single women continued to rise, they became less a force in the economic history of American women.[2] The history of the

The Journal of Economic History, Vol. XL, No. 1 (March 1980). ISSN 0022-0507.

The author is Associate Professor, Department of Economics, University of Pennsylvania, and Research Associate, National Bureau of Economic Research. An earlier draft of this work has benefited from the comments of participants at the Columbia University Faculty Seminar in Economic History, the Cliometrics Conference at the University of Chicago, and a University of Pennsylvania workshop. NSF Grant SOC 78-15037 has supported this research and Nadja Zalokar provided able research assistance. Limitation of space has resulted in the omission of various supporting materials which can be found in Claudia Goldin, *Feminine Economy: An Economic History of American Women* (in progress) and "Women in the American Labor Experience: Issues, Life Cycle Participation, and Earnings Functions" (mimeo, April 1979).

[1] Little is now known about the labor force participation of women prior to 1870, but existing evidence suggests that the percentage of married women then at work was higher in large cities.

[2] See Table 4 of Goldin, "Women in the American Labor Experience," paper presented at the 1979 Cliometrics meetings. Labor force participation rates for single women by age, nativity, and race are given below for the entire U.S. and for cities of over 100,000 in 1890. It can be seen that part of the rise in the labor force participation of single women after 1890 was probably a function of the movement of population to the cities.

Labor Force Participation Rates of Single Women, 1890

	Entire U.S.		Urban U.S.	
Age:	*15–24*	*25–34*	*15–24*	*25–34*
Native-born, Native parents	24.0	42.3	42.9	48.0
Native-born, Foreign parents	41.9	55.7	54.0	62.0
Foreign-born	71.1	78.9	82.2	79.0
White	35.0	53.3	58.0	64.1
Black	55.5	78.8	82.5	67.8

Source: *Federal Census of Population, 1890*, vol. 1, parts 1 and 2.

female labor force from 1870 to 1920 was shaped by single women, and, correspondingly, that from 1920 to 1970 by those who were married. Accompanying these changes in the composition of the labor force was an evolution of occupations, events that were not in the least unrelated. The first period witnessed the peaking of the employment of women in manual, manufacturing occupations and the second the peaking of clerical employment.[3]

During the Progressive Era the young and unmarried working woman was the subject of much social concern. The conditions of industrial work for single women, their health, their morals, and the sufficiency of the pay of those living away from home were the heightened issues of a period witnessing the rise of factory employment and increased immigration to large cities. Prior to the 1870s women were employed in very few industries, but as more were hired in trades previously occupied by men, increased concern was expressed about the relative efficiency of the sexes, the related issue of pay differentials, and the impact of female labor on the economic position of men.

This concern about single working women led to the collection of data on their industrial and social condition, and it is perhaps ironic that these documents were ultimately used to draft legislation limiting their employment. These reports are remarkable depositories of information on work and home life, and it is fortunate that two of the most detailed records span the high-point of single women's work in American history. Carroll Wright's Bureau of Labor document *Working Women in Large Cities* (1889) and the nineteen-volume report of the Secretary of Commerce and Labor, *Woman and Child Wage Earners* (1910), studies of women in 1888 and 1907 respectively, form the basis of this article on women in the midst of the era of single women's work.[4]

Characteristics of Single Working Women, 1888 to 1907[5]

Single working women at the turn of this century were historically unique in terms of their home lives and occupations. They worked at a time when there were primarily two types of position available to urban women—manual factory work and service employment—and their occupations, unlike those in the then nascent clerical sector, did not particularly prepare them to reenter the labor force after marriage.[6] Their jobs

[3] See Elyce Rotella, "Women's Labor Force Participation and the Growth of Clerical Employment in the U.S., 1870–1930" (Ph.D. diss., Univ. of Pennsylvania, 1977).

[4] *Fourth Annual Report of the Commissioner of Labor, 1888. Working Women in Large Cities* (Washington, 1889), and *Report on Condition of Woman and Child Wage-Earners in the U.S. in 19 Volumes*, Senate Documents Vols. 86–104 (Washington, 1910/11).

[5] This section is a highly condensed version of material in Goldin, "Women in the American Labor Experience," and *Feminine Economy* (in progress).

[6] Among all white working women in the U.S. in 1890, approximately 1/3 were employed in domestic and personal service, 1/3 in manufacturing and mechanical trades, 1/10 in trade and transportation, 1/10 in professional jobs, and the rest in agriculture. Only a trivial fraction were clerical workers.

were predominantly task-oriented, were frequently paid for by the piece (between 35 percent and 47 percent of women in manufacturing in 1890 worked on piece rates),[7] and were almost uniformly distinct from those occupied by men. They learned their trades on-the-job in the factory, store, or home; although their educations preceded the rise of vocational schools for women, the data in this article demonstrate that schooling was a clear advantage to them in the labor market.

Women frequently began their labor market experience when young, working continuously until they married. But their age at first marriage was late; indeed it was the latest of all birth cohorts of American women, and the percentage of these women who never married was correspondingly high. These women worked in the labor market when it was common for a young woman to work full-time in her parents' home instead. About 35 percent of all urban, single women 16 to 24 years old were neither at school nor working outside their homes in 1900, although this figure declined to about 5 percent by 1930. Therefore a large fraction of these women were still attached to their parents' homes, working in them or, if they worked outside, giving their entire salaries to their families. But at the same time, fully 38 percent of all single urban working women over 16 years old in 1900 lived away from their parents, with their employers or in the homes of others. Even though part of this rather large figure is accounted for by servants, housekeepers, teachers, and cottonmill towns, the nature of employment alone did not determine residence. And, as a footnote to this attempt at generalization, a hallmark of this group of single women was cultural heterogeneity.

Issues and Sources

Questions on both the demand and supply sides of the labor market are suggested by the unique position of single women during this period of American history. I have concentrated here almost exclusively on the supply side to offer answers to the following questions.

1) What was the nature of work and of skill formation? What were the functions of piece work and task-oriented jobs?
2) What governed the choice of occupation for a single woman among jobs in manufacturing, in a store, or as a servant?
3) What were the payoffs to women (or their families) from entering the labor force when young and remaining at work until marriage, and what were the gains to parents from having their daughters specialize in home or market work?
4) Why were occupations segregated by sex?
5) What determined whether working women lived at home with their families or in boarding houses?
6) How did education and ethnicity affect earnings?

[7] The lower bound is from the *Federal Census of Manufactures, 1890*, Part I, Table 5, pp. 92–114, and the upper bound adjusts this figure for the understatement of pieceworkers in cotton and other textile mills. The figure for men is about 11%.

Data from two federal studies enable the estimation of a relationship between earnings, experience on-the-job, and other variables. These earnings functions will provide insights to these issues.

Carroll Wright's *Working Women in Large Cities* (hereafter the *1888 study*), the first federal report on working women, investigated the conditions of women "who work in great city manufactories upon light manual or mechanical labor and in stores" (p. 9). The study included 343 industries in 22 cities and contained information on 17,427 women, of whom 88 percent were single.[8] It was not until the Secretary of Commerce and Labor's multi-industry report *Woman and Child Wage Earners, (1907 study)*, that women were again a direct concern of a federal agency.[9] Only city-industry averages can be used in the *1888 study*, the original surveys having never been located, but the *1907 study* contains most of the raw data collected for 6 industries, in total information on about 10,000 single women. The present article is based on all the observations for men's clothing in Chicago, and for cotton textiles in Massachusetts and North Carolina, 1785 observations on single women of all ages. The *1888 study* includes women living away from home; the observations used for the *1907 study* are only for those living at home.

Earnings Functions: Theory and Results

The earnings equations estimated are variants of a general form implied by a model of human capital formation with a linearly declining investment ratio. The simplest statement of such an earnings function is:

$$\text{Log } Y_t = \beta_0 + \beta_1 s + \beta_2 e + \beta_3 e^2 + \sum \alpha_i x_i + \nu, \tag{1}$$

where Log Y_t is the log of earnings at time t, e is total work experience, s is years of schooling, the x_i are personal and family characteristics influencing job efficiency, and ν is the error term. The coefficient on schooling, β_1, can be interpreted as its rate of return, and one can also derive the rate of return to experience and the initial investment ratio from β_2 and β_3.[10] The data used in the estimation procedure are weighted city-industry averages for 1888 and micro-level observations for 1907. The following summarizes the major findings of the results given in Table 1.

[8] The cities included, with the regional divisions used to estimate the earnings functions in Table 1, are: *South*—Atlanta, Baltimore, Charleston, New Orleans, Richmond, Savannah; *North*—Boston, Brooklyn, Buffalo, Newark, New York, Philadelphia, Providence; *Midwest*—Chicago, Cincinnati, Cleveland, Indianapolis, Louisville, St. Louis, St. Paul; *West*—San Francisco, San Jose.

[9] This statement excludes reports using census materials, in particular *Statistics of Women at Work* (Washington, 1907) based on the 1900 Census.

[10] See in particular Jacob Mincer, *Schooling, Experience and Earnings* (New York, 1974). Under a particular set of assumptions, Mincer (p. 91) has shown that:

$$\beta_2 = \left[r_t k_0 + \frac{k_0}{T}(1 + k_0)\right] \text{ and } \beta_3 = -\left[\frac{r_t k_0}{2T} + \frac{(k_0)^2}{2T^2}\right],$$

where r_t = rate of return to experience; $k_0 = (C_0/E_0)$ = the initial investment ratio which is assumed to decline linearly with time, $k_t = k_0 - k_0(t/T)$. At time T investment is zero. If $T = 10$, the results in Table 1, col. 3 yield $k_0 = 0.33$ and $r_t = 0.14$; if $T = 7$, $k_0 = 0.35$, $r_t = 0.06$.

TABLE 1
EARNINGS FUNCTIONS FOR WOMEN IN 1888 AND 1907
(Dependent variable = log annual earnings)

Independent Variables for {*1888 Study* / *1907 Study*}	*1888 Study* *Mean of Dependent Variable:* 5.52 (1)	(2)	*1907 Study* *Mean of Dependent Variable:* 5.30 (3)	(4)
Constant	4.7837*	5.4805*	−1.5350*	−2.0140*
	(0.1202)	(0.1247)		
1) Experience	0.0855*	0.0778*	0.0890*	0.0936*
	(0.0089)	(0.0082)	(0.0043)	(0.0042)
2) Experience² × 10⁻²	−0.4387*	−0.4386*	−0.2809*	−0.2929*
	(0.0007)	(0.0006)	(0.0002)	(0.0002)
3) Schooling[a]	0.1553*	0.1249*	0.0564*	0.0446*
	(0.0014)	(0.0232)	(0.0133)	(0.0130)
4) Schooling² × 10⁻²	−0.7148*	−0.6249*	−0.3609*	−0.2792**
	(0.0014)	(0.0013)	(0.0017)	(0.0016)
5) Log days lost / Log days worked	−0.0731*	−0.0793*	1.2133*	1.2189*
	(0.0108)	(0.0100)	(0.0169)	(0.0165)
6) % Born in state / Native-born, Native parents		−0.1557*	−0.0225	−0.0036
		(0.0441)	(0.0506)	(0.0495)
7) % Born out of state / Foreign-born		0.1872*	−0.0910*	−0.0216
		(0.0622)	(0.0456)	(0.0452)
8) % Native mothers / Foreign-born × Years in U.S.		−0.1627*	0.0006	−0.0011
		(0.0334)	(0.0015)	(0.0014)
9) % Live at home / Presence of mother		−0.3325*	−0.0763*	−0.0419
		(0.0567)	(0.0300)	(0.0296)
10) % Assist at home / Age began work		−0.1124*		0.0295*
		(0.0316)		(0.0032)
11) Store × schooling	0.0347*	0.0251**		
	(0.0154)	(0.0141)		
Number of Observations	1107	1107	1785	1785
R^2:	0.996[b]	0.996[b]	0.836	0.845
s.e.e:	0.762	0.697	0.313	0.306

Notes: 1888—All variables weighted by $\sqrt{n}$, where n = number of women in each industry-city category. The mean of the weighted dependent variable is 18.78. Other variables entered: three regional dummies, percent in bad health, percent married, widowed, separated or divorced, and percentage with previous occupations.

1907—Other variables entered: state or city dummies.

Standard errors are in parentheses under coefficients. All starred coefficients (*) are significant at the 5% level; those with (**) are significant at the 10% level.

[a] Schooling is measured as a residual (age that work began minus seven years) for 1888 but directly for 1907. The 1907 data, however, give months attended which has been converted to years by dividing by 12. This procedure understates the impact of schooling because school months per year were less than 12. Note that even though the coefficients differ for the two years, the marginal returns are about equal.

[b] This measure of R^2 overstates the "explained variance" because the weighting procedure increases the variance in the dependent variable. If, instead, one were to compute a measure of R^2 by applying the coefficients from this GLS estimation to the unweighted data, one would get an R^2 of about 0.35. The R^2 from an OLS regression on the unweighted data would, of course, be greater.

Sources: See text.

Earnings data for women doing manual work in both 1888 and 1907 indicate that there were large advantages to remaining in the labor force. Earnings rose steeply with experience on the job, peaking or leveling off early. The occupations women held during this time may be colloquially termed unskilled or, at best, semiskilled, but they involved substantial learning-by-doing, and only after several years of job training did individuals become proficient. In various industries (for example, men's clothing), moving up on the earnings function involved job mobility. "Occupational promotion in coat making necessitates changes in the character of the work done and involves a period of reduced productivity and reduced wages" (*1907 study*, vol. 2, p. 477). In others, such as weaving, it involved supervising more machines, or making more and better pieces (for example, shoes).

Learning on-the-job was considerable for individuals entering at any age. Although maturity was a factor in the earnings-experience function, it was not an overriding one. Delaying entry into the labor force for one year added less than 3 percent to earnings, whereas working for that year would have added over 9 percent.[11] In other words, a 14-year-old working for two years would earn at a maximum 6 percent less than a 16-year-old working for two years, but the 14-year-old working for two years would earn 12 percent more than a 16-year-old just entering the labor force.

Moreover, the shape of the earnings profile was not merely a function of some screening mechanism used to identify fast quitters. Various economic theorists have posited that employers who have fixed hiring costs and heterogeneous labor with characteristics that are not easily identifiable will maximize profits by having two types of earnings functions, one flat and one rising. This screening mechanism ensures the self-selection of laborers, with the slow quitters opting for the rising function. The widespread use of piece rates for women is of critical importance in this regard.[12] Piecework rates may have been used by firms to screen workers initially and then to maintain employment by continuously rewarding effort. Employers desiring to attract female labor might have altered work organization to include more task-oriented and incentive pay jobs to reward effort where occupational mobility was excluded by the limited nature of job attachment. But the use of piece rates implies that differences in earnings were a direct function of productivity and not a mere construct. Furthermore, domestic service was an alternative occupation that had a relatively high but flat earnings profile, and it might have served to attract the casual worker. Lucy Salmon, in summarizing her 1889 survey

[11] The 3% figure is a maximum because the *1907 study* does not include information on prior occupations. To the extent that there was a return to experience on other jobs the coefficient on the age at beginning work would include it.

[12] See, for example, Joanne Salop and Steven Salop, "Self-Selection and Turnover in the Labor Market," *Quarterly Journal of Economics*, 90 (Nov. 1976), 619–27, who state that "the firm could pay for piecework, thereby allowing the worker to receive the full value of his own marginal product and eliminating the firm's interest in this information [turnover costs]" (p. 627).

of domestic service, indicated precisely these market forces in determining the allocation of women among occupations.[13]

Although the earnings functions for both years display similar characteristics, that for 1907 rises more steeply and peaks later than that for 1888. The 1888 experience variable measures years in a particular occupation, and when total job experience is substituted, the profiles are virtually identical for the two years. A third type of occupation, store work, also existed for single women during this period, and it appears that store work in 1888 differed substantially from that in 1907. Although in 1888 there was a bonus to store workers with more schooling (var. 11, cols. 1 and 2), earnings did not differ by experience; that is, the profiles had the same shape but that for store work was about 3 percent greater. By 1907 there was more room for advancement in store work. Earnings were initially lower by 8 percent but rose by 1.8 percent with each year of experience over and above the same gradient in the factory (eq. 2).

$$\text{Log (weekly earnings)} = \underset{}{1.506} + \underset{(.0058)}{0.0996\ \text{Exp.}} - \underset{(.0004)}{0.0038\text{Exp.}^2}$$

$$- \underset{(.0277)}{0.0758\ \text{Store}} + \underset{(.0063)}{0.0181\ (\text{Exp.} * \text{Store})} \qquad (2)$$

$R^2 = 0.316$; number of observations = 1319; standard errors are in parentheses.

Store = 1, if woman was working in a department or retail store.

Exp. = years experience in this occupation.

Source: *1907 study,* vol. 5, pp. 268–98. New York City sample of "women living at home."

The scant existing information on the earnings of men with similar characteristics during the same time period suggests that their earnings rose less rapidly but peaked later than women's.[14] Occupations and industries were often highly segregated by sex. It is likely that these divisions were less a reflection of inherent differences in ability than they were a by-product of segregation by method of payment and the specialized nature of work. Men were infrequently found in the tedious, task-oriented jobs which women held. Because of their greater expected attachment to the labor force, they had greater incentive to perform efficiently in non-piece

[13] Lucy M. Salmon, *Domestic Service*, 1897 ed. (rpt. New York, 1972), stated:

> In the two occupations the wages in which have been compared with those in domestic service [teaching and factory work] while the general average wages are low, it is possible to reach through promotion a comparatively high point. The fact that the wage plane is a high one is one inducement for women of average ability to enter the occupation [servant]. On the other hand, the fact that the wage limit, high as it is, is soon reached must act as a barrier in the case of others (pp. 103–04).

[14] See Joan Hannon, "The Immigrant in the Promised Land: Human Capital and Ethnic Discrimination in the Michigan Labor Market" (Ph.D. diss., Univ. of Wisconsin, 1977), Table 3.5 for male earnings equations in 1889.

rate work and stood more likely eventually to receive "prizes" in the form of promotions and monetary rewards.

Among those under 16 years old, earnings were somewhat higher for girls than for boys, but boys received a higher return on their education. Boys invested more in training than girls did, and given their respective life-cycle labor force participation rates, these may have been optimal strategies. But the implicit investment choice was made more by parents than by youngsters. Parents were a large factor in the intergenerational transmission of cultural norms, and the earnings functions are suggestive in this regard. Young women who lived at home earned less than those who boarded (var. 9, col. 2) and, understandably, those who assisted at home earned even less (var. 10, col. 2). Those who lived away from home may have been a biased sample of all young women in terms of differing with their parents' decisions and their innate ability. Those whose mothers were alive earned less than did those without mothers at home (var. 9, cols. 3 and 4), an indication that these girls worked at home part-time and either worked fewer hours in the factory or worked less intensively.

Education had a smaller impact on earnings than is generally observed for contemporary data, but it was nonetheless important. Ethnicity, however, was not a separate factor in determining earnings. Although the results in col. 3 indicate that the foreign-born (var. 7) earned 9 percent less than native-born with native- or foreign-born parents, this differential disappears when relative maturity is considered, that is, when the age at which work began is entered. The foreign-born began work younger; given their level of experience, they earned somewhat less. The results in col. 4 indicate no residual differences in earnings due to ethnicity, although there were differences in labor force participation by ethnicity.

Summary Remarks

In summary, work in the labor market for women from 1870 to 1920 was the realm of the unmarried, whose occupations involved much on-the-job training but little long-range advancement. The estimated earnings functions are consistent with the life-cycle labor force participation of these women. But the comment by one astute observer, that

> [In] most cases, probably, woman's expectation of marriage is responsible for her lack of skill, but in some instances, doubtless, her enforced lack of skill is responsible for her longing for marriage as a relief from intolerable drudgery (*1907 study*, vol. 9, Helen Sumner, p. 32),

indicates this harmony need not have been universally felt or long-lived.

REVIEW ESSAY

WOMEN'S WAGE WORK AS MYTH AND HISTORY

By ALICE KESSLER-HARRIS*

Arno Press has recently printed some 53 volumes of literature pertaining to women and some 105 volumes pertaining to labor in America. Among these are a dozen or so, originally published in the late nineteenth and early twentieth centuries and having to do with the lives of wage-earning women.[1] They are an impressive collection. Written and compiled by sociologists, economists, and interested observers, they are replete with statistical tables, firsthand observations, and documents written by working women themselves. Their rich data offer irrefutable testimony to the consistency of women's collectively unfortunate experience as wage laborers. But in the years before the First World War, such data were not unusual.

Almost anyone during those years could have told, if asked, that more and more women—married and unmarried, immigrant and native born, poor and not-so-poor—were entering the paid labor force. And almost everyone would have agreed with the popular wisdom: women's natural role was to take care of home and children. Wage work, sometimes an unfortunate necessity, ought to be regulated and controlled so that women's family roles were not impaired. From the mid-1880s on, state and federal bureaus of labor statistics, and social welfare organizations of all kinds gathered and published data that detailed the harsh con-

*My thanks to Milton Cantor, Blanche Wiesen Cook, Jacques Marchand, Sonja Michel, Sumner Rosen and Bert Silverman for reading and commenting on earlier drafts of this article.

[1] The two series to which I refer here are Leon Stein and Philip Taft, eds., *American Labor: From Conspiracy to Collective Bargaining* and Annette Baxter and Leon Stein, *American Women: Images and Realities.* Among the best-known volumes in these series are John Andrews and W.D.P. Bliss, *History of Women in Trade Unions* (1910); Helen Sumner, *History of Women in Industry in the U.S.* (1910); Carroll Wright, *The Working Girls of Boston* (1889); Elizabeth Butler, *Women and the Trades* (1909); Helen Campbell, *Women Wage Earners* (1893); Edith Abbott, *Women in Industry: A Study in American Economic History* (1910).

ditions under which women were employed.[2] Clothed in the garb of objective investigation, most of these studies were frankly reformist in aim. Written in a period when long hours and hard physical toil were the norm for most workers, they reflected a genuine concern with the problems women faced in attempting to meet family responsibilities while earning a living. They raised issues of morality, of health, of excessive fatigue, and of inadequate food and housing in support of legislation to protect future mothers and homemakers. Information compiled in these sources supported a vast array of health and safety legislation for employed women. In turn, the legislation helped to close off certain kinds of jobs to women while encouraging them to enter others.

Prepared initially for broadly political purposes, these volumes —now ably represented by the Arno series—have since formed the underpinnings of scholarly knowledge about wage-earning women in industrial America. Their statistics, firsthand testimony, and descriptions of work place experiences are invaluable. Yet the datum has proven a mixed blessing for historians. The volumes were written out of a set of assumptions, perfectly valid for their day, that guided the tone of scholarship about wage-earning women thereafter. These assumptions need to be viewed critically. With a few exceptions, the literature on wage earning women accepted the social imperative of the nuclear family sustained by wives and mothers, and implicitly and explicitly acknowledged that women's primary function was in the home. Wage work for women, it was argued, must be constructed so as not to impair family functions. In agreeing that women could play only limited roles in the work force, the literature conceded that those women whom necessity forced into the marketplace labored at an inevitable disadvantage. Physical weakness, home responsibilities, lack of assertiveness, were part of a natural sorting process that regulated their access to certain kinds of jobs. A free market economy assumed that women's primary roles as housewives and mothers inhibited success in an open and com-

[2] Not yet reprinted, to my knowledge, are more of the 19 volumes of the *Report on the Condition of Women and Child Wage Earners in the U.S.*, 61st Congress, 2nd Session, Senate Document #645 (Washington, D.C., 1910, 1911, 1912) or 6 of the 8 volumes of the Pittsburgh Survey (1907-08); and such scattered sources as Elizabeth Beardsley Butler's *Saleswomen in Mercantiles Stores, Baltimore, 1909* (New York, 1912); Mary Van Kleeck, *Artificial Flower Makers* (New York, 1913), *Women in the Bookbinding Trade* (New York, 1913).

petitive wage labor force. Women would always be less productive than men and therefore could not be expected to earn as much. The appropriate response of a liberal society, therefore, was to provide access to vocational education and to legislate such protective remedies as shorter hours and healthful working conditions in an attempt to alleviate the worst impact of the market.

Few economists, those days, faced with the urgent necessity of confronting woman's deteriorating options in the marketplace, could have done other than to recommend bolstering her position. It was, after all, self-evidently true that most women had, or could expect to have, homes and families. Yet the literature served to perpetuate the underlying myths that anchored women so firmly in disadvantaged positions. As it was itself blinded to the possibility that women were not naturally disadvantaged, so it obscured the possibility that women were not operating in a competitive labor market at all. Employers who took advantage of prevailing myths to assign women to special labor market positions confirmed the realities of poverty and degradation that kept women in menial jobs. Interest in alleviating the wage-earning woman's lot centered on adjusting the realities of her daily and increasing work experience to prevailing myths about what women should be doing. Little attention was given to economic, psychic, or familial solutions that might bring home and work into harmony.

The present position of wage-earning women confirms the results. Although women have been working in growing numbers —they are now 46% of the wage labor force—their relative position in the work force may only now be starting to change. Women have consistently remained in sex-stereotyped, menial jobs where their economic well-being has been kept above sheer immiseration by legislation that regulated hours and wages. A general rise in standards of living of all workers obscures the continuing lowly condition of women wage-earners, but a glance at any set of statistics (the best efforts of the women's movement notwithstanding), reveals that their relative status as regards to pay, job discrimination, and unionization has remained virtually unchanged.[3]

[3] The best sources for historical data are the *Handbooks on Women Workers* compiled by the

Historians who accepted the assumptions of a competitive marketplace wrote books like Elizabeth Butler's *Women in the Trades,* Alice Henry's *The Trade Union Woman,* and Elizabeth Baker's *Protective Labor Legislation,* that argued the case for greater legislative efforts on behalf of working women. Their questions revolved around issues such as how women's family roles have influenced their work force participation, or whether wage work mitigates against adequate mothering and good morals.[4] Discrimination, economic deprivation, and conscious self-image were all accounted for by women's special relationship to the home which was in the end responsible for their lower productivity and permanently dependent status.

The net result has been an empirical literature rooted in the need to justify women's wage labor activities as a product of economic necessity. Sometimes justification took the form of reassuring readers about the historical validity of women's work. "Women have of course, always, worked," says Sophonisba Breckenridge definitively. Helen Sumner agrees: "Women have always worked and their work has probably been quite as important a factor in the total economy of society as it is today." And the theme persists down to the present: "Women are in the labor force to stay," notes Robert Smuts in a widely used account of women's work. Often the literature tried to refute contentions that women's wage labor threatened the successful performance of work at home. Additional wages, it was argued, kept impecunious families together: work was a consequence of financial need. Not infrequently, this literature celebrated the great contributions of women who had always worked.[5]

Women's Bureau of the Department of Labor. See bulletin #218: Janet Hooks, *Women's Occupations Through Seven Decades* (Washington, D.C., 1947), and most recently Bulletin #297, the *Handbook on Women Workers (Washington, D.C., 1975).* See also, the following newspaper articles: June Kronholz "Though More Women Work, Job Equality Fails to Materialize," *Wall Street Journal*, July 6, 1976; 1; Eileen Shanahan, "Gap in Earning Between the Sexes Reported Up Threefold Since '55," New York *Times*, Nov. 29, 1976, 18; and Peter Kihss, "Women's Wages Fall Even farther Behind," New York *Times*, April 3, 1977, 35.

[4] Some notable exceptions include Vera Shlakman, *Economic History of a Factory Town: A Study of Chicopee, Massachusetts*, Smith College Studies in History, Vol. 20, (October 1924-July 1935) 31-34; Theresa Wolfson, *The Woman Worker and the Trade Union* (New York, 1926); and Constance McLaughlin Green, *Holyoke, Massachusetts: A Case History of the Industrial Revolution in America* (New Haven, 1939).

[5] Abbott, *Women in Industry*, vii; Sumner, *History of Women in Industry*, 11; Robert Smuts, *Women and Work in America* (New York 1971 [1959]), xv. See also Caroline Dall, *Women's Right to Labor, or Low Wages and Hard Work* (Boston, 1860), and Johanna Lobsenz, *The Older Woman in Industry* (New York, 1974 [1929]). For recent examples of

From a historiographical perspective the consistency of attempts to reassure readers that women have always worked, reveals something of the circular reasoning that has made it possible for the literature to sustain women's actual labor market roles. Since women were expected to participate in the work force only when to do so was economically useful and socially appropriate—a result of circumstance not an exercise of right—investigators gathered data that offered evidence that this was in fact what women were doing. The questions that informed their investigations emerged from a value orientation that accepted prevailing social norms. They overlooked the experiences of those ethnic groups that imposed few limits on the economic role of women, and tended to ignore a variety of ways in which some urban women combined family roles with economically productive activities.[6]

Empirical research has centered on convincing skeptics that economic necessity, not frivolous neglect of the home forced women into paid labor. How many times, through how many generations have researchers had to prove that women did not work for "pin money"? The subtly debilitating questions that emerged continue to undermine women's already tenuous conviction that paid work is an honest life need for them. Examples include the sociologist's concern with the impact of women's employment on the family (implying potential neglect of female responsibility), and the economists' with her effect on the structure of the wage labor force (can the economy absorb all those women? will they lower wages? compete with men?) Historians become obsessed with statistics about female-headed households, women adrift, and declining fertility rates marshaled to refute the widely held belief that the natural role has always been that of housewife. The scholarly research that emerges from the continuing need to justify women's wage work provides, in short, a perfect example of how the social sciences have functioned, in Joan Kelly-Gadol's words, "as myth reinforcing patriarchy."[7]

"great contributions" literature see Cecyle Neidle, *America's Immigrant Women* (New York, 1976), and Barbara Wertheimer, *We Were There* (New York, 1977).

[6] I am thinking here of the Jewish wife's consistently superb contribution to Ma and Pa stores, of Italian women who worked in canneries where they could supervise their children and of black women who routinely cared for each other's children.

[7] "The Social Relation of the Sexes: Methodological Implications of Women's History," *SIGNS*, 1 (Summer 1976), 814. Some powerful illustrations of such myth reinforcement occurred during the Great Depression. See Claire Howe, "Return of the Lady," *New Outlook*, 164 (October 1934), 34-38; R.J. Davies, "Are Women Taking Men's Jobs?" *Political*

But the need to reassure readers about women's work force participation has a practical impact too. It results in policy decisions that affect women's ability to work, and that perpetuate a cumulative cycle of discrimination. The subliminal message is clear: women have been doing it for a while, so there isn't any real danger that they'll take men's jobs, become unfeminine, neglect their homes, and so on. The historical result has been to seek legislation that insured that women did not in fact threaten to transcend acceptable bounds. Preferred approaches in the early twentieth century included regulating women's access to jobs or restricting the conditions under which women could work. Such protective legislation, widely favored by feminists, economists, and social welfare activists who genuinely cared about the well-being of wage-earning women, had the immediate advantage of mitigating the low wages and harsh conditions that might otherwise jeopardize women's capacity to raise children and run the home. The consequence, felt largely by the poor, was to confirm women's competitive disadvantages in the marketplace and to relegate them to the lowest economic sectors.

More recently explicit references to sex-related physical and personality characteristics, have been invoked to stratify women in the areas of the labor market they are just beginning to enter. Women, who now hold 1.2 per cent of the nation's construction jobs, for example, find themselves subject to physical violence from threatened male workers.[8] And those who attempt to enter the sanctuaries of male management confront attitudes such as those of Roy Killian. The preface to his book, a publication of the American Management Association, declares that the book

> rests heavily on the fact that there are pertinent, job related differences between men and women, that these can be identified, and that with appropriate leadership these differences can benefit all concerned. It demonstrates that women can be understood and their behaviour on the job can be predicted.[9]

Quarterly, 2 (January 1931), 126-130; Sarah Comstock, "Marriage—OR Career?" *Good Housekeeping*, 94 (June 1932), 32-33, 156-162; "What do the Women of America Think about Careers?" *Ladies Home Journal*, 56 (November 1939), 12.

[8] "Women Win Fight for More Construction Jobs, Less Harassment," New York *Times*, August 23, 1977, 30.

[9] *The Working Woman: A Male Manager's View* (American Management Association, 1971), v.

Finally, the imputation that it is somehow women's responsibility or fault that they happen to be or have been in the work force—a matter for apology instead of analysis—obscures the historical process that shapes the work force as a whole. That process, as Herbert Gutman has emphasized, incorporates ethnic and working class values in familial decision making.[10] Working class culture defines parameters that employers must acknowledge, and in particular it tends to circumscribe women's choices in the labor market. But indigenous cultural norms are neither unchanging nor unreflective of labor market needs and opportunities. Indeed, it is precisely in the search for explanations about the intersection of culture and economic reality that material about women can be of greatest use. Dramatic alterations in the relationship between paid and unpaid work for women since the late nineteenth century, differential entry patterns and occupational participation rates for women of different ethnic groups and economic strata speak about the whole culture in which women share. They offer rich material about shifting patterns of capital-labor relationships. They help to illuminate questions of stratification, segmentation, and tracking. They address the configuration of family and technological changes with which everyone interacts. The flux of women into and out of the paid labor force should encourage questions about the dynamism of change. Yet the constant need to reassure seems to have confirmed the inevitability of things as they are and inhibited inquiry into the process of change.

One could state the case for a different approach to the study of women wage-earners more strongly. The historical literature has tended to offer constructs about women in the labor force that assume that they were entering a male bastion in which they could never be more than auxiliary troops. The result has been to measure women's wage labor against an idea of the labor force that already existed. The idea was static, and essentially male-defined: opportunity in the labor market would be weighed against the (more or less) desirable jobs through which men could

[10] See "Work, Culture and Industrializing America," *American Historical Review*, 78 (June 1973), 531-588. Tamara Hareven has argued that familial control of the work process has been extensive. See especially, "Laborers of Manchester, New Hampshire, 1912-1922: The Role of the Family and Ethnicity in Adjustment to Industrial Life," *Labor History*, 16 (Spring 1975), 249-265.

improve their own positions; it embodied a sense of progress judged by advances in wages, and it invoked mobility as an individual category for which men acquired training and skill.

Measured by these standards, the data about women seem endlessly repetitive. In the aggregate, they were not good competitors, their wages were consistently low, they were ensconced in dead-end jobs. Because women's natural roles have historically been identified as outside the labor force, we can trace back their involvement in wage labor over the 200-year span that marks the transition from cottage industry to contemporary technology. We can see entry and departure patterns for women in relationship to class and ethnicity. We have illustrations of how women succumbed to the pushes and pulls of the labor market, of how and who resisted it; and we know where and for whom the mechanisms of restricted access to the labor force begin to break down. In other words, we can describe quite accurately what happened to women. In limited ways we can even explain why it happened. We have answers in terms of an accepted labor force structure. We know, for example, that women were played off against men —used as strikebreakers or employed as substitute workers— that effective rationale were developed for low pay and lack of training.

But although the body of data about women's wage labor is fairly complete, its uses are limited. It provides very little understanding of the way the labor market has been altered by women. It fails to explain the relationship of unpaid labor at home to paid labor market participation for both men and women. Nor does it illuminate the intertwined ideological and economic coercion that have led male and female workers to collude with employers in perpetuating discriminatory policies.

These questions require a conception of a labor force in flux— a labor force on the model of Thompson or Hobsbawm that has choices to make, that can influence decisions as to production, and of which women are an essential and dynamic piece. To conceive of women as part of this process, given their relative historical absence from wage labor, requires exploration of the interaction of homework with waged work. This perspective leads us to ask about how institutions, ideas and role expectations change in response to a changing technology. If offers for analysis a labor force in which men and women have often played different roles and in which we need to explore how and why those roles changed in relation to market demands and societal expectations.

These new assumptions find support in recent studies that have begun to modify the model of a free labor market organized on neoclassical lines. Instead of viewing all workers as competitive with one another, engaged in a race in which women's real and ascribed home roles proved a weighty handicap, some economists have posited a stratified labor force in which people are relegated to particular tracks, often quite early in life.[11] Race, ethnicity, class, education and sex all influence the terms on which an individual enters the race, and though none alone are determining, all affect a worker's prospects and position. The market itself is seen by these labor market segmentation theorists as so structured that there is little or no competion of "secondary" workers for jobs in the primary (unionized, white collar, major firms) sector, while the same barriers preserve primary workers from the risk of joining the secondary (menial, insecure, low paid) sectors. Most people enter and remain in the same sector; limited movement between sectors sustains the myth of upward mobility.

Dual labor market theory, and its more flexible cousin, labor market segmentation theory, leave many questions unanswered and generate their own critiques. Yet for students of women and of work, they offer some useful insights. Applied to women, the argument holds that they have not competed with men for jobs, but seek, and are offered work in different sectors of the economy as well as in different occupations in these sectors. Like blacks and new immigrants, they have largely been confined to low-paid jobs in the secondary labor market.

This perspective, confers a new importance on women's unpaid work at home. To sustain racial, ethnic and sexual divisions in the labor force required a system of social reproduction that

[11] For the framework on which this theory rests see Peter Doeringer and Michael Piore, *Internal Labor Markets and Manpower Analysis* (Lexington, Mass., 1971); useful applications of the theory are contained in Richard Edwards, Michael Reich and David Gordon, eds., *Labor Market Segmentation* (Lexington, 1975). Particular applications of the theory as they apply to women are illustrated by Janice Madden, *The Economics of Sex Discrimination* (Lexington, 1973). For a brief defense of the Neoclassical position see Glen Cain, "The Challenge of Dual and Radical Theories of the Labor Market to Orthodox Theory," *American Economic Review*, 65 (May 1975), 16-22.

reinforced expectations and behavior patterns of each group. Traditionally this has been women's job. Since family expectations and training are seen, in the labor market segmentation schema, as important elements in where workers enter the labor force, the homemaker's attitude toward her own unpaid labor is understood as a key element in the labor market. A mother who teaches her children to be neat, thrifty, disciplined, and obedient to authority produces good workers. Women's work at home assumes a place in relation to the wage labor force which is more than merely functionally supportive of men who work. It is integrally related to the development of social attitudes about work in different class and ethnic groups.

The assignment of the unpaid home role to women has "natural" and historical validity: it also serves to regulate women's labor market participation. Employers could and did take advantage of the ideology of the "home" to ensure the development of an efficient labor force, calling into play all the psychic and social networks—schools, media, religion—calculated to reinforce home roles. In the framework of labor market segmentation it is in the interest of the employing group not merely to maintain the home ideology, but to specify the kinds of behavior patterns needed for each labor market sector. Girl children, if a little hyperbole can be forgiven, ought to be sweet, submissive, and nonassertive.

To sustain a self-reinforcing cycle, the work force experience of women who enter the labor force continues to renew and validate the experiences women have when they work at home. To provide another kind of experience would subvert the ideological structure on which labor market behavior rests. To return for a moment to our initial mountain of data: had the scholars of the turn of the century argued that women should have free access to all jobs they would have threatened to undermine not only the stratified structure of the labor market, but the homes which supported the edifice. Wittingly or not, those who wrote about women at the turn of the century, affirmed their support for an existing machinery that divided workers from each other. The contemporary women's movement, which challenges myths about women's place as it demands new roles at home and new opportunities to work, seems now to be engaged in the kind of fundamental critique that may, in the end, disrupt the cycle.

From a historical perspective, labor market segmentation theory encourages us to take a new look at workers' lives. It opens the door to understanding how home and work roles articulate with one another. Among other things, job stratification imposes limits on family choice and on income. It artificially reduces wages for women without raising them for men, and it reinforces rationale about sex differences. It establishes limits on aspiration difficult to transcend, and which go far toward helping us to understand the parameters of mobility for working people throughout much of industrializing America. Nineteenth-century trade unionists who accused women of competing for jobs, or of strikebreaking, may have spoken from within these limits, and historians can fruitfully view them as participants in the stratification process. Housework appears as another layer (perhaps not the lowest) among work hierarchies. The perspective of labor market segmentation theory exposes hierarchical work structures, long seen as natural, as reflecting the needs of the American capitalist economy. The idea that women and men operate in separate labor markets, with its corollary that we condition ourselves to accept assigned roles, makes sense of socially accepted attitudes about women's lesser capacities for management, their reluctance to assume responsibility, and their lack of assertiveness. It explains much of what we know both about where women have worked in the past and about why their individual and collective struggles have had so little impact on their position in the labor force.

Segmentation theories about the operation of the labor market move us toward a more satisfactory analysis of how employers exploit race, ethnicity, and sex to achieve efficiency and profit. Unlike the older literature, which reinforced stereotyped patterns by urging that women's jobs be regulated to suit family needs, recent studies address the issue of how cultural patterns and values surrounding women's lives are themselves subject to exploitation in the labor market. They therefore open questions about how labor policies simultaneously help to sustain the self-images that underlie women's restrictive roles. The measure of new constructs about women's place in the economy lies in their ability to explain how work is part of the entire social role of women and how women's social reproduction is in turn integral to the operation of the labor force. In the comments that follow, I have focused on recent literature that touches on these questions.

Economists Jerolyn Lyle and Jane L. Ross, begin their study of *Women in Industry* with a brief and lucid discussion of theories of discrimination that rejects explanations for women's place that stem from the neoclassical model.[12] Beginning with the dual labor market theory assumption that all firms discriminate, they set out to find out why some discriminate more than others. Exploring the sources of differences in the amount of occupational discrimination among firms opens a series of new questions and permits the authors to examine a long series of market variables. The geographical location of a firm, its size and administrative structure, its place in relation to other firms and in relation to the Federal government, and to particular management practices, all come under scrutiny as potential contributors to discriminatory policy.

In the end, the authors identify several patterns of discrimination that historians can readily recognize. Where large numbers of women are employed in sex-typed jobs, the proportion of female managers tends to be small. The largest industrial firms seem to have the largest proportion of women in responsible positions; perhaps, the authors suggest, because size contributes to mobility at upper levels. There are other conclusions, all quite specific and leading to some affirmative action policy recommendations. The authors propose new legislation and training programs for women as well as federal enforcement of existing laws. These are clear, precise, well-substantiated recommendations. Yet, as the authors conclude, "the most important changes which will bring about equal employment opportunities lie . . . in changes in social attitudes about women and work." A historian might argue that labor market dynamics are only one factor in matching people with jobs. Cultural norms, family patterns, affluence and demography play parts in creating expectations of social roles. Yet it is comforting to note that these two economists are as concerned with internal labor market dynamics in explaining women's position as they are with blaming a set of

[12] Jerolyn R. Lyle and Jane L. Ross, *Women in Industry: Economic Patterns of Women in Corporate America* (Lexington, 1973).

seemingly sacred attitudes. A reader might wonder how attitudinal change relates to economic and technological shifts, how and when people alter their notions of who should work and at what job.

These questions become more urgent when one reviews the recommendations of the Twentieth Century Fund Task Force on Women and Employment. Set up in 1970 to consider the status of working women, the task force published its conclusions in a 1975 volume entitled *Exploitation from 9 to 5.*[13] The authors urge a series of steps designed to provide women with access to all sectors of the labor market. The recommendations are buttressed by half a dozen very good essays documenting past practices of discrimination and detailing problems currently requiring attention. These do not pretend to originality but constitute a concise compendium of available information on women's current labor market situation. The recommendations are comprehensive and very specific. The authors suggest that firms inventory their personnel, analyze their job structures for built-in discrimination, set up training programs for women and minorities, adopt flexible work schedules, and investigate the possibility of on-site child care. Nowhere do the recommendations assume that women alone will benefit from child care. Indeed, to the authors' credit, the report rejects the notion that child and home responsibilities are women's alone.

The report's recommendations are directed toward employers and federal officials. It assumes, I think rightly, that access into the intertwined networks of business policy and social attitudes can best be achieved by a direct confrontation with the villains themselves. Yet what pressure can be brought to bear? People responsible for policies created in their own self-interest, can hardly be expected to alter those policies out of good will. Neither the courts nor legislative bodies have consistently defended women's right of access to jobs. The key is to understand and confront the social sources of labor market policies. In that context, the task force's primary recommendations to employers "that they use their resources to act immediately to end sex discrimination" appears as futile as it would be desirable. Why should they

[13] The Twentieth Century Fund Task Force on Women and Employment, *Exploitation from 9 to 5* (New York, 1975).

do so? It all boils down to social attitudes again, and here the authors leave us stranded. They suggest that women demand more, and that employers alter their old behavior patterns to conform to new social values. The book shies away from noting that those old social patterns have effectively and efficiently created a pool of relatively skilled labor suited to certain kinds of jobs. For employers to alter those patterns might be to subvert their own ends, unless one argues that labor force needs are themselves changing. Short of that, only organized pressure from women will achieve a reallocation of social priorities (day care, paid maternity leaves, flexible time schedules) that must accompany new demands. Like Lyle and Ross, the Twentieth Century Task Force gets to the point of understanding, but does not break through the economic tensions that sustain the social roles at whose feet they lay responsibility for women's exploitation in the labor force.[14]

Barbara Wertheimer and Ann Nelson, looking at the participation of women trade union members in their unions, confront directly the problem of how to get women to demand more.[15] Wertheimer and Nelson's useful study of seven New York City locals is based on their survey of 1,500 union members and on interviews with a variety of male and female leaders. They are optimistic about the possibility of including women in the trade union power structure. Although conceding that woman's homework and child care are important, the authors reject the notion that they are primary causes of the low rate at which women get involved in leadership positions. Rather, the authors blame the resistance of male leadership to female encroachment on their turf. Yet they argue that union leadership would make room if they could find women with the "necessary assertiveness for union work." Here we confront a piece of the "social attitudes" problem and Wertheimer and Nelson do not hesitate: "Women must look to themselves," they assert, "if they are to take advantage of opportunities. They must ready themselves."[16]

One cannot quarrel with the sentiment expressed, but there is room for skepticism about both conclusions. The authors seem

[14] *Ibid.*, 95-96, 4, 5.
[15] Barbara M. Wertheimer and Anne H. Nelson, *Trade Union Women: A Study of Their Participation in New York City Locals* (New York, Praeger, 1975).
[16] *Ibid.*, 144, 145.

to take too literally union leaders' assurances that they would welcome women into leadership positions. The mainstream of the American trade union structure has not historically been on the cutting edge of change and there is little reason to assume that its role will change. Male dominated unions, like the employers with whom they negotiate, benefit from a stratified labor force. Admitting large numbers of women into leadership positions would minimally disrupt the self-renewing cycle by which women's social roles sustain their disadvantaged labor market positions. One has to question whether the organized labor movement would willingly engage in such subversion.

Amazingly enough, the authors followed through on their conclusions. They set up a project, briefly described in this volume; I would have liked a much fuller account. The Trade Union Women's Studies Program, sponsored by the Cornell Industrial and Labor Relations School, offers general education courses designed to encourage assertiveness and self-awareness as well as to train potential leaders. A useful book to use in these classes would be *America's Working Women,* edited by Rosalyn Baxandall, Linda Gordon, and Susan Reverby.[17] This volume illustrates the range of possibility as to women's perceptions of, and responses to, a variety of social roles over time. The collection provides a valuable antidote to the work of economists who examine labor markets as though they were self-perpetuating, and unresponsive to social change. *America's Working Women* presents a tradition of physical and mental labor, of active and creative women who attempt to exercise some control over what they do and who have no illusions about their place in the labor force. Its pages reveal how little we remember about past struggles. By undermining myths about women's historical confinement to limited spheres the book supports arguments for changing the social attitudes that legitimize sex role divisions in a hierarchical structure. It challenges assumptions that women's roles have always been restricted or that restrictions have operated in the same way for different ethnic groups in different periods of time.

The volume is filled with carefully selected documents that illustrate the scope of women's working lives. Its definition of

[17] Rosalyn Baxendall, *et al, America's Working Women: A Documentary History 1600 to the Present* (New York, 1976).

work is cultural: it includes living conditions, unpaid labor at home, and family relationships as well as work place problems and union organizing within its pages. Chapter introductions and headnotes preceding each selection are uniformly informative and intelligent. The volume conceives of the work place and of organizing problems as factors among many that illuminate women's wage labor roles.

Many of the sources used here will be familiar to students of working class history and yet their juxtaposition and pithy quality as edited for this volume make several clear points. The documents describe women's productive labor at home in the preindustrial period and suggest how it is transformed into wage work. They reveal a constant interaction between the expansion of women's jobs and the creation of home technology. They present such dramatic variations in attitudes toward home and work that one is forced to reject notions of women's place.

Thematic consistencies in women's work are instructive. For example, the following description from Alice Morse Earle of making linen reveals the hard physical labor involved in home production:

> The skeins of linen thread went through many tedious processes of washing and bleaching before being ready for weaving; and after the cloth was woven it was "bucked" in a strong lye time and time again, and washed out an equal number of times. Then it was "belted" with a maple beetle on smooth flat stone . . .[18]

Two hundred years later the kind of work had changed and factory production had replaced home production, but the issue of overwork for women remained. In World War II, for example, convenience foods were developed as a partial solution to the following problem reported by the Women's Bureau:

> With no husband at home to cook for her, Mrs. Smith, tired hot and dirty after a long day in the plant, must either stand in line at some restaurant or shop for food when she finishes work. Then the chances are that the butcher and the grocer are out of nearly everything. As a result she is suffering from malnutrition.[19]

Again and again, in this volume, we see women act together to influence the development of certain work processes. There is a description of women who united in an attack against factory

[18] *Ibid.*, 14.
[19] Quoted from Kathryn Blood, *Community Service for Women War Workers* (Washington,

gates in 1846 to break the twelve-hour day. The authors reproduce one of my favorite accounts of women's responses to petty harassments in the workshop from Agnes Nestor's autobiography: "Any new method which the company sought to put into effect and disturb work routine seemed to inflame the deep indignation already burning inside us. Thus . . . when a procedure was suggested for subdividing our work so that each operator would do a smaller part of each glove . . . we began to think of fighting back." And there is a wonderful first-person account of a telephone operator in training in 1921 which details the way in which women were disciplined into those polite impersonal roles. But resisting discipline was equally part of woman's experience. Meat wrappers reported that "the checker would come around with a stopwatch. You learned to wrap a package of bacon using a lot of extra motions because it was a time study thing. When he wasn't there we eliminated all those motions and did it simply . . . The older women would show the new women. It was a tremendous relationship of solidarity."[20]

Even the best collection of documents has built-in limitations. This one speaks only of discrete experiences, begging questions about how changes occurred. Neglected areas are inevitable: here they encourage curiosity. Work technology, for example, scarcely appears. Abundant illustrations of the active lives of women who worked, have no parallel in material detailing what manufacturers thought about their female workers. The book stresses women's protests about their work, noting, only in passing, the institutional structures in which they worked. Nevertheless, Baxandall, Gordon, and Reverby admirably illustrate what historians have to teach those who study the present without perspective. *America's Working Women* informs questions about women in the economic marketplace with a sense of the flexibility of the labor market over extended periods of time. In this longer perspective, the role women played in shaping the work force as well as in working in it assumes wholly different proportions. Women, having participated in a full range of economic activities in the past, must look in other places to discover why myths about their role have persisted.

In contrast to *America's Working Women,* which explores the

D.C., 1944), in *Ibid.*, 14.

[20] *Ibid.*, 61, 178, 236-240, 273.

phenomenon of work for women, W. Elliot and Mary Brownlee, *Women in the American Economy: A Documentary History, 1675-1929* focuses on exploring women's increasing participation rates. The book is more limited in chronological and conceptual scope than *America's Working Women.* It neglects the early colonial period and it stops short of the exciting events of the Great Depression. Its coverage of minority women is limited to two pieces; there is heavy emphasis on the upper ranks of women who worked and much of the material on unskilled labor is about that group, not by them. The book lacks the cultural tidbits on family life and leisure that dot the pages of *America's Working Women.*

But its limitations reflect the underlying premises of the book as the authors state them at the end of their introduction. Out of "the forces of marketplace capitalism," they believe, will come the end of restrictions on women. In their words, "the premium attached by capitalism to the optimal use of human resources, unchecked by cultural restrictions, should lead to institutional innovations." This seems to mean that women will be free when capitalism finds it profitable or necessary to free them. I am not sanguine either that this will happen quickly or that it will happen in ways that would benefit most of us. In the past, "optimal use of human resources" has more often involved playing people off one another in competing groups rather than recognizing and rewarding talent. The short run interest of increased profits has been modified by the need to ensure an efficient, manageable, and self-producing labor force. One suspects that institutional innovations that come from the needs of marketplace capitalism will speed up the full and final conversion of workers into a commodity divided into interchangeable units. The authors recognize the development of sex segmentation in the work force as early as the 1890s; they view the twentieth-century labor market as gradually overcoming such division; and they seem insensitive to the influence of home relationships. They ride roughshod over the culture of immigrants who, they say, found "the Victorian family ideal compelling," and distort the history of the 1930s which, they assert "only reinforced the forces that tended to confine women to the family as the high rate of unemployment caused government, private employers and unions to restrict opportunities for women."[21] Most evidence, including their own tables, indicate that in the aggregate, women made small gains in the depression period. The point, however, is not to debate rising or falling rates, but to understand the terms on which women participated in the wage labor force. Social and cultural values have lives and wills of their own, which influence as well as respond to the labor market.

Increasing sophistication on that question comes from recent work on the home. The long and venerable literature documenting the economic losses and gains of home and wage work is now being cross-fertilized by analysis of the social value of work at home.[22] Dual labor market theory provides a framework for rejecting the idea that work at home is no work at all. It eliminates the absurdity of early twentieth-century censuses when enumerators who went from door to door asking if women and children were gainfully employed were instructed to respond quite literally. For those who worked in the home, census takers filled the column headed "occupation" with the word "none."[23] Neither scholars nor census enumerators are ignoring the work of housewives any longer. The central questions now emerging have to do with how the labor market benefits from its use of unpaid labor, and with the relationships of an economic structure built on small households to a consumer economy. Social scientists are beginning to comprehend the answers to these questions in a framework informed by emerging insight into work culture, and enriched by the growing literature on ethnic related familial norms.

Among the most fruitful of new work is Anne Oakley, *Women's Work.*[24] The first two chapters of this volume describe the

[21] W. Elliot Brownlee and Mary M. Brownlee, *Women in the American Economy: A Documentary in History, 1875-1929* (New Haven, 1976), 39, 29, 38. For an analysis of women in the depression see Ruth Milkman, "Women's Work and the Economic Crisis: Some Lessons from the Great Depression," *Review of Radical Political Economics*, 8 (Spring 1976), 73-97.

[22] In addition to Charlotte Perkins Gilman, *The Home* (New York, 1873), see such long-forgotten sources as Hazel Kyrk, *Economic Problems of the Family* (New York, 1933 [1929]), and the newly rediscovered Alva Myrdal and Viola Klein, *Women's Two Roles: Home and Work* (London, 1956).

[23] This applied to the 1910 and 1920 censuses. See Joseph Hill, *Women in Gainful Occupations 1870-1920*, Census Monographs, IX (Washington, D.C., 1929), 21.

[24] Annie Oakley, *Women's Work* (New York, 1974). Much of the recent analysis is informed by a series of articles that appeared in the pages of the *New Left Review* in 1973-1975. See especially Wally Secombe, "Housework under Capitalism," #83, 3-24; and Jean Gardiner, "Women's Domestic Labor," #89 47-58. Although sometimes overly concerned with what was or was not productive labor in the Marxian sense, these articles performed an inestimable function in laying the theoretical framework for analyzing housework as "work."

breakdown of family work in the pre-industrial period and detail the transition in jobs of women who work in and around the home in the period of industrialization. Oakley insists that the full-fledged housewife is to be understood in terms usually reserved for factory workers: job satisfaction, division of tasks, efficiency are some key concepts. The bulk of the volume is a series of interviews (based on Oakley's more technical *Sociology of Housework)* in which housewives reveal some of the conflicts they face in their work. The clear distinction here between housewifery as a social role and the work that housewives do lends itself to understanding how work at home has been rationalized as noneconomic. The role is clearly gratifying to many women; the job seems to be largely disliked. Oakley uses history to buttress her case against housewifery. Her task is made easier because she draws most of her evidence from England. An American scholar would have to account for different and persistent ethnic traits, which seem to validate the role even when the work has virtually disappeared. Yet, even in England, neither the role nor the work have been unchanging. Both can change again.

In contrast, Barbara Ehrenreich and Deirdre English, in an article entitled "The Manufacture of Housework," illustrate the difficulty of measuring women's work at home in the language of the wage labor force.[25] Attempts to make the home efficient were one thing. Catharine Beecher had pioneered kitchen design as early as the 1850's. But when home management experts attempted to apply scientific management procedures to household tasks, the result was to multiply the actual number of jobs women did. According to Ehrenreich and English, the time saved by turning women into their own managers was immediately spent by them in deciding what to do before they did it. Challenged about the absence of sufficient real work to do in the home, home management experts responded by arguing that women should spend their time preparing themselves to decide what to do.

In sum, the literature I have reviewed questions accepted notions about the determining influence of women's home and child care roles on their labor market behavior. Along with current demographic, technological and ideological shifts, it increases the pressure to understand women's role in the context of

[25] *Socialist Revolution* 6 (October-December 1975), 5-40.

larger economic and social issues. New work indicates that the twin doors of biology and destiny are not so much barriers to the labor force, as instruments used to give it structure. Historians need now to probe how labor market roles have reinforced the cultural patterns and values of sex-role differentiation. In breaking out of the circular logic that has justified continuing discrimination against women, scholars can begin to create a new set of parameters for understanding labor market behavior.

"WHERE ARE THE ORGANIZED WOMEN WORKERS?"

Alice Kessler-Harris

"The organization of women," wrote Fannia Cohn, an officer of the International Ladies Garment Workers Union to William Green, newly elected president of the American Federation of Labor, "is not merely a moral question, but also an economic one. Men will never be certain with their conditions unless the conditions of the millions of women are improved."[1] Her letter touched a home truth and yet in 1925, the year in which Cohn's letter was written, the A. F. of L., after nearly forty years of organizing, remained profoundly ambivalent about the fate of more than eight million wage-earning women.

During these four decades of industrial growth, the women who worked in the industrial labor force had not passively waited to be organized. Yet their best efforts had been tinged with failure. Figures for union members are notoriously unreliable, and estimates fluctuate widely. But something like 3.3 percent of the women who were engaged in industrial occupations in 1900 were organized into trade unions. As low as that figure was, it was to decline even further. Around 1902 and 1903 trade union membership among women began to decrease, reaching a low of 1.5 percent in 1910. Then, a surge of organization among garment workers lifted it upwards. A reasonable estimate might put 6.6 percent of wage-earning women into trade unions by 1920. In a decade that saw little change in the relative proportion of female and male workers, the proportion of women who were trade union members quadrupled, increasing at more than twice the rate for trade union members in general. Even so, the relative numbers of wage-earning women who were trade union members remained tiny. One in every five men in the industrial workforce belonged to a union, compared to one in every fifteen women. Although more than 20 percent of the labor force was female, less than 8 percent of organized workers were women. And five years later, when Fannia Cohn was urging William Green to pay attention to female workers, these startling gains had already been eroded.[2]

Figures like these have led historians of the working class to join turn-of-the-century labor organizers in lamenting the difficulty of unionizing female workers. Typically, historians argue that the traditional place of women in families, as well as their position in the workforce, inhibited trade unionism. Statistical overviews suggest that these arguments have much to be said for them. At the turn of the century, most wage-earning women were young, temporary workers who looked to marriage as a way to escape the shop or factory. Eighty-five percent of these women were unmarried and nearly half were under twenty-five years old. Most women worked at traditionally hard-to-organize unskilled jobs: a third were domestic servants and almost one quarter worked in the garment and textile industries. The remainder were scattered in a variety of industrial and service jobs, including the tobacco and boot and shoe industries, department stores, and laundries. Wage-earning women often came from groups without a union tradition: about one half of all working women were immigrants or their daughters who shared rural backgrounds. In the cities, that figure sometimes climbed to 90 percent.[3]

For all these reasons, women in the labor force unionized with difficulty. Yet the dramatic fluctuations in the proportions of organized working women testify to their potential for organization. And the large numbers of unions in which the proportion of women enrolled exceeded their numbers in the industry urge us to seek further explanations for the small proportions of women who actually became union members.[4]

No apparent change either in the type of women who worked or in the structure of jobs explains the post-1902 decline in the proportion of unionized women. On the contrary, several trends would suggest the potential for a rise in their numbers. The decline began just at the point when union membership was increasing dramatically after the devastating depression of 1893-1897. The proportion of first-generation immigrant women who were working dropped after the turn of the century only to be matched by an increase in the proportion of their Americanized daughters who worked. Married women entered the labor force in larger numbers suggesting at once a more permanent commitment to jobs and greater need for the security unions could provide. Large declines in the proportion of domestic workers reduced the numbers of women in these isolated, low-paying, and traditionally hard-to-organize jobs. At the same time, increases in office and clerical workers, department store clerks, and factory operatives, offered fertile areas for promoting unionization among women. Strenuous organizing campaigns by and among women in all these areas achieved few results.

Although cultural background, traditional roles, and social expectations hindered some unionizing efforts, they were clearly not insurmountable barriers. Given a chance, women were devoted and successful union members, convinced that unionism would serve them as it seemed to be serving their brothers. In the words of a seventeen-year-old textile worker, "We all work hard for a mean living. Our boys belong to the miners' union so their wages are better than ours. So I figured that girls must have a union. Women must act like men, ain't?"[5] In the garment workers union where women were the majority of members, they often served as shop "chairladies" and reached positions of minor importance in the union structure. Faige Shapiro recalled how her union activity began at the insistence of a business agent but quickly became an absorbing interest. In these unions, women arrested on picket lines thought highly enough of the union to try to save it bail money by offering to spend the night in jail before they returned to the line in the morning.[6]

In mixed unions, women often led men in militant actions. Iowa cigar makers reported in 1899 that some striking men had resumed work, while the women were standing pat.[7] Boot and shoe workers in Massachusetts were reported in 1905 to be tough bargainers. "It is harder to induce women to compromise," said their president, "they are more likely to hold out to the bitter end . . . to obtain exactly what they want."[8] The great uprising of 1909 in which 20,000 women walked out of New York's garment shops occurred over the objections of the male leadership, striking terror into the hearts of Jewish men afraid "of the security of their jobs."[9] Polish "spool girls" protesting a rate cut in the textile mills of Chicopee, Massachusetts, refused their union's suggestion that they arbitrate and won a resounding victory. Swedish women enrolled in a Chicago Custom Clothing Makers local, lost a battle against their bosses' attempts to subdivide and speed up the sewing process when the United Garment Workers union, largely male, agreed to the bosses' conditions. The bosses promptly locked out the women forcing many to come to terms and others to seek new jobs.[10] At the turn of the century, female garment workers in San Francisco and tobacco strippers, overall and sheepskin workers, and telephone operators in Boston ran highly successful sex-segregated unions.[11]

If traditional explanations for women's failure to organize extensively in this period are not satisfying, they nevertheless offer clues to understanding the unionization process among women. They reveal the superficiality of the question frequently asked by male organizers and historians alike: "Why don't women organize?" And they encourage us to adopt economist Theresa Wolfson's more sensitive formulation: "Where are the organized women workers?"[12] For when we stop asking why women have not organized themselves, we are led to ask how women were, and are, kept out of unions.

The key to this question lies, I think, in looking at the function that wage earning women have historically played in the capitalist mode of production. Most women entered the labor force out of economic necessity. They were encouraged by expanding technology and the continuing division of labor which in the last half of the nineteenth century reduced the need for skilled workers and increased the demand for cheap labor. Like immigrant men, and blacks today, women formed a large reservoir of unskilled workers. But they offered employers additional advantages. They were often at the mercy of whatever jobs happened to be available in the towns where their husbands or fathers worked, and they willingly took jobs that offered no access to upward mobility. Their extraordinarily low pay and exploitative working conditions enabled employers to speed up the process of capital accumulation. Their labor was critical to industrial expansion, yet they were expected to have few job-related aspirations and to look forward instead to eventual marriage. Under these circumstances, employers had a special incentive to resist unionization among women. As John Andrews, writing in the 1911 Report on the Condition of Women and Child wage earners, put it: ". . . the moment she organizes a union and seeks by organization to secure better wages she diminishes or destroys what is to the employer her chief value."[13]

If the rising numbers of working women are any gauge, women for the most part nicely filled the expectations of employers. Traditional social roles and the submissive behavior expected of women with primary attachments to home and fmaily precisely complemented the needs of their bosses. To those women whose old world or American family norms encouraged more aggressive and worldly behavior—Russian Jews, for example—unionization came easier. Yet, for the most part, women fought on two fronts: against the weight of tradition and expectation, and against employers. If that were not enough, there was yet a third battlefront.

Unionists, if they thought about it at all, were well aware of women's special economic role. Samuel Gompers, head of the American Federation of Labor, editorialized in 1911 that some companies had "taken on women not so much to give them work as to make dividends fatter."[14] In a competitive labor market unionists tended to be suspicious of women who worked for wages and to regard them as potentially threatening to men's jobs. "Every woman employed," wrote an editor in the A. F. of L. journal, *American Federationist*, "displaces a man and adds one more to the idle contingent that are fixing wages at the lowest limit."[15]

Since employers clearly had important economic incentives for hiring women, male trade unionists felt they had either to eliminate that incentive, or to offer noneconomic reasons for restricting women's labor-force participation. In the early 1900s they tried to do both. In order to reduce the economic threat, organized labor repeatedly affirmed a commitment to unionize women wage earners and to extract equal pay for them. Yet trade unionists simultaneously argued that women's contributions to the home and their duties as mothers were so valuable that women ought not to be in the labor force at all. Their use of the home-and-motherhood argument had two negative effects: it sustained the self-image on which the particular exploitation of women rested, and it provided employers with a weapon to turn against the working class as a whole.

Buttressed by the grim realities of exploitative working conditions and the difficulties of caring for children while working ten or more hours a day, and supported by well-intentioned social reformers, the argument to eliminate women from the work force, in the end, held sway. It was, of course, impossible to achieve, so the A. F. of L. continued to organize women and to demand equal pay for equal work. But genuine ambivalence tempered its efforts. The end result was to divide the working class firmly along gender lines and to confirm women's position as a permanently threatening underclass of workers who finally resorted to the protection of middle-class reformers and legislators to ameliorate intolerable working conditions. The pattern offers us some lessons about what happens to the work force when one part of it attacks another.

The published sources of the A. F. of L. reveal some of the attitudes underlying A. F. of L. actions, and I have focused attention on these because I want to illustrate not only how open and prevalent the argument was, but because the A. F. of L.'s affiliated unions together constituted the largest body of collective working-class opinion. We have amassed enough evidence by now to know that the A. F. of L. was a conservative force whose relatively privileged members sacrificed the larger issues of working-class solidarity for a piece of the capitalist pie. In the creation of what labor economist Selig Perlman called "a joint partnership of organized labor and organized capital," the Federation cooperated extensively with corporation-dominated government agencies, sought to exclude immigrants, and supported an imperialist foreign policy.[16] Its mechanisms for dealing with the huge numbers of women entering the labor force are still unclear. Yet they are an integral part of the puzzle surrounding the interaction of ideological and economic forces in regulating labor market participation.

In the period from 1897 to 1920, the A. F. of L. underwent dramatic expansion. It consolidated and confirmed its leadership over a number of independent unions, including the dying Knights of Labor. Membership increased from about 265,000 members in in 1897 to more than four million by 1920, and included four-fifths of all organized workers. In the same period, the proportion of women working in the industrial labor force climbed rapidly. Rapid and heady expansion offered a golden opportunity for organizers. That they didn't take advantage of it is one of the most important facts in the history of labor organizing in America.

Union leaders were sure that women did not belong in the work force. Anxious about losing jobs to these low-paid workers, they tried instead to drive women out of the labor force. "It is the so-called competition of the unorganized defenseless woman worker, the girl and the wife, that often tends to reduce the wages of the father and husband," proclaimed Samuel Gompers.[17] And the *American Federationist* was filled with tales of men displaced by women and children. "One house in St. Louis now pays $4 per week to women where men got $16," snapped the journal in 1896. "A local typewriter company has placed 200 women to take the place of unorganized men," announced an organizer in 1903.[18]

The Federation's fears had some basis. In the late nineteenth and early twentieth century, new technology and techniques of efficiency pioneered by Frederick Taylor eroded the control and the jobs of skilled workmen, replacing them with managerial experts and the unskilled and semiskilled. Skilled members of the A. F. of L. who might appropriately have directed their anger at the way technology was being manipulated, lashed out instead at women who dared to work. Gompers offers a good example. In an article published in 1904, he declared, "The ingenuity of man to produce the world's wealth easier than ever before, is utilized as a means to pauperize the worker, to supplant the man by the woman and the woman by the child. . . ."[19] Some of the least appropriate bitterness was expressed by Thomas O'Donnell, secretary of the National Spinners Union whose constituency, once largely female, had been replaced by men after the Civil War. The advent of simple electric-powered machinery caused him to complain that "the manufacturers have been trying for years to discourage us by dispensing with the spinning mule and substituting female and child labor for that of the old time skilled spinners. . . ."[20]

Real anxieties about competition from women stimulated and supported rationalizations about woman's role as wife and mother. Working men had argued even before the Civil War that women belonged at home, and both the harsh conditions of labor and the demands of rearing a family supported their contention. But the women who worked for wages in the early 1900s were overwhelmingly single, and often supported widowed mothers and younger siblings with their meagre pay. An argument that could have been used to improve conditions for all workers was directed at eliminating women from the work force entirely. By the early 1900s it had become an irrepressible chorus. "The great principle for which we fight," said the A. F. of L.'s treasurer in 1905, "is opposed to taking . . . the women from their homes to put them in the factory and the sweatshop."[21] "We stand for the principle," said another A. F. of L. member, that it is wrong to permit any of the female sex of our country to be forced to work, as we believe that the man should be provided with a fair wage in order to keep his female relatives from going to work. The man is the provider and should receive enough for his labor to give his family a respectable living."[22] And yet a third proclaimed, "Respect for women is apt to decrease when they are compelled to work in the factory or the store. . . . More respect for women brings less degeneration and more marriages . . . if women labor in factories and similar institutions they bring forth weak children who are not educated to become strong and good citizens."[23] No language was too forceful or too dramatic. "The demand for female labor," wrote an official of the Boston Central Labor Union in 1897, is "an insidious assault upon the home . . . it is the knife of the assassin, aimed at the family circle."[24] The *American Federationist* romanticized the role of women's jobs at home, extolling the virtues of refined and moral mothers, of good cooking and even of beautiful needlework and embroidery.[25]

These sentiments did not entirely prevent the A. F. of L. from attempting to unionize women. Gompers editorialized on the subject in 1904: "We . . . shall bend every energy for our fellow workmen to organize and unite in trade unions; to federate their effort without regard to . . . sex."[26] Yet the limited commitment implied by the wish that women would get out of the work force altogether was tinged with the conviction and perhaps the hope that women would in the end, fail. The Federation's first female organizer, Mary Kenny, had been appointed as early as 1892. But the Federation had supported her only half-heartedly and allowed her position to expire when she gave up the job to marry. It was 1908 before the organization appointed another woman, Annie Fitzgerald, as full-time organizer. While Gompers and others conceded the "full and free opportunity for women to work whenever and wherever necessity requires," Gompers did not address himself to the problem of how to determine which women were admissible by these standards, and his actions revealed that he thought their numbers relatively few.[27] The A. F. of L. repeatedly called for an end to discriminatory pay for women and men: "Equal compensation for equal service performed."[28] The demand was a double-edged sword. While it presumably protected all workers from cheap labor, in the context of the early 1900s labor market it often functioned to deprive women of jobs. The Boston Typographical Union, noted one observer, saw "its only safety in maintaining the principle of equal pay for men and women. . . ."[29] Officials must have been aware that equal compensation for women often meant that employers would as soon replace them with men. It was no anomaly, then, to find an A. F. of L. organizer say of his daughters in 1919 that though he had "two girls at work [he] . . . wouldn't think of having them belong to a labor organization."[30]

When the A. F. of L. did organize women, its major incentive was often the need to protect the earning power of men. Women were admitted to unions after men recognized them as competitors better controlled from within than allowed to compete from without. "It has been the policy of my associates and myself," wrote Gompers in 1906, "to throw open wide the doors of our organization and invite the working girls and working women to membership for their and our common protection."[31] *American Federationist* articles that began with pleas that women stay out of the work force concluded with equally impassioned pleas to organize those who were already in it. Alice Woodbridge, writing in 1894, concluded an argument that women who worked for wages were neglecting their duties to their "fellow creatures" with the following statement: "It is to the interest of both sexes that women should organize . . . until we are well organized there is little hope of success among organizations of men."[32] The A. F. of L. officially acknowledged competition as a primary motivation for organizing women in 1923. "Unorganized they constitute a menace to standards established through collective action. Not only for their protection, but for the protection of men . . . there should be organization of all women. . . ."[33]

These were not of course the only circumstances of which men suspended their hostility toward women's unions. Occasionally in small towns female and male unions in different industries supported each other against the hostile attacks of employers. Minersville, Pennsylvania miners, for example, physically ousted railroad detectives who tried to break up a meeting of female textile workers.[34] The women in this case were the daughters, sisters and sweethearts of miners. Far from competing with men for jobs, women were helping to support the same families as the miners. Similarly, women and men in newly established industries could cooperate more effectively in unionizing together. The garment industry saw parallel but equally effective organization among its various branches. Though female organizers complained bitterly of the way they were treated, male leadership depended on the numerical majority of female workers to bargain successfully with employers and did not deny women admission. Yet, even here, union leadership successfully eliminated "home work" without offering to the grossly underpaid and often needy female workers who did it a way of recouping their financial losses.

Occasional exceptions notwithstanding, the general consequence of union attitudes toward women was to isolate them from the male work force. Repeatedly women who organized themselves into unions applied for entry to the appropriate parent body only to be turned down or simply ignored. Pauline Newman, who had organized and collected dues from a group of candy makers in Philadelphia, in 1910 offered to continue to work with them if the International Bakery and Confectionery Workers union would issue a charter. The International stalled and put them off until the employers began to discharge the leaders and the group distinegrated.[35] Waitresses in Norfolk, Virginia suffered a similar fate. Mildred Rankin, who requested a charter for a group of fifteen was assured by the local A. F. of L. organizer that she was wasting her time. "The girls were all getting too much money to be interested," was his comment on denying the request.[36] New York's International Typographical Union refused to issue female copyholders a charter on the grounds that they were insufficiently skilled. When the group applied to the parent A. F. of L. for recognition, they were refused on the grounds that they were within the ITU's jurisdiction. The Women's Trade Union League got little satisfaction when it raised this issue with the A. F. of L.'s executive. council the following year. Though the Federation had agreed to issue charters to black workers excluded from all-white unions, it refused to accord the same privilege to women. The parent body agreed only to "take up the subject with the trade unions and to endevaor to reach an understanding" as far as women were concerned.[37]

A strong union could simply cut women out of the kinds of jobs held by unionized men. This form of segmenting the labor market ran parallel to, and sometimes contradicted the interests of employers who would have preferred cheap labor. A Binghamton, New York printing establishment, for example, could not hire women linotype operators because "the men's union would not allow it."[38] The technique was as useful for excluding racial minorities as it was for restricting women.[39] Like appeals to racist beliefs, arguments based on the natural weakness of women worked well as a rationale, as the following examples will indicate. Mary Dreier, then President of the New York Chapter of the Women's Trade Union League, recalled a union of tobacco workers whose leaders refused to admit women because "they could only do poor sort of work . . ., because women had no colour discrimination."[40] A Boston metal polishers union refused to admit women. "We don't want them," an official told a Women's Bureau interviewer. "Women can only do one kind of work while men can polish anything from iron to gold and frame the smallest part to the largest," and besides, he added, "metal polishing is bad for the health."[41]

Women were often excluded from unions in less direct but equally effective ways. The International Retail Clerks Union, charged an initiation fee of $3, and dues of 50¢ a month. Hilda Svenson, a local organizer in 1914, complained that she had been unable to negotiate a compromise with the International. "We want to be affiliated with them," she commented, "but on account of the dues and initiation fee we feel it is too high at the present time for the salaries that the girls in New York are getting."[42] Sometimes union pay scales were set so high that the employer would not pay the appropriate wage to women. Joining the union could mean that a female printer would lose her job, so women simply refused to join.

Though the A. F. of L. supported its few female organizers only half-heartedly, male organizers complained of the difficulty of organizing women. Social propriety hindered them from talking to women in private or about moral or sanitary issues. Women felt keenly the absence of aid. When the Pennsylvania State Federation of Labor offered to finance the Philadelphia Women's Trade Union League's program for organizing women, its secretary pleaded with Rose Schneiderman to take the job. "We have never had a wise head to advise, or an experienced worker," she wrote.[43]

But even membership in a union led by men guaranteed little to women. Such well known tactics as locating meetings in saloons, scheduling them at late hours, and ridiculing women who dared to speak deprived women of full participation. And unions often deliberately sabotaged their female members. Fifteen hundred female street railway con-conductors and ticket agents, dues-paying members of New York City's Amalgamated Street Workers Union, complained in 1919 that their brother union members had supported a reformers' bill to deprive them of their jobs. When the women discovered they had been betrayed they resigned from the union and formed their own organization sending women throughout the state to Albany "to show them that they . . . were able to take care of their own health and morals." To no avail. Eight hundred of the 1500 women lost their jobs and the remaining 700 continued to work only at reduced hours.[44] Supporting union men was not likely to benefit women either. Mary Anderson, newly appointed head of the Women's Bureau, got a frantic telegram from a WTUL organizer in Joliet, Illinois, early in 1919. The women in a Joliet steel plant who, in return for the promise of protection, had supported unionized men in a recent strike, were fighting desperately for jobs that the union now insisted they give up. The company wanted to retain the women, but union men argued the work was too heavy for them.[45]

As the idea of home-and-motherhood was used to exclude women from unions, so it enabled unionized workers to join legislatures and middle-class reformers in restricting women's hours and regulating their working condition through protective labor legislation. The issue for the Federation's skilled and elite corps of male workers was clearly competition. Their wives did not work for wages, and most could afford to keep their daughters outside the marketplace. In an effort to preserve limited opportunity, they attacked fellow workers who were women, attempting to deny them access to certain kinds of jobs. Abused by employers who valued women primarily for their "cheap labor," women were isolated by male workers who were afraid their wages and their jobs would fall victim to the competition. Arguments used by male workers may have undercut their own positions, confirming the existence of a permanent underclass of workers and locking men psychologically and economically into positions of sole economic responsibility for their families. Appeals to morality and to the duties of motherhood obscured the economic issues involved, encouraging women and men alike to see women as impermanent workers whose major commitment would be to families and not to wage earning. Women would, therefore, require the special protection of the state for their presumably limited wage-earning lives.

The argument reached back at least as far as the 1880s and it was firmly rooted in the idea that the well-being of the state depended on the health of future mothers. But the line between the interests of the state and those of working men was finely drawn, and occasionally a protagonist demonstrated confusion about the issue. A few examples will illustrate the point. The cigar maker, Adolph Strasser, testifying before a Congressional Committee in 1882, concluded a diatribe against the number of women entering the trade with a plea to restrict them. "Why?" asked his questioner. "Because," replied Strasser, "I claim that it is the duty of the government to protect the weak and the females are considered among the weak in society."[46] Nearly forty years later, a Women's Bureau investigator reported that the Secretary of the Amalgamated Clothing Workers Union, fearful that women were taking jobs from men, had argued that women were "going into industry so fast that home life is very much in danger, not to mention the propagation of the race."[47] As the idea spread, it took on new forms, leading a Boston streetcar union secretary to acknowledge that "he would not care to see [women] employed as conductors. . . . It coarsened [them] to handle rough crowds on cars.[48] But in more sophisticated form, the argument for protective legislation appeared as a patriotic appeal to enlightened national self-interest. "Women may be adults," argued one A. F. of L. columnist in 1900, "and why should we class them as children? Because it is to the interest of all of us that female labor should be limited so as not to injure the motherhood and family life of a nation."[49] Sometimes pleas were more dramatic. In a piece entitled, "The Kingdom of God and Modern Industry," Ira Howerth, a sociologist writing for the *American Federationist*, asserted:

> The highest courts in some of our states declare that a law limiting the hours of labor for these women is unconstitutional. It may be so, but if it is so, so much the worse for the state. The state or nation that permits its women to stunt their bodies and dwarf their minds by over-exertion in insanitary[sic] stores and mills and factories is thereby signing its own death warrant. For the degeneracy of women is the degeneracy of the race. A people can never be any better than its mothers.[50]

Gompers, as well as other Federation officials, at first opposed the idea of legislation. But in the period following World War I, their attitudes changed, perhaps as a result of what seemed like an enormous increase in the number of women in the industrial labor force. The A. F. of L. encouraged the Department of Labor to set up a Women's Bureau to defend the interests of wage earning women.[51] The Bureau, on investigation, found that many union officials viewed unionization and protective legislation as alternate means to the same goal: better working conditions. Sara Conboy, United Textile Workers' official and a WTUL activist, told a Women's Bureau interviewer that she believed in "legislation to limit long hours of work for women where and when the union [was] not strong enough to limit hours."[52] Some unionized workers thought legislation surer and faster or remarked that it was more dependable than possibly untrustworthy union leaders. A. J. Muste, then secretary of the Amalgamated Textile Workers Union of America perferred unionization, but was said to have believed that legislation did not hinder organization and might be esesntial in industries with many women and minors.[53] But some women union leaders were not so sanguine. Fannia Cohn of the International Garment Workers Union only reluctantly acquiesced to the need for protective legislation. "I did not think the problem of working women could be solved in any other way than the problem of working men and that is through trade union organization," she wrote in 1927, "but considering that very few women a are as yet organized into trade unions, it would be folly to agitate against protective legislation."[54] Cohn laid the problems of female workers on the absence of organization.

In any even, exclusion from unions merely confirmed the discomfort many women felt about participating in meetings. Italian and Southern families disliked their daughters going out in the evenings. Married and self-supporting women and widows had household duties at which they spent after-work hours. Women who attended meetings often participated reluctantly. They found the long discussions dull and were often intimidated by the preponderance of men. Men, for their part, resented the indifference of the women and further excluded them from leadership roles, thereby discouraging more women from attending. Even fines failed to spark attendance. Some women preferred to pay them rather than to go to the meetings.[55]

Self-images that derived from a paternalistic society joined ethnic ties in hindering unionization. Wage-earning women, anxious to marry, were sometimes reluctant to join unions for what they felt would be a temporary period. Occasionally, another role conflict was expressed: "No nice girl would belong to one," said one young woman.[56] An ILG organizer commented that most women who did not want to join a union claimed that "the boss is good to us and we have nothing to complain about and we don't want to join the union."[57] A woman who resisted unionization told an an organizer that she knew "that $6 a week is not enough pay but the Lord helps me out. He always provides . . . I won't ever join a union. The Lord doesn't want me to."[58] A recent convert to unionism apologized for her former reticence. She had always scabbed because church people disapproved of unions. Moreover she and her sister had only with difficulty, she told an organizer, overcome their fear of the Italian men who were organizing their factory.[59]

Exceptions to this pattern occurred most often among women whose ethnic backgrounds encouraged both wage labor and a high level of social consciousness, as in the American Jewish community for example. Young Jewish women constituted the bulk of the membership of the International Ladies Garment Workers Union in the period from 1910 to 1920. Their rapid organization and faithful tenure is responsible for at least one quarter of the increased number of unionized women in the second decade of the twentieth century. And yet, they were unskilled and semi-skilled workers, employed in small, scattered shops, and theoretically among the least organizable workers. These women, unionized at their own initiative, formed the backbone of the ILGWU, which had originally been directed toward organizing the skilled, male, cutters in the trade.

As it became clear to many laboring women that unionists would offer them little help, many women turned to such middle-class allies as the Women's Trade Union League. Established in 1905, the WTUL, an organization founded by female unionists and upper-middle-class reformers, offered needed financial and moral support for militant activity. Its paternalistic and benevolent style was not unfamiliar to women and those who came from immigrant families seemed particularly impressed with its Americanizing aspects. Young immigrant girls spoke with awe of the "fine ladies" of the WTUL and did not object to the folk-dancing classes that were part of the Chicago League's program.[60] But help from these nonwage earning women came at a price. Working women who became involved in the WTUL moved quickly from working class militance to the search for individual social mobility through vocational training, legislation, and the social refinements that provided access to better paying and rapidly increasing clerical and secretarial jobs. Rose Schneiderman illustrates this syndrome well. Beginning as a fiery organizer of the hat-and-cap makers, she moved through the WTUL to become Secretary of the New York State Department of Labor. Like the WTUL, which had begun by organizing women into trade unions, she began in the 1920s to devote herself to attaining protective legislation, even borrowing some of the arguments used by men who did not wish women to compete with them.

By this time many working women were themselves moving in the direction of legislative solutions to exploitative working conditions. It seemed to be the most accessible solution to the problems of exploitation. Female workers interviewed by the Women's Bureau at first felt that both women and men should be included in any legislation. Later, they asked that office workers be exempted.[61] Other women acquiesced reluctantly. "I have always been afraid," wrote a supervisor in a Virginia silk mill, "that if laws were made discriminating for women, it would work a hardship upon them." By 1923 she had changed her mind: ". . . it would in time raise the entire standard rather than make it hard for women."[62] As women came to accept the necessity for legislation, they, like men, saw it as an alternative to unionization and rationalized its function in terms of their female "roles." A Women's Bureau agent noted of the reactions to a 48-hour law passed in Massachusetts that "the girls felt that legislation establishing a 48-hour week was more 'dignified' and permanent than one obtained through the union as it was not so likely to be taken away."[63] By the mid-1920s only business and professional women remained staunchly opposed to protective legislation.

Within this framework of trade-union ambivalence and the real need of wage-earning women for some form of protection employers who were particularly anxious that women not unionize pressed their advantage. Using crude techniques, rationalized by the home-and-motherhood argument, they contributed more than their share toward keeping women out of unions. In the small businesses in which women most often worked, employers used a variety of techniques to discourage organization, some of them familiar to men. Department store employees whose union membership became known were commonly fired. Many stores had spy systems so that employees could not trust their coworkers. Blacklists were common. A representative of the year-old retail clerks union testifying before a Congressional Committee in 1914 was afraid even to reveal the number of members in her union. Owners of New York's garment shops, fighting a losing battle by 1910, nevertheless frequently discharged employees who were thought to be active organizers or union members.[64]

Other tactics were no more subtle. Employers often played on ethnic and racial tensions in order to prevent women from unionizing. Rose Schneiderman who formed the Hat and Cap Makers Union in 1903, fought against bosses who urged immigrant workers to stick to the "American shop"—a euphemism for an antiunion shop. Jewish owners sometimes hired only Italian workers who were thought to be less prone to unionization than Jews.[65] Others hired "landsmen" from the same old country community, hoping that fraternal instincts might keep them from striking. Blacks were played off against whites. Waitresses picketing Knab's restaurant in Chicago were met with counterpickets paid by the employers. A representative of the waitresses union reported indignantly that the employer "placed colored pickets on the street, colored women who wore signs like this 'Gee, I ain't mad at nobody and nobody ain't mad at Knab.' " When the nonunion pickets attracted a crowd, police moved in and arrested the union members. The women were further discouraged by trials engineered by employers who had previously given "every policeman a turkey free."[66]

Police routinely broke up picket lines and outdoor union meetings. Women who were accused of obstructing traffic or were incited into slapping provocateurs were arrested. More importantly, women who might have been interested in unionization were intimidated by police who surrounded open air meetings or by department store detectives who mingled obtrusively with potential recruits. Department store owners diverted workers from street meetings by locking all but one set of doors or sending trucks, horns honking full blast, to parade up and down the street in which a meeting was scheduled.[67]

Small employers formed mutual assistance associations to help them resist their employees' attempts to unionize. The Chicago Restrauant Keepers Association, for example, denied membership to any "person, firm or corporation . . . having signed agreements with any labor organization."[68] Garment manufacturers in both New York and Chicago created protective associations to combat what they called "the spreading evil of unionism."[69] In small towns, the power of town officials was called into play. Ann Washington Craton, organizing textile workers in Minersville, Pennsylvania, was warned by the town burgess: "You are to let our girls alone . . . Mr. Demsky will shut the factory down rather than have a union. . . . The town council brought this factory here to provide work for worthy widows and poor girls. We don't intend to have have any trouble about it."[70]

Employers justified continued refusal to promote women or to offer them access to good jobs on the grounds that women's major contribution was to home and family. When they were challenged with the argument that bad working conditions were detrimental to that end, they responded slowly with paternalistic amelioration of the worst conditions and finally by acquiescing to protective labor legislation. Often concessions to workers were an effort to undercut mounting union strength, as for example when department store owners voluntarily closed their shops one evening a week. Some employers introduced welfare work in their factories, providing social workers, or other women, to help smooth relationships between them and their female employees. Mutual benefit associations, sometimes resembling company unions, were a more familiar tactic. Though they were presumably cooperative and designed to incorporate input from workers, membership in them was compulsory and dues of ten to twenty-five cents per month were deducted from wages. In return employees got sickness and health benefits of varying amounts but only after several months of continuous employment. A 1925 investigation of one widely publicized cooperative association operated by Filene's department store in Boston revealed that in all its twelve years, only store executives had ever served on its board of directors.[71]

Manufacturers seemed to prefer legislation regulating the hours and conditions of women's work to seeing their workers join unions. One, for example, told the Women's Bureau of the Department of Labor that a uniform 48-hour week for women would equalize competition and would, in any event only confirm existing conditions in some shops. Some went even further hoping for federal legislation that would provide uniform standards nationwide.[72]

When occasionally employers found it in their interests to encourage unionism they did so in return for certain very specific advantages. One of these was the union label. In the garment industry the label on overalls in certain parts of the country assured higher sales. To acquire the right to use it, some employers rushed into contracts with the United Garment Workers and quite deliberately urged their workers into the union.[73] New York garment manufacturers negotiated a preferential union shop, higher wages, and shorter hours with the ILGWU in return for which the union agreed to discipline its members and to protect employers against strikes. The garment manufacturers' protective association urged employers to "make every effort to increase the membership in the union so that its officers may have complete control of the workers and be enabled to discipline them when necessary."[74] Southern textile mill owners, otherwise violently opposed to unions, were similarly interested in the disciplinary functions of unionism. They would, an observer reported, modify their opposition "if the purposes of the union were to improve the educational moral and social conditions of the workers."[75]

In general, however, employers made valiant attempts to keep women out of unions. The paternalism, benevolence, and welfare they offered in compensation were supported by other sectors of their society, including the trade unions. Middle-class reformers and government investigators had long viewed the harsh conditions under which women worked as detrimental to the preservation of home and family, and government regulation or voluntary employer programs seemed to many an adequate alternative. Unions played into this competitive structure adopting the home-and-motherhood argument to restrict women's labor-force participation. In the process they encouraged women to see their interests apart from those of male workers.

Limited labor-force opportunities, protective labor legislation and virtual exclusion from labor unions institutionalized women's isolation from the mainstream of labor. Not accidentally, these tendencies confirmed traditional women's roles, already nurtured by many ethnic groups and sustained by prevailing American norms. Together they translated into special behavior on the part of female workers that isolated them still further from male workers and added up to special treatment as members of the labor force.

In acquiescing, women perhaps bowed to the inevitable, seeking for themselves the goals of employers who preferred not to see them in unions, of male workers who hoped thereby both to limit competition and to share in the advantages gained, and of middle-class reformers who felt they were helping to preserve home and motherhood. Echoing labor union arguments of twenty years earlier, Women's Bureau head Mary Anderson defended protective legislation in 1925 on the grounds that such laws were necessary to conserve the health of the nation's women.[76]

A final consequence for women was to lead them to search for jobs in non-sex-stereotyped sectors of the labor market. Employers' needs in the rapidly expanding white-collar sector led women increasingly toward secretarial and clerical work. Vocational education to train women for office jobs, teaching, and social work expanded rapidly in the early twentieth century. Working women rationalized these jobs as steps up the occupational ladder; state and local governments and employers provided financial aid; and middle-class women launched a campaign to encourage women to accept vocational training.[77] It took an astute union woman like Fannia Cohn to see what was happening. She drew a sharp line between her own function as educational director of the International Ladies Garment Workers Union and the functions of the new schools. Her hope was to train women to be better union members, not to get them out of the working class.

The parallel development of protective legislation and vocational education confirmed for many working women their marginal positions in the labor force, positions they continued to rationalize with obeisance to marriage and the family. As Alice Henry said of an earlier group of female wage-earners, "they did not realize that women were within the scope of the labor movement."[78] Fannia Cohn understood what that meant. That hard-headed and clear-sighted official of the ILGWU prefaced a call for a revolution in society's view of women with a plea for an end to competition between working women and men. Because it was destructive for all workers, she argued, "this competition must be abolished once and for all, not because it is immoral, yes inhuman, but because it is impractical, it does not pay."[79] But in the first two decades of the twentieth century, the moral arguments prevailed—releasing some women from some of the misery of toil, but simultaneously confirming their place in those jobs most conducive to exploitation.

NOTES

I wish to thank the Louis M. Rabinowitz Foundation and the American Philosophical Society for essential financial support, and Jan Shinpoch for assistance in research.

Abbreviations: WB/NA: Women's Bureau collection, Record Group no. 86, National Archives; CIR: Final Report and Testimony of the Commission on Industrial Relations. Senate Documents, vol. 21, 64th Congress, 1st session, vol. 3, 1914: *AF American Federationist*.

[1] Fannia Cohn to William Green, March 6, 1925. Fannia Cohn collection, New York Public Library, Box 4.

[2] Figures are derived from John Andrews and W. D. P. Bliss, *History of Women in Trade Unions*, Report on the Condition of Women and Child Wage Earners in the U. S. (Washington, D.C.: G.P.O., 1911), vol. 10, pp. 136-39; Leo Wolman, *Ebb and Flow in Trade Unionsim* (New York: National Bureau of Economic Research, 1936), pp. 74, 116; Leo Wolman, *The Growth of American Trade Unions, 1880-1923* (New York: National Bureau of Economic Research, 1923), chapter 5. Wolman estimates that about 40 percent of organized women were in the three garment industry unions: ILGWU, Amalgamated Clothing Workers, and United Garment Workers, unions that had been either literally or virtually nonexistent before 1910. See Wolman, and Alice Henry, *Women and the Labor Movement* (New York: George Doran, 1923), chapter 4, for discussions of the difficulty of collecting trade union figures. Henry illustrates the numbers of women in specific unions.

[3] The proportion of foreign-born and native-born daughters of foreign-born women declined slightly in this period and women continued to shift from manual sectors to low-level clerical sectors of the work force. See U. S. Census, *14th Census of Populations* (Washington, D.C.: G.P.O.: 1920), vol. 3, p. 15. Such occupations as taking in boarders, homework, and working on husband's farms or in family businesses are not counted by census takers. Including these legitimate forms

of labor would create drastic upward revisions in the proportion of working women, but we have no way of knowing by how much. The figures include black women, more than 40 percent of whom worked for wages, compared to about 20 percent of white women. However, about 32 percent of married black women worked, compared to less than 6 percent of married white women. Black wage-earning women are far more heavily concentrated in agricultural and domestic service jobs than their white counterparts. Figures are from Joseph Hill, *Women in Gainful Occupations: 1870-1920*, Census Monographs, no. 9 (Washington, D.C.: G.P.O., 1929), chapters 5 and 9; Janet Hooks, *Women's Occupations Through Seven Decades*, Women's Bureau Bulletin, no. 218 (Washington, D.C.: G.P.O., 1947), pp. 37, 39.

[4]Andrews and Bliss, *History of Women in Trade Unions*, pp. 138-39. Even before the great uprising of 1909-1910, women, who made up 63 percent of the workers in the garment trades, represented 70 percent of the trade union members. This is all the more remarkable because their skill levels did not, by and large, match those of men. 32.5 percent of hat and cap makers were women, and 54 percent of union members were women. Women made up 50 percent of bookbinders, and 40 percent of the trade union members in that industry.

[5]Ann Blankenhorn, miscellaneous notes, chapter 2, p. 12, file no. 23, box no. 1, Ann Craton Blankenhorn collection, Archives of Labor History, Wayne State University. For another example, see interview with Netti Chandler, Virginia Home visits, Bulletin no. 10, accession no. 51A101, WB/NA.

[6]Interview with Faigele Shapiro, August 6, 1964. Amerikaner Yiddishe Geshichte Bel-pe, YIVO, pp. 2, 7.

[7]*AF* 6 (November 1899): 228.

[8]Quoted in Andrews and Bliss, *History of Women in Trade Unions*, p. 173.

[9]New York Women's Trade Union League, *Report of the Proceedings*, 4th Annual Conference of Trade Union Women, October 9, 10, 1926, p. 18.

[10]Vera Shlakman, *Economic History of a Factory Town: A Study of Chicopee, Massachusetts*, Smith College Studies in History, vol. 20, no. 1-4 (October 1934-July 1935), p. 216; Andrews and Bliss, *History of Women in Trade Unions*, p. 166.

[11]Andrews and Bliss, *History of Women in Trade Unions*, p. 168; Massachusetts Women's Trade Union League, *The History of Trade Unionism among Women in Boston* (Boston: WTUL, n.d., but c. 1907), pp. 22, 23.

[12]Theresa Wolfson, "Where are the Organized Women Workers?" *AF* 32 (June 1925): 455-57.

[13]Andrews and Bliss, *History of Women in Trade Unions*, p. 151.

[14]*AF* 17 (November 1911), p. 896. James Kenneally, "Women and Trade Unions," *Labor History* 14 (Winter 1973), describes, but does not explain, the A. F. of L.'s mixed feelings.

[15]Eva McDonald Valesh, "Women and Labor," *AF* 3 (February 1896): 222.

[16]Selig Perlman, *A History of Trade Unionism in the U.S.* (New York: Macmillan, 1923), p. 166. For illustrations of A. F. of L. policies see James Weinstein, *The Corporate Ideal in the Liberal State: 1900-1918* (Boston: Beacon Press, 1968), especially chapters 1 and 2; Ronald Radosh, *American Labor and United States Foreign Policy* (New York: Vintage, 1970); Stanley Aronowitz, *False Promises* (New York; McGraw Hill, 1973).

[17]Samuel Gompers, "Should the Wife Help Support the Family?" *AF* 13 (January 1906): 36. See also Stuart Reid, "The Joy of Labor? Plutocracy's Hypocritical Sermonizing Exposed—A Satire," *AF* 11 (November 1904): 977-78.

[18]"Mainly Progressive," *AF* 3 (March 1896): 16; "What Our Organizers are Doing," *AF* 10 (April 1903): 370.

[19]Editorial, *AF* 11 (July 1904): 584.

[20]"Trade Union History," *AF* 9 (November 1902): 871.

[21]John Safford, "The Good that Trade Unions Do," part 1, *AF* 9 (July 1902): 353, 358; "Talks on Labor," *AF* 12 (November 1905): 846.

[22]William Gilthorpe, "Advancement," *AF* 17 (October 1910): 847.

[23]Safford, "The Good that Trade Unions Do," part 2. *AF* 9 (August 1902): 423.

[24]Edward O'Donnell, "Women as Breadwinners: The Error of the Age," *AF* 4 (October 1897): 186. The article continued: "The wholesale employment of women in the various handicrafts must gradually unsex them as it most assuredly is demoralizing them, or stripping them of that modest demeanor that lends a charm to their kind, while it numerically strengthens the multitudinous army of loafers, paupers, tramps and policemen."

[25]Safford, "The Good that Trade Unions Do," part 1, pp. 357-58.

[26]Gompers, "Should the Wife Help Support the Family?" p. 36.

[27]Ibid. See also Louis Vigoreux, "Social Results of the Labor Movement in America," *AF* 6 (April 1899): 25.

[28]"Women's Labor Resolution, *AF* 5 (January 1899): 220; "Talks on Labor," *AF* 10 (June 1903): 477.

[29]Massachusetts, WTUL, *History of Trade Unionism Among Women in Boston*, p. 13; Elizabeth Baker, *Technology and Women's Work* (New York: Columbia University Press, 1964), p. 33.

[30]Mildred Rankin to Mrs. Raymond Robins, March 30, 1919, Margaret Dreier Robins Collection, University of Florida, Gainesville, Florida. In 1918, two women members of the federation offered a resolution to the national convention urging the addition of two women to the all-male executive board. It was quietly suppressed.

[31]Gompers, "Should the Wife Help Support the Family?" p. 36.

[32]Alice Woodbridge, "Women's Labor," *AF* 1 (April 1894): 66-67; Valesh, "Women and Labor," p. 222; and Massachusetts WTUL, *History*, p. 32. 2.

[33]WTUL Action of Policies, pp. 3, 8, box 4, accession no. 55A556, WB/NA: Proceedings of the A. L. of L. convention, 1923. See also Massachusetts WTUL, *History of Trade Unionism among Women in Boston*, p. 32.

[34]Blankenhorn manuscript notes, chapter 4, p. 17, box 1, file no. 24. Such examples of family unity are not unusual in the mine/mill towns of Western Pennsylvania and the Appalachian mountains. Women helped to picket during strikes, provided essential support services, and sometimes spearheaded attacks against mine management.

[35]Pauline Newman, interview, undated, Amerikaner Yiddisher Geschichte Bel-pe, p. 21, YIVO. Gladys Boone, *The Women's Trade Union League in Great Britain and the U. S. A.* (New York: Columbia University Press, 1942), p. 166, recounts a similar incident as having taken place in 1918. I suspect that it might be the same one and that her date is incorrect. Andrews and Bliss, *History of Women in Trade Unions*, p. 149, notes that women practically disappeared from this union between 1905 and 1910—a period in which master bakers were rapidly being eliminated by machinery.

[36]Mildred Rankin to Mrs. Raymond Robins, March 30, 1919, Robins papers.

[37]Boone, *The Women's Trade Union League*, p. 167; Alice Henry, *Women in the Labor Movement* (New York: Doran, 1923): 102.

[38]Interview with Vail Ballou Press, Effects of Legislation: Night Work Schedule, New York. NA/WB.

[39]See for example Rankin to Robins, March 30, 1919; and M. E. Jackson, "The Colored Woman in Industry," *Crisis* 17 (November 1918): 14.

[40]New York Women's Trade Union League, *Report of the Proceedings*, 4th Conference, p. 14.

[41]Undated interviews, unions, for Bulletin no. 65, NA/WB.

[42]Testimony of Hilda Svenson, C.I.R., p. 2307; the testimony was taken in June 1914.

[43]Florence Sanville to Rose Schneiderman, November 28, 1917, Rose Schneiderman collection, Tamiment Institute library, box A 94. For examples of union discrimination see Massachusetts WTUL, *History of Trade Unionism among Women in Boston*, p. 13; Andrews and Bliss, *History of Women in Trade Unions*, pp. 156, 157; Alice Henry, *The Trade Union Woman* (New York: Burt Franklin, 1973), p. 150.

[44]Testimonies, box 15, accession no. 51A101, WB/NA. The women had been hired when the war broke out.

[45]Emma Steghagen to Mary Anderson, January 15, 1919, WTUL Action on Policies, accession no. 55A556, WB/NA.

[46]United States Education and Labor Committee, *Report Upon the Relations Between Capital and Labor* (Washington, D.C.: G.P.O., 1882), vol. 1, p. 453. See Andrews and Bliss, *History of Women in Trade Unions*, p. 94, for Strasser's often-quoted "We cannot drive the females out of the trade but we can restrict their daily quota of labor through factory laws," and p. 155 of the same volume for Samuel Gompers' fears of female competition as expressed in 1887.

[47]Interview is with Mr. Salerno, Amalgamated Clothing Workers, interviews, unions, accession no. 51A101, WB/NA.

[48]Interview with Mr. Hurley, July 1919, Women Street Car Conductors, accession no. 51A101, WB/NA.

[49]Sir Lyon Playfair, "Children and Female Labor," *AF* 7 (April 1900): 103. See also Martha Moore Avery, "Boston Kitchen Help Organize," *AF* 10 (April 1903): 259, 260.

[50]Ira Howerth, "The Kingdom of God in Modern Industry," *AF* 14 (August 1907): 544.

[51]Mary Anderson, "The Federal Government Recognizes Problems of Women in Industry," *AF* 32 (June 1925): 453.

[52]Individual interviews, Massachusetts, April 12, 1920, accession no. 5A101, WB/NA. Her preference rested on the union's ability to ask for wage raises to compensate for the reduction in hours.

[53]Individual interviews, Massachusetts and New Jersey, accession no. 51A101, WB/NA. See especially interviews with A. J. Muste, Mr. Sims, Secretary of the Weavers union, and Amalgamated meeting of workers at Princeton Worsted Mills. These are undated but must have occurred in early 1921.

[54]Fannia Cohn to Dr. Marion Phillips, September 13, 1827, Fannia Cohn Collection, box 4.

[55]Interviews with Tony Salerno, Amalgamated Clothing Workers Union and Hat and Cap Makers Local 7, Boston, individual interviews, unions, accession no. 51A101, BW/NA. Massachusetts WTUL, *History of Trade Unionism among Women in Boston*, p. 11.

[56]Lizzie Swank Holmes, "Women Workers of Chicago," *AF* 12 (August 1905): 507-10; Eva McDonald Valesh, "Women in Welfare Work," *AF* 15 (April 1908): 282-84; "Mainly Progressive," *AF* 3 (March 1896): 16.

[57]Shapiro, p. 25.

[58]*Justice* (April 19, 1919): 2.

[59]Blankenhorn manuscript notes, chapter 13, p. 4, box 1, file 25.

[60]For example, see Mary Dreier, address to New York WTUL in *Report of the Proceedings*, 4th conference, 1926, p. 14. Dreier refers in this speech to the difficulty the WTUL had getting female workers to serve on the executive board at first. See Nancy Schrom Dye, "Creating a Feminist Alliance: Sisterhood and Class Conflict in the New York WTUL, 1903-1914," *Feminist Studies* 2 (1975): 24-38. Keneally, "Women and Trade Unions," treats the WTUL's relations with the A. F. of L. at length.

[61]Individual interviews, California, effects of legislation, accession no. 51A101, WB/NA.

[62]Quoted in a letter from Mary Van Kleek to Mary Anderson, February 2, 1923, Mary Van Kleeck collection, Smith College, unsorted.

[63]Breman and O'Brien, individual interviews, Massachusetts, accession no. 51A101, WB/NA. Such sentiments must, however, be treated cautiously. We know, for example, that the National Consumers' League in Philadelphia orchestrated an anti-E.R.A. letter-writing campaign by wage-earning women in 1922. The league urged women to write letters arguing that the E.R.A. would limit or eliminate protective labor legislation. See Barbara Klazcynska, "Working Women in Philadelphia: 1900-1930," (Ph.D. dissertation, Temple University, 1975). Janice Hedges and Stephen Bemis point out that most "protective" legislation has now been invalidated by EEOC decisions. "Sex Stereotyping: Its Decline in Skilled Trades," *Monthly Labor Review* 97 (May 1974): 18.

[64]Sylvia Shulman, testimony, CIR, pp. 2285, 2292; Hilda Svenson, testimony, CIR, pp. 2311,

2317; Elizabeth Dutcher, testimony, CIR, p. 2392. Exceptions sometimes occurred in small western towns where workers would not patronize nonunion stores. Dutcher testified that 75 employees of Macy's were discharged in 1907 after they attended a union ball. Svenson, CIR, p. 2307; Lillian Mallach to David Dubinsky, December 18, 1964, YIVO. See also minutes of the Waistmakers Conference, January 10, 1911, ILGWU, Ladies Waist and Dress Makers Union file, Rose Schneiderman collection, Tamiment, box A 95.

65 Rose Schneiderman with Lucy Goldthwaite, *All for One* (New York: Paul Erickson, 1967): 59; Shapiro, p. 9.

66 Elizabeth Maloney testimony, CIR, pp. 3246-47. See also M. E. Jackson, "The Colored Woman in Industry," pp. 12-17.

67 Agnes Nestor, testimony, CIR, p. 3389; Elizabeth Dutcher testimony, CIR, p. 2405.

68 Elizabeth Maloney testimony, CIR, p. 3245.

69 Leon Stein, *The Triangle Fire* (Philadelphia: J. B. Lippincott, 1952), Nestor, CIR, p. 3382.

70 Blankenhorn, manuscript notes, chapter 4, p. 17, file 24, box 1.

71 Nestor, CIR, p. 3382; Svenson, CIR, p. 3382 and Svenson, CIR, p. 2308, reveal the degree to which this was an attempt to undercut union strength; see also an unsigned typescript entitled "Personnel and Management in a Retail Store : A Study of the Personnel Policies and Practices of William Filene's Sons Co., Boston, Mass.," p. 14, in the Mary Van Kleeck collection, unsorted, Smith College; and Marie Obenauer and Charles Verrill, *Wage Earning Women in Stores and Factories*, Report on the Condition of Women and Child Wage Earners (Washington, D.C.: G.P.O., 1911), vol. 5, p. 48; Svenson, CIR, p. 2309.

72 See Cambridge Paper Box Company, Long Hour Day Schedule, accession no. 51A101, WB/NA.

73 Andrews and Bliss, *History of Women in Trade Unions*, p. 169.

74 U. S. Department of Labor, Bureau of Labor Statistics, Bulletin no. 145, 1914, p. 37.

75 *The Cotton Textile Industry*, Report on the Condition of Women and Child Wage Earners, (Washington, D.C.: G.P.O., 1910), vol. 1, p. 608.

76 Mary Anderson, "Industrial Standards for Women," *AF* 32 (July 1925): 21.

77 See Massachusetts WTUL, *History of Trade Unionism among Women in Boston*, pp. 7, 32; New New York WTUL, *Report of the Proceedings*, 4th Conference, p. 21.

76 Henry, *Woman and the Labor Movement*, p. 108.

79 Typescript of "Complete Equality Between Men and Women," from the December 1917 issue of the *Ladies Garment Worker*, Fannia Cohn collection, box 7.

ORGANIZING THE UNORGANIZABLE: THREE JEWISH WOMEN AND THEIR UNION *

by ALICE KESSLER-HARRIS

Women who were actively engaged in the labor struggles of the first part of this century faced a continual dilemma. They were caught between a trade union movement hostile to women in the work force and a women's movement whose participants did not work for wages. To improve working conditions for the increasing numbers of women entering the paid labor force, organizers painstakingly solicited support from labor unions that should have been their natural allies. At the same time, they got sympathetic aid from well-intentioned women with whom they otherwise had little in common. The wage-earning women who undertook the difficult task of organizing their co-workers also faced yet another problem: they had to reconcile active involvement in labor unionism with community traditions that often discouraged worldly roles.

Understanding how women who were union organizers experienced these tensions tells us much about the relationships of men and women within unions and throws into relief some of the central problems unionization posed for many working women. It also reveals something of what feminism meant for immigrant women. Evidence of conscious experience, frequently hard to come by, exists in the papers of three women who organized for the International Ladies Garment Workers Union: Pauline Newman, Fannia Cohn, and Rose Pesotta. All were Jews working for a predominately Jewish organization. Their careers span the first half of the twentieth century. Taken together, their lives reveal a persistent conflict between their experiences as women and their tasks as union officers. Their shared Jewish heritage offers insight into the ways

* This paper is a revised draft of one presented at the Conference on Class and Ethnicity in Women's History, SUNY, Binghamton, Sept. 21-22, 1974. The author gratefully acknowledges the generous support of the Louis H. Rabinowitz foundation.

women tried to adapt familiar cultural tradition to the needs of a new world.

Like most of the women they represented, Newman, Cohn and Pesotta were born in Eastern Europe. Cohn and Newman emigrated as children before the turn of the century, Pesotta as a teenager in 1913. In the United States, poverty drove them to the East Side's garment shops. There they worked in the dress and waist industry, a rapidly expanding trade in which Jewish workers predominated until the 1930s, and in which women made up the bulk of the work force.[1]

Their experience was in many ways typical. Among immigrant Jews in New York, Philadelphia, Boston, and other large cities only the exceptional unmarried woman did not operate a sewing machine in a garment factory for part of her young adult life.[2] In the old country, where jobs were scarce, daughters were married off as fast as possible. In America they were expected to work, for the family counted on their contributions. Many young girls emigrated as teenagers to go to an uncle or older sister who would help them to find a job so that a part of their wages could be sent back to Europe.[3] The wages of others helped to pay the rent, to buy food and clothing, to bring relatives to America, and to keep brothers in school. An eldest daughter's first job might mean a larger apartment for the family–"a dream of heaven itself accomplished."[4] When they married, young women normally stopped working in the

[1] In 1913, 56.56% of the workers in the industry were Jews and 34.35% were Italian. 70% or more were women. See Hyman Berman, "Era of the Protocol: A Chapter in the History of the International Ladies Garment Workers Union, 1910-1916" (unpublished PhD diss. Columbia Univ., 1956), pp. 22 and 24. Jewish women were much more likely to be working inside a garment shop than were Italian women who often preferred to take work home. 53.6% of all employed Jewish women were in the garment industry in 1900. Nathan Goldberg, *Occupational Patterns of American Jewry*, (N.Y., 1947), p. 21. The relative proportion of women in the garment industry declined between 1900 and 1930. In addition to dresses and waists, women were heavily employed on kimonos, housedresses, underwear, children's clothing, and neckwear. Melvyn Dubovsky, *When Workers Organize: New York City in the Progressive Era*, (Amherst, 1968), p. 73 ff has a good description of conditions in the garment industry.

[2] The industry was characterized by the rapid turnover of its employees. In 1910 about 50% of the dress and waist makers were under 20 years old. The best estimate is that less than 10% of the women working on dresses and waists were married. See U.S. Senate, 61st Congress, 2nd Session. *Abstracts of the Report of the Immigration Commission*, Doc. #747, 1911, Vol. II, p. 336; Berman, p. 23.

[3] The proportion of women in the Jewish immigration between 1899 and 1910 was higher than in any other immigrant group except the Irish. See Samuel Joseph, *Jewish Immigration to the U.S., 1881-1910* (N.Y., 1914), p. 179. This can be accounted for in part by the high proportion of family emigration, and in part by the numbers of young women who came to America without their parents, to work. Rose Pesotta, Rose Cohn, Emma Goldman fall into this category.

[4] Unpublished autobiography #92, YIVO archives. See also #160, p. 8; Etta Byer, *Transplanted People* (Chicago, 1905), p. 28.

garment shops. As in the old country, they were still expected to contribute to family income. Married women often took in boarders, helped in their husbands' businesses, or ran small shops.

A combination of factory work before marriage and the expectation of a different kind of paid labor afterwards, presented problems for Jewish women, who, like Newman, Cohn, and Pesotta wanted to take advantage of the new world's possibilities. Women who earned wages could dream of self-sufficiency.[5] Adolescents hoped that the transition to America would bring about a previously unknown independence and offer them new and different roles. Rose Pesotta (the name had been changed from Peisoty) arrived in America in 1913, aged 17. She had left Russia, she said, because she could "see no future for [herself] except to marry some young man ... and be a housewife. That [was] not enough.... In America a decent middle class girl [could] work without disgrace." [6]

Expectations of independent self-assertion were frustrated when marriage intervened and women were confined to more restricted roles. But aspirations towards upward mobility may have provided the death blow. The legendary rapidity of Jewish economic success perhaps did women a disservice by encouraging husbands to deprive their wives of the limited economic roles marriage permitted–contributing, incidentally, to the American version of the "Jewish mother." Yet the hard physical labor required of women who worked for wages at the turn of the century led them to escape from the work force as soon as possible. A folk song, reportedly first sung in Eastern Europe at the turn of the century, and later heard in New York's sweat–shops records one woman's wish for a husband:

> Day the same as night, night the same as day.
> And all I do is sew and sew and sew
> May God help me and my love come soon
> That I may leave this work and go.[7]

Women who hoped they would soon marry and leave the shops joined trade unions only reluctantly and male union leaders thought them poor candidates for membership.[8]

---

[5] Flora Weiss, interview in Amerikaner Yiddishe Geschicnte Bel-Pe, YIVO archives, June 15, 1964, p. 4. See also Anzia Yezierska, *Bread Givers* (N.Y. 1932), p. 28.

[6] Rose Pesotta, *Bread Upon the Waters* (N.Y.: 1944), p. 4. The novels of Anzia Yezierska, who arrived in America from Russian Poland in 1901, beautifully express these aspirations. See *Bread Givers; All I Could Never Be* (N.Y., 1932); *Arrogant Beggar* (Garden City, N.Y., 1927); and her semi-fictional autobiography: *Red Ribbon on a White Horse* (N.Y., 1950).

[7] Ruth Rubin, *A Treasury of Jewish Folksong*, (N.Y., 1950), pp. 43, 97.

[8] See for example, Rose Schneiderman as quoted in "Finds Hard Job unionizing Girls whose Aim is

To choose a militant and active future among a people who valued marriage and the family as much as most Eastern European Jews did must have been extraordinarily difficult.[9] Women who chose to be continuously active in the labor movement knew consciously or unconsciously that they were rejecting traditional marriage. In her autobiography, Rose Schneiderman, just beginning a career in the Women's Trade Union League, recalls her mother warning her she'd never get married because she was so busy.[10] One woman organizer, who did marry, made the following verbatim comment to an interviewer who asked her about children: "I wouldn't know what to do with them. First of all I never . . . we were very active, both of us, and then the unions. I don't think I . . . there were always meetings . . . so we had no time to have children. I am sorry now. . . ."[11] Even after so many years, her discomfort at talking about her unusual choice was apparent. Despite difficulties, many in the first generation of immigrants, Newman and Cohn among them, did not marry and there are numerous examples of women whose marriages did not survive the urge to independence. Rose Pesotta divorced two husbands, and anarchist Emma Goldman and novelist Anzia Yezierska one each before they sought satisfying lives outside marriage.

These women were not entirely outside the pale, for while on the one hand, American-Jewish culture urged women into marriage, that culture's injunction to self-sufficiency encouraged extraordinary militancy. In this respect Jewish women may have been luckier than most. They came from a class conscious background in which competitive individualism and the desire to make it in America was only one facet. A well-developed ethic of social justice was equally important and played its part in producing perhaps the most politically aware of all immigrant groups. Socialist

to Wed," New York *Telegram*, June 18, 1924; Julia Stuart Poyntz, "Marriage and Motherhood," *Justice*, March 18, 1919, p. 5; Matilda Robbins, "My Story," unpublished manuscript, Matilda Robbins collection, Wayne State University Archives of Labor History, p. 38. Mechanics of organizing women are illustrated in Alice Kessler-Harris, "Where Are All the Women Unionists?", *Feminist Studies*, III (Fall, 1975), 92-110.

[9] Although the same tensions existed for women of other cultural backgrounds, one does not always get the impression that non-Jewish women were quite so torn. Mary Kenney, for example, continued to be active after she married John O'Sullivan. The most prominent Jewish women who remained active after marriage married outside their ethnic group. Anna Strunsky Walling and Rose Pastor Stokes are two examples. In some ways Emma Goldman's life acted out the protest many women must have felt but expressed in more limited ways. See Blanche Wiesen Cook, "Emma Goldman and Crystal Eastman," unpublished paper delivered at the Organization of American Historians meeting, April 1973.

[10] Rose Schneiderman with Lucy Goldthwaite, *All for One* (N.Y., 1967), p. 50.

[11] Interview with Pearl Halpern in Irving Howe collection, YIVO (undated), p. 8.

newspapers predominated in the Yiddish-speaking Lower East Side. Jews were well represented in the Socialist Party at the turn of the century and were among the best organized of semi-skilled immigrants.[12] On the Lower East Side, as in Europe, women absorbed much of their community's concern for social justice.[13] A popular lullabye provides a clue to the extent to which women experienced a prevailing class consciousness:

Sleep my child sleep,
I'll sing you a lullabye
When my little baby's grown
He'll know the difference and why

When my little baby's grown
You'll soon see which is which
Like the rest of us, you'll know
The difference between poor and rich.

The largest mansions, finest homes
The poor man builds them on the hill
But do you know who'll live in them?
Why of course the rich man will!

The poor man lives in a cellar
The walls are wet with damp
He gets pain in his arms and legs
And a rheumatic cramp.[14]

There is no way of knowing whether Cohn, Newman or Pesotta knew that song, but it is likely that they sang the following tune:

No sooner in my bed
Than I must up again
To drag my weary limbs
Off to work again

To God will I cry
With a great outcry!
Why was I born
To be a seamstress, why?

Should I once come late
'Tis a long way

[12] Report of the Immigration Commission, Vol. 11, p. 317, indicates that in 1910 23.9% of Jewish men belonged to trade unions as opposed to 14% of Italian men.
[13] See for example unpublished autobiography, #160, YIVO, pp. 8 and 12.
[14] Rubin, *A Treasury of Jewish Folksong*, p. 23.

They dock me straight off
A full half-day!

The machines are old
The needles they break
My bleeding fingers–
Oh, how they ache!

I've nothing to eat
I'm hungry all the day
They tell me: forget it
When I ask for pay! [15]

Like the women who sang them, the songs had travelled to America, steerage class. In the garment shops of the Lower East Side, they could sometimes be heard over the noise of the machines, reflecting always the conscious desire of working women not only to get out of the shops but to make life in them better.

Faced with the exploitative working conditions characteristic of the early twentieth century United States, many women turned naturally to unionism. The ILG, founded and nurtured by socialist Jews from New York's Lower East Side, offered an appropriate organizing agency, and early expressions of enthusiasm indicate something of its romantic appeal. "I think the union is like a mother and father to its children. I'd give my whole life for the union," said one young woman in 1913.[16] Half a century after she joined the union in 1908 an eighty-year-old woman wrote to David Dubinsky, the ILG's president, "And I still have my membership book of that year. And I will keep it with reverence until the end of my days." [17] Another recalled her experience on the picket line: "I felt as if I were in a holy fight when I ran after a scab." [18]

It could be said of the early 1900s that Jewish women courted the unions that should have been courting them. Rose Schneiderman solicited the signatures of 25 capmakers before the union would acknowledge them or provide aid.[19] Her friend, Pauline Newman, recalled that when she and

[15] *Ibid.*, p. 97. These songs, with their hope of escape, should be compared with the hopeless and agonized verse of Morris Rosenfeld. See *The Teardrop Millionaire and other poems* (N.Y., 1955), pp. 14, 19.

[16] "Manhattan's Young Factory Girls," The New York *World*, March 2, 1913.

[17] Lillian Mallach to David Dubinsky, December 18, 1964, Glicksberg, mss., YIVO.

[18] Weiss, YIVO, p. 11. The same woman recorded the influence the legend of Mother Jones had had on her, p. 20.

[19] Schneiderman, *All for One*, p. 49. Officially, ILGWU policy was to organize whoever was in the shop, regardless of sex. It was easier in practice to discriminate against women since they were often employed in sex-segregated jobs.

her friends "organized a group, we immediately called the union . . . so that they could take the members in and naturally treat them as they would treat any member who joined the union. Our job was to attract women which men were not willing . . . to do." [20] But unions did not treat women even-handedly. During a capmakers strike, for example, when married men got strike benefits amounting to $6.00 per week, women, even those who supported widowed mothers and young siblings, got nothing.[21]

Women who had had to struggle to create and enter trade unions, who were baited, beaten, and arrested on picket lines, and who had already rejected traditional roles sought help from other women, identifying their problems as different from those of male workers. Large numbers indicated their need for organization by participating in spontaneous strikes. Workers on women's clothing (largely female) tended to strike without union support more than half again as many times as workers on men's clothing (largely male).[22] In the early years of organizing, attacks against other women often elicited support from co-workers. Clara Lemlich, whose proposal to strike sparked the 1909 uprising of 20,000 in the dress and waist trade, had been badly beaten by thugs. A woman who had participated in the Chicago garment strike of 1911 recalled that violent attacks against other female strikers had persuaded her not to return to work until the strike was won. As she and her fellow workers were negotiating with their employer to call a halt to the strike, they heard a terrific noise. "We all rushed to the windows, and there we [saw] the police beating the strikers–clubbing them on our account and when we saw that we went out." [23] A sense of female solidarity joined the oppressed together. A 1913 striker who said she was "in good" at her job refused to work without a union "for the sake of those that didn't have it good." [24] In jail women strikers passively resisted when their captors tried to separate them.[25]

Yet solidarity among women was limited by ethnic and class antagonisms that persistently interfered with the best efforts of organizers, and of which the organizers themselves were often guilty. Organizers repeatedly complained that their work was hampered by ethnic conflict among

[20] Pauline Newman, Interview, Amenkaner Yiddishe Geshichte Bel-Pe, June 26, 1965, YIVO, p. 19.

[21] Schneiderman, *All for One*, p. 61.

[22] Isaac Hourwich, *Immigration and Labor: the Economic Aspects of European Immigration to the United States* (N.Y., 1922), p. 373. These figures are for the period from 1880-1905.

[23] *Life and Labor* February 1911, p. 52.

[24] "Manhattan's Young Factory Girls," The New York *World*, March 2, 1913.

[25] Weiss, YIVO, p. 28.

women. Jewish women thought they were superior unionists. They treated non-Jews in the garment shops suspiciously complaining, for example, that Polish women would listen to their speeches quietly and then report them to the boss.[26] Italian women were felt to be unreliable allies, and fear that they would not join in a strike sometimes hindered other garment workers from going out.[27] In the 1909 uprising, Italian and Jewish women, divided by language barriers, met separately. The ILG, without an Italian-speaking organizer, selected women to harangue the Italians in English daily until the Italians agreed not to desert the strike.[28] Julia Poyntz, the ILG's first educational director, used the pages of *Justice*, its official journal, to argue in 1919 that "our Italian sisters who are still suffering from the age long seclusion of women in the home need a long and serious education to enable them to function intelligently as members of the working class in the shop and in the political field." [29]

"American" women, as the organizers persistently called them, were hardest of all for Jewish women to unionize. It was a necessary assignment in order to prevent some shops from undercutting the wages of others, enabling them to charge lower prices for finished goods. But it was dreaded by Jewish organizers who saw "shickses" as at best indifferent to unionism, and more often as strike breakers and scabs.[30] Success at organizing "Americans" evoked unconcealed glee. Pauline Newman wrote to Rose Schneiderman from Massachusetts that they had "at last succeeded in organizing an English-speaking branch of the waist makers union. And my dear not with ten or eleven members—but with a good sturdy membership of forty. Now what will you say to that!" [31] Long after most Jewish women were comfortable within unions, Rose Pesotta complained that she was having a "hell of a job" with the Seattle workers she had been sent to organize. They were, she said, the "100% American white daughters of the sturdy pioneers. They are all members of bridge clubs, card clubs, lodges, etc. Class consciousness is as remote from their thoughts as any idea that smacks with radicalism." [32] Women from such an ethnic background

26 Faigele Shapiro, Interview, Amerikaner Yiddishe Geshichte Bel-Pe, August 6, 1964, YIVO, p. 9.

27 Constant D. Leupp, "Shirtwaist Makers Strike," in Edna Bullock, ed., *Selected Articles on the Employment of Women* (Minneapolis, 1919), p. 126.

28 Louis Lorwin, *The Women's Garment Workers: A History of the International Ladies Garment Workers Union* (N.Y., 1924), p. 156.

29 Julia Stuart Poyntz, "What do you do with Leisure," *Justice*, February 22, 1919, p. 13.

30 Unpublished autobiography, #160, YIVO, p. 13.

31 Pauline Newman to Rose Schneiderman, September 20, 1910. Rose Schneiderman Collection, Tamiment, Box A94. Hereinafter referred to as P.N. and R.S. respectively.

32 Rose Pesotta to David Dubinsky, February 6, 1935, Rose Pesotta Collection, New York Public Library, General Correspondence. Hereinafter referred to as R.P.

could severely inhibit the success of an organization drive. Pesotta complained that she could not call a strike as women would not picket. "No one will stand in front of the shop . . . as they will be ashamed. Not even the promise of getting regular strike benefits moved them." [33]

Isolated from the mainstream of the labor movement and divided from other working women who came from less class conscious backgrounds, Jewish women gratefully accepted help from middle class groups like the Women's Trade Union League. But the financial and moral support of the WTUL came at a price.[34] Jewish women had been nurtured in the cradle of socialism, and for them, alliances with other women were largely ways of achieving a more just society. Many middle class members of the WTUL, in contrast, held that political, social, and biological oppression of women was the major problem. They saw labor organization among women as a way of transcending class lines in the service of feminist interests.

Contemporary testimony and filtered memory agree that the WTUL provided enormously valuable organizing help.[34] Yet the tensions were not easily suppressed. Rose Schneiderman, working for the WTUL in 1911 needed reassurance from a friend: "You need not chide yourself for not being able to be more active in the Socialist Party. You are doing a much needed and splendid work." [35] And it was always clear to those who continued to work for the union that the women of the WTUL had only limited access to and limited understanding of the Jewish labor movement. "Remember Rose," wrote Pauline, "that no matter how much you are with the Jewish people, you are still more with the people of the League. . . ." [36] And again, Pauline comforted her friend: "They don't understand the difference between the Jewish girl and the gentile girl. . . ." [37]

Neither the trade union nor solidarity from other women offered adequate support to the exceptional women who devoted themselves to organizing. How did they choose between the two? And at what cost? They worked in a lonely and isolated world, weighing the elements of their

[33] Jennie Matyas to R.P., February 25, 1935.

[34] See Weiss, YIVO, p. 32 for one encomium. For the WTUL side of the story see Nancy Schrom Dye, "Creating A Feminist Alliance: Sisterhood and Class Conflict in the New York Women's Trade Union League, 1903-1914," paper presented at the Conference on Class and Ethnicity in Women's History, SUNY, Binghamton, September 22, 1974; and Robin Miller Jacoby, "The Women's Trade Union League and American Feminism," *Feminist Studies*, III (Fall, 1975), 126-140.

[35] "Joe" to R.S., November 8, 1911. R.S., A94.

[36] P.N. to R.S., April 17, 1911. R.S., A94.

[37] P.N. to R.S., February 9, 1912. R.S., A94.

success against the conflict and tension of their lives. They were not typical of rank and file union women, nor symbolic of others' lives. The three female ILG organizers I have selected, each chose not to conform to traditional patterns and to pursue what for women was an extraordinary lifestyle. Their particular struggles crystallize the tensions other women faced, and more easily resolved in the service of a familiar destiny. As their relationship to the union is filled with conflict so their attitudes towards women reflect the way feminism is experienced by working women. Their lives illustrate a continuing uncertainty over the sources of their oppression.

Pauline Newman became the ILG's first female organizer in the aftermath of the "Great Uprising" of 1909. She had a stormy relationship with the union until she settled down in 1913 to work for the Joint Board of Sanitary Control—a combined trade union and manufacturers unit designed to establish standards for maintaining sanitary conditions in the shops. Fannia Cohn worked for the union from 1919 to the end of her life. For most of that time she was educational director though she also served as an executive secretary and briefly as a vice president. Rose Pesotta (some 10 years younger than the other two) became a full time organizer in 1933 and a vice president of the union in 1934. She remained active until 1944 when she returned to work in the shops.

Their lifestyles varied. Pauline Newman, warm, open and impulsive, had a successful long-term relationship with a woman with whom she adopted a baby in 1923. Fannia Cohn lived alone—a sensitive, slightly irritable woman, concerned with her ability to make and retain friends. Rose Pesotta married twice and afterwards fell in love with first one married man and then another. Cohn and Newman called themselves socialists. Pesotta was an anarchist. No easy generalization captures their positions on women, or their relationships to the union. But all felt some conflict surrounding the two issues.

From 1909 to 1912 just before she went to work for the Joint Board, Newman vacillated between the union and the middle class women of the WTUL. Frequently unhappy with a union that often treated her shabbily she nevertheless continued to work for them throughout her life. "I cannot leave them," she wrote in 1911, "as long as they don't want to accept my resignation." "Besides," she rationalized a few months later, "they are beginning to realize . . . women can do more effective work than men, especially where girls are involved." [38] Yet later that year she angrily

[38] P.N. to R.S., April 17, 1911 and P.N. to R.S., August 9, 1911. R.S., A94.

severed her connection with the ILG for which she had been organizing in Cleveland. "They wanted me to work for *less* than the other organizers get," she wrote angrily to her friend Rose Schneiderman, "and while it was not a question of the few dol[lars] a week with me, I felt that I would lower myself before the others were I to go out on the price offered to me. . . ." Her anger increased as the letter continued to describe the women selected by John Dyche, the union's executive secretary, to replace her: "Well they too are not bad looking, and one is rather liberal with her body. That is more than enough for Dyche." [39] Two months later she was still angry. ". . . The International does not give a hang whether a local lives or dies . . . ," she wrote to Rose.[40] And several weeks after that: "I for one would not advise you to work for any Jewish organization." [41] But within a few months she was back at work again for the ILG.

She had little choice. Though she disliked the union's attitude towards women, she had equal difficulty relating to the middle class women who were potential non-union allies. Not that she disagreed with them on the women's issues: she was more than sympathetic. An ardent supporter of the ballot for women, she could not, she said later, recall any woman (save for Mother Jones) "in any of our organizations who was not in favor of getting the vote." Like her friends she was convinced that the ballot would "add greatly to our effectiveness for lobbying or sponsoring labor legislation." [42] Moreover, she not only willingly accepted aid and support from women who were not workers but she actively solicited it, even quoting Christ in order to induce church women to help garment workers.[43] To gather support for striking corset workers in Kalamazoo, Michigan in 1912, she visited women's clubs. When local officials and the mayor had been unable to help resolve the strike she "decided that the best thing to do would be to ask the ladies who wear corsets not to buy that particular brand." [44]

Yet the task of reconciling class and feminist interests exhausted her. "My work is horrible," she complained from Detroit a few months before

[39] P.N. to R.S., November 14, 1911. R.S., A94. Three months later, the ILG fired the new organizers and Pauline crowed "I tell you, Rose, it feels fine when you can say to a secretary of an International to 'go to hell with your job together' and after have the same man beg you to work for them again!" P.N. to R.S., February 22, 1912. R.S., A94.

[40] P.N. to R.S., January 17, 1912. R.S., A94.

[41] P.N. to R.S., February 9, 1912. R.S., A94.

[42] Newman interview, YIVO, pp. 21 and 22. See also P.N. to R.S., May 17, 1911, R.S., A94, where Newman expresses sadness at not being able to attend a conference to discuss the "woman problem." "You must tell me about it in your next letter."

[43] P.N. to R.S., April 11, 1910. R.S., A94.

[44] Newman interview, YIVO, p. 2.

the Kalamazoo strike. "The keeping sweet all the time and pleading for aid from the 'dear ladies' and the ministers is simply sickening." [45] Her greatest praise went to the St. Louis, Missouri WTUL. It was, she said, "a strictly working class organization in spirit as well as in action." When she sent off an article praising it to the WTUL journal, *Life and Labor,* Margaret Dreier Robbins suppressed it.[46] Newman, in a remarkable letter to Rose Schneiderman written in 1911, explored her feelings about the effect of the WTUL on women workers. Mrs. Robbins, she noted, "has made all the girls of the League think her way and as a consequence they do not use their own mind and do not act the way they feel but the way Mrs. R. wants them to." She frowned at the League's Saturday afternoon teas (which served "a glass Russian Tea") and disapproved of giving the girls folk dancing lessons. "It is of course very nice of her," conceded Newman, "but that is the instinct of charity rather than of unionism." [47]

Her disagreements were not simply matters of style. She was more than willing to give way when she thought a well-spoken woman could influence a stubborn manufacturer. But she thought it bad strategy to raise issues of morality when they threatened to interfere with negotiations over wages and hours. It may have been true, she argued, that a factory owner's son and his superintendent had taken liberties with female employees: "There is not a factory today where the same immoral conditions [do] not exist. . . . This to my mind can be done away with by educating the girls instead of attacking the company." [48]

Caught between the union and middle class allies, Newman called for help—a pattern repeated by other women involved in the labor movement. Her letters to Schneiderman are filled with longing: "all evening I kept saying if only Rose were here . . . ;" and with loneliness: "No matter how good the people are to me, they do not know me as yet." [49] At times one can only guess at the toll her job took. She wrote repeatedly of trying to "get away from the blues" and complained, "I am just thrown like a wave from one city to another. When will it end?" [50] Respite came at last in the form of the Joint Board of Sanitary Control. With the struggles to organize behind her she could spend her energies improving working

[45] P.N. to R.S., March 5, 1912. R.S., A94.

[46] P.N. to R.S., November 7, 1911. R.S., A94. Newman had already had a similar experience with the *Ladies Garment Worker (Justice*'s predecessor) which mutilated an article on the League she had written for them.

[47] P.N. to R.S., December 1, 1911. R.S., A94.

[48] P.N. to R.S., July 11, 1912. R.S., A94.

[49] P.N. to R.S., October 19, 1910 and April 11, 1910. R.S., A94.

[50] P.N. to R.S., October 29, 1911 and November 7, 1911. R.S., A94.

conditions for women in the factories.

Feelings of displacement and the need for support may have preceded the drive by women members of ILG's Local 25 to create first an educational department and then a vacation retreat. The men in the union had no patience with the demands at first. One active woman recalled the men's snickers: "What do the girls know–instead of a union they want to dance." [51] But the women persisted, insisting that the union would be better if the members danced with each other. The women proved to be right. By 1919 Unity House, as the vacation home was called, had moved to quarters capable of sleeping 900 people and two years later Local 25 turned it over to a grateful International.

Unity House may have symbolized a growing solidarity among working class Jewish women. In any event, the feminism of ILG members seems to have become a problem for just at the peak of its success, *Justice*, the Union's official journal, began to attack middle class women. Could it have been that some union leaders feared that working women were seeking alliances with others of their sex and would eventually cease to identify their interests with those of working men? "Women who work," an editorial intoned early in 1919, are not like "that type of woman, who to her shame be it said, is less a person than a thing." [52] Increasingly *Justice*'s writers insisted that working women had it in their own power to defend themselves. When female pickets faced attacks by gangsters, *Justice* insisted that the solution was in the hands of the strikers themselves. It urged women to "take a little trip down to City Hall and get the vote that will put these fellows out of business." [53] Julia Poyntz, *Justice*'s writer on women's affairs, was adamant that middle class women no longer interfere with their sisters. "The interests of the women of the working classes are diametrically opposed to those of the middle classes. . . ." [54] A month later she attacked a Women's International League for Peace and Freedom conference for virtually excluding working women and their problems.[55] Although the journal continued to solicit support for the WTUL and the ILG continued to send women to the Bryn Mawr Summer School, attacks did not cease. A 1923 article protested the absence of working women at a conference on women in industry: "The ladies who employ domestics came to Washington to speak about higher wages, shorter hours, and

[51] Shapiro interview, YIVO, p. 17.
[52] "On Lightheaded Women," *Justice*, March 8, 1919.
[53] Julia Poyntz, "The Unity Corner," *Justice*, March 29, 1919, p. 3.
[54] "The Problem of Life for the Working Girl," *Justice*, February 1, 1919, p. 3.
[55] *Justice*, March 15, 1919, p. 5.

better working conditions for their help. The domestics, of course, or their representatives were not invited." [56]

It was just in this period that Fannia Cohn climbed to a position of authority in the ILGWU. In many ways she was fully aware of women's issues. In 1919, in the aftermath of a successful shirtwaist strike, she pleaded for tolerance from male union members. Recalling the militancy of the young female strikers she wrote: "Our brother workers in the past regarded with suspicion the masses of women who were entering the trades. They did everything to halt the 'hostile army' whose competition they feared." [57] Wasn't it time, she asked, finally to accept fully the women strikers who had so often been jailed and beaten. An ardent supporter of the Bryn Mawr Summer School and a regular contributor to the WTUL, Cohn had friendly relations with many of its officers.[58] In 1926 she protested the absence of women's names on a list of anti-war petition signatures, and later she was to fire off a rapid telegram insisting that Anne Muste be included in a tribute offered to her husband.[59] Her experiences strike familiar chords. She complained of the difficulty of holding independent views from the men she worked with but noted "It is still more painful to have women, too, assume a similar attitude toward their sex." [60] She laughed with a friend whose husband was called by his wife's surname ("let men have the sensation of changing their lifelong name for a new one"), and supported Mary Beard's proposed world center to preserve a record of women's achievements.[61]

Cohn's strong empathy for women's feelings surely derived from her own uncomfortable experiences in the ILG. Theresa Wolfson, later to become a well-known economist and an expert on the problem of working women, glimpsed this suffering in 1923. "Never have I realized with such poignancy of feeling," she wrote to her, "what it means to be a woman

[56] B. Maiman, "Conference on Women in Industry," *Justice*, January 19, 1923, p. 4.

[57] Fannia Cohn, "With the Strikers," *Justice*, February 22, 1919.

[58] Fannia Cohn to R.S., January 24, 1929, Fannia Cohn papers, New York Public Library, Box 4; see also E. Christman to F.C., October 2, 1915, F.C., Bx. 1.

[59] James Shotwell to F.C., December 31, 1926, F.C., Bx. 1; F.C. to James Maurer, March 6, 1931, F.C., Bx. 5.

[60] F.C. to Helen Norton, February 9, 1932, F.C., Bx. 5. The rest of the letter reads in part: "It hurts me also to know that while 'men' frequently come to each others' assistance in an emergency, 'women' frequently remain indifferent when one of their own sex is confronted with a similar emergency. Of course, a woman is expected to assist a man in his accomplishments, but she (the woman) is forced in her aspirations—in social and economic field—to struggle along. She is compelled to depend upon her own resources, whether this be material, moral or intellectual."

[61] F.C. to Dorothea Heinrich, February 3, 1937, F.C., Bx. 5; F.C. to Mary Beard, January 23, 1940, F.C., Bx. 5.

among men in a fighting organization as last Monday when I heard your outcry and realized the stress under which you were working."[62] In a letter she hesitated at first to mail, Cohn shared some of her angry frustration with a woman who taught at Brookwood Labor College. Cohn had urgently requested the college's faculty to make two studies of union women for her. The faculty had repeatedly postponed the request. "I wonder whether they would treat in the same manner, a 'man' who would find himself in a similar position . . ." She wrote, "The labor movement is guilty of not realizing the importance of placing the interest of women on the same basis as of men and until they will accept this, I am afraid the movement will be much hampered in its progress."[63]

Despite the anguish caused by her male colleagues and her strong sympathy with women's causes, Cohn came down on the side of the labor movement when a choice had to be made. She rejected a request to segregate men and women workers in evening classes: "I am a great believer that men and women working together in the labor movement or in the classroom have much to gain from each other."[64] In 1925 she appealed to William Green, the AFL's president, "not as an officer speaking for her organization [but as] a woman trade unionist" protesting conferences called by ladies. "When the deplorable conditions of the unorganized working woman are to be considered," she objected, "a conference is called by many ladies' organization who have no connection with the labor movement and they are the ones to decide 'how to improve the conditions of the poor working woman.' "[65] A year and a half later she regretfully refused an invitation to attend a WTUL conference on working women, cautioning the delegates to "bear in mind that it is very difficult nowadays to even organize men and they should remember that in proportion there are not enough men organized in our country as yet."[66] On the question of protective legislation for women, Cohn only reluctantly sided with the middle class reformers who favored it: "I did not think the problem of working women could be solved in any other way than the problem of working men and that is through trade union organization, but considering that very few women are as yet organized into trade unions, it would be folly to agitate against protective legislation."[67]

---

[62] Theresa Wolfson to F.C., November 19, 1923. F.C., Bx. 1.
[63] F.C. to Helen Norton, February 9, 1932. F.C., Bx. 5.
[64] F.C. to Evelyn Preston, September 21, 1923. F.C., Bx. 4.
[65] F.C. to Wm. Green, March 6, 1925. F.C., Bx. 4.
[66] F.C. to R.S., October 5, 1926. F.C., Bx. 4.
[67] F.C. to Dr. Marion Phillips, September 13, 1927. F.C., Bx. 4.

These contradictory positions were not taken without inner struggle. Cohn knew well the sacrifice she was making to stay in the labor movement. "Did you ever think of the inner pain, worry and spiritual humiliation . . . ?" she lamented in 1922.[68] Her remedy, like Newman's, was close friendship. "You know that I . . . must be in constant touch with my friends," she wrote. "If I can't have personal contact then the medium of letters can be employed." [69] Or again, "To satisfy my own inner self, I must be surrounded by true friends . . . [who] never for a moment doubt my motives and always understand me thoroughly." [70] Cohn found refuge in the education department of the ILG where she could continue the battle and yet remain sheltered from the worst of the storm.

Rose Pesotta took no shelter and asked no quarter. By 1933 when she began full-time organizing for the ILG, it had become clear to many that women, married and unmarried, were in the work force to stay and the ILG willingly committed both money and resources to organizing them.[71] Membership campaigns no longer focused on the East Coast cities. In the garment centers of the Far West and in places like Buffalo and Montreal, Jews took second place to Mexican, Italian, and "American" women. But Pesotta was a Russian Jew who worked for a still Jewish union and, like her predecessors, she suffered the turmoil of being a woman in ambivalent territory. Sent by the ILG to Los Angeles in 1933, she moved from there to organize women in San Francisco, Seattle, Portland, Puerto Rico, Buffalo, and Montreal before she became involved with war mobilization.

None could question her awareness of women's particular problems. Persuaded by the argument that there were no women on the union's General Executive Board, she accepted a much-dreaded nomination for Vice President. "I feel as if I lost my independence," she confided to her diary.[72] She often berated the union leadership for its neglect of women: "our union, due to the fact that it has a WOMAN leader is supposed to do

68 F.C. to Theresa Wolfson, May 15, 1922. F.C., Bx. 4.

69 F.C. to Evelyn Preston, September 9, 1922. F.C., Bx. 4; see also F.C. to E.P., February 19, 1924.

70 F.C. to Theresa Wolfson, May 15, 1922. F.C., Bx. 4.

71 Fannia Cohn, "A New Era Opens for Labor Education," *Justice*, October 1, 1933, p. 9. The article may be more hopeful than real. Cohn said in part ". . . the women strikers, many of whom were married and their younger sisters, too, increasingly realized that no longer do they want a strong union as a temporary protection for themselves but as a permanent safeguard for their present and future families." There is no question, however, that the industry's workers were increasingly drawn from married women and older women.

72 R.P., diary, June 9, 1934, Rose Pesotta Collection, New York Public Library. In her autobiography, *Bread Upon the Waters*, p. 101, Pesotta wrote that "the voice of a solitary woman on the General Executive Board would be a voice lost in the wilderness."

everything, organizing, speechmaking, etc., etc." [73] She was not shy about asking for courtesies that men might have had trouble obtaining. Women who earned meager wages could not be expected to pay even modest union initiation fees, she urged at one point. At another, she demanded that ILG pay not only the expenses but make up the lost income of a Spanish woman elected to attend the biennial ILG convention.[74] And she knew the advantages of solidarity among women, making personal sacrifices to "win the support of the ladies who might some day be of great help to the girls." [75]

Repeatedly, however, Pesotta and her fellow West Coast organizers sacrificed the feminist issues in the interests of generating an enthusiastic and loyal membership. To keep striking women happy they agreed to double strike benefits before Easter Sunday "for the girls to buy something." [76] When newly organized women brought their husbands to discussion meetings, the men were made welcome.[77] In 1933, Pesotta compromised to the extent of abandoning the negotiating process to men and confining her own activities to organizing women because "our late President Schlesinger once told your humble servant to stop this kind of business and go home and get married. I hate to hear that from an employer." [78] Her perspectives were not always those of other women. While WTUL officials were praising the NRA codes, Rose Pesotta condemned them. Organizing in Seattle and witness to how badly the codes were abused, she complained "the women are satisfied that the N.R.A. gave them 35 hours and better wages, why pay dues to a union that does nothing for the workers?" [79]

Pesotta carried the scars of the woman organizer. "A flitting happy little whirlwind," her friends called her. It was an image that did not fit. "Nobody knows how many cheerless, sleepless nights I have spent crying

[73] R.P. to Rae Brandstein, April 9, 1934.

[74] R.P. to David Dubinsky, April 26, 1934.

[75] R.P. to David Dubinsky, March 3, 1934. Pesotta on this occasion stayed in a YMCA because it was "respectable."

[76] R.P. to Jennie Matyas, April 16, 1935.

[77] R.P. to Paul Berg, February 15, 1934.

[78] R.P. to David Dubinsky, September 30, 1933. Pesotta's snippy attitude comes through in the rest of that letter. "Now, my dear President, you will have to come across with the help we need namely; financial, moral and the representative for a week or two. After we'll pull this through you will come to visit these whores and I am confident that you will see with your own eyes that enthusiasm is not such a bad thing after all."

[79] Rose Schneiderman called the codes "the Magna Charta of the working woman" and characterized them as "the most thrilling thing that has happened in my lifetime." New York Evening *Journal*, October 24, 1933, p. 15 (clipping in R.S., A97); R.P. to David Dubinsky, February 1, 1935.

in my loneliness . . . ," she confided to her diary.[80] Unlike Newman and Cohn, she sought solace in men and depriving herself of close women friends exacerbated her isolation. Tormented by the gossip of her female colleagues she struggled with her self-image. Occasionally she confessed "I feel so futile . . . ," or sorrowed "everybody has a private life. I have none." [81] In an effort to avoid entangling herself with a married man she exiled herself to Montreal in 1936. It was no use. She wrote from there to her lover: "Why must I find happiness always slipping out of my hand . . . I'm sinking now and who knows where I will land." [82] For ten years, Rose Pesotta battled against police alongside her union colleagues. Then she returned to the comparative peace of the garment shop from which she had come.

By the middle 1930s, with unionism apparently secure and the ILG's membership expanding rapidly, it looked as though women might at last begin to raise issues peculiar to them within the confines of the union. Fannia Cohn wrote a play in 1935 which raised critical issues. Intended for presentation at union meetings, it described a husband and his "intellectually superior" wife. Both worked, but, because the wife had to devote her evenings to caring for the home, the husband rapidly developed more interests and became increasingly discontented with his spouse. The wife, wrote Cohn, brought with her the resentment and "the protest of a woman worker, wife and mother against an economic condition that compels her to work days in the shop and evenings at home." [83] Chivalry, Rose Schneiderman had said, "is thrown away" when a girl enters the factory or store: "Women have to work and then are thrown on the dust heap the same as working men." [84] Working men were by no means chivalrous in 1935, but enough women had been organized in the ILG so that the union, no longer afraid of imminent disintegration and collapse, could lend an ear to the women's issues. Perhaps in consequence the solidarity of women within the unions diminished.

Those who came before walked an uneasy tightrope–slipping first to one side and then to the other. Tempted sometimes by the money and

[80] R.P., diary, November 3, 1931.

[81] R.P., diary, February 24, 1934, March 12, 1934, August 9, 1934.

[82] R.P. to Powers Hapgood, February 21, 1937.

[83] F.C. to Jess Ogden, June 25, 1935, F.C. A second play described how two sisters, both of whom worked, nevertheless waited on their brother at home because they had to atone for earning less than he did.

[84] Quoted in a clipping entitled "Says Chivalry stops at Door of Workshop," from an unidentified newspaper, 1912. R.S., A97.

support of middle class women, at others by the militance of a changing labor union leadership; alternately repelled by "ladies" and repeatedly hurt by their union's male leadership, women who tried to organize their sisters were in a precarious position. They were not feminist–they did not put the social and political rights of women before all else. They did draw strength and support from the solidarity of women inside unions and outside them. Their lives illustrate the critical importance of "female bonding" and of female friendship networks. Newman and Cohn, who had particularly strong relationships with women and who managed to find relatively passive roles within the union, maintained their relationship with the ILG far longer than Pesotta who relied on men for support and who stayed in the front lines of battle. All were class conscious, insisting that the class struggle was preeminent. When their class consciousness and their identification as women conflicted, they bowed to tradition and threw in their lot with the working class.